THE HEIRS OF
MUHAMMAD

THE HEIRS OF MUHAMMAD

ISLAM'S FIRST CENTURY AND THE ORIGINS
OF THE SUNNI–SHIA SPLIT

BARNABY ROGERSON

THE OVERLOOK PRESS
Woodstock & New York

This edition first published in paperback in the United States in 2008 by
The Overlook Press, Peter Mayer Publishers, Inc.
Woodstock & New York

WOODSTOCK:
One Overlook Drive
Woodstock, NY 12498
www.overlookpress.com
[for individual orders, bulk and special sales, contact our Woodstock office]

NEW YORK:
141 Wooster Street
New York, NY 10012

Library of Congress Cataloging-in-Publication Data

Rogerson, Barnaby.
The heirs of Muhammed : Islam's first century and the origins of
the Sunni-Shia schism / Barnaby Rogerson.
p. cm.
1. Aisha, ca. 614-678. 2. Ali, Caliph, 600(ca.)-661. 3. Islam—History
I. Title.
BP55 .R635 2007   197.09/021 dc—22   2006051520

Manufactured in the United States of America
ISBN 978-1-59020-022-3
10 9 8 7 6 5 4 3 2 1

For my mother

'Heaven lies at the feet of mothers'
The Prophet Muhammad

ACKNOWLEDGEMENTS

It is not easy, writing about the early history of Islam. I have got used to spotting that eyebrow flicker of incredulity when I meet Muslim writers and they hear that I have written a biography of the Prophet Muhammad followed by a book about the first four Caliphs. I know exactly what they feel, but are too polite to say. So I have started saying it for them. It should take a dozen lives of scholarship before I attempt so much as a single chapter. I should first spend a century immersed in the thirty-volume histories of Waqidi, Tabari and Ibn Sa'd, and another hundred years on the commentaries on the commentaries of these masters, backed up by an exact and critical knowledge of each of the seven dozen-volume editions of the Hadith. I should know Ibn Ishaq and the Koran by heart and then torture the texts of the early grammarians for the exact shade of meanings of early Arabic verbs before penning so much as a single line. I cap it all by admitting that I can read the prime texts only in English translation. So my first debt of gratitude must always be to those who have laboured in the exacting – but too often uncelebrated – craft of translation.

My second is to my friend Rose Baring who has given me the precious gift of time. Time in which to read and write, think, make notes and obsess while she has taken on the real burden of our lives, running a home, caring for our children and teaching them to write and play music not to mention her daytime responsibilities of running Eland: our jointly owned publishing company.

I would of course also like to thank my ever cheerful agent Michael Alcock and Steve Guise, my attentive publisher at Little, Brown, who are the professional godfathers who have overseen the gestation of this book. Bruce Wannell and Robert Hoyland of the University of St Andrews were both kind enough to make a detailed and exacting read of the first draft. Their notes, inquiries and suggestions have greatly enriched the final work, though in such a survey of narrative history as I have attempted there will be always be many matters on which we can never agree. They have offered me their learning and I now claim any remaining errors of fact and analysis as my own. As well as thanking Reginald Piggot for drawing the elegant maps and the eager assistance of Jenny Fry and Clara Womersley in the publicity department of Little, Brown, I would also like to testify to the friendship, advice and animated conversations that I have enjoyed within that small group of independent-minded writer-publishers that can still be found in the side streets of London. Robert Irwin, Michael Hagg, Nicola Beauman, Mark Ellingham, William Facey and Charlie Boxer also know both sides of the counter.

CONTENTS

LIST OF MAPS

PREFACE

I had been looking forward to meeting her for months, though when I did, it was the evening that the bombs had begun to fall on her home town. The first hour was spent in polite denial, as we chattered on about art, culture and history in their elegant London drawing room furnished with modern pieces from Syria as well as heavier relics from an Ottoman past interspersed with her own massive canvases. But it was only when we ended up packed into their small sitting room, staring at a giant television screen filled with orange flashes as their homeland was bombed, that I began to learn.

It was clearly not the first time that Baghdad had been bombed before her eyes. Her husband would excitedly point out some feature of the city to us, such as the ministry that he had laboured in, working on various agricultural schemes. It stood beside the excavations of an Abbasid palace and he prayed that this might not be considered a target. It was the only one that the Mongol cavalry had left, though soon there might be nothing left of this last fragile trace of Baghdad's medieval glory. The 'City of Peace' that now knew nothing but war. Now and then they would both defiantly agree to turn off the television, produce another plate of food for their guests, fill their glasses and the conversation would be resumed on a calmer, cultural level. We talked about our shared love for palm trees and later he proudly showed me a copy of the travels of his grandfather, that he had carefully edited with the assistance of his brothers. This could not be compared to English travel literature of the same period. His grandfather was a nationalist hero of Iraq, a man who had struggled against both the old Ottoman power and the British neocolonial protectorate that had followed it. The title 'travels' was no more than a polite literary fiction, for the questing experience of a young man who had been banished from his homeland and was looking for possible political answers from the other Arabs in the Middle East. Then the television would be switched on again for another round of CNN-reported explosions, in and around Baghdad. 'This is not new. It has always been like this for us Iraqis, to suffer. To struggle and to suffer.'

Later she took us out to the corridor and began to turn around canvas after canvas that had been facing the wall. They were still wet, a gallery of hieratic figures drawn from the inspirational images of Mesopotamian civilisation: the priests, kings and goddesses of Sumer, Akkad, Chaldea, Babylon mingled with Islamic symbols and totems, all of them consumed by flames and anguish. That they were still wet was a tribute to her enormous energy but she dismissed this with a flick of her eyes as she staggered under the weight of her stretched canvases. 'I paint because I cannot sleep. Now that the bombs have come again, I only see her.'

Later, much later, we heard who the 'her' was. We also heard of the years of work, the internal battle between her role as a mother and wife and that of an artist, the war waged within herself between the freedom to work that London gave her and the relevance and sustenance that could only come from living in her homeland. And then finally had come the night of recognition; a brilliantly successful show in London, saluted by the whole expatriate Arab world. But that very same night, coming home from the euphoria of a lifetime of effort, she had switched on the midnight news and heard that a rocket had gone astray – one of the chance side effects of the no-fly zones placed by the allies over bits of Iraq. Then suddenly she realised that the debris of this rocket-destroyed house in Iraq was hauntingly familiar. The television cameras were playing over the remains of her sister's house.

Her entire family had been destroyed by a stray rocket on the night that she had finally been saluted as an artist. She had been given an hour or two of total happiness before it was all swept away. Now years later the bombs had started falling on Baghdad again and she felt her personal grief being shared by tens of thousands. Her response had been to paint, to paint through day and night, creating elements of her sister's face intertwined among all the past glories of Iraq. It was a harrowing, if not tortured vision, but it is 'what we are born for', she said. 'We are born to this fate, we who are the people of Ali, who were born to struggle, to struggle and then to suffer.'

In the sitting room the television had gone back on again and so the explosions had returned to dominate the conversation. As we made our farewells, her husband led me back to his cherished library with its rows of revered history books, well-thumbed novels in Arabic, English and French and the glossy well-illustrated surveys of the glories of Islamic art, architecture and calligraphy. The top right-hand shelf looked empty, though it was not. It was the place of honour where an old leather-bound book lay flat. It was his grandfather's copy of the sermons of Ali. 'I would not surrender one line from that book for all the rest in this room,' he declared. If it had been said by a bearded teacher in his barren schoolroom one would have nodded in polite agreement, but somehow, coming from such a Westernised Iraqi, it had even more power. The evening was an education; it was about the inescapable nature of suffering. How the true and the good must always suffer.

I also began to understand something of the emotional nature behind the story of the Heirs of the Prophet.

It is a tragic tale. It can also be complex, for within Islam there are two different historical narratives, the Shia version and the Sunni version, and these were only really codified into rival interpretations of history some two hundred years after the death of the Prophet. About the Prophet Muhammad himself there is very little disagreement between the two traditions. The unity that they share over the events of the lifetime of the Prophet Muhammad ends symbolically at the hour of his death. The Shia believe that the Prophet died in the arms of Ali, the Sunni that he died with his head in the lap of Aisha. A believing Muslim will typically grow up with the knowledge of only one of these – and in my experience is often pleasantly surprised and genuinely interested to hear the other narrative. It has been my aim to honour both traditions and to sit like a tailor darning together two pieces of cloth into one. For in this instance it is possible that both traditional accounts are literally true.

INTRODUCTION

'Genuine tragedies in the world are not conflicts
between right and wrong. They are conflicts
between two virtues'
Christian Friedrich Hebbel

'God knows best which is right'
traditional Muslim saying

The Heirs of the Prophet Muhammad is a tale filled with remark-able individuals, who each take their turn to bob and weave in the flood of history before the relentless tide of events. It is a quite extraordinary epic, a fantastic fusion of tragedy, love and noble self-sacrifice; of destructive war, of scarcely credible conquests, of unbelievable wealth, of suffering, ambition, bravery, chivalry and trickery such as never can be nor ever has been exceeded.

It is the story of a small tight-knit band of believers who had followed the Prophet Muhammad into exile from Mecca to Medina, fought for him for ten years and then struggled to organ-ise and direct the Muslim community after his death. They started as a band of some eighty penniless refugees and would end up in command of a hundred thousand warriors. It is a tale of quite stag-gering achievement, of how the scattered, poor and anarchic tribes of Arabia conquered the known world under the banners of Islam. Of the genius-like commanders who led them to victory over the legions of the Byzantine Empire and then those of Sassanid Persia, while back in the oasis of Medina a series of wise old Caliphs founded new cities and organised an empire that would endure for six hundred years. Though the Arab conquest might now appear to be an unstoppable force of predetermined historical inevitability, it is one that is also riddled with bizarre instances of chance; where victory hangs in the balance of a summer wind, on ground conditions or on the stamina of the nomadic Bedouin warriors after a four-day running battle. On such foundations are empires built and kingdoms lost.

The four great Caliphs of Islam, Abu Bakr, Omar, Uthman and Ali, will each dominate the historical stage by turn. Each was a true heir to some aspect of their revered master's character though none could hope to match the full range of Muhammad's unique nature. Each would also find out how the exercise of power would transform their character. The meek, pious and utterly loyal Abu Bakr would be transformed into a brilliant strategist who outwitted all the wily old tribal warlords of Arabia. Omar, the second Caliph, is an iconic archetype of faith in flesh if ever there was one. A grand, implacable puritan of towering strength and conviction who would hold on to the Prophet's example of incorruptible poverty and absolute integrity even though he failed to imitate his master's compassion and great empathy with women. For if there was one thing that delighted Muhammad more than anything on this earth it was the company and friendship of his clever, articulate and free-speaking wives. Uthman, the third Caliph, was a kind, pacific, generous and clever man who proved himself an inspired administrator. Despite his one great failing – an uncritical love for his own clansmen – he must be honoured as a martyr and saluted as the steadfast guardian of the Koran. Ali, the fourth Caliph, is the linchpin of the whole tale, a figure crafted from the purest principles of honour, truth, bravery, integrity and faith. He is the knight gallant that stands behind all our tales of chivalry, both of the East and the West. Like all such men, he was not fated to prosper in our venal world, ridden as it is with secret ambitions, private fears and covert jealousies. When he is struck down by the assassin's blade, the 'Rightly Guided Era' of Islam is finished for ever.

But aside from these four great historical figures other memorable characters will also emerge. Khalid, the brilliant but merciless general who conquered Arabia and then the Byzantine Near East for his masters, would yet lose himself by his pride. He first became notorious when he bedded a captive virgin over the field of battle impregnated with the blood of her fallen tribe. Amr, who was destined to conquer Egypt three times, is a near-perfect example of just how talented the traditional merchant chiefs from the Quraysh tribe of Mecca could be – despite the intriguing mystery of his birth. On the eastern front with Persia no one could hope to match the stature of Ibn Harith, a pure-blooded Bedouin Arab chieftain who seems to have come from out of the pages of some pre-Islamic ode. Then there is the almost fictional villainy of that womanising power politician, the ex-bandit Mughira, who yet remains endearing from the pure zest with which he cut his way through life. He would ultimately use his talents in the service of the cautious, superbly efficient and sagacious Muawiya, who despite being the son of the Prophet's most determined pagan enemy would establish the rule of the Umayyad dynasty. Within our Western tradition perhaps only Augustus Caesar can stand beside Muawiya as a political genius of the first water.

The Heirs of the Prophet is also a story centred on love, especially a conflict in love between Muhammad's two closest followers, between his first disciple Ali and his devoted wife Aisha. This fatal enmity would accidentally pave the way for the first schism within the ranks of Islam out of which would come Islam's two paths, and ultimately assist in the triumph of Muawiya over the saintly Companions of the Prophet.

To appreciate the true resonances of this tale we must first become familiar with the landscape of Medina, the oasis capital of the Caliphate, know the story of Ali's exceptionally close relationship with the Prophet Muhammad, appreciate the nature of the Arab Bedouin warriors who achieved the Arab conquest, but also understand how the Prophet Muhammad existed and was supported by the love of Aisha and his other wives. Each of these four introductory chapters takes a different perspective but all conclude around that most decisive moment in the whole of this tale, the Prophet's death in Medina on Monday 8 June 632.

Only then are we ready to launch upon the narrative of events that follow in rapid succession immediately after the death of the Prophet. For once the first Caliph has been placed in office as the 'successor' the whole community is launched upon the path of conflict and expansion, which once initiated has its own extraordinary internal momentum. So that the young Muslim community is catapulted on to the pages of world history in a blaze of blood, glory and power.

On one level, it is a triumphant progress to match the conquests of Alexander the Great, though on another level it is also the ultimate test of any spiritual faith to be tried by the distracting temptations of pride, wealth, fame, ambition and dominion. It is as if the temptations that Satan offered to Christ during his forty days in the wilderness were made flesh.

Fifty years after the Prophet's death an empire had indeed been forged but the Kaaba, the house of God at Mecca, had been burned to the ground and the Prophet's own beloved grandson Husayn had been spurned, betrayed and beheaded.

It is this concept, of how speedily the example of the Prophet Muhammad was betrayed by mankind, which lies right at the heart of this epic tale and of why Muslims are still today divided between Sunni and Shia from out of the events of the seventh century. All Muslims agree that with the assassination of Ali in 661 the era of holiness is over. Within but a generation after the death of the Prophet the rule of the enlightened is finished, and the tough-minded generals, the scheming politicians, the police chiefs and the old dynasts are back in the seats of power. No one doubts this, whether they are Sunni or Shia.

The difference is in how they would look back upon the period of the Heirs of the Prophet. The Sunni, for all the slow creeping decay in spiritual values, honour this first generation of Muslims and consider the example set by Abu Bakr, Omar, Uthman and Ali (and the other Companions of the Prophet) to be of use in how mankind can best conduct himself on earth. Their heroes are these Rashidun, the first four Rightly Guided Caliphs, and the scholar-sages who would later protect this heritage from the corruption of the world.

The Shia concentrate on the sense of immediate loss, of the vision betrayed within a day of the Prophet's death. They argue that only Ali was qualified to uphold the spiritual values that underpinned the whole future direction of Islam. On one level it is an undeniably gloomy vision, this triple betrayal of Ali (for his claims to leadership were to be passed over three times) which was to be later compounded by the murder of his son Husayn. However, on another level it allows the Shia to reach for the very stars, to freely speculate about 'what if?', and to aspire to create a holy state such as Ali might have instituted on this earth. To understand some of its attraction, try to put it into a British perspective by recalling the romance of a lost cause – think of King Arthur linked up with the Stuarts and Jacobites and espousing an evangelical Christian-Communism.

After the story of the Heirs of the Prophet is finished there are two appendices. The first traces how the events of the seventh century connect with some of the better-known Islamic movements and leaders of today. This is followed by the story of 'How do we know?', which traces our knowledge of these times back to the chain of storytelling within the old oasis city of Medina which directly links us to Aisha, the beloved of the Prophet.

In order to keep the main structure of the book free from a flood-tide of unfamiliar Arabic names I have deliberately concentrated the narrative around a dozen key characters. I have also got rid of all accents and used recognisable names wherever possible rather than list the full glory of the Arabic patronymic, which delights in recording both the ibn/bint (whose son or daughter you are, the Nasab) and the Abu/Umm (who you have fathered or mothered, the Kunya) as well as your grandparents, your tribe and home town. I have also plumped for some old-fashioned English spellings of Arabic words which have long been superseded in scholarly circles. In particular I have chosen to spell the second Caliph as 'Omar' rather than the canonical ''Umar' purely because I think it might rest easier on the reader not to have two of the principal characters both beginning with a 'U'. Similarly I have dropped the current orthodox spelling of Qur'an for the more homely, Anglicised 'Koran', and preferred the old-fashioned 'Beni' to 'Banu'. This might annoy a handful of specialists but then this book was never addressed to their attention. My aim has always been to try to include as many potential listeners as possible and to free this vitally important story from what a newspaper editor recently explained to me as the two greatest obstacles facing any current writing about Islam, that his readership is either 'bored or afraid'. Only when the Western world can move beyond this threshold of boredom and fear and offer up some degree of respect to Muhammad and Ali – that is so freely bestowed upon Moses and Jesus within the Islamic world – will this world become a more just and safer place.

PART I

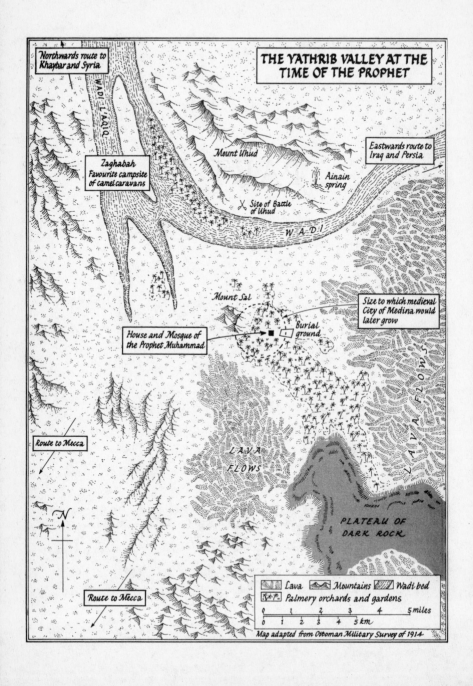

THE YATHRIB VALLEY AT THE
TIME OF THE PROPHET

Northwards route to
Khaybar and Syria

WADI L'AQIQ

Zaghabah
Favourite campsite
of camel caravans

Mount Uhud

Eastwards route to
Iraq and Persia

Ainain
spring

Site of Battle
of Uhud

WADI

Mount Sal

Size to which medieval
City of Medina would
later grow

House and Mosque of
the Prophet Muhammad

Burial
ground

LAVA FLOWS

Route to Mecca

N

LAVA
FLOWS

PLATEAU OF
DARK ROCK

Route to Mecca

Lava   Mountains   Wadi bed
Palmery orchards and gardens

0   1   2   3   4   5 miles
0   1   2   3   4   5 km

Map adapted from Ottoman Military Survey of 1914

1

Medina: Oasis Capital
of the Muslim State

It was on a moonlit desert night in AD 622 that the Prophet Muhammad had first received the loyalty of the men of Medina. They had met in secret in the high reaches of the valley of Mina, at Aqaba, just outside Mecca. There the Prophet had replied to the sworn oaths of the assembled men with 'I am yours and you are mine. Whom you war against, him I war against. Whom you make peace with, him I make peace with.' With these words the Muslim community was born, and his personal bonds with Mecca were loosened and a new loyalty pledged to Medina.

A decade later he would make another moonlight appointment with his followers – though this time it was outside Medina and it was only the Prophet who would speak. He had awoken one midsummer night directed by an inner conviction that he should go out to the cemetery and pray over the dead. He left the rest of the household sleeping but woke a trusted companion and together they wandered out through the dusty lanes overhung with the dark silhouettes of palm trees for a mile towards the burial ground of Baqi al-Gharqad. Over the dead, which for him included two daughters and an infant son, as well as wives, dear friends and loyal followers, Muhammad called out a clear greeting: 'Peace be upon you, O people of the graves. Rejoice in your state, how much better is it than the state of men now living. Dissensions come like waves of darkest night, the one following hard upon the other, each worse than the last.' Then he prayed quietly to Allah to exercise mercy over this field; for among the many sublime titles of absolute power, God may also be addressed as Ar-Rahim (the merciful) and Al-Ghaffar (the forgiver). After a while the two old men returned back to the house-mosque. When Muhammad awoke just before dawn he was transfixed by a violent throbbing headache. Ten days later he would be dead. In the ten years between that first moonlit oath at Aqaba and those midnight prayers for the dead, the oasis of Medina had risen under the leadership of Muhammad to become the governing capital of all Arabia.

The Prophet Muhammad and all his chief followers were from the trading city of Mecca. They were born in Mecca, brought up in Mecca and had their whole lives transformed when they converted to Islam at Mecca. All the Caliphs who would succeed the Prophet Muhammad were from Mecca as were the chief generals of the Arab conquest and all his most influential wives. Even the great dynasties that would ultimately rule for centuries over the early empires of Islam, be they the fiercely antagonistic Umayyad, Abbasid or Fatamid clans, were all descended from Meccan families. The haj pilgrimage to Mecca, one of the five pillars of the Muslim faith, continues to this day to stress the whole Mecca-focused nature of early Islam. In comparison the oasis of Medina seems to hardly rate at all. Although everywhere acknowledged as the second city of Islam it also remains curiously unfocused, slipping in and out of the historical record like some sketchily painted backdrop to the principal events. (Though they were intertwined by history, there was a hard ten-day ride across the desert between the two cities.)

This hidden nature of Medina only adds to its fascination. For it was against the everyday reality of this oasis community that at least half of the Koran was revealed. For the verses of the Koran are divided into two quite different tones, the verses revealed at Mecca in the twelve years 610–22 and those that were delivered in Medina in the ten years 622–32. The Meccan verses could seemingly be addressed to any age and body of mankind. They have a strong universal appeal and are the central lodestone around which all the great mystics of Islam, such as Rumi or Ibn Arabi, have built their own spiritual reflections and poetical commentaries. By contrast the Koranic verses from the Medina period tend to be much more specific, detailed and placed into the physical and political realities of seventh-century Arabia. Many of the Medina verses can be seen to be a divine answer to a specific problem of the Muslim community in Medina as framed by the Prophet in prayer and meditation to God. These divine answers are the Koranic bedrock which still underlies the daily conduct of the whole vast worldwide society of Islam. So it is of critical importance to our understanding of true Islam to know how this first community of Muslims at Medina were behaving. For it was their moral behaviour that so often posed the question that God would answer with a revelation. With this sort of crucial understanding of the Koran on offer, there seems little need to stress the importance of looking with eagle-eyed attention at everything one can ever learn about Medina. It was the place where the Prophet took a band of penniless refugees who hitherto had to practise their faith in secret and under constant persecution and hostility in Mecca. In Medina they were finally free to worship as they pleased. All the distinctive habits of Islamic civilisation were created in the freedom of

Medina. It was the place where the Prophet built the first mosque, where the Prophet lived freely, where he developed the rituals of prayer, burial, daily conduct, marriage and pilgrimage. Here he established not only the intimate domestic details of daily faith but also the yearly cycle of festivals. Medina was also the seat of the Islamic state; the centre from which every single military expedition was sent out. It was to Medina that the chiefs, sheikhs and diplomats of tribal Arabia came to make their peace and bargain their submission. It was at Medina that the Prophet established the details of how to rule, how to judge, how to tax and how to govern an Islamic state. In just ten years of the Prophet's own personal guidance, the community of Muslims at Medina grew from eighty impoverished refugees to a movement to be numbered in tens of thousands. If Mecca was the crucible in which Muhammad was transformed from an orphan boy to a Prophet, Medina was the forge by which the Prophet transformed tribal Arabia into a theocratic state.

Medina means 'the city' in Arabic. It is an affectionate abbreviation of Medinet al-Nabi, 'the City of the Prophet', though throughout the lifetime of Muhammad it was never a town, let alone a city, but a scattering of hamlets spread across an agricultural oasis – one of the many oases that are placed like islands in the sea of the Nejed Desert of central Arabia. In the decades after the death of Muhammad, the city of Medina would gradually grow around its nucleus, the house-mosque of the Prophet, but throughout his own lifetime there was no specific urban centre. So Medina referred to the entire oasis community that was strung along the Yathrib valley. A contemporary Christian historian from this early period records both these names and offers up the explanation that Yathrib was named after the fourth son of Abraham, while Medina was derived from Midian – the biblical name for the Arabs of the desert. None of these statements is in conflict with that central Islamic tenet that the Prophet Muhammad was not a founder of a new religion but a reformer of the old monotheist tradition that reaches back through Jesus, Moses, Abraham to our common first-father, Adam. As a traditional Muslim saying has it:

Our Lord Abraham is the beloved of God
Our Lord Moses is the mouthpiece of God
Our Lord Issa [Jesus] is the spirit of God
But our Lord Muhammad is the Prophet of God

If you had approached seventh-century Medina from the vantage point of the hills to its south, it would at first have looked like an 8-mile-long river of green, for at that distance the dusty grey-green of the palm leaves merged together to form a forest. As you rode closer this verdant unity dissolved, and the oasis broke up into a collection of ill-defined villages, with some standing like detached islands off from the main archipelago. If the sporadic spring rains had been good the whole area around the central palmery would have been cultivated with plots of barley among fields of grass on the wadi beds. These would be cropped in May just as the summer scorched this marginal, unfenced occasional ploughland into the burnt yellows and browns of the desert steppe.

Approaching ever closer, you passed beside ancient cemeteries: fields of neglected stone beside which the circular clay floors of the threshing grounds looked polished with continuous use. As you finally rode into the centre of the oasis, the dense forest dissolved into a patchwork of small intensely worked gardens where the palm trunks formed a canopy below which lesser crops of fodder and vegetables grew in the dappled light. Many of these enclosures included a simple hut made of woven palm fronds, where gardeners might shelter by day and dogs by night. The modest courtyard houses of Medina were clustered together for defence around the distinctive fortified manor-houses of the oasis – which were known as *atam*. There were over seventy of these fortress farmhouses scattered throughout the length of the Yathrib valley. In the desperate periods of internal fighting before the coming of Islam, the possession of an *atam* was the measure by which the rival tribes, dissident clans and confederations measured their strength. The densest area of settlement was on the higher southern edge of the valley where the cleanest water, the best gardens and tallest *atam* could be found. This was the Aliyah, which was also the oldest area of settlement, though the Prophet would not make his home there. On that joyous day of celebration when he first rode into the Yathrib valley he had given his camel Quswa her head and allowed her to choose their future home. Quswa chose an old date-drying yard off a back alley that stood roughly in the middle of the oasis.

A hill, Mount Sal, stood on the northern edge of the oasis. It was on this low but strategic eminence that the Prophet had pitched his leather tent as a watchtower and military headquarters when the whole oasis was under siege. However, the real geographical signpost of Medina was Mount Uhud, which rose three miles to the north. Uhud had two escarpments which reached south towards the oasis to frame a bowl, a natural theatre where the Battle of Uhud had been fought out between the Muslims and the pagan Arabs of Mecca. Here the rough grave-cairns of the seventy-four martyrs who had fallen during that day's fighting (including the Prophet's uncle Hamza) could be found, as well as the chuckling waters of Ainain – the double spring. The west face of Mount Uhud served as Medina's harbour. Here the three wadis, or dry river beds, that framed the Yathrib valley joined together at Zaghabah, a natural camping ground where expeditions and caravans could patiently assemble. It was close enough for merchants to ride in and trade at the various clan markets, as well as to make those last farewells and last-minute changes to faulty harnesses that are always necessary at the start of a journey – but not so close to the oasis that the grazing pack camels became a nuisance to the gardens or the caravan became afflicted by the visits of idle youths, dogs and the curious. Here also the gravel and sandy floor of the wadi l'Aqiq pointed travellers neatly on their way: either north towards Khaybar oasis or south towards Mecca. From this perspective you could understand how well placed Medina was to act as a trading centre. Immediately south of the oasis began the lava flows: a massive extrusion of eroded basalt that stretched hundreds of miles south. Determined travellers could make their way across this territory but the sharp, black stones and the bleak grazing made it very hard going with a real risk of damaging the hoofs of your pack animals. However, just to the north of Medina the way opened for the first really inviting east–west crossing of the Nejed Desert; and the road to Iraq and Persia. Indeed so obvious are Medina's charms that many historians have wondered how it came to be that dry, arid, mountain-embraced Mecca ever came to dominate the Arabian carrying trade when Medina had seemingly all the geographical advantages on her side.

Mecca's one great advantage was the quality of her political leadership. The Quraysh of Mecca, for all their clan rivalries, usually succeeded in presenting a united face to the outside world. Unlike Medina, which was so riven by the political infighting of the clans that it could not pretend to any coherent policy.

In Mecca the agricultural poverty of the desert valleys had always worked to drive the men out to seek employment in the wider world. The Quraysh of Mecca were to be found everywhere in the Middle East where there was a sniff of trade: be it the ports of Abyssinia, the hill towns of the Yemen, a castle in Syria or the court of a Persian governor in Iraq, there you would find them, trusted figures who were equally at home with the Bedouin tribes of the desert, urbane merchant dynasts and the outposts of bored frontier guards. The rich chieftains of Mecca had a correspondingly diverse portfolio of holdings: perhaps a small estate in Palestine, a house in a walled town of Syria, some grazing grounds in Mesopotamia, an orchard in the Yemen or in the hill town of Taif; and then there were their herds, some of which would be held in hand, others cared for by distant Bedouin tribes. Mecca and its leadership prospered or perished from its role as trusted traders.

Medina by contrast was rich enough in agricultural produce that the success or failure of its caravan carrying trade was not such a vital concern. Although the men of Medina also worked on the caravan routes and were involved in grazing the surrounding desert with their herds, their primary concern was always their oasis gardens. This provided them with very different priorities, for there was no such thing as an off-season in the life of a Medina gardener. The gardens had always to be protected from man and beast; the neat picket fences of palm fronds and high mud walls had to be continually repaired against the recurrent assault of nimble goats, pushy mules, inquisitive camels and envious neighbours. Above all the oasis gardens had to be watered; for it was truly said of the palm that it will flourish only if its head is in the sun and its feet are in the water, which in Medina required months of back-breaking work at the well-heads. This subterranean water was Medina's true wealth but it was jealously guarded. Typically the one recorded row between the Muslim refugees from Mecca and the indigenous Muslims of Medina began over a seemingly petty dispute over a leather bucket of water. Some wells were communally maintained by a clan or a neighbourhood but most were private ventures that needed constant attention – and the work of repair was expensive and dangerous. In their first years as exiles in Medina the pious Muslim refugees, most of whom had been

ruined by a decade of persecution and trade embargo, were driven
by necessity to work as day labourers in the gardens of their hosts.
Ali for instance had to earn his keep by hauling water. The wealthy
and clever Uthman earned enormous gratitude from the young
Muslim community when he paid for the construction of a new
well and then gave it over for the sole use of the poor Muslim
refugees from Mecca. The jealousy over water rights and garden
fences was emblematic of the whole political system within
Medina, just as the smooth operation of Mecca's spring and
autumn caravans revealed a native genius for consensus politics.

Before the arrival of the Prophet the oasis of Medina was in a
political mess. Although a precise chronicle of this clan warfare has
not survived, there is no shortage of factual information from pre-
Islamic Medina. In fact there is an overabundance, for the family
histories of hundreds of early Muslims from Medina were proudly
recorded for posterity. Though unlike Mecca there was no
Quraysh-like supertribe which could link all the clans together
under the cousinly umbrella of a family tree with one common
male ancestor. For pre-Islamic Medina was then still a partly matri-
lineal society, so that around half the population of the oasis traced
its descent through their mothers and grandmothers. Property in
Medina was also inherited in a different way from that of Mecca,
for in the oasis it was usually held by uncles for the future benefit
of their nephews (their sisters' children) rather than for the children of their own wives. To add a further twist of complexity to
these early genealogies some of the oasis women appear to have
had three husbands – simultaneously. In short it has proved impossible to use all these individual family stories to piece together a
coherent history of the clan conflict within the oasis.

Muhammad may have shared in some of these traditions, for
his great-grandmother from the Najjar tribe was from the oasis.
He had other close family connections with the place, for his

mother, Amina, would die on a journey to Medina which she had
undertaken to introduce her young son to some of his uncles
there.

Nor did the division of this oasis community between two
deadly rivals, the Aws and Khazraj (the Capulets and the
Montagues of pre-Islamic Medina), seem to underwrite any firm
alliance of clans. The celebrated antagonism between the Aws and
the Khazraj appears to have been a shifting concept, and seems to
denote no more than a pair of labels for the battlefields. The real
diplomatic life of the oasis seethed within the complexities of eight
major clans (some on the point of amalgamation, others busily
fracturing themselves into new units) assisted by thirty-three
smaller groups all politicking against one another. They could be
linked by *jiwar* (the temporary protection of a neighbour), by *hilf*
(a full mutual alliance), which might lead to the two parties
becoming *hulafa* (confederates), or by a carefully watched armed
neutrality. To this already confusing picture you must add the separate allegiances made between each oasis clan and the rival
Bedouin tribes of the surrounding desert.

There was also the presence of three determinedly independent Jewish clans – Beni Nadir, Beni Qurayzah and Beni
Qaynuqa – to take into account. The Jewish clans of pre-Islamic
Medina were highly confident Arabs of Jewish faith who freely
intermarried with their pagan Arab neighbours and had their
own traditional allies among the Bedouin tribes of the desert.
The old traditions of Medina recalled that these three clans had
once ruled the entire oasis, holding fifty-nine fortified *atam* with
just thirteen in the hands of the pagan Arabs. This was the period
when the Arab kings of Kinda kept the peace in central and southern Arabia as the client allies of the Persian Empire in the fifth
century. The Jews within Arabia were always the natural allies of
Persia and this was probably the time when the Beni Qurayzah

and Beni Nadir clans were confirmed in their possession of most of the richest land in the Aliyah – the oldest and most southerly part of the oasis.

The Beni Qaynuqa by contrast had hardly any land at all and lived off the product of the nearby gold and silver mines. They were renowned as smiths, miners and jewellers and their market held outside their fortified *atam* was one of the most important metal-trading centres in all of central Arabia. Recent radiocarbon dating from carbon residue locked into mining slag from the nearby mine of Mahd al-Dhahab, Medina's 'cradle of gold', has pinpointed the reopening of the works to around AD 450, which fits neatly into this scenario of the Jewish clans of Medina prospering during the pro-Persian rule of the Kinda kings. Nor are the early Muslim chroniclers silent, for Ibn Sa'd wrote about Medina's two silver mines and how 'much money came . . . from the mines of Qabaliyya and Juhayna, while the mine of the Sulaym tribe was opened during the Caliphate of Abu Bakr (632–4). He received alms money from it and deposited it in the treasury, hence distributing it to the people.' Another account describes how the Prophet Muhammad was in the habit of giving a couple of ounces of cast silver to each member of a tribal delegation as a 'going-away' present at the end of their meeting. This fits in with his known habits of generosity and reckless hospitality, but it also suggests that he was in control of a regular supply of silver bullion.

Clearly one has to be careful how one conceives of Medina in this era. For this agricultural oasis was no backwater but seems to have had great wealth and considerable technical knowledge at its disposal. A selective inflow of gold and silver bullion into the oasis society would also go a long way to explaining the vindictive cycle of wars. These conflicts had climaxed in the war of Hatib just before the arrival of the Prophet. It had started with four separate clan grievances being fought out but gradually escalated into an all-out war as various Bedouin allies were drawn into the fight. The pitched battle of Bu'ath was the bloody and inconclusive culmination of this escalating conflict. The killing that day included so many of the leading warlords that it effectively brought about a truce. In particular the death of the chief of the Bayadah clan, whose predatory instincts had led his small but militant clan to build up a solid block of nineteen *atam* on the western edge of the oasis, allowed Medina a relaxation from his schemes and machinations. Other numerically strong clans, such as the Najjar, had wisely stayed away from that final round of the fighting, as had the most statesmanlike of all the clan leaders, Abdallah ibn Ubayy of the Ba'l Hubla.

The invitation to welcome Muhammad to Medina does appear to have been a genuinely collective decision. It was also one that was taken gradually and peacefully. It had begun in the summer of 620 when half a dozen men from Medina were deeply impressed by their chance meeting with Muhammad at the time of the annual pilgrimage to Mecca, holy to both pagan Arabia and the Muslim faith. They deliberately returned again the following year to hear more from this remarkable man though this time their numbers had doubled to a dozen men, ten Khazraj and two from the Aws. At the end of their visit they promised to follow the teachings of the Prophet and specifically 'to associate nothing with God, that we would neither steal, or commit fornication, nor slay our offspring nor utter slanders'. To continue their spiritual education and to teach them the daily practice of prayers, Muhammad sent one of his most trusted followers, Musab, who rode back with this small caravan and dwelt with them for some eleven months. Musab's mission bore spectacular fruit, for the following year, sixty-three men and two women from Medina joined the annual pilgrimage in order to meet Muhammad and pledge their faith in Islam. Clearly some of the political leadership within Medina had been very impressed by the way that the small community under Musab's tutelage had been able to unite Aws and Khazraj in common worship. So that within this group of sixty-five of the faithful there were also twelve *nuqaba*, 'representatives' of the most powerful Medina clans.

Even so it is always useful to remember that Muhammad was not immediately entrusted with anything like full powers nor was the population of Medina committed to following his religious teachings. The oath of Aqaba of 622 contained two principal conditions: first that Muhammad was acknowledged to be a Prophet; and second that he was accepted as the chief arbitrator by all the clans of the oasis. At that emotive moonlit oath there were dozens of devout Muslim converts, though the presence of the twelve *nuqaba* also gave the event a very strong political element.

Muhammad was also to be treated like an honorary clan chieftain by the people of Medina; this was not a side clause from the Aqaba oath but due to his unquestioned leadership over the Muslim exiles from Mecca who in effect formed yet another clan within the complex patchwork of Medina's society. The number of refugees from Mecca was at first very small: about eighty men who could bear arms. Later when Muhammad's authority had grown enormously he never stepped aside from that first contractual oath with the *nuqaba* of Medina and respectfully continued to work through the clan chieftains of the oasis rather than rule directly over the population.

Once Muhammad arrived in Medina no one was forced to become a Muslim or to follow Muhammad on campaign. The only things they were obliged by the oath at Aqaba to do was to acknowledge him as a Prophet of God and bring their disputes to him first and to unite in a common defence when either the

Prophet or the oasis was threatened by outsiders. Even when the whole oasis had embraced Islam, the Prophet scrupulously respected the legal basis of his position in Medina. If there was a campaign being sent beyond the oasis, the Prophet would exhort the men of Medina to volunteer for battle, he might even try to shame them, but he would never command them to go. His leadership over the men of Medina was inspirational, never absolutist, and was always the more powerful because of this. Right from those very first years, the men of Medina were, however, an absolutely vital component to the military strength of Islam. In the lists of those who fought at that first engagement – the battle of the wells of Badr – there were just 86 exiles from Mecca but 238 clansmen from Medina.

Support for the Prophet, and for Islam, reached beyond the hitherto unbroken demands of clan allegiance. And looking back over those proudly preserved lists – of which warrior fought in which of the early battles of Islam – it is clear that these early heroes came from every clan and that no clan predominated. But there were a few clans who proved themselves conspicuously pro-Muslim. The small Salimah clan always fielded more than its share of warriors due to its devotion to the Prophet, while members of the Saidah clan (another small clan) would rise high due to the passionate support that its chief, Saad ibn Ubadayah, would give to Muhammad. The Saidah clan were also close neighbours to the Prophet, for their marketplace was conveniently close to Muhammad's house-mosque. But even the redoubtable Saad ibn Ubadayah had had his moment of weakness. It was remembered that he had not actually fought at the battle of the wells of Badr because he was out of action from a snake bite – though malicious rumour had it that he was actually still watching which way the political wind would blow. The Najjar would also gain prominence but this was more out of luck than their own judgement, for the Prophet's house-mosque stood in their neighbourhood and so the future city of Medina would rise up from out of their old gardens.

Nor must one forget the dissident voices within the clans of Medina. Asma, daughter of Marwan, a forceful poet and a prolific mother, was one of the most inflammatory voices of this opposition. The early Muslim historian Waqidi quotes one of her acerbic taunts:

> *Fucked men of Malik and Thabit*
> *And of the Awf and Khazraj*
> *You obey a stranger who does not belong among you,*
> *Who is not of Murad, nor of Madhhij*
> *Do you when your own chiefs have been murdered, put your*
>   *hope in him*
> *Like men greedy for meat broth when it is cooking?*
> *Is there no man of honour who will take advantage of an*
>   *unguarded moment*
> *And cut off the gull's hopes?*

After the victory of Badr (in 624) one of her own clansmen crept into her house, tiptoeing across the spread-eagled forms of her sleeping children, and stabbed Asma through the heart. The next day this assassin confessed his deed to the excited crowd of clansmen that had assembled before her house: 'It was I that killed the daughter of Marwan. Decide what is to be done with me, but do not keep me waiting.' But not a man moved to demand vengeance on behalf of the five sons of Asma on a man of her own clan. The Prophet himself dismissed ideas of a penalty being imposed for this murder by declaring that as far as he was concerned 'Two goats shall not come to blows for her.'

A month later, the second vocal opponent of Muhammad's

presence in Medina, Abu Afak, would also be killed in his sleep. Among other verses, he had written,

I have lived a long time, but I have never seen
Either a house or gathering of people
More loyal and faithful to
Its allies, when they call on it,
Than that of the children of Qayla [the people of Medina]
As a whole.
The mountains will crumble before they submit.
Yet here is a rider come among them who has divided them.
[saying] 'This is permitted; this is forbidden to all kinds of
   things.
But if you believed in power
And in might, why did you not follow a tubba?'*

Another opponent from within Medina was Abu Amir, nicknamed 'ar-Rahib', the monk. Ar-Rahib should have been an early candidate for conversion. He was a classic example of a *hanif* (a native-born monotheist). For ar-Rahib, just like the Prophet, looked to the old pure religion of Abraham (that pre-dated Judaism and Christianity) as the role model for Arabia, took spiritual retreats (hence his nickname) but rejected celibacy as unworkable in the passionate environment of the Bedouin of Arabia. However, after a few early conversations with Muhammad he grew resentful and decided to abandon Medina altogether, taking his followers (a not insignificant body of between fifteen and fifty men) to Mecca, where he became an active ally of the pagan opposition – before finally riding north into Syria. A jealous, if independent-minded, free spirit to the end.

---

* 'Tubba' is the name-title of a dynasty of Yemeni rulers.

These three individuals – Asma bint Marwan, Abu Afak and ar-Rahib – were in a tiny minority. The vast bulk of the oasis population were enthusiastically behind the internal peace that had been provided by the leadership of the Prophet Muhammad. There were also many genuinely pious individual converts to Islam, who can be numbered in their hundreds and are still proudly listed as Companions of the Prophet. There was also a sizeable group within the oasis who are referred to in the Koran and in the first histories as the 'Hypocrites'. They had converted more for an easy life than for any interest in a reflective moral life and a living faith. According to the popular picture of such Hypocrites they performed only the most minimal prayers, gave alms grudgingly, fasted reluctantly and failed to attend the all-night recitations of the Koran which were such a striking feature of the early community.

It is possible that the label of 'Hypocrites' has been taken too literally. Some scholars argue that 'slow to contribute' is in any case a more appropriate translation of the Arabic term, which is also linked to the root *naqaf*, which describes various types of hole or lair. It may also have included many who were not anti-Muslim but just attached to the old ways and agricultural traditions of the oasis and slow to pay the charitable tithe. We have very little literary evidence about the old pagan habits of Medina, especially when compared with those of Mecca and its surrounding shrines. Nor do we have any reliable traditions about the destruction of the old shrines with the coming of Islam or even the title of the tutelary goddess of the oasis – as we do for pre-Islamic Mecca and Taif. It seems possible that the old agricultural rituals of Medina were not so much destroyed as quietly absorbed beneath the public attachment to Islam. The Muslims of Mecca, who by their background and education were all linked to herding and the mechanics of the caravan trade, were often completely ignorant

of farming techniques and customs. It may be that this very ignorance made them unnecessarily suspicious of the Muslim people of
Medina, for they could never be confident about what was a real
process of farming and what was an old pagan ritual, an element
of the worldwide fertility cult where the fecundity of the earth was
renewed with sacrifices.

To those unaware of the yearly cycle of farming activities,
such joyous (and vitally necessary) occasions as the fertilisation
of the female palm tree with the pollen of the male could easily
be mistaken for a spring bacchanalia. While those who had
not participated in the sense of physical relief at the gathering-
in of a successful harvest might confuse a celebratory supper
served up before a midsummer midnight fire with some pagan
offering to Saturn (especially if culinary tradition required
the baking of a succulent young dog in a subterranean trench-
oven for such an event). Even the simple act of fertilising a field
might appear to be a mysterious pagan practice to those
unused to it, as the produce of the dung heaps, the old bones
and hearth fires were broken up, mixed together and then
carefully buried beneath the soil to 'strengthen' next year's
crops.

Adding to the difference between the agricultural habits of the
oasis farmers and the rituals of the Islamic year, they were based
on different calendars. Farming has to stay true to the dictates of
the solar calendar, while Islam was fixed to an unchanging cycle
of lunar months which remains free of any distinctive season.
This slight antagonism survives today, when the faith of the
farmers is often depicted as slightly childish by the religious leaders of society who are habitually associated with townsmen: with
the traders, artisans and those in the learned professions. It may
be that some similar suspicions kept the Muslims of Mecca from
fully understanding the faith of the Muslims of Medina. Alcohol

was certainly much more readily available in the oasis (with its rich annual harvest of dates and barley) than in mountain-encircled Mecca. This would also explain the growing sternness of the three Koranic pronouncements against alcohol, as the community moved from Mecca to the greater temptations within Medina.

The habit of the women of Medina taking multiple male partners was also in strong contrast with the paternalistic traditions of Mecca, as was the tradition of creating your given name from your female ancestor not your male line. Indeed, once seen in the specific light of Medina, many of the Koranic pronouncements on marriage and divorce can be viewed not so much as restricting female rights as making the previously feckless men of Medina aware of – and also for the first time financially responsible for – their offspring. Islam, especially in Medina, sought always to strengthen the family against the clan. The sexual freedom of the pre-Islamic society obviously had its own great attractions, especially for the young, the rich and the beautiful. However, the Prophet recognised the obverse of these freedoms: neglected penniless widows and cast-off mothers, the herds of uncared-for, underfed and unloved orphans, the burial of unwanted newborn infants and the untamed and fatherless adolescents that roamed the streets were too high a price.

The oasis of Medina was the theatre where a new moral order was first tested on Arabia. The stresses and strains that existed between the Muhajirun (Muslims of Mecca) and the Ansar (Muslims of Medina), and between a core of devout converts and a less ardent majority, and also between the Bedouin and town-dwellers, swirl around just beneath the surface historical record. These antagonisms would play a powerful role in altering the shape of early Islamic society. The Muslims of Mecca were certainly convinced that the Muslims of Medina were not fit to become the Heirs of the Prophet, even though they had numerically and militarily functioned as the backbone of early Islam. This may have been based on nothing more valid than tribal prejudice. What is certain is that the one Muslim from Mecca who we know had a very direct experience of agricultural labour in the oasis, and who maintained an impeccable morality throughout his life, was never touched by such prejudice. Ali, the true Heir of the Prophet, always championed the rights of the Muslims of Medina. Perhaps this was another reason why his candidacy would be overlooked. Certainly all the three other Caliphs, Abu Bakr, Omar and Uthman, hardly ever gave a position of responsibility to anyone from Medina. Ali's egalitarian nature would long be frustrated.

2

Ali: First Disciple
of the Prophet

At the very moment of Muhammad's death the two traditions of
Islam each branch out with their own rival stories. The Sunni
believe that the Prophet died resting on the lap of Aisha. The Shia
believe that he expired leaning against the shoulder of Ali. This
contradiction is emblematic of the whole schism within Islam but
it is also not unusual in the Arabic tradition, where it was a
common practice for a historian to tell at least two or three variant
tales about any decisive event, and then leave the reader to make
their own decision – with the pious disclaimer that 'The truth is
known only to God.'

In this case it is possible to believe both accounts. On the morning of Muhammad's death, Ali and Aisha may have put aside their
mutual hostility as they silently supported the man they both
loved. Later their partisan supporters told only the narrative that
featured just one of them.

Whether Ali was with the Prophet at the hour of his death or
not, he was undoubtedly a true intimate in the last days of
Muhammad, as he had been throughout his life. It was Ali, with

his great-uncle Abbas, who was there to support the fever-ridden
body of Muhammad as he was moved from the room of his wife
Maymuna to be nursed in Aisha's hut. It was also on Ali's shoulder
that the Prophet leant when a few days later he made his last visit
to the mosque and instructed Abu Bakr to lead the prayers in his
place. When Muhammad breathed his last it was Ali who immediately took responsibility for the washing of the dead and the
burial preparations. No one could ever doubt Ali's devotion to
Muhammad and the many bonds that connected them: Ali was
the Prophet's cousin, the Prophet's son-in-law, arguably the
Prophet's first male believer, the father of the Prophet's only male
grandchildren, the Prophet's most intimate disciple and the first
heroic warrior champion of Islam (alongside his great-uncle
Hamza). Ali had also served the Prophet as an army commander,
missionary, diplomat and administrative secretary. It is said that
while he prepared the Prophet's body for the grave his grief poured
out into spontaneous verse:

May my parents be sacrificed on you, Messenger of God
For with your death things have come to an end
Which could not have ended with the death of any other
    person.
The chain of prophethood has been snapped.
News of the unseen has ceased,
Revelations from the Almighty have been severed
You gave a message of hope to the people
You showed them the right path
You established a new order
You are the saviour of humankind
You established equality among the people
You ushered in a revolution
You were our guide when alive

You will guide us even after death
If you had not ordered patience in the hour of grief
I would have shed blood from my eyes
The entire world is now dark without you
Your passing is a loss beyond measure
But we will resign ourselves to the will of God
From God you came and to God you have returned,
May your soul rest in peace close to your creator

Until Muhammad's death there had never been a time when Ali's life had not been filled by the presence of the Prophet. They were first cousins, for Ali's father was the elder brother of Muhammad's father, Abdullah, though the two families were so close that they almost constituted a single unit. For Ali's father, Abu Talib, had acted as a father to Muhammad after the successive deaths of father, mother and grandfather had orphaned the young boy. From the age of eight Muhammad was entirely dependent on Abu Talib for food, shelter and his education. As the leading sheikh of the clan, Abu Talib's protection remained upon Muhammad as he became a man, and a merchant. Later, when he became a Prophet, it was only Abu Talib's continual protection that preserved his nephew's life and those of his followers. Muhammad's cousins from this family would become like his brothers and sisters: Talib was about the same age, Aqil a little younger, as was the only girl of the family, Fakhita (with whom the teenage Muhammad fell in love), while Jafar was the family's darling. Ali was an afterthought, born half a generation after the rest of his siblings. By the time of Ali's birth, Muhammad was twenty-nine years old and had already been married to Khadijah for four years. Legends would later collect around Ali's birth story. How his mother was performing a ritual circulation around Mecca's holy Kaaba shrine when the birth pains came upon her – and so was forced to use the shelter of God's own temple to give birth to Ali. Another tale records how the infant Ali could not open his eyes – until he was seated in the lap of his cousin Muhammad, whose face was the first that he saw.

When Ali was a boy he moved over from his father's house to Muhammad's. He was aged five, eight or eleven, according to the various prime sources, so an exact chronology for Ali's life remains elusive, even if there is little doubt about the order of events. Some chroniclers record that this was to relieve Ali's father Abu Talib, then reportedly suffering from a bad run of business, from the pressure of feeding another mouth. It is difficult to give full credit to this and it may well be a slur against the business efficiency of the Hashim clan that was added by their dynastic rivals at a later date. Certainly Abu Talib, the leader of the Beni Hashim clan, remained one of the most respected sheikhs in Mecca until the day of his death – and if he wanted for anything as simple as food Muhammad and his wealthy and famously generous wife Khadijah would have been honoured to provide; as would the rest of his clan. Ali may have moved to his cousin's house partly to assuage the grief that lay there, for though all his four daughters survived, all three of Muhammad and Khadijah's sons had by then died. There may be an even simpler explanation: the young Ali might have preferred to spend his time in a house filled with cousins of his own age rather than the adult siblings that occupied his father's house. The two houses were not in any case very far apart, which would have allowed him to happily ricochet between them at will. There was a pleasing symmetry about the arrangement, for just as Muhammad had learned the caravan trade by serving an apprenticeship for his uncle Abu Talib, now it was Muhammad's turn to teach Abu Talib's son.

This was probably the time when Ali was taught to read and write – skills available only to a wealthy minority. There are also stories of how the young Ali was an intimate and very early witness to his cousin's private piety, for he would bring supplies of food and water to the caves where Muhammad prayed and meditated in the many years before he became a Prophet. Ali's exposure to the detailed workings of the caravan trade would, however, have been fairly minimal. When Muhammad's first revelation came upon him, in 610, Ali was still a young boy. Five years later, in 615, when Muhammad was instructed by his angelic messenger to become a full-time preacher – the time when Muhammad presumably surrendered his last direct involvement in the Meccan caravan trade – Ali would have been about thirteen.

This was to have an enormous bearing on Ali's future prestige as a leader among his contemporaries. No one could doubt his ancestry, but what he did lack was a manhood spent in the Arabia-wide caravan trade, of finding out the necessary ways of surviving within this highly competitive mercantile world, of bargaining in the markets, of dealing with nomad guides, hiring camels, buying fodder, not to mention the customs officials in the Yemen, in Persian-controlled Iraq, in the Byzantine culture of Syria, in Abyssinia and the harbours of the Red Sea. He would never grow into manhood with an innate understanding that the world was governed as much by coin as by faith, that even the most noble warlord had his price in silver bullion and that envy, jealousy and treachery were more common human traits than compassion, honesty and a righteous passion. Ali's nature was created in an exceptional household, which equipped him with many precious spiritual attributes, but it did not make of him a natural politician who understood the venality that underpinned human motivation.

Of faith Ali had an abundance. Even as an awkward fifteen-year-old he was not ashamed to make a public testimony of support for Muhammad's teachings. And this was after all the high dignitaries of his Hashim clan (that included his father and his powerful uncles, such as the sardonic worldly-wise Abu Lahab and the tough hero-huntsman Hamza) had sat through dinner and listened to Muhammad preaching with not so much as a single voice raised in support. Ali's older brother Jafar would later convert and become such a key figure within the small community of Muslims that he would be given the task of leading the refugees who took shelter in the Christian kingdom of Abyssinia in 616. For those who remained in Mecca, the trade boycott placed by the pagan majority over the Muslims and the Beni Hashim clan that continued to protect them was a time of great trial. Muhammad's wife Khadijah's great fortune was entirely dissipated at this time, and we also know that Abu Bakr's dropped from 50,000 to 6000 dirhams. The year 619 with the death of both Abu Talib and Khadijah must have been as testing a time for the nineteen-year-old Ali as it was for his revered master. Ali lost both father and adopted mother, the Prophet lost his adopted father and wife. The verse that Ali is considered to have composed for this occasion still survives:

> *My eyes well with tears*
> *I weep for the chief of the Bateha valley*
> *Whose name was Abu Talib:*
> *And they weep for that flower of womanhood*
> *Whose name was Khadijah;*
> *The woman first to accept Islam;*
> *And first to pray.*
> *Both Abu Talib and Khadijah were pure souls.*
> *Their passing away has created a great void.*
> *At the pain of their separation*
> *I spend the whole night in weeping.*
> *They succoured the Holy Prophet.*

They were a source of strength to Islam.
After them the world has been plunged into darkness.
From God they came and to God they have returned;
May their souls rest in peace.

The last line was more of a heartfelt wish from a loyal son than a statement. For though Abu Talib had remained a steadfast protector of both his nephew and his hundred or so followers, he stoutly refused to embrace Islam even on his deathbed. Ali must have feared the fate that awaited his non-Muslim father, even one so well loved by the Prophet as Abu Talib.

The years after Khadijah's and Abu Talib's deaths were to become ever more desperate for the embattled community, so that once the Yathrib oasis emerged as a place of safe exile for the Muslims of Mecca they quickly and quietly migrated to this refuge. Ali and Abu Bakr were the last of the able-bodied male believers to stay behind in Mecca with Muhammad. It was at this critically vulnerable point, with all their followers out of the city of Mecca, that the pagan opposition decided to strike Muhammad down. Choosing one young man from each of the clans (so that responsibility for blood vengeance would be difficult to apportion), they surrounded the Prophet's house. Arab honour would not allow them to strike at him within the sanctity of his home – especially one filled by his women – so they waited for him to emerge into the street after dawn. They patiently watched for the first signs of movement from the figure wrapped up in Muhammad's cloak on the bed mat. When the cloaked figure arose and shrugged off his cloak in the morning light to reveal young Ali not the bearded Prophet, the band of assassins immediately realised that they had been fooled. Muhammad had made his escape with Abu Bakr in the night. Ali was able to tell them that the Prophet had already left for Yathrib (now known as

Medina) – a calculated half-truth that greatly facilitated the Prophet's safe journey, for he was hiding in a nearby cave.

It was left to Ali, as the last professed Muslim man to remain in Mecca, to tidy up a few last affairs of the refugee community before making his own way to the safety of Yathrib – a heroic solitary journey that he made by foot. When Ali eventually arrived at the Yathrib oasis the pairing system by which the Prophet had placed the penniless Meccan refugees among the indigenous people of Medina – who acted as both hosts and tutors in the very different agricultural environment of their oasis – had been completed. In some cases the pairing worked like a dream: the devout Medina Muslim Sad ibn ar-Rabi offered his paired brother from Mecca half his wealth and even one of his two wives. In this case the offer was politely rejected. Instead Abder-Rahman ibn Awf politely enquired from his host where the market was – for as a Quraysh merchant he suspected that he could quickly earn a living from his wits there. At the end of that first day's trading he brought back a goatskin of butter and a cheese which he presented to his host.

There was great interest among the men of Medina to see which of them would be paired with the Prophet, but Muhammad did not wish to establish any favourites or exacerbate the already fierce clan rivalries within the oasis. So he chose the late arrival, his young cousin Ali, to be his official 'pair'. In doing so he also consciously placed both himself and Ali at an economic disadvantage, for they had no one who could provide them with barley and dates. The two of them embraced poverty as a necessary part of their struggle for religious freedom. To earn his daily bread Ali worked at the well-heads, hauling up leather buckets of water in exchange for dates – a job that was usually performed by beasts of burden or slaves. Ali was proud to return to Muhammad and share his wages as their evening meal. Ali also bought rushes from the markets, which in the evening he would weave into mats that could be resold at a slight profit. He was also the foremost labourer in the construction of the courtyard house-mosque for the Prophet. This modest building, believed to have been roughly fifty yards square, rose from out of the free labour of the Muslims, both the Meccan refugees (Muhajirun) and the men of Medina (the Ansar – the helpers) working side by side. Stories survive of Ali cutting out the foundations for the walls and later working as a hod-carrier, ferrying loads of mud bricks to the skilled masons. The Muslims chanted as they worked, 'There is no life but the life of the next world, O God have mercy on the Muhajirun and the Ansar.' Ali also composed other verses to sing out: 'Whoever builds a mosque, And works whether sitting or standing, puts up with the pain of labour, while others shirk work, for fear of dust and pain, Both of these verily cannot equal each other.' It is strong testimony for how soon Ali had become associated with the rights of the workers and the devoted believers against the half-hearted Muslim converts who 'fear dust and pain'.

Ali had no such fears. As well as labouring with the sweat of his brow for his own sustenance he was also soon recognised as one of the leading warriors among the Muslims. After the house-mosque was finished he was selected – alongside Zubayr ibn al-Awwam (also among the inner core of early believers, the Companions) – to scout out the desert routes that might be used by the great Quraysh caravan, due to return from Syria to Mecca that spring of 624. Having found out that it would pass through the wells of Badr, they hurried back to Medina, where after a hurried council of war the Muslims decided to try to intercept it. For the Prophet knew that if he captured their treasure-filled caravan, he would at last get a sympathetic hearing for his message of peace from the proud, pagan lords of Mecca. The intimacy of these early days of Islam is revealed by the size of the Muslim army – just 313 men, of whom only a small proportion were mounted on camels. When the battle lines were drawn the three champions who advanced to fight in single combat included Ali and his uncle Hamza. Like Homeric heroes of old they dispatched their opponents and those who advanced to take their place, before the general melee commenced. It was a day when brother was pitted against brother. No empty metaphor this, for Ali's two elder brothers, Talib and Aqil, actually fought in the ranks of the pagan Quraysh. The body of the former was to be identified among the seventy slain that day, the latter among the prisoners who would later be profitably ransomed. When the booty was finally distributed Ali had won himself a camel, a sword and a precious suit of body armour. He had also won a formidable reputation as a swordsman, and the Prophet publicly saluted his young cousin as 'Haider-I-Karrar' – 'the lion that returns again and again to the fight'. It was the first attested battle that he had ever been engaged in, so clearly Ali must have been well taught and continuously exercised in the arts of war as a young man.

Ali now felt confident enough to tackle one of the great passions of his life, his love for his cousin Fatimah, the youngest of the daughters of the Prophet and a woman he knew as well as a sister. In this, as in so many things, Ali's life unconsciously followed the pattern set by Muhammad before him, who as a young man had fallen in love with his cousin Fakhita – though Muhammad had been considered too poor a catch to be given her hand. Ali's mother was the ambassador to Muhammad for this highly delicate mission, for the Prophet had already turned down requests for Fatimah's hand from both Abu Bakr and Omar. In this case Muhammad took the proposal to Fatimah herself. He almost certainly knew the answer before he asked his daughter. She answered with a downward glance and a silent pause. Fatimah was not like her other, older sisters. From her childhood she had been totally engaged in her father's spiritual teachings. The only other believer of her age who understood her total immersion in Islam was the young cousin who had grown up in her household. Ali also shared Fatimah's love for her mother, Khadijah, which was another great bond between them – especially after the Prophet took other wives.

Ali still had no money, nothing for a dowry, nothing for the customary gifts of jewels for his bride or the expenses of a marriage. Fortunately the merchant prince Uthman stepped in at this moment. Fixing the value of Ali's newly won body armour at a generously high price, he insisted on buying it for five hundred dirhams. Four hundred could then be set aside as a dowry for Fatimah, leaving a hundred for all other expenses. Later Uthman presented the armour back to Ali as a wedding present. Ali was scandalised by the scale of this generosity and refused to accept the gift, though Uthman (an early believer like Ali and now also his brother-in-law) patiently insisted and finally persuaded Ali to accept the armour back in the name of God. As Uthman so charmingly explained, 'it would sit and rust in the house of a merchant like myself while in the possession of Ali it would see valiant service in the cause which we both serve'.

The marriage was conducted by the Prophet himself, who gave a short sermon after the communal prayers before concluding, 'Now in obedience to the Will of God I perform the marriage of Fatimah with Ali and ask you all to bear witness that I have given Fatimah in marriage to Ali against a dower of 400 pieces of silver coin. May God create love between the pair, bless them, purify their offspring, make their progeny a mine of wisdom and a source of God's blessings.' Of the world's blessings they had but a very small store. In the first years of their marriage Ali continued to labour for hire, while Fatimah ground barley with a hand-mill for other households. There was not time enough in the day for their clothes to be regularly washed or for them to be able to gather kindling to keep their hearth fire alight. Even in bed their poverty showed. Their blankets were not ample enough to cover Ali's warrior's physique, so he had to choose between exposing his legs or his head and shoulders. Fatimah, whose childhood in Mecca must have been filled with all the comforts of a wealthy Quraysh household, now went to bed with her shoulders bruised from carrying pitchers of water from the well-heads and her hands blistered from turning the stone hand-mills. When she asked her father for help he offered her what was most precious to him, additional prayers.

Khadijah and Fatimah are the ultimate archetypes for Muslim women. For both Sunni and Shia Muslims they are inspiring examples of the near-perfect woman. Fatimah has always been the most popular girl's name throughout the Muslim world. Scholars would later speculate on the pre-Islamic origins of her name. 'Fatimah' is derived from the verb *fatima*, to wean a child. This was seen as a portent. Fatimah's example would help wean the people from the material things of this world to address the real concerns of the thereafter. The enormous honour in which she is held can at times seem almost inappropriate for a strictly mono-theistic religion. Islam's most respected university, Cairo's Al-Azhar, was named in her honour. With such titles as Al-Mubarakah (the blessed), Az-Zakiyah (the virtuous), As-Siddiqah (the righteous), Ar-Radiyah (the satisfied), Al-Muhaddithah (the eloquent), Az-Zahra (the blossomed) and al-Tahirah (the pure) it is easy to see how the cult of Fatimah has often been compared to that of the Virgin Mary. The analogy is all the more potent because they have many similarities: Fatimah, just like the Virgin Mary, has a revered mother (Khadijah to the Virgin's mother St Anne) and gives birth to a beautiful boy child destined for a heroic sacrificial death (Husayn and Jesus) while another child is fated to survive (Hasan and St James) and father children.*

Ali's prowess on the battlefield at Badr was remembered. When the Prophet wished to isolate the Beni Qaynuqa clan (one of the three wealthy Jewish clans within Medina oasis with a special expertise as metalworkers) he chose Ali to command the operation. It needed to be quick, bloodless but totally efficient if Muhammad's role as the recognised arbitrator within the oasis community as agreed in the oath of Aqaba was going to be upheld. The young Ali placed the Beni Qaynuqa strongholds under such a tight siege that within a fortnight they were forced to sue for terms. It was an impressive tactical achievement, that required discipline and a sure organisational hand, for though Ali would have been in command of some Ansar (Muslims from Medina) he had essentially toppled one of the most powerful of the clans with a scratch force of refugees who had three years' experience of the oasis. After the Beni Qaynuqa were expelled, their confiscated land was parcelled up among the penniless Meccan refugees, who at last had gardens and palm orchards of their own – and would henceforth become less of a burden to their Medina Muslim paired hosts.

Ali had never had such a host and must have been delighted that he could now haul water to irrigate his own garden, rather than work as a hired hand for others. The extra food and security was well timed. Fatimah was pregnant and would give birth to their first child, Hasan, in 625 and a year later to Husayn, followed by two girls, Zaynab and Umm Kulthum. Hasan and Husayn were the only male descendants of the Prophet Muhammad. In the

---

* Occasionally there has been a powerful near-fusion of identity. At the shrine of Our Lady of Fatima – in Portugal, a Catholic country that has incorporated many aspects of its Moorish Muslim past – a divine female communicated prophecies to awestruck shepherds.

traditional society of Arabia their births would have enormously increased the already high esteem in which their parents were held. It would also have only been natural if the childless wives of Muhammad were a little inwardly envious – even while they shared the joy that these infants brought to their beloved Prophet. They were another thorn in the enmity that would develop between Aisha and Ali.

In the battle of Uhud, that resulted in a defeat for the Muslim army in 625 by the pagans of Mecca, no blame could be attached to the personal conduct of Ali. For once again he had been chosen as one of the three champions of the Muslims who engaged the enemy warriors in single combat as a prelude to the battle. He stood firm where all too many of his comrades broke ranks when the cavalry of the Quraysh fell upon them; indeed his personal example meant that he became the standard-bearer around which a defiant nucleus held firm. Just as David and Saul are credited with killing their thousands and tens of thousands, one need not believe the later traditions that claimed Ali had personally slaughtered two hundred of the enemy that day. Much more moving than these swollen statistics is the memory that the two nurses in the Prophet's household (Umm Salim and Umm Atiya) did not dare to dress the sixty-three wounds that had cut into Ali at the end of that day. In the aftermath of the battle, Ali would be tended by Muhammad. As his wounds were cleaned he asked through gritted teeth that 'God grant me patience to bear this suffering for it was indeed only by a favour from God that he gave me the courage to stand and fight in spite of these wounds and not to leave the battle.' As an Amen to that, Muhammad named him 'Asad Allah' – 'Lion of God'. While in the oasis the street poets sung,

there is no sword better than the sword of Ali
and there is no young man superior to Ali.

During the siege of Medina in 627 by the coalition of Meccan and pagan Bedouin tribes Ali once again played a military role. He was one of the section commanders put in charge of digging a portion of the protective moat – and then later for supervising its defence. Throughout this morale-testing siege the Muslim forces remained tactically on the defensive. Not so in the aftermath. The last remaining enclave of Jews in Medina (who had been in correspondence with the besiegers – though they had not actually broken ranks) was placed under Muslim siege. Ali reportedly directed the blockade, which after twenty-five days brought them to surrender – though this also seems to have been precipitated by his successful midnight attack against one of their *atam*. Having neither negotiated nor fought their way out, the Beni Qurayzah were now defenceless. The harsh judgement delivered over them by Sad ibn Muadh (a clan chieftain of Medina who had been their ally of old) was to be administered by Ali. It was he and Zubayr ibn Al-Awwam (an early believer of whom we will hear much more later) who oversaw the enslavement of six hundred of the women and children of the clan and who organised the execution of all the men of the Beni Qurayzah – some two hundred of whom were beheaded that night and their bodies rolled into trench pits that had been dug across their own marketplace. Ali and Zubayr as well as wielding swords themselves arranged that at least two men of the Beni Qurayzah were killed by each of the major clans and sub-clans of Medina – so that the whole oasis shared in the blood guilt. Such a night must have tested the resolve of even the most steadfast faith, though once again the comparatively small numbers of professed Muslims would have gained from the confiscation and distribution of Jewish property. It was probably in the aftermath of the destruction of the Beni Qurayzah that Fatimah at last acquired a girl to work for her and help her bring up Husayn – then just one year old, while Hasan would have been two. The old Quraysh practice of finding a wet nurse for their children among the Bedouin of the desert was not possible in this time of war.

Throughout the eight-year period from 622 to 630 there was a constant sniping war of raids and counter-raids between the Medina oasis and the surrounding world. Ali does not seem to have played a major role in this. The Prophet led many of the campaigns himself and distributed commands among his close companions. Zayd was favoured more than any other man with by far the most commands. Zayd stood outside the Quraysh clan system and could harbour no unsuitable political ambitions; indeed his status as Muhammad's ex-slave boy (even though he had later been adopted) would have been held against him by the status-attuned desert Arabs. (Zayd had grown up among the tents of the Kalb tribe of northern Syria. He was captured by a raiding party of the Beni Qayn, who sold him at auction at Mecca's annual trade fair of Ukaz. He entered the household of the Prophet as a fifteen-year-old slave boy – a wedding present from the Prophet's wife Khadijah.) The Prophet could also trust Zayd's actions and maybe even intuitively know them in advance – for Muhammad had personally trained Zayd when they had worked together in the caravan trade. I have found no record of how Ali and Zayd felt about each other, although they grew up together in the household of Muhammad, and loved him as a master and an adopted father figure years before they learned to also revere him as a Prophet of God. It may be that their difference in age and Zayd's greater experience of the caravan trade and administrative command counterbalanced Ali's literacy and acknowledged brilliance as a poet, speaker and a daring swordsman. Where the young Ali was all zeal, Zayd was the more cautious-minded older brother. Zayd was necessarily a bit reserved, to protect himself from the innuendoes flung at him about his period as a slave, and

quietly spoken, especially when compared with the excitable
Bedouin under his command. He was also totally reliable and
thorough in his planning. One might ask what would have
happened if Zayd had not been killed at the battle of Mutah
just before the death of the Prophet. For if the 'brothers' Zayd and
Ali had stood shoulder to shoulder it is hard to imagine that
anyone, let alone Abu Bakr and Omar, would have stood as candidates for the Caliphate against them . . . and then Islam would
have known no schism. Even Aisha, proud though she was that
her father had become the first Caliph of Islam, thought this way,
for she declared, 'It never happened that the Holy Prophet
included Zayd in an army going to battle but not as its commander. Had he been alive at the time of the Prophet's death, he
would have been selected by the Holy Prophet as his Caliph.'
Omar seems to have concurred when years later he honestly
explained to his own son that the Prophet loved 'Usama more
than he loved you and he loved his father [Zayd] more than he
loved your father [Omar].'

But to return from speculation to known events: Ali was trusted
by the Prophet Muhammad with an independent command in
627, but in that same year Zayd had been given seven such com-
missions. In the winter months Ali led a force of some one
hundred mounted warriors out of the oasis of Medina. They did
not leave in secrecy but made a noisy departure under the guise of
setting out as a warrior-protected trading caravan – though once
they were safely out of sight they pushed north in a series of forced
night marches towards Fadak. Their objective was not to raid this
oasis (which would be conquered the next year) but to neutralise
the Bedouin tribes that dominated this part of the desert. Having
captured a lone tribesman of the Beni Sad, Ali used this young
man to lead them to the tribal camping grounds. The subsequent
raid caught the Beni Sad totally unprepared and in the aftermath

the tribal sheikhs made their protestation of Islam and Ali drove back to Medina 100 camels and 2000 goats. A fifth were handed over to the Prophet, the rest shared out among the warriors. In the formal catalogue of the campaigns of the Prophet (one of our earliest historical sources) this expedition is listed as the Sariya-i-Fidak.

It was undoubtedly considered to be a successful operation but no more than a small incident set against the greater struggle. The Prophet's quixotic pilgrimage to Mecca in the following spring (into the arms of the hostile pagans who still ruled the city) brought out many of the personal qualities of the leading Companions, especially during the negotiations that brought about the truce of Hudaibiya. Abu Bakr showed unstinting support, Omar championed greater militancy while Uthman was selected by the army as the most diplomatic voice within the Muslim community. Ali revealed another facet of his nature by acting as a confidential secretary to the Prophet. It was he who wrote out the Muslim draft of the treaty, altered various clauses during the negotiations, and who was close enough to the Prophet's thinking to understand that the implicit 'recognition of Islamic Medina' that was awarded in the treaty by the pagans of Mecca was a triumph (both for peace and realpolitik) that eclipsed the one or two irritating side clauses.

Just two months after Hudaibiya had been signed, Ali was once again back in his more celebrated role as the great warrior-champion of Islam even if Zayd outranked him in generalship. In the campaign against Khaybar he was formally chosen by the Prophet to act as the standard-bearer of Islam and given a great new battle flag – the eagle that had been fashioned from one of the cloaks of Muhammad's beloved young wife Aisha. Was this mere coincidence or was the Prophet discreetly trying to patch up the coolness that had developed between Aisha and Ali?

Muhammad remained the overall commander of this expedition, which specifically comprised only the same 1400 warriors who had followed him to Hudaibiya. The conquest of Khaybar oasis, as well as a campaign to extend the faith, was designed to be a reward for those who had proved their faith in his leadership. There was to be no set-piece battle at Khaybar oasis, just a series of sieges, some fortresses facing the combined might of the Muslim army while others were assaulted by smaller detachments. The two forts of al-Watih and al-Sulalim were particularly well defended and held out for ten days, successfully repelling attacks led by Abu Bakr and Omar. When it was Ali's turn to serve as commander it was his attack that finally broke into the citadel – though up until that time he had been out of action suffering from an eye infection. Years later, when one of the soldiers recalled the vicious hand-to-hand fighting of that day, he remembered, 'We went with Ali when the apostle sent him with his flag and when he got near the fort the garrison came out and fought them. A Jew struck him so that his shield fell from his hand, so Ali laid hold of a door by the fort and used it as a shield. He kept it in his hand as he fought until God gave victory, throwing it away when all was over. I can see myself with seven others trying to turn that door over, but we could not.' There were some legendary encounters with Jewish strongmen during the Khaybar campaign – such as the duel with the warrior-poet known as Marhab who came out of his fortress boldly declaring:

Khaybar knows that I am Marhab
An experienced warrior armed from head to foot,
Now piercing, now slashing,
As when lions advance in their rage.
The hardened warrior gives way before my onslaught;
My motherland cannot be invaded.

... before he was slain by a Muslim warrior. The successful conquest of the oasis of Khaybar (and the peaceful submission of the neighbouring oasis of Fadak) ended the days of poverty for the Muslims. For not only was a rich booty of material seized (and many slave girls taken) but henceforth half the harvest of both oases was to be sent as tribute to Medina – which the Prophet carefully divided up into 1800 shares, one for each of the 1400 warriors who had accompanied him on the expedition, with extra shares for the 200 cavalry horses. In addition fields were put aside for members of his family as well as for Aisha, Fatimah and Ali. The produce of the oasis of Fadak, which had surrendered without its fields being trampled underfoot by either 'horse or camel', became the privy purse of the Prophet's expanding household. Henceforth Ali and his wife Fatimah could expect an annual delivery of sackloads of dates and barley in the autumn, this income varying each year with the harvest and the attention of the assessor.

The following year, 629, was to be an even greater time of transition for Ali. For the Muslim community had progressively transformed itself from an embattled group of refugees to the rising power within central Arabia. The defection of some of the leading warrior-commanders of pagan Mecca, men such as Khalid ibn al-Walid and Amr ibn al-As, to the Muslim side must have appeared opportunistic to those who had suffered decades of battle wounds and persecution at their hands. The campaign that autumn, an ambitious expansion northwards into the old territory of the Ghassanid kingdom, was to result in defeat. The Prophet's adopted son Zayd had once more been trusted with the command but at the battle of Mutah bled to death from 'loss of blood from the spears of the enemy'. Whereupon Ali's older brother Jafar took 'the standard and fought with it until when the battle hemmed him in when he jumped off his roan horse and hamstrung her and fought till he was killed'. Ali had not been among the 3000 soldiers that Zayd had led north and so it was left to Khalid, one of the brand-new Muslims, to make his name by organising the safe return of this army. Once back in Medina Khalid was saluted by the Prophet as the 'sword of God'.

In 630 when the Prophet led his army into Mecca it was Ali who carried the standard of Islam – though this meant that he had not been asked to be one of the four military commanders that day. When it came to the cleansing of the interior of the Kaaba of all its idols it was Ali who was honoured to be the sole Companion of the Prophet in this task. According to a traditional account he was forced to stand on the Prophet's shoulders to clear out the upper shelves of the sanctuary – and years later would recall feeling that at that moment he had the power to reach up into the very heavens. This cleansing was then extended to the surrounding countryside as the little rural sanctuaries were destroyed by bands of Muslim horsemen. Khalid, who alone of the four commanders had spilled blood during the occupation of Mecca, once again proved brutally efficient when entrusted with the destruction of the old pagan shrines of the Banu Jazaima Bedouin nomads – but overstepped the mark by executing some of his old adversaries even after they had formally converted and laid down their arms. To make amends, the Prophet dispatched Ali as a true ambassador of Islam. Ali at once paid them blood money and then dwelt among them as a missionary, patiently explaining the practical details of the new religion as well as its deeper mission. His generosity was such that Ali 'made good their loss even for a dog's bowl' and then paid some more out for 'the claims of which neither he nor they knew at the time'.

Later that campaigning season Ali once again returned to war. First as a soldier at the battle at Hunayn, where the now over-large Muslim army (boosted by all the new Muslims converted after the capture of Mecca) was nearly routed by a surprise attack of

Bedouin. Then at the siege of the walled town of Taif, which (unlike Khaybar) was well defended by its inhabitants. They possessed machines that could fire hot iron down on the attackers and were also well trained as archers – so that the Muslim siege had to be called off after a depressing number of casualties. Despite this reverse, it was soon to become clear that the oasis of Medina was now the capital of an ever-expanding central Arabian state as delegation after delegation came from the tribes and kingdoms to make their peace with the Prophet. It was an exceptionally active time for the close Companions of the Prophet, who were appointed to tutor these delegates in Islam. The members of one such embassy were greatly concerned that though they wore their finest gold ornaments and their most exquisite silk robes, the Prophet never granted them so much as a greeting, let alone an audience. Ali took pity on them (they were from the old Kinda dynasty) and explained that Muhammad associated such flamboyant wealth with the power of Satan to tempt mortals into envy, greed and discord. When they appeared the next day in simple white cotton robes they were at once greeted by the Prophet and bidden to sit at his side.

The Prophet also kept up his tactic of sending missionary raids to harry the Bedouin tribes into listening to his message. In August 630 Ali was given command of 150 horsemen and instructed to enter the territory of the Tai and destroy their pagan shrines. The Tai tribe (also labelled Beni Tayyi on tribal maps of old Arabia) still glowed with the fame of their old chief, Hatim al-Tai. Hatim had become a legend throughout Arabia for the reckless generosity with which he entertained travellers and was saluted by the Prophet as a natural Muslim though he had died before he had a chance to hear Muhammad's message. Hatim's son Adi now presided over the Tai tribe but avoided a confrontation with Ali's armed band by prudently retiring into the protection of Byzantine

Syria. So Ali was able to round up the leaderless tribe and its flocks and march them back to Medina. The Prophet, in honour of Hatim's natural pre-Islamic goodness, would later release all these prisoners. Such a chivalric gesture won over the hearts of the Tai, who delighted in the honour that had been done to their famous chieftain's reputation. In due course they would make their own way back to Medina to hear Muhammad's preaching.

Right at the end of that incident-packed year of 630 the Prophet determined to lead a military expedition back into the borderlands of Byzantine Syria where Zayd had met his death the year before. The equipping of this force tested the resources of the fledgling Muslim state to their full – so much so that the Prophet had to appeal to his followers for funds with which to feed, equip and mount a force that may have numbered more than 20,000 men. Ali was left behind to look after the Prophet's family and household but was so stung by the street gossip – that he had become a useless burden and that Muhammad wanted rid of him – that he at once rode out with his armour and offered his services to his master. It reveals a curious sensitivity in Ali, who more than any other Muslim should have been self-confident enough to rise above such slurs. Muhammad at once reassured Ali, 'They lie. I left you behind because of what I had left behind, so go back and represent me in my family and you in yours. Are you not content, Ali, to stand to me as Aaron to Moses, except that there will be no Prophet after me?' The comparison worked on a number of levels, not least because Moses remained childless while Aaron stands as the proud progenitor of all the genealogies of Israel. It must also have seemed to many that Ali was being designated as heir.

The following spring Abu Bakr was chosen to lead the Muslims in pilgrimage to Mecca, though after this caravan had left, the Prophet received a revelation which he wanted all the pilgrims of

Arabia to share. Ali was given the task of catching up with the caravan – which he did by borrowing the Prophet's very fast slit-eared camel. When he reached Abu Bakr he was immediately asked whether he had 'come to give orders or to convey them' – so used were all the Companions to instantly accepting change in their command structure. In such incidents one clearly sees that there was no established system of rank among the Companions – who were all instantly at the disposal of their master, ready either to lead or to obey. Ali answered that he had merely come with a new Koranic verse which he had been ordered to read at the plain of Mina to the assembled pilgrims. This particular revelation banned pagans from performing the pilgrimage the next year and forbade the old tradition of public nakedness in the ritual circulation of hills and shrine.

Later in the year (631) Muhammad's messengers brought back the submission of the people of Oman as well as that of many of the princes and tribal lords who ruled over the valleys and mountain kingdoms of the Yemen. Now assured of a sympathetic audience, the Prophet had little use for armies and even less for war. He specifically instructed the first missionary, 'Deal gently and not harshly; announce good news and do not repel people. You are going to one of the people with scriptures who will ask you about the key of heaven. Say to them it is our witness that there is no divinity but God, who has no partner.' Khalid, who was sent to subdue the famous Yemeni city of Najran with 400 cavalrymen, was given specific orders 'to invite them to Islam three days before he attacked them'. Khalid followed Muhammad's instructions to the letter and sent back a report: 'They have surrendered and have not fought and I am staying among them instructing them in the apostles' positive and negative commands and teaching them the institutions of Islam . . .'

Five months later, Ali was dispatched at the head of 300 soldiers to pass through Najran and from there proceed south in order to bring the Maddhij tribe to Islam. The chronicles are irritatingly silent about the details of this expedition, apart from the fact that it was to be entirely peaceful – like the two before it. The gap has been filled with traditional accounts that record a series of three-day-long debates, as first Ali converted a Christian priest and then a Jewish rabbi by his skilful espousal of the superior merits of Islam. At the end of this four-month tour of missionary duty, there was an arrangement that Ali was to rendezvous with the Prophet, who would be leading the pilgrimage to Mecca. In order to make this appointment on time, Ali hurried ahead and placed a companion in charge of his troops. When his soldiers later approached Mecca, Ali rode back out to greet them but was astonished to find that they were all dressed in gleaming new white linen robes of Yemen, 'in order that they might appear seemly when they mingled with the people'. Ali was furious that they had broached the bundles of Yemeni linen, the charitable tithe, that he felt honour-bound to deliver totally intact to the Prophet. He ordered them to hand back their proud new uniforms and dress in their old travel-worn clothes. The soldiers were furious and showed their resentment by later taking their complaint straight to the Prophet, who told them, 'Do not blame Ali, for he is too scrupulous in the things of God, and in the way of God, to be blamed.' It was on one level a testimony to Ali. Though on another, the incident damaged Ali's reputation as a man 'too scrupulous' to be trusted with the realities of political life and military command.

This pilgrimage of 631 was to be the Prophet's last and he was accompanied by many of his followers who were most dear to him, including his daughter Fatimah and Aisha, who had been distraught with worry that the arrival of her monthly period would have disqualified her. When Muhammad had fulfilled all the ritual

actions in a clear manner he delivered his celebrated moral summary of what it is to be a Muslim in 'The Farewell Sermon'. After
the sacrifices had been made and consumed in the canonical rest
period, the pilgrim caravan set out on the long road back to
Medina. This journey, like all desert crossings, was broken by the
daily necessity of halts but at a halfway point a longer camp was
decreed, so that the caravan – now spread out over several miles –
could collect itself together. At this camp at Ghadir Khumm (the
pool in the valley of Khumm) the Prophet revealed one of the last
verses of the Koran with its potentially mysterious references: 'O
Messenger of God, make known what has been revealed to you
from your Lord, for if you do not, you will not have conveyed His
message. God will protect you from mankind. Lo, God guideth
not the unbelieving folk.'

Muhammad then gave a sermon of which there is no definitive
record though some of it is preserved in a number of sayings – of
which there are variant Sunni and Shia versions. In outline it was
clearly a repetition of the Meccan sermon and his lifetime of
preaching, exhorting mankind to fear only God and trust only in
the Koran. But it also warned the assembled believers that in the
future they would be tested by hard times, unjust wars, accusations
of doctrinal falsehood but that ultimately truth would prevail.
Muhammad also received a premonition that his death was not far
off. Some sort of declaration was made in favour of Ali by
Muhammad: 'O God, be a friend to whomever he [Ali] befriends,
and an enemy of whomever he takes as an enemy,' which was
prevented from being made into a clear oath of succession only
by the direct intervention of Omar, talking the Prophet out of
such an action.

Some historical sources (the ones that lean towards the Sunni
position) pass over the event altogether, others deny that it happened, while still others suggest that Muhammad was simply

making it clear that Ali was to be the future patron (*mawla*) of his immediate kinship group – the Beni Hashim clan of the Quraysh. For the Shia it is a defining moment in history. It is the source of their belief that spiritual authority is passed down by a formal designation, *nass*, which began at Ghadir Khumm when the Prophet Muhammad chose Ali to succeed him as the next Imam. Just as Ali would in due course make his own designation from his own children, the only living male descendants of the Prophet Muhammad, and from them on down the line of their descendants. He did so in order to create a hereditary theocratic leadership that also included an explicit appointment and an element of apostolic anointment. Future generations of Shiite Muslims would see this Imam as much more than an elective leader: 'He was the pillar of God's unity [*tawhid*] . . . immune from sin and error . . . possessed of the power of irrefutable arguments . . . alone gifted with wisdom to interpret the Koran for each generation . . . and may be likened to the ark of Noah: he who boards it obtains salvation and reaches the gate of repentance.'

What did or did not happen at Ghadir Khumm is a matter of the utmost importance but it can no longer be resolved as a historical fact that will be accepted by both communities within Islam. Instead it has become one of the litmus tests that distinguish a Sunni from a Shia. The truth is known only unto God.

When Muhammad had returned to Medina he gave orders that Zayd's young son, the eighteen-year-old Usama, be given the command of an army that would raid the desert frontiers of Palestine 'into the borders of Balqa and al-Darum'. There were mutterings of dissent from the army that 'He has put a young man in command', especially when they would be facing once again the only external adversary which had yet worsted a Muslim Arab army. Perhaps the Prophet was specifically complaining of these dissident voices when he prayed over the cemetery, 'O people of the graves!

Happy are you that you are so much better off than men here. Dissensions have come like waves of darkness one after another, the last being worse than the first.'

Later the Prophet's visit to the mosque – in the grip of his mortal fever – would be to urge his men on with their preparations for this Palestine campaign. Usama did in fact lead an army out of Medina but by common agreement this force camped down at al-Jurf (just a half-stage halt outside the oasis) in order to see 'what God would decide' about the Prophet's illness.

As we have heard, Ali was in constant attendance upon the Prophet in the last ten days of his life. At one point, when it seemed that the Prophet had made a recovery, Ali was taken aside by his canny uncle Abbas, who told him that 'I recognised death in the apostle's face as I used to recognise it in the faces of the sons of Abdul Muttalib [the Prophet's paternal uncles].' Abbas urged Ali to go to the apostle to find out if the 'authority is to be with us'. Ali answered, 'By God, I will not. If it is withheld from us none after him will give it to us.' This defiantly principled statement carries the true colour of Ali's indomitable character. The Prophet died with the heat of noon that day.

Aisha in her account of the Prophet's last hours did allow that there was another man in her hut that fateful morning, who gave Muhammad a toothpick, though she did not name this man. Aisha was also quoted as saying that 'the apostle died in my arms. Then I laid his head on a pillow and got up beating my breast and slapping my face along with the other women.' This testimony clearly does not exclude the fact that Ali might also have been at the Prophet's bedside when he died. According to some Shia sources, when Ali felt the dead weight of the Prophet on his shoulder he recited an elegiac farewell which began 'Dearer than my father and mother/your smell is sweet alive and dead' and which was accompanied by a waft of sweet odour that rose through the hut, the like of which they had never experienced before and would never smell again.

It was certainly Ali and Abbas who took care of the funeral arrangements, for in this both the Sunni and Shia historians are in full agreement. Ali asked that his cousin al-Fadl (one of Abbas's sons) be sent for to assist him, and acceded to the requests from the people of Medina that they should be allowed a share in this honour. For they had shouted through the door, 'We implore you for our share in the Messenger of God,' and so Ali allowed one Aws ibn Khawali to enter, who carried in a jug of fresh well water. Ali did not strip the corpse naked but respectfully washed the body under the covering of the long shirt that Muhammad was wearing when he died. It was then anointed with myrrh and wrapped in three garments, one from Oman, one from Yemen and then finally a striped mantle from Bahrain. The body of Muhammad then lay on its deathbed from sunset that Monday until Wednesday night. The decision to bury Muhammad within the confines of Aisha's little bedroom hut – in fact right beside his deathbed – has never been satisfactorily explained. It ran against all the codes of the ancient world that had kept the cities of the living and the places of the dead in proximity, but also very strictly apart. Aisha herself was clearly kept in ignorance and explained after-wards that 'We did not know that the Messenger of God was being buried until we heard the sound of shovels in the middle of the night.'

Some historians have argued that Ali and his family were already reacting against the seizure of the political leadership by Abu Bakr and Omar (which we will examine later) – and were determined that the new leaders should not be allowed to enhance their legitimacy by publicly leading the funeral cortège of the Prophet Muhammad and the prayers over his graveside.

This view is too exclusively political in mood. Instead the passionate immediacy of twenty years of Muhammad's preaching which constantly stressed the nearness of the day of judgement and past instances of divine wrath must be considered. The followers of Muhammad also knew enough about the biographies of previous prophets (all of whom the Prophet had so greatly honoured) that they must have harboured extraordinary expectations in their hearts. If Jesus had been resurrected from the dead, or as the Koran explicitly declares, 'God raised him up to himself', and if Elijah had been summoned to heaven in a fiery chariot, 'and Moses was a hundred and twenty years old when he died . . . and the children of Israel wept for Moses in the plains of Moab for thirty days', there must have been many believers who expected an equally charismatic ending for their Prophet.

There is also an account that records that Ali, Talha, Zubayr and other notables among the Companions sat up to watch over the body of the Prophet which may contain a partial memory of a core of disciples watching over the body with secret expectations of some miraculous transformation after the third day. Even Omar initially shared in these wild millenarian hopes, though he at first believed that Muhammad was 'sleeping' and would rise up from the dead after forty days. Whether the quick burial in the night was executed in despair by the Companions after the third day when no miracle had occurred (for we must also bear in mind that Muhammad died in the midsummer heat of central Arabia) we can never know. It would, however, explain why the events immediately after the Prophet's death were so muddled. Some of the believers were waiting for Muhammad's bodily resurrection (in the canonical mystical intervals, such as the third, the thirtieth or the fortieth day) while some were no doubt paralysed with doubts now that their great Prophet had proved to be mortal. Many others must have feared that the end of the world was nigh. At this critical point there were very few believers who could be gathered together to make rational and formal decisions about their collective political future.

This intensely confusing period marks the second great fork in the road between the Sunni and Shia historical narrative. At the absolute core of Shia belief is that it was Ali's right to be the Prophet's spiritual heir. The Sunni also acknowledge this but consider Ali not to be the lone heir but one among a handful of four devout followers who would all be Heirs of the Prophet – the Rashidun – the first four Rightly Guided Caliphs. In something of the same manner the Orthodox Church and the Anglican Church acknowledge the primacy of St Peter but also look to the other Apostles as equal members of a Church council, not just obedient deputies.

Before examining the vexed issue of the Caliphate, it is instructive to consider the armies of Arabia that underpinned the spectacular growth of the Early Islamic Empire. Then we will look at the relationship between the Prophet and Aisha and his other wives in order to broaden our understanding of this extraordinarily influential period of history, and how the chance interactions of two characters would contribute another strand to the coming schism.

3

Arabian Soldiers of the Seventh Century

'Tastier than old wine, sweeter than the passing of wine-
cups is the play of sword and lance, the clash of armies
at my command. To face death in battle is my life, for
life is what fulfils the soul'

Al-Mutanabbi

The Arab conquest of the Middle East in the name of Islam is
one of the most decisive events of Mediterranean and Asian history. It is also curiously one of the least understood and studied.
Think back for a moment to those charts that map the campaigns of Hannibal, of Alexander the Great, of the Duke of
Marlborough, of Frederick the Great and Napoleon. Think of
those plans that show the disposition of the troops on the morning of Agincourt, on the doomed beachheads of the Dardanelles,
of Picket's division at Antietam, of Hastings and Bannockburn.
They would fill up a whole book. Then think of the Arab conquest of the Persian Empire and the Byzantine Near East; an

event that has changed world history. In most cases the page is blank.

So try instead to imagine an army of conquering Arabs. The images for this come quickly to mind. On the summit of sand dunes wait wave upon wave of Arab cavalry. Their green standards flutter in the wind and contrast with the puritanical regularity of their dress, a romantic swirl of black cloaks, white kaftans and turbans. Here and there flashes of sunlight are reflected off curved scimitars of steel. A soldier rises up on his stirrups in order to test the sweep of his sword arm. Your eye then moves up to a massed squadron of camels on the summit. You focus in on a veiled Arab chief on his camel, a profile like a hawk. The hand of this chief is raised slowly and then drops suddenly with a sweeping gesture that again recalls the swoop of a raptor. As one this vast force of Arab cavalry, a desert storm of camel-riders, falls down upon the valleys and farmland like a tidal wave. Their victory over the exhausted and war-devastated provinces of the Middle East seems as inevitable as the dawn. It is a powerful image, and one that is found in dozens of films, historical documentaries and countless scores of posters, book illustrations and cheap prints.

It is also wrong. Wrong in detail. Wrong in substance. Wrong in mood. The real story is much more interesting, though be warned that the more you look into the details, the less certain you become of any easy answers. After a lifetime of dedicated research, one historian has concluded that it is 'well nigh impossible for us to come to any firm conclusions about the reasons for the military success of the early Islamic armies'. We do not have to go quite so far down this academic corridor of perpetual doubt, though what is quite certain is that the Arab Conquest was never a foregone conclusion. It was a very finely poised thing, which seemed one day to hang in the balance of the wind, or the ground conditions, or the stamina of the troops, but rests on no historical inevitability.

For an Arab audience the issue is too obvious to need any comment. Their heroic ancestors were fighting for God and with God, in the knowledge that if they died, they won heaven, while if they survived, they conquered the known world. These conquests were later recorded in a number of proud chronicles. These tales are fundamental to the pride felt by an Arab. It was a time of the utmost heroism, a period of legendary valour, and the first writers were determined to give full rein to the epic quality of the conquests. These first chroniclers of conquest were interested in the heroic deeds of individuals, not battle formations or supply lines. Their opponents were also the opponents of God and so are habitually portrayed as the complete cardboard cut-out anti-hero: vain, foolish, treacherous, cruel and cowardly.

Western historians have found these chronicles a less than satisfactory source material, mutually contradictory and clearly written for a specific tribal audience to a well-established literary prototype. They were also first written down about a hundred years after the events they describe. To any historian trying to establish an exact chronology, or even an orderly sequence of events, this period is a minefield. Those with an academic reputation to lose usually pass over it with indecent haste, which is a pity because it is of central importance to an Arab's sense of identity. It is also such a vivid and compelling tale and so little known in the West that I will risk constructing a narrative where a better scholar would keep his silence. But first we must re-examine our images of those first Arab armies of Muslims coming from out of the desert.

It is an error to imagine that the Arab armies of early Islam were noticeably different from those of Persia or Byzantium. When he could afford to, an Arab warrior would be dressed in exactly the same state-of-the-art war gear as a Byzantine or a Persian soldier. From the surviving poetry we know that armour was greatly prized and that which had been earned by an ancestor, who had served abroad in the armies of Persia and Byzantium, was passed down through the generations as a treasured heirloom. Arms and armour were the jewellery of men, the first thing that an Arab soldier would acquire if his purse were full.

The preferred armour in the seventh century was made from plates of metal neatly sewn on to a long leather jerkin. Greaves that guarded the shins were also worn, though solid plate armour, like a breastplate, had by this time become a thing for the parade ground only. Helmets, nicknamed eggs – *bayda* – by Arab soldiers, were also highly prized. The best were fitted with nose-guards, but even these would have been composed of riveted metal plates rather than cast as a single piece of metal. We hear of Arab shield walls from literary sources but otherwise the Arabs tend to be rather reticent about describing their shields, almost as if they were unmanly, though with the preponderance of archery they must have been carried by everyone. They were simple lightweight discs, no more than a yard across and made of wood and leather, with the more elaborate boasting a central metal plate.

The spear – *rimah* – was a vital weapon of war. A determined group of foot soldiers armed with spears was proof against any frontal assault by cavalry, though they were vulnerable to the attack of light cavalry equipped with bows. There were three principal grades of spear: a lighter javelin that could be thrown at close quarters; a heavier 'hunting spear' that could be used to slash as well as stab an enemy; and great 20-foot-long spears that could be hung with a flag to make battle standards. The bows of the period look small by medieval standards, but the double-'S'-shaped *qaws* of the Arabs could kill at a range of 250 yards. Arrows were either 'Arab' or 'Persian', though this slight technical difference, probably in the design of the arrowhead, is now lost to us.

The weapon held in the greatest reverence by the Arabs was the sword. The scimitar and the curved dagger, now synonymous with

a well-dressed Arab gentleman, was the invention of later centuries. The sword used by the first Muslim Arab armies was a
straight blade with two cutting edges and a simple handle. It was
commonly carried from the shoulder on a strap and worn in
tandem with a long sheathed knife which was strapped to the
upper thigh. Echoes of this habit were until recently preserved in
the central Sahara, where a fully dressed Tuareg warrior carried a
broadsword, a spear and a shorter blade strapped to his leg. The
symbolism of the sword – *sayf* – has never been lost. Muslim rulers
continue to present each other with gilded swords at state cere-
monies. While the essential element of the coronation of an
Ottoman sultan was when the sheikh at Eyup hung the sword of
Osman on the shoulders of a new ruler. Dhu'l Fiqar, the sword of
the Prophet, and the double-pointed sword of Ali would later
achieve iconic status within Islam, depicted on battle standards
and royal decrees wrapped up in wafts of calligraphy. In the first
century of Islam the well-wrought swords of Hindi, the blades
made in India and imported through Ceylon, were the most
highly regarded of all. Next in value were the blades known as
Baylaman and Mushrafi, by smiths in Syria, Sind and the Yemen.
A good example could cost as much as a hundred gold coins
while a common sword knocked up in the markets of Egypt or
Iraq could be acquired for just under three gold coins. Even this
was no mean price. A gold dinar, a wafer-thin coin about a centi-
metre in diameter, was worth around twenty silver dirhams (which
were 3 grams in weight and 2 centimetres in diameter). Even in
the cities a skilled worker could not expect to be paid more than
one-twelfth of a dirham a day.

The Muslims had no new weapons, no new armour, no new
technical equipment with which we can explain away their military success. All armies in the Middle East made use of the same
weapons and the same body armour. If anything the Muslims

were less well equipped than their adversaries. Not that that would have shown up so much on the battlefield. For it is now thought that in the two really crucial battles there might have been almost as many Arab-speaking auxiliaries within the Persian and Byzantine armies as there were Arabs in the Muslim armies.

What about the image of the Arab armies as one vast cavalry force? This remains true on one level but there are some important qualifications to take on board.

The first Muslim armies were indeed highly mobile. There were no problems with supply lines and baggage trains, for the Muslim army was entirely composed of men who moved vast distances as a matter of course. They could travel quickly, bringing their own equipment and essential supplies of millet, flour and dates with them. In the first decades they were neither paid nor expected any salary and required no bonus in coin before battle, unlike their adversaries.

In earlier tribal wars within Arabia the whole community had been involved. The women of the tribe were there to cook, to nurse the wounded, to urge their menfolk into brave actions, to greet the victors with ululations, to bury the dead, to protect the herds and if need be defend the tents aided by the very old and the very young. This was not the case with the Muslim armies.

They were not hampered by any concern for the safety of their tents. They were entirely formed of men of declared Muslim faith who had first been summoned together at the new capital of Medina. Here they were placed under the command of specific generals chosen by the Caliph himself. The armies were then dispatched on missions and could be recalled or redirected by the orders of the Caliph. Booty was divided up among the victors on a proportional basis that sent a fifth back to the Caliph at Medina.

It has been calculated that although the distances involved are vast, it took just a week for a determined messenger to pass from

Medina to an army camp in Syria or Iraq. It also appears that in the first years of war it was rare for whole Bedouin tribes to be recruited at once into an army, though it was common for the men of the same tent groups and clans to volunteer, march and fight together. A Muslim army in the first decade of conquest (the ten years that followed the death of the Prophet in 632) might well be composed of clans from all over Arabia, from the Yemen, the Hijaz, the Syrian desert, plus a hard core of older Muslim converts from Mecca and Medina.

In the first decade of fighting no roll-call of soldiers was kept, nor were the warriors mustered into specific units or into regiments. Apart from the general and a handful of named successors (should he fall in battle) there is no record of other officers. It is presumed that this was sorted out during the period of march. Perhaps we presume too much, perhaps the Arab Muslim armies needed no officers or sergeants. They all knew their task, how to fight, and they were all brothers under Islam. Certainly time and time again in the reports of battles you hear how general after general of a Muslim army had been killed but the army fought on regardless. Not so their hierarchically organised adversaries, whose armies could be paralysed by the death of their leader or by a breakdown in communication.

This self-sufficiency of command within the Muslim forces must have been an enormous advantage in the murderous anarchy of hand-to-hand fighting. From the accounts that have come down to us the order of battle was a fixed process. Horsemen to the fore, then a line or two of archers, then the mass of infantry divided into three groups: left wing *maysara*, right wing *maymana* and the centre, *qalb*. The numbers deployed were not normally so vast that the men could not recognise their general by sight. Muslim armies of 4000 seem quite common. The largest Muslim army assembled, for the battle of Yarmuk in 637, is reckoned to have numbered somewhere between 20,000 and 40,000 men. To put this force in the field, the Caliph had to pull out all the stops, patiently assembling this irreplaceable army over six months.

There is also another mental image one ought to adapt to get a truer picture: that of the conquering Arab sitting atop his camel. It is a powerfully imprinted image, the proud Lord of the Desert looking down from the height of his camel saddle. It is true that camels have a natural advantage in any engagement with cavalry because horses unused to the desert detest the smell of camels. The Byzantine army had learned this to their cost a century before, during their long-running border war against the nomad tribes of the Sahara. In those far-flung engagements they found out that their cavalry force could not be compelled to attack a corral of camels. This defensive tactic was never used in Arabia, largely because the Arabs were always on the offensive and the native Arab horses had become well used to camels. It is a surprise to realise that Muslim Arab armies never used camels on the field of battle. Camels were vital: they were invaluable pack animals but they were for transport not attack, used like lorries or troop carriers not like a tank or an armoured car. They were used to quickly move troops up to battle positions, keeping the men and the horses fresh and not weary from long marches. In some of the surviving poetry, a warrior will be described as leading his horse on a rein beside his camel.

Another curious fact to assimilate is that the Muslim armies, although mounted and highly mobile, could not really be considered cavalry as we now understand it. They were just too flexible. A force of Arab 'cavalry' would rush up to the front but then dismount and advance on foot to give battle. Similarly Arab 'infantry' could suddenly mount up and ride off. However, it must be stressed that seventh-century battles were only ever decided in the life-and-death struggle between foot soldier pitted against foot soldier. Parties of horsemen could turn flanks, scout out the enemy, defend marching camps but they could not win battles – or at least not until they dismounted to fight. Cavalry, as we know it, would have to await the development of the stirrup. This simple improvement in saddle stability is a highly contentious issue among military historians. It seems clear that they had already been invented by this period but it also appears that they were still made of leather or rope not of iron. It would be another century before stirrups would provide a firm enough footing for a horseman to take the impact from his lance and sword and still keep his seat. Only then could cavalry be used as a devastatingly aggressive instrument of battle.

Nor need we instinctively feel that the Muslim armies were largely made up of impulsive Bedouin. It is true that they formed the vast majority of the soldiers of the line. But we must also remember that the infant Muslim state was based on the population of the two cities of Mecca and Medina. All the principal Muslim commanders came from these two communities and proved to be men of the very highest calibre. And they could sometimes bring extraordinarily detailed knowledge to their commands. For instance, one of the earliest Muslim governors of Syria knew the area intimately as his family possessed estates at Balqa in the Transjordan. While the Muslim general who conquered Egypt had no need for maps, scouts or spies. He had it all in his head, from a lifetime of experience taking merchant caravans into Gaza and then on into Egypt.

What about weaknesses? The major Muslim weakness was numerical. Even pulling all its resources together, the Caliphate could never equal the great armies that Persia and Byzantium were separately able to pitch against the Muslims. Again reliable battlefield figures are a much contested ground among historians, though it is generally accepted that the two empires – when at full stretch – could each probably have as many as 100,000 soldiers under arms. For instance it is extremely doubtful that if the result at the decisive battle of Yarmuk had been reversed, the Caliphate would have had the resources to attempt a second invasion of Syria. At that time the Caliph was so strapped for men that he had to reverse one of his strongest prejudices and recruit from the pagan Arab tribes that had revolted on the death of the Prophet. After this resounding victory the flood of new recruits ended this problem. Old Arab allies of the fallen empires, Bedouin tribes that had been sitting on the fence, Arab converts from Christianity, even a whole regiment of Persian imperial guards decided to join the Muslim army once fate had so decisively declared herself.

A second potential weakness, well known and commented on at the time, was the Arab ignorance of fortifications. In the first decade of warfare the generals of the Muslims never knew how to besiege a walled city or fortress. This could have been a problem but seldom was. In fact this weakness seems to have been strategically beneficial. Muslim armies consistently sidestepped the complications of a long siege in order to concentrate their energy on the destruction of rival field armies. Walled cities, once deprived of the hope of deliverance, prove all too vulnerable. The simple Arab tactic of setting up a nearby base to raid the outskirts of a city, even if it was spun out over a year or more, was an efficient way to get the city fathers to come to terms by pillaging their suburban farms, orchards and merchant caravans. It was also enormously important that the Muslim generals were trusted to keep their word. The deal struck at the time of the surrender, invariably about the level of annual tribute that was to be paid out, had all the force of statute law.

So how did the Muslim armies achieve their conquests? We have seen how they were worse equipped, less numerous, knew nothing of siegecraft and had no new technical inventions or tactical manoeuvres to spring on their enemies. They were highly mobile and highly motivated, it is true, but when it came to the actual field of battle they basically fought it out hand-to-hand on foot. Here they appeared to have more in common with a Norman soldier, with their body armour, trusty spear and straight sword, than our image of a desert cavalier.

One of the stock explanations is that the Muslim armies attacked war-shattered empires that had been weakened by plague and religious controversy. There is some truth in this but not enough to make a convincing explanation. Bubonic plague had swept through the Eastern Mediterranean, wiping out perhaps a third of the population. The major epidemics were in the previous generation, between 540 and 560, and though some historians argue that it hit the densely packed cities of Persia and Byzantium with particular savagery, it is unlikely that even the desert wastes of Arabia could completely immunise the Arabs. Everyone suffers equally from plagues. The Arab armies that occupied the Holy Land would in any case be decimated by plague in 639.

The idea that Byzantium could be weakened by religious controversy is another enduring myth. The whole gorgeous millennial culture of Byzantium lived and breathed religious controversy right from its foundation by the first Constantine to its death 1100 years later under Constantine XII. Though in the province of Egypt, as we will see, the government's politico-religious policy had a clear and disabling effect.

The evidence of war-shattered economies is harder to determine. The empires had just fought a particularly savage twenty-five-year war but then Sassanid Persia and Byzantium had been doing this on and off for several hundred years. What was so new? The extent of the collateral damage must surely be at least partly offset by a pair of well-trained imperial armies tempered and toughened by years of conflict.

Archaeological evidence in the Near East has also been slowly revealing that the Early Byzantine period was one of exceptional prosperity. Syria and Palestine were thickly populated – the rival estimates come in somewhere between 3 million and 10 million. Although some cities, most noticeably Jerusalem, had been devastated by the Persian-Byzantine war most of the region had been able to bend with the prevailing wind. For the only proven political art for the survival of cities was careful non-involvement, coupled with a clear understanding that be they friend or be they foe, all armies are ultimately predatory and are fed by the local inhabitants. Though administratively divided up into a cluster of ten provinces,* the Byzantine Near East was militarily united. The 'Magister Militum Per Orientem' (Master of the Soldiers of the East) commanded 20,000 men, the best of whom were concentrated on the desert frontier with Persia. The Byzantine army was composed of regiments – *bandum* – of 400 men, each with its own combat history, distinctive badges and coloured uniforms. There was also flexibility within this regimental structure, for each platoon of sixteen men was responsible for their own tents and catering, which they carried with them in a small cart. In times of war, three or four regiments were combined to form a brigade, which was the basic unit for the march and for the battle, and to which an ambulance corps was attached.

The first Muslim incursions were therefore not directed against dusty, neglected frontier posts and a handful of third-rate border guards. Instead they actually coincided with the determined reoccupation of the old frontier posts by the battle-hardened Byzantine army. Indeed the first Muslim raid was made only two months after the Persian and Byzantine Empires had made peace. The

*Syria I, Euphratensis, Syria II, Theodorias, Phoenice, Phoenice-Libanensis, Palestina I, Arabia, Palestina II and Palestina III.

well-tried military strategy of the Roman Byzantine Empires was of defence-in-depth. Allied Arab tribes policed the desert, while forts and walled towns protected a 100-mile-deep frontier zone. These defences could not seal a province from a determined assault but they did provide time. Time for the mobile field army to move up and face off any invader on its own terms.

All the components of this system of defence-in-depth were vital, though it is increasingly thought that the role of the allied Arabs had become ever more important during the sixth and seventh centuries. Far from being just a desert patrol, the allied Arabs had been invited deeper and deeper into Syria. Indeed it seems that many cities directly supported a *hira*, an Arab camp, outside their walls. From surviving records we know that a camp of Arabs existed outside Emessa (Homs) and another one guarded the approaches to the city of Gaza. These camps would empty, move and change location with the seasons and the availability of grazing. Even within living memory, such camps of nomadic herdsmen were a regular feature of the agricultural life of the southern Mediterranean. They would help with the brief but labour-intensive olive oil harvest while their flocks would be allowed to glean the wheat fields in exchange for the dung that was dropped – which was next year's fertiliser. The Arab camps were also a labour pool where messengers could he hired or expert guides and stockmen engaged to escort a caravan of city merchants.

In the Byzantine period an annual stipend paid to the local chiefs by the city turned these camps of the Arabs into a part-time militia that watched over farms and the approach roads. In the wise words of a Byzantine scholar, one Evagrius Scholasticus, the empire had long since realised that 'the best way to fight the Arabs was to use other Arabs against them'. There was only one flaw to this policy, for it presumed a perpetual disunity among the Arab tribes. If something were to unite the Arabs they would prove a very formidable foe; for they knew the land, the quick ways, the hidden ways, the population's fears and hopes very much better than the official garrisons. The Byzantine Emperor Maurice had not managed Arab affairs at all well. In 581 he had dropped the annual subsidy of Roman gold that had supported the power of the Ghassanids, the Christian Arab kings of the Syrian desert, and then compounded his errors by arresting and exiling their chief, al-Mundhiri. In 584 the border capital of Bostra was raided by the Ghassanid tribe, infuriated at the duplicity of the Emperor. However, despite this treatment, the Byzantine relationship with the Ghassanids was patched up. They continued to remain inflexibly loyal to the Empire. Indeed the last of the line, Prince Jabala ibn al-Ayham, continued to fight for the Byzantine Empire against the Muslims even when its cause was plainly lost.

Before we return to that day of destiny in the oasis of Medina, Monday 8 June 632, let us remind ourselves of the immediate political and military background between the nascent Muslim state and the Byzantine Empire.

Just three years before, in 629, the Prophet Muhammad had sent a number of missionaries to the Bedouin tribes of Syria. These were repelled by a shower of arrows. This was in the nature of Arabian tribal politics. Of a different nature was the messenger who had been dispatched to the Byzantine governor with a personal letter for the Emperor Heraclius outlining the Muslim faith. The Muslim messenger, under the age-old sanctity of the heralds, took the customary route north from Medina towards the frontier city of Bostra. Here something went wrong. An official, perhaps a military officer, perhaps a Ghassanid sheikh, or maybe even the governor, had the herald executed. This insult enraged the Muslims and may have been designed to inflame a dispute. The

Prophet dispatched an army of 3000 men under the command of Zayd, on a revenge raid. There may also have been a tactical agenda to this mission: to acquire a quantity of the coveted swords of Mashrafiyah manufactured in the Syrian borderlands for the expanding Muslim army.

They were expected. A league of pro-Byzantine Arab tribes shadowed Zayd's column and opposed them, though the Muslim army managed to force its way through. Although any element of surprise had now gone Zayd led the column right up to the shore of the Dead Sea. Here they were attacked by the Patricius Theodorus, in command of the regular army assisted by his Arab allies. The fighting was so fierce that Zayd was slain, as were the two other warriors who succeeded him by turn as commander. The battle of Mutah was a defeat and the Muslim army retreated to Medina.

The Byzantine strategy of defence-in-depth had worked like clockwork. There was no time for immediate countermeasures. The Prophet sent one of his most confident and ambitious officers, Amr ibn al-As, to hold this desert frontier with just three hundred men while he proceeded with the major coup of his career, the conquest of Mecca in 630. Later that year in the worst possible conditions – in the midst of an Arabian summer – he personally led an army back north towards the Syrian frontier. This has often been dismissed as no more than a military gesture, a face-saving parade, for the Muslim force never penetrated the Byzantine frontier. This is to misread its objective. The purpose was not to blunder back into another defeat against the imperial army but to pave the way for greater victories in the future. The Prophet brought his impressively large army to win over the Christian Arab tribes of the Syrian desert who had thwarted the invasion of 629. They had harassed the Muslim army on its way to Syria and had provided vital intelligence that allowed the Patricius

Theodorus to be fully prepared and win the battle of Mutah. If the Prophet could neutralise these tribes, the playing field of war would become level; if he could win them over to his side he would achieve a decisive advantage. If he could not, the defeat at Mutah in 629 was likely to be repeated again and yet again.

This midsummer campaign must have witnessed a series of very intense negotiations. The Prophet was passionately keen to convert these Christian Arab tribes to Islam, but he was also keen to win them over as political allies. At the very least he did not want to push them further into a dependent alliance with the Byzantine Empire. The stakes were high in these desert frontier negotiations of 630.

On the other side of the frontier the Byzantine Emperor Heraclius had settled down and made the northern Syrian city of Antioch his imperial headquarters. Having personally vanquished the Persian Empire in a series of dazzling campaigns – the like of which had not been seen since the time of Alexander the Great – the fifty-five-year-old Emperor must have appeared at the very apogee of power. Stories, most of them true, flickered around his person. How he had changed the course of a battle by personally charging at a Persian-held bridge. A deed so astonishing in its recklessness that even the enemy general is recorded to have said to a group of Greeks, 'Look at your Emperor. He fears those arrows and spears no more than would an anvil.'

Eight years of warfare had seen Heraclius lead armies back and forth across Anatolia, Armenia, Syria and deep into the Persian Empire. He had proved himself an extraordinarily imaginative commander, nor should we forget that he was fully experienced in campaigning in the arid steppes and desert fringes. He had been raised as a child in the service of the Byzantine army of North Africa, where his father had been an outstandingly effective exarch. Indeed Heraclius had first come to the attention of the world when he decided to oppose the tyrant who had seized the throne of the emperors and led a march from Carthage right across the Libyan Sahara and recruited 3000 camel-borne Luwata tribesmen to his cause.

In 630 this battle-hardened emperor made his triumphant pilgrimage to Jerusalem, returning the True Cross to its rightful home after it had been recovered from the Persians. He advanced on the holy city not astride a white horse, as a conqueror, but on foot as a pilgrim. He approached Jerusalem from the Emessa road but his feet never touched the ground. He walked over a roadway buried under carpets and strewn with fragrant herbs by the jubilant citizens of Byzantine Syria. Once within the city he carried the cross up the Via Dolorosa to the doors of the rebuilt Holy Sepulchre, where he handed over Christendom's most holy relic to the Patriarch. Afterwards he returned to Antioch.

Despite the nearby presence of this charismatic Byzantine emperor, his victorious army and court, the Prophet Muhammad was able to win over a number of important new local allies in 630. Many of these, like Yhanna ibn Ruba, bishop of Aqaba, accepted the Prophet's political leadership but succeeded in retaining their Christian faith, though they had to agree to pay a poll tax. The Prophet's negotiating position was greatly strengthened as news of the submission of southern Arabia (and control of all the trade routes) became known. He was also much assisted by the Emperor Heraclius's post-victory economies, which included cutting off the annual subsidy that had been paid to the Christian Judham and Qudaah tribes for guarding the Syrian desert.

More of these vital negotiations continued over 631 and 632, the last two years of life for the Prophet. It might have been during these years that the Prophet's letter was finally delivered to the Emperor at Antioch. This incident figures very large in traditional Muslim belief along with the questions that the Emperor asked about the Prophet Muhammad's character from one of his most bitter opponents among the pagan Quraysh. At the end of this public hearing Heraclius declares, 'I knew he would appear, but I did not know he would be from among you. If what you have said is true, he will soon rule the ground beneath these two feet of mine . . .' This personal sympathy to Islam was soon drowned out by a clamorous roar of opposition from the bishops, generals and grandees of his court.

Whatever the truth behind this widespread popular tradition, the Emperor Heraclius remained at the city of Antioch. His immediate concern was to preside over a series of councils where he tried to iron out the differences between the Christian churches. He also wished to oversee the peaceful departure of the last Persian garrisons from his eastern provinces. The Byzantine border of Syria must have buzzed with rumours and been criss-crossed with intelligence agents in 632 and the following summer of 633.

That winter a Muslim force occupied Areopolis (also known as Maab), a border post just east of the Dead Sea. The stage was now set, the local allies were in place. Key elements of the Christian Arab tribes of the Syrian desert had been neutralised. A deal had been struck, political submission to the Islamic state in exchange for tolerance of Christianity. The Prophet Muhammad, as well as inspiring his people with a new religion, which would provide them with a unique experience of Arabian unity, had also proved himself a master tactician and an accomplished diplomat.

4

Aisha and the Other Mothers of the Faithful

On the tenth day of his mortal fever the Prophet had forced himself up from his sickbed – a mattress stuffed with husks in Aisha's hut – to attend the dawn prayers then being called in the open courtyard outside. He was not well enough to lead the prayers, and having appointed Aisha's father Abu Bakr to deputise for him, he returned to Aisha's hut immediately after the prayers were over. There he had laid his head on her breast and clasped her hand firmly in his own. In order to reduce the heat, for it was close to midsummer's day, and his body was racked with fever, he lay quite still all that morning. Then his head grew heavy and Aisha heard him murmur 'Lord, grant me pardon' as the grip on her hand loosened for the last time.

She was only eighteen years old. Muhammad's death brought Aisha's matrimonial and sexual life to an end. She would never love again, yet she was to be loved and honoured by the whole Muslim community as one of the Mothers of the Faithful – as all the Prophet's wives were to be addressed. Her pre-eminence within that group was never disputed. She would live on for another fifty-six years, outliving practically all her friends, cousins and the Companions of the Prophet, to die as a venerable old woman aged seventy-four. Her memories of those years with Muhammad became a bright jewel that was polished and reflected upon throughout Aisha's long life.

In those first eighteen years there had seldom been a time when her life had not been filled with the presence of the Prophet. It had been a life of high adventure and exhilaration. Of occasional marches with the army, filled with the scent of camels, leather harnesses, danger and war, set against a life that was otherwise lived around the confines of the walled compound that was Muhammad's house. It was a place that was both mosque, meeting ground and the courtyard in which all the intense elements of Arabian family life were staged. Deaths, births, betrothments, wedding feasts as well as the humdrum daily concerns of grinding grain to make flour, spinning wool, the weaving of palm fronds and leather, caring for children, the making and embroidering of clothes, tending fires and cooking pots, the keeping of pets, greeting of travellers, caring for the sick, the safe storage of dates and grain from pests, the giving of food to the poor, not to mention such out-of-house chores as milking, fetching well water, the gathering of firewood and bargaining in the weekly markets. For the first six years in Medina the household's income derived from the skilled working and selling of leather.

This household stood at the political and religious centre of the oasis of Medina. After Muhammad's death, it would be drained of its domestic role and gradually transformed into the first monumental mosque of Islam. Though the nine small mud-brick huts, with their palm-frond ceilings and doorways sealed by a simple woollen drape, would long stand as graphic testimony to the simplicity and austerity of his lifestyle. The everyday actions that had occurred in this courtyard house would become vital role models for the personal conduct of future Muslims. While they lived (and two of them, Aisha and Umm Salamah, would outlive all the principal male characters in this story) the Prophet's widows formed an impromptu court of high appeal, drawn out of their individual and collective memories of his thoughts, speech and actions. On this level alone they must be considered as Heirs of the Prophet – though as we will see Aisha would also pursue a direct and disastrous involvement in political and military events.

Aisha's faith was absolute. She was arguably one of the first Muslims to have been born straight into belief – rather than converted from the pagan beliefs of pre-Islamic Arabia. For her parents were among the very first Meccans to profess themselves Muslims and they were also the intimate friends of the Prophet. Aisha, like many a child of the Quraysh, had been sent out from Mecca by her parents to be wet-nursed in the comparative health of the desert by a Bedouin mother. By the time Aisha had been returned to her mother's house the full force of the Meccan persecution had fallen upon the small Muslim community. The Muslims had become outcasts within Mecca and had clustered for self-defence among the households of Muhammad's Beni Hashim clan. Aisha's father, Abu Bakr, was one of the Prophet's closest advisers, and as neighbours in this harrowing time they would have been in and out of each other's household several times a day. Especially as the Prophet had just lost the great emotional supports of his life: his beloved first wife Khadijah and old Abu Talib, his uncle.

Aisha's mother, Umm Ruman, stood slightly apart from the pecking order that was jealously maintained among the rival clans within the Quraysh tribe of Mecca. She was a Bedouin of the desert, the daughter of Amir of the Kinana tribe. Aisha's father, Abu Bakr, also had a somewhat equivocal position. He was a pure-bred member of the Taym clan within the Quraysh tribe of Mecca as his mother and father were cousins. He was also a very successful businessman who before the arrival of Islam had accumulated a capital fortune of 40,000 dirhams. This by any reckoning within Arabia was a sizeable fortune (we know that a whole city bought immunity from attack for a year for a similar sum), though within the venture-capitalist aristocracy of Mecca it put him only in the middling rank. Aisha's father also clearly lacked those vital connections that made you a man of respect within pagan Mecca. For instance there is the humiliating tale of how he had been bound hand to foot (like a goat on its way to the butcher) and left beside his cousin and fellow Muslim Talha ibn Ubaydallah to be mocked by every passer-by. This could never have happened to a man whose clan were fully behind him. They would have certainly exacted vengeance for such a dishonour whatever their clansman's beliefs. There is also the intriguing matter of his nicknames: al-Siddik, 'the truthful', was a source of justifiable pride at the end of his life, though the earlier Atik, 'freed slave', might have been the source of his equivocal social position, especially if he had been made a captive as a young man and had later to be liberated by his kinsmen. This is no more than hypothesis; pious commentators have no trouble in reading Atik as nothing to do with his social status but a recognition that Abu Bakr was destined to be 'freed from hell'.

Abu Bakr was a *tadjir*, a merchant of Mecca who was also an expert on tribal genealogy and the history of the Bedouin clans. This was no amateur enthusiasm but a necessary skill in the planning of which route a caravan should take, which guides to recruit and which of the rival tribal sheikhs actually had enough authority to make them worth your while cultivating. This sort of task, as a fixer and a negotiator who helped set up the transport details of a caravan, rather than as a merchant-trader on his own behalf, might well have been Abu Bakr's experience before he embraced

Islam. As a fellow trader in Mecca he would have known his friend Muhammad extremely well, for they were but three years apart in age. The depth of his devotion to the faith revealed by Muhammad was never in any doubt. That fortune, carefully accumulated from a lifetime of labour, was not kept cautiously to one side but was recklessly spent on feeding his brother Muslims during the years of persecution and buying the liberty of such persecuted Muslims as Bilal from out of pagan bondage. By the time he himself left for Medina, he had but 6000 dirhams to his name.

Although Abu Bakr and his wife Umm Ruman revered the Prophet with an absolute faith, this was not true of the entire household. Some time in this period, Abu Bakr's first wife, Kutayla bint (daughter of) Abd al-Uzza of the Amir clan, began to drift apart from her husband. When the time came to make the move to Medina Aisha's stepmother had chosen to stay behind in pagan Mecca with her two young children, Abdallah and Asma. One can only guess at the domestic scenes that were behind this decision but it would not have been lightly taken. The young Abdallah would take his mother's side in this issue. Indeed he would even fight on the pagan side against the Muslim forces at the battles of Badr and Uhud. It was against the background of such a family row that we hear of the first story about Aisha. On one of his frequent visits to her home in Mecca, the Prophet saw the young Aisha crying bitter tears outside the front door. She had been punished by her mother for telling tales to her father which had upset him. Out of sight of the child the Prophet later asked Umm Ruman to be gentle with Aisha for his sake.

In those last years of Aisha's childhood in Mecca, the widowed Muhammad would have often eaten in the house of Abu Bakr as a guest. Since the death of his own beloved Khadijah, his own household had been intermittently under the care of a

number of relatives. His aunt Khawlah had been especially help-
ful. Khawlah bint Hakim was the sister of Muhammad's mother.
She and her husband were early converts to Islam but
Muhammad remained her affectionate nephew as well as her
spiritual adviser. He had even taken on the delicate task of
explaining to his uncle by marriage, who was a very passionate
Muslim, that Islam (unlike Paulist Christianity) did not require
or even approve of celibacy within marriage. Perhaps such frank-
ness on her nephew's part allowed Khawlah to be candid in
return, and to suggest that Muhammad should himself take a
wife after the first period of intense mourning for Khadijah was
over. When he asked for more specific advice, she had put forward either Aisha for her virginal beauty or Sawdah, a
middle-aged widow, who knew how to run a house and might
prove a motherly help to his daughters. The Prophet accepted
both candidates. Aisha, then just six, was betrothed. She stayed
with her parents though she remembered the change in her status
as she was thereafter encouraged to play indoors rather than
range through the streets as a wild tomboy.

Three years later Aisha's father would be chosen as
Muhammad's sole companion in the secret emigration from
Mecca to Medina. It was a testament to the absolute trust that
Muhammad placed in him but also an acknowledgement of Abu
Bakr's profound knowledge of every track and back-way in the surrounding mountains. Aisha may also have been privy to the almost
reckless bravery of her half-sister Asma, who not only denied any
knowledge of the fugitives when questioned but also managed to
slip through all the guards and secretly take provisions to the cave
where her father and the Prophet were hiding. In one instance she
even ripped up her own clothes in order to make a rope with
which to let down a basket of food into the cave.

Once Muhammad and Abu Bakr had safely arrived in Medina

and established themselves they sent word for their families to join them – though this process took months rather than weeks. Although both Muhammad and Abu Bakr had been hunted as fugitives by hundreds of pagan horsemen and Bedouin bounty hunters, Arab chivalry concerning women was absolute. Abu Bakr's son might have remained a pagan opponent of Islam but he was also proud to serve as the escort of his family. He guarded his stepmother Umma Ruman, his full sister Asma and his half-sister Aisha safely to Medina assisted by his Muslim cousin Talha.

Aisha dwelt with her mother and father for a year in the little house in the hamlet of al-Sunh in the Medina oasis where Abu Bakr had made his home. The Prophet had not forgotten his betrothed but was waiting for the huts around the mosque court-yard to be finished and for the chance to acquire sufficient funds to present Aisha's parents with the customary bride price. Even after the victory of Badr, a year after the migration to Medina, and the distribution of spoils from the battlefield and the ransoms, he found himself lacking. According to tradition Abu Bakr had to privately lend the Prophet the bride price before the marriage could go ahead. Aisha could always vividly recall that day. 'I was playing on a see-saw and my long streaming hair became dishevelled.' Then her mother and her closest friends and neighbours came and 'took me from my play and made me ready'. She was given a new dress made from the fine red-striped cloth traded out of Bahrain and an onyx necklace before her mother led her to a newly built hut around whose doorway there was a seated company. In front of these witnesses her mother placed her in the lap of the Prophet and then blessed the pair of them: 'These are your family, may God bless you in them, and bless them in you.' A bowl of milk was offered from which the Prophet drunk before passing it to Aisha. At first she shyly declined but he gently insisted, so she sipped and then it was passed to her elder sister Asma, who was sitting beside her. Then it was passed to all the other guests, who afterwards rose up and departed. Later the Prophet led Aisha into the bridal hut and she became a woman.

In later life Aisha liked to compare the modesty and simplicity of that day with the lavishness and complexity of the celebrations that would later wrap themselves around the Muslim ritual of marriage. As for many who have known poverty and also great wealth there was a bittersweet pleasure in contemplating these strong contrasts. She would always be fascinated by such celebrations. She keenly recalled her first sight of the dancelike exercises of the Abyssinian Muslim soldiers held in the mosque courtyard, where the Prophet drew her protectively to his side as she watched their drill. There is another beguiling story that as a young bride she was seen by the Prophet tiptoeing precariously to peek over a wall in order to catch sight of the boisterous marriage festivities of a neighbour. Instead of reproving her, Muhammad helped her secure a better view. Upon this delicate instance of tacit permission rests the whole doctrinal support for the celebration of Muslim marriages with music, for otherwise the Prophet in his recorded sayings came down against lascivious music. Indeed one might say the only party a pious Muslim family is doctrinally permitted to throw is a wedding party – and so these events pack in all the celebratory inclinations of the populace. In traditional societies they would be made to stretch out over a whole week of interrelated activities – such as the day of the bath or the day when the bride is formally presented to her mother-in-law.

Neither Aisha nor any of the Muslim historians thinks it worth commenting on the great age gap between a bride who was, at most, aged ten and a groom aged fifty-four. It was clearly not an issue, any more than it was for an Archbishop of Canterbury to do the same less than a century ago in Victorian Britain. However, in our post-Industrial Revolution society, where we are permitted to vote, to drink and are forced into schools according to a formula calculated by your government-registered birth date, it is almost impossible to think back to how other societies quantified these issues. I had an inkling of the old simplicity when I travelled through a desert community that still followed a nomadic lifestyle based on their herds of camels and goats. No one knew their birth-day or was much concerned with which year they were born – though cousinage was known to the nth degree. They laughed at the stupidity of my questions, such as 'When does a boy take the veil?' and 'What age do the girls marry?' – for their answer was clarity itself: 'A boy takes the veil when he becomes a man, a girl gets married when she has become a woman.'

Although physically a woman, Aisha kept hold of her toys and her playmates. She remembered how her friends would hide away when her impressive husband entered her room but that the Prophet would ask her to gather them together again – and then join in their games. Another instance she liked to recall was him sitting contently in the corner as she finished her game based around her collection of little toy ponies – though in Aisha's eyes they were horses from King Solomon's stables. In these early years all practical matters of the household were handled by the mater-nal figure of her co-wife, Sawdah, who also cared for the Prophet's daughters and brought much-needed income from her skilled work as a weaver of fine dyed leather strips into wind curtains, mattress straps and ornate harnesses.

Three years into her marriage and Aisha still remained childless. This would have been a vital influence on both Aisha and Muhammad – though it is not so much as mentioned in passing by any of the earliest Muslim historians. Their silence was no doubt a reaction to pagan propaganda from Mecca which would surely not have let this telling issue – why God had withheld the gift of children to the Prophet and his young wife – lie uncommented on. The honorific title of Umm (mother of) or Abu (father of) was the most prized possession of any Arab.

In the winter of 625 the Prophet took a third wife. Aisha was always to be fiercely competitive with each new rival to her love for Muhammad, though Hafsah, his third wife, may have proved herself something of an exception. She had already been widowed, her young husband had died in battle (though the earliest records are not quite sure if it was at Badr or Uhud), but she had also earned a reputation as a slightly charmless plain speaker with a temper attached. She was also literate – a rarity among Arab men, let alone women, in those days. So she was proving rather difficult to place, especially as her father Omar shared all these characteristics. Omar had approached Uthman (a rich and well-respected early Muslim) with the offer of Hafsah's hand but had been rejected – which Omar perhaps correctly took to be something of a social slight and so was then doubly infuriated when Abu Bakr (his social equal) also politely declined. Muhammad, seeing the trouble that was brewing up between his immediate confidants, then stepped in, asking for Hafsah's hand himself while simultaneously offering Uthman one of his own daughters. It was a consummate piece of in-house diplomacy. Aisha for her part quickly saw that Hafsah could never be a threat. Stories from this period cast them together as friends, either guiltily breaking a fast with a meat dish (and later confessing) or sending their co-wife, the motherly Sawdah, into a fit of nerves about the coming of *dajjal* – a devilish false prophet whose arrival was much feared.

Hafsah is all too often dismissed as an Arab bluestocking, as an embarrassment to her father and a trial to her husband – although in this very archetype she may yet serve as a role model for future generations of Muslim women. Her absolute belief in Islam harmoniously coexisted with a bright, ever-questioning mind. When Muhammad entered her room one day and declared that he hoped none of those who had taken the oath of loyalty beneath the thorn tree at Hudaibiya would be punished in hell (the oath had been an especially taxing time for even the most pious Muslims – especially for Hafsah's own father, Omar), Hafsah objected. She quoted a Koranic verse to the Prophet, 'None of you can avoid to pass over it [hell].' The Prophet accepted the correction but in his turn quoted back, 'But we shall save those who guarded against evil.' This casual dialogue was to be carefully remembered and reflected upon and remains the basis for Muslim belief in a form of purgatory. All believers will have to cross 'over it [hell]'– but the righteous will in some way be protected from the full horror of the experience. This is popularly conceived to be a bridge of fire that stretches over the yawning gulf of hell to reach paradise.

It also seems that in later life Hafsah was the prime source who provided her full brother, Abdullah, with a great many of the 'sayings' of the Prophet that can be directly traced back to his memory. But that is not all, for the traditions refer to the very first written Koran in existence – none other than Hafsah's own private copy, which pre-existed Uthman's 'first definitive edition'. In this light, Hafsah, far from being a gawkish embarrassment to the household, increasingly appears as a major intellectual figure in the codification of Islam. She would survive the Prophet by thirty-five years, renowned for the vigour with which she fasted and devoted herself to prayer to her very end.

About a year after Hafsah's marriage the Prophet took Zaynab bint Khuzaymah as an additional wife. She was the daughter of a Bedouin sheikh, though there is some confusion about her previous history. She might have had two husbands before the Prophet, for like Hafsah she was a war widow, though again we are not certain if her husband (or husbands) died at Badr or Uhud. Zaynab was a genuinely pious woman and renowned for her charity to the poor but did not cause many ripples in the Prophet's household in which she lived for only a year before her death. In any case her quietist character was quickly overshadowed by the arrival but a month later of Umm Salamah (sometimes written Umm Salme) in January 626. The sisterly bond that had developed between Hafsah and Aisha is vividly expressed in their joint reaction to Muhammad's new partner.

'When the Prophet of God married Umm Salamah I was exceedingly sad. Having heard much of her beauty, I was initially gracious to her, desiring to see her for myself. And by God, I saw that she was twice as beautiful and graceful as she had been reported to be. I mentioned this to Hafsah, who said, "By God no, this is nothing but jealousy clouding your vision for she is not as they say." Then Hafsah too was gracious to her, and having called to see her, she said to me, "I see her not as beautiful as you say, not even anywhere near it; though she is unquestionably beautiful." I saw her afterwards and, by my life, she was as Hafsah had said. But still I was jealous.'

Aisha never made her peace. Umm Salamah was a remarkable woman. Her marriage to her first husband – who was the eleventh to embrace Islam – was a celebrated love match. Her proud Quraysh family in pagan Mecca had initially refused to allow her to emigrate to Medina to join her Muslim husband (and even kidnapped her child from her), but they were so impressed by her genuine grief that they later relented. Even so none of her clan would escort Umm Salamah and her boy-child to Medina so she was forced to buy her own camel. Fortunately just four miles out of Mecca at the halt of Taneem she met one of those gallant chivalric Arab gentlemen who patrolled – or sometimes pillaged – their way across the deserts of old Arabia. Though still a pagan, Uthman bin Talha escorted her the whole way to Medina and at each stop 'used to sleep at a distance under some other tree' while throughout the day he spurned his own mount 'and with the bridle in his

hand used to walk in front of my camel'. He also knew exactly
where Umm Salamah's husband was to be found in Medina but
politely turned back once they had arrived outside the oasis hamlet
of Amr bin Awf, carefully avoiding the necessity of being thanked
and rewarded for what he considered to be no more than his
chivalric duty. Umm Salamah's husband was one of the heroic
early warriors of Islam who fought at both Badr and Uhud. In a
later fight the heavy wounds that he had received at these battles
reopened and would not heal. During their time together in
Medina Umm Salamah gave birth to two young daughters.

In widowhood she was wooed by both Omar and Abu Bakr –
both of whom she refused – before finally being persuaded by the
Prophet to join his household. She had initially protested that 'I am
advanced in age and have orphaned children', to which Muhammad
had replied, 'As for your age, I am older than you, and as for your
orphans, they shall be the responsibility of God and his messenger.'
So Umm Salamah came to the household as a middle-aged mother
with responsibilities and a certain dignity. She soon found the company of Muhammad's serious-minded daughter Fatimah to be the
most congenial and their friendship ripened. In part this may have
been because they were both bringing up young families. Many
years later Umm Salamah's son Omar would recall the times he had
sat in the lap of his stepfather and shared the simple meals of the
household. The friendship between Umm Salamah and Fatimah
would develop as a rival axis of influence to that of Aisha and
Hafsah – one of the shadow faultlines which would later grow in the
famous historical cleavage between Shia and Sunni.

The opportunity to travel with the Prophet on his military
campaigns and missionary journeys was taken by lot. Though it
seems many of the wives preferred to stay at home, leaving Aisha
and Umm Salamah to be the most well travelled of his wives. It is
certainly noticeable how often it was Umm Salamah who was the

companion of Muhammad on all the really decisive expeditions;
such the pilgrimage that ended with the truce of Hudaibiya (628),
or in the headquarters tent during the siege of Medina in the year
of the battle of the Trench (627) and also at the conquest of
Khaybar oasis (628). Umm Salamah proved herself an exceptionally wise counsellor to the Prophet; indeed her advice at Hudaibiya
for Muhammad to go ahead and perform his own sacrifice (in the
face of a near-mutiny from his army) delivered in the privacy of
her tent appears to have been crucial to the happy resolution of
that day. She was also gifted with a prodigious memory, so that in
the years after the death of the Prophet, she (alongside her rival
Aisha, who had a similar genius for accurate recall) became one of
the two centres of Islamic learning. As Marwan (one of the earliest authorities) used to pronounce, 'So far as the wives of the
Prophet are living among us, we should not consult anybody else.'
Nor is there even so much as a flicker of prudery in her cherished
memories of her physical life with the Prophet. Muslims must
wash after sex but the exact timing and degree of cleanliness
required was a continual source of concern to early believers – as
ritual uncleanliness was (and still is) considered to invalidate all the
benefit of fasting and prayer. She remembered asking the Prophet
whether she had to unfasten her long hair (which was gathered
tightly together and scented) in order to wash it thoroughly after
sex. To which he replied no, that it was perfectly adequate to leave
it as it was but soak it carefully to the roots with three applications
of water. On a later occasion, once again answering some concerned petitioner after the death of Muhammad, she remembered
that rather than get up and wash himself in the night, the Prophet
after the act used to sleep till morning without taking a bath even
when he was keeping the fast. And mind, she continued, that this
bath used to be taken not because of ejaculation but because of
copulation. When this was independently confirmed by Aisha's

memory it immediately became accepted practice among the whole of the community. The leading male authority of the day candidly admitted that he had been in the wrong, for 'Actually, they are the one who know about it better than anyone else.'

In times of trouble Umm Salamah advised believers to recite her favourite passage from the Koran, 'To God we belong and to him is our return.' This has now become a universal graveside prayer and a benediction to the dying. She was also secure enough in her faith to question the Prophet, famously enquiring of him why women only merited half the inheritance of men; was it because they did not fight in battles? On another issue when she asked 'Why is there no mention of women in the Koran?' her query resulted in an immediate tightening up of definitions, so that Sura (chapter) 35 specifically states, 'For Muslim men and women, for believing men and women.' Umm Salamah's role in our under-standing of the Prophet's message to all humankind (clearly she would not approve of such shoddy terms as 'mankind') is almost without equal. She would live on longer than any other of the Companions or the Mothers of the Believers, surviving until her eighty-fourth year, just a few months after Aisha. She was a living library of knowledge until her last days, with at least 378 recorded sayings of the Prophet directly attributed to her and other streams of memory, history and knowledge passed on to the world through such male spiritual confidants as Abdullah ibn Abbas.

Less than a year after the marriage to Umm Salamah, the house-hold was again to be augmented. The arrival of Zaynab bint Jahsh remains one of the most controversial events in the life of Muhammad – to Westerners. This beautiful cousin of the Prophet had migrated to Medina but initially had no household to stay in. Muhammad arranged for her to marry his adopted son, Zayd. The Prophet placed enormous trust in Zayd but his love was not always shared by many of his more socially conservative followers. Zaynab, a proud granddaughter of the sheikh of the Beni Hashim, could never quite overlook the fact that Zayd was not of the Quraysh, but had first come to Mecca as a captive slave boy who had been bought at the fair of Ukaz by Khadijah and given to Muhammad as a wedding present. So when Muhammad fell passionately in love after a chance meeting with Zaynab, exclaiming 'Praise be to God who disposeth of men's hearts,' it seemed a blessing. Zayd could at last get rid of his imperious and unloving wife, especially now that he knew that she would go straight into the Prophet's household. Muhammad at first refused, telling Zayd to 'Keep your wife and fear God'. Zayd listened respectfully but soon after he and Zaynab separated.

For a while nothing was done. Nothing needed to be. Muhammad already had the four wives permitted to a Muslim and was then aged sixty (for Sawdah had separated and the first Zaynab was dead). Zayd was only ten years younger than the Prophet and Zaynab was just short of her fortieth year. Then a couple of months later, while he was talking to Aisha, a revelation suddenly came upon the Prophet, and when he recovered himself he called out, who will give Zaynab the good news that God has declared that, 'We have married her to thee'? When this news was brought to Zaynab in her house she gave thanks to God and then took off her silver bracelets and anklets and presented them as a gift to the messenger, for such was the extravagant custom of the time. Aisha would later find Zaynab's boasts about having been 'given by God' a little tiresome. At the time her famous retort to Muhammad had been 'Truly thy Lord makes haste to do thy bidding.' Read by a Western audience this can be made to sound ironical, though a pious Muslim can read this and take comfort in God's special concern for the Prophet.

Shortly after this extraordinary event the seventy-three verses of Sura 33 of the Koran were revealed to Muhammad – some claim immediately after the marriage of Zaynab, though others have argued with conviction that Sura 33 is a composite collection of verses from several different historical revelations. This famous revelation is addressed to all believers, though several verses pour their special attention on the women of his household. It contains the poignant cry 'Muhammad is not the father of any of your men, but he is the Apostle of God' and so in a sense a father to all believers. His childless wives are also to share this adoptive role: 'his wives are [as] the mothers of the believers'. They are counselled, 'O wives of the Prophet! You are not like any other of the women: if you will be on your guard, then be not seductive in speech, lest he in whose heart is a disease yearn: but speak a good word. And stay in your houses and do not display your finery like the displaying of the ignorance of yore; and keep up prayer and pay the poor rate, and obey God and his Apostle. God only desires to keep away the uncleanness from you, O people of the House! And to purify you a purifying.' These commands are specifically addressed to his wives, who occupied an honoured role and yet were housed in an exceptionally public space, existing in their small huts within the open courtyard that served as the Prophet's house, a communal assembly point and a prayer hall.

Verse 53 instructs, 'Believers! Do not enter the house of the Prophet unless permission is given to you for a meal, not waiting for its cooking to be finished – but when you are invited, enter, and when you have taken your food then disperse, not seeking to listen to talk . . . and when you ask them [his wives] for any goods, ask of them behind a curtain, this is purer for your hearts and their hearts.' This is considered to be in response to the chaotic evening of Zaynab's wedding celebration when the guests long outstayed their welcome. Whatever the historical basis of this revelation it has now become one of the cornerstones of Muslim social etiquette. At a Muslim gathering the offering of food will be delayed as long as possible, to allow enough room for conversation, for Muslim guests will know that they are expected to depart immediately after the last course.

The much quoted advice to Muslim women in verse 59 is even more specifically related to the geographical location and simplicity of the Prophet's house at Medina. This courtyard house with its simple row of bedroom huts had no lavatory, so all the inhabitants were forced to go out and use the surrounding bushes. In the night and in a hurry, his wives were not always as modestly covered as they might be. On one such occasion a wife had been mistaken as a woman of the street or a slave girl and crudely propositioned. So this verse can be read as simply advising his household to wear a shawl-like wrap so that they are recognised for who they are: 'O Prophet! Say to your wives and your daughters and the women of believers that they let down upon them their over-garments; this will be more proper, that they may be known, and thus they may not be given trouble . . .' This course of action had long been urged upon Muhammad by the puritanical Omar, who in the seclusion of a dark night had once stumbled across the squatting bulky form of Sawdah – much to his surprise and disgust.

From such practical instructions would later generations of legal consultants and arid scholars construct the constraints upon medieval Muslim women – of which all too many survive today. Other Koranic verses dealing with suitable public dress, such as in the Sura of Light (24:31), which advises believing women to 'wear their head coverings over their bosoms' and both believing men and believing women to 'cast down their looks and guard their private parts', are mild enough instructions to encourage a natural modesty – especially when you remember that the Prophet was addressing an audience brought up in the extremely free sexual environment of the oasis of Medina.

*

When the Prophet was accompanied on his campaigns and missionary journeys by his wives, they travelled by day in howdahs – light canopied seats made from cane and stretched leather that rose above a camel's back. Aisha, being the youngest, lightest and most adventuresome, took the comparative discomfort of these journeys in her stride. In January 627 the Prophet had heard that the Beni Mustaliq, a powerful subclan of the Khuzaa tribe, who controlled the caravan route along the Red Sea coast, were preparing a raid on Medina. He decided to strike first, and carried off thousands of sheep, goats and camels as well as 200 captives. Both Aisha and Umm Salamah accompanied the Muslim army on this successful raid – as the soldiers were all too aware. The presence of the young Aisha had done nothing to assist their military efficiency. For just as this force was getting ready to move on, after a short rest stop at dusk, Aisha found to her horror that her favourite necklace – an elegant chain of onyx – had slipped from her neck. In the growing darkness she could not find it but was desperate with a cold superstitious dread. It had been given to her on her wedding day. The Prophet considerately gave the order for his army to camp where they were, though they had been geared up to use these cool hours of the night to push on with their march and catch their enemy off guard. As there was no water or well-head at hand that night, Aisha's name was roundly rebuked on all sides. In the morning light the necklace still could not be found. But then when Aisha's mount was finally made ready it was discovered that her camel had actually been sitting upon the necklace. Though publicly scolded by her father about this incident, Aisha clearly remained the darling of her husband's eye. For just a few days later the army watched in delighted surprise as Muhammad and Aisha emerged from their tent and challenged each other to a race along a valley of golden sand. Years and years later she remembered this arresting scene and how 'I girded up my robe about me and the Prophet did likewise. Then we raced, and he won the race. "This is for that other race," he said, "which you did win from me,'" referring back to some happy memory they shared.

As the march neared its end they were but a day's ride away from Medina. At one of the customary halts Aisha dismounted from her howdah and climbed a dune so as to be out of sight of the men while she answered the call of nature. Just when she was almost back in her howdah she realised that her precious necklace had once again slipped off and so she slowly retraced her clear footprints in the sand while she searched for the onyx stones at every step. In the meantime the march had continued without her. When she returned to the empty campsite she behaved quite properly by seating herself down where her howdah had been and patiently awaiting rescue. Her absence had not been noticed so as the hours stretched on Aisha wrapped herself from the full force of the sun in the covering of her veil and fell asleep. The rescue, when it came, arrived from an unexpected direction. A young Bedouin of the Beni Sulaym tribe, Safwan ibn Muattal, came across the sleeping form of young Aisha. She awoke suddenly when Safwan was standing over her, but once her eyes were open he immediately recognised Aisha and stepped back crying out, 'Verily we are from God and unto Him we are returning. This is the wife of the messenger of God.'

Safwan then gallantly offered Aisha a seat on his camel while he escorted her on to the next halt. When these two figures emerged out of the horizon, the whole camp buzzed with the talk of it, especially as no one had yet noticed that Aisha was missing from her howdah.

Once they returned to Medina the incident was at first forgotten as the triumphant expedition force settled down to the division of the spoils. The Prophet was in her room when Aisha opened the door to Juwayriyah, the captive daughter of the chief of the Beni Mustaliq. Aisha remembered her: 'She was a woman of great loveliness and beauty. No man looked on her but that she captivated his soul, and when I saw her at the door of my room I was filled with misgivings.' Juwayriyah had come to seek the Prophet's help in the matter of her ransom – which had been pitched very high by her Muslim captor. Muhammad offered to pay it himself and at the same time offered to marry her, though her proud Bedouin father would have none of it. He rode into Medina and paid the full ransom first. Only then would he agree to his daughter's marriage – free of any constraints. Such generosity and nobility struck at the roots of Arabic pride in good manners. The sheikh of the Beni Mustaliq was to be repaid in an unexpected form, when a hundred of his tribesmen were freely released by their Muslim captors. They had been impressed by his spirited conduct but also wished to hold no one captive who might have been related to the Prophet's new wife. As Aisha commented, 'I know of no woman who was a greater blessing to her people than she.'

Then came the moment of Aisha's great trial.

Soon after Juwayriyah had been welcomed into the Prophet's household – after a new hut had been built for her – Aisha was laid low by a fever. Sensing a reduction in the Prophet's concern for her, and once again afflicted with a raging jealousy of the new bride, she took herself off to her parents' house to be nursed by her mother. Twenty days later she was up and about again but by then the oasis was alive with rumours that Safwan was her secret lover and that she had betrayed the Prophet. Modern commentators make much of the political ramifications and how the rumour was circulated by the 'Hypocrites' or half-converted Medina locals, who may have wanted to diminish the Prophet's standing. There may be some truth in this, though it is equally clear that many of the disseminators were good Muslims seemingly caught up by a simple love of gossip and intrigue – such as the Prophet's otherwise loyal poet Hassan Ibn Thabit, one of Aisha's own cousins, and Hamnah, sister to the Prophet's cousin-wife Zaynab.

Whatever the source, the Prophet for his part was clearly disturbed. He never claimed to be able to read the secrets of the human heart or possess any miraculous powers. When questioned he freely confessed, 'I know only what God giveth me to know.' Usama, son of Zayd, jumped to her defence, declaring, 'This is all a lie – we know nothing but good of her.' As the adopted grandson of the Prophet his opinion was listened to but as he was about the same age as Aisha it did not carry gravitas. Aisha's maid, Burayrah, when questioned by Muhammad declared resoundingly, 'By him that sent thee with the truth, I know only good of her; and if it were otherwise God would inform his Messenger. I have no fault with Aisha but that she is a girl, young in years,' but then went off at a conversational tangent of her own, adding that 'when I am kneading dough and I bid her watch it she will fall asleep and her pet lamb will come and eat it. I have blamed her for that more than once.'

After prayers in the mosque the Prophet indirectly questioned his congregation, declaring that he 'knew naught but good of my household, and naught but good of the man [Safwan] they speak of, who never entereth a house of mine but I am with him'. The congregation nodded its agreement but then quickly dissolved into disorder as the Aws and Khazraj factions within Medina's clans used the dispute to sharpen their old rivalry and fling at each other accusations of backstabbing.

Then it was the turn of Ali, Muhammad's beloved son-in-law through his marriage to Fatimah, to be questioned. Ali did not really doubt Aisha's innocence but gave his master some brutally frank advice, 'God hath not restricted thee, and there are many women besides her.' Ali was effectively advising the Prophet to divorce Aisha and choose himself a less contentious partner. This off-the-cuff but candid remark was to be held against him for the rest of his life. Aisha was never to forgive Ali. Their enmity would develop into one of the great faultlines that would divide the community of Islam into Sunni and Shia.

Muhammad, like most of Medina, was in daily expectation of a revelation to sort out this tangled affair. But weeks and weeks went by. Eventually after a month apart he went to talk to Aisha himself, finding her in her hut in the company of a pair of grave parents and one lone but sympathetic neighbour. Aisha had been crying for two nights and a day. The Prophet addressed her formally but with compassion. 'Aisha, if you are innocent, God will absolve you but if you are guilty, ask forgiveness from God and repent, for God pardons those who confess and repent.' To Aisha's ears it sounded as if she had already been judged and she was furious that neither of her parents spoke in her defence but meekly answered her appeals with 'I know not what answer to make.'

She had no need of any spokesperson. All of a sudden her tears dried up and she found herself calmly declaring, 'I see that you have listened to the talk about me until it has taken hold of you so that you now believe in it. If I declare my innocence (and God Most High knows that I am) you will not believe me. But if I confess you will surely believe me. There remains nothing to do but to follow the example of Joseph's father and say, "Patience is becoming and God's help is to be implored."'

It was well said and timely – though later she would chastise herself for forgetting Jacob's name, though 'Joseph's father' proved perfectly adequate at the time. Then she went to the back of the hut and lay down on her bed. Shortly afterwards her supplication was answered. The hut went totally silent as the Prophet was visibly gripped by a long-awaited revelation. In Aisha's words, 'He was seized with the pangs which seized him at such times, and as it were pearls of sweat dripped from him although it was a wintry day'. Then when he was relieved of the pressure his face rose up and he was smiling. He called out, 'Good tidings, Aisha. God Most High has exonerated you.'

Her parents were beside themselves with relief and hurriedly called out to Aisha to rise from her mat and thank the Prophet. Their anxiety had clouded their understanding of the nature of revelation – for it was God's word not Muhammad's. Aisha with theological accuracy and a chilling dignity chided these two believers (her own parents) who had, half an hour earlier, not come to her aid. She declared, 'I shall neither come to him nor thank him. Nor will I thank the both of you who listened to the slander and did not deny it.' She paused to let this sink in and then added, 'I shall rise and give thanks to God alone.'

Aisha had come of age. The experience also hardened the growing split within the household of the Prophet. Henceforth Aisha would be a devoted friend to Usama and her old enmity with Zaynab was buried in remembrance of the good things Zaynab had said of Aisha when she was at her most dejected and exhausted. For Ali, however, she developed a fierce and implacable hatred.

In the immediate aftermath the revelation that came upon Muhammad in Aisha's hut was revealed in all its verses as Sura 24. It is a little Koran in itself, a glorious dancing mixture of exact law codes for future ethical conduct, metaphysical descriptions and passages of great sublimity. For instance verse 35: 'God is the light of the heavens and the earth; a likeness of his light is as a niche in which is a lamp, the lamp is in a glass and the [glass] as it were a brightly shining star lit from a blessed olive tree, neither eastern or western, the oil whereof gives light though fire touch it not – light upon light – God guides to his light whom he pleases, and God

sets forth parables for men, and God is knowing of all things.'
While unbelief is described as 'like utter darkness in the deep sea:
there covers it a wave above which is another wave, above which is
a cloud, [and layers of] utter darkness one above another; when he
holds out his hand, he is almost unable to see it, and to whomso-
ever God does not give light, he has no light.' Elsewhere in this
chapter, eighty lashes are prescribed as the punishment for those
who bear false witness to a charge of adultery, four witnesses are
required for any future accusation of adultery, and a hundred
lashes prescribed as the punishment for convicted adulterers.
Husbands and wives may testify against each other four times but
on the fifth time they solemnly have to call down the curse of God
upon themselves if they lie. Though as so often in the Koran this
outward legal severity can always be waived by the calls of mercy,
such as in verse five, 'Except those who repent after this and act
aright, for surely God is Forgiving, Merciful.'

Aisha must have especially delighted to the sound of this whole
sura. The verse that freed her, by God's command, from accusations of infidelity, had also been uniquely delivered to the Prophet
in her presence. No other wife was ever so honoured by God
speaking to his messenger in her presence.

The composition of the household was in the following years to
be constantly augmented and Aisha had always to be on her guard
against another rival toppling her from her prime position. The
next wife to arrive, Raihanah bint Zayd, was a tragic figure. She
was a Jew from the Beni Nadir who had escaped the exile that was
imposed upon her wealthy tribe by marrying into one of the other
great Jewish clans of Medina, the Beni Qurayzah. When that clan
also fell before the Muslims in the aftermath of the failed pagan
siege of Medina oasis (627) Raihanah passed to Muhammad as
part of his share of the booty while her Jewish husband – and all
his fellow cousins and clansmen – were executed. Whether out of

grief at their fate or a deliberate desire not to antagonise any of his existing wives, Raihanah preferred to legally remain a concubine rather than become a free Muslim wife. Her meek demeanour allowed her to exist quietly in the Prophet's house and she would die five years later, a shadowy figure in that household that otherwise blazed with such strong characters.

The other Jewish woman in the harem, Safiyah bint Huayy, was not so self-effacing, though she came into the Prophet's family in just the same way – as war booty. Safiyah's family had been decimated by the Muslims: her father, first husband and brother had been executed with the fall of the Beni Qurayzah while her second husband, Kinanah, one of the paramount Jewish chiefs of Khaybar oasis, had been put to death for hiding treasure from the Muslims. The seventeen-year-old widow had at first been awarded to the Muslim warrior Dihyah al-Kalbi, who was acknowledged to be the most beautiful man in all Arabia – whom the Prophet compared in looks to the Archangel Gabriel. Safiyah saw things in another way. She recounted a disturbing dream about how the moon had travelled from above Medina to Khaybar, where it had fallen in her lap. This was at once taken to refer to Muhammad and so she was exchanged with another captive. Her original given name had been Zaynab but with the evidence of this prophetic dream to hand she was renamed the 'selected one' – Safiyah. She also proved physically pleasing to the Prophet, for he would celebrate this new marriage when the army was just a day's march out from Khaybar – having only just survived an attempted poisoning. The Muslim army had camped at the halt of Sebha. Here two of his wives who were travelling with the army prepared Safiyah for the marriage bed, combing her hair with sweet-smelling oils and anointing her with scent before leading her to Muhammad's tent. It was said that neither bride nor bridegroom could sleep that night. During the journey back to Medina, the Prophet was at pains to make Safiyah feel honoured. She often sat behind him (within a canopy) so that he could advise her on the correct way to ride. He also arranged a marriage feast, though shortage of supplies meant that his troops brought their own rations, just butter, dates and milk, which were placed together in a communal kitchen and then shared out among the assembled host. At each halt he gallantly stooped before Safiyah's camel and offered his knee as her mounting block. Safiyah was completely overwhelmed and declared that 'I have not seen any other person who had such good manners.'

Aisha was typically torn apart with anxiety with this new young rival, especially after Umm Salamah had taunted her by declaring, 'She is beautiful indeed and the Messenger of God loves her very much.' So when Safiyah was first brought to Medina, and lodged in a house apart from the others, Aisha arranged to join the welcoming party in order to inspect this new rival. Although heavily veiled and uncharacteristically keeping to the background she was spotted by Muhammad hiding among the crowd. Later he would casually intercept her on the way home and call out, 'Aisha, how didst thou find her?' to which she dismissively replied, 'I saw in her a Jewess like any other Jewess.' Muhammad corrected her, for Safiyah had professed herself a Muslim. Still it was clearly a weak point and her co-wives would taunt Safiyah by addressing her as 'Daughter of Huyayy' – for her dead father was an old adversary of the Muslims. The Prophet taught her an effective riposte: 'Tell them,' he advised, 'that my father is Aaron and my uncle is Moses' – two of the great Jewish prophets that are also honoured by all Muslims. This anti-Jewish spat proved to be but a passing storm, for Aisha soon found that Safiyah's youth and high spirits matched her own. She became co-opted into the party of Aisha's friends. She never found that loyalty to her own people conflicted with her beliefs as a Muslim. In later life she kept Friday as holy as any believer but she also put aside the Sabbath as the day when she would receive her Jewish friends and distribute charity to her impoverished kin.

Not so the next of the Prophet's women, who came from the inner circle of Mecca's clan societies. His marriage to the thirty-five-year-old Umm Habiba was celebrated hard on the back of his new union with Safiyah. Indeed she was awaiting him when the Muslim army returned from its victorious conquest of Khaybar. She had been long awaited and a new hut stood already built for her use in the Prophet's house-mosque. The marriage to Umm Habiba was essentially a political union, for although she was a Muslim widow deserving of honour – she had been an early believer who had endured persecution and thirteen years as an exile in Abyssinia – she was also a daughter of Abu Sufyan (the leader of pagan Mecca) and a cousin of the noble Uthman. By making a marriage alliance with the leader of pagan Mecca Muhammad was paving the way for a negotiated settlement. By all accounts Habiba was a serious-minded figure who piously enquired from the Prophet such legalistic details as the correct period of mourning a Muslim woman should follow (which was three days except for a husband, who can be mourned for three months and ten days). These enquiries may have come out of her long exposure to Abyssinian culture, for her first husband, though he arrived as a Muslim refugee, had converted to Coptic Christianity during the long years of exile. Once within the compound Umm Habiba instantly joined the party of Umm Salamah, whom she had known as a child. She thus earned the enmity of Aisha.

On her deathbed (some thirty years after her marriage) she at last made her peace with Aisha, appealing to her old enemy, 'Since we have been co-wives of the Prophet and I might have uttered some harsh words against you, I ask you now to forgive me for the hurt I might have caused you.' Aisha forgave her and the old rivals blessed each other for the first and last time with conviction, 'May God keep you happy.' On her gravestone was recorded not that she was a daughter of the great Abu Sufyan, or a wife of the Prophet Muhammad, or that she was one of the Mothers of the Believers or a cousin of the third Caliph. Instead it was inscribed with just her given name and that of her mother, 'Ramla daughter of Safiya'.

Aisha and her supporters – Hafsah, Safiyah and Sawdah – had now coalesced into a gang of four. Sawdah was almost a step-mother to her. The Prophet's cousin Zaynab was a wild card floating whichever way her tongue led her but on the other side were Umm Salamah, Umm Habiba and the Prophet's daughter Fatimah.

It was an acknowledged division but as well as strong underly-ing passions it had its lighter moments. Muhammad loved honey and Umm Salamah used to keep a little store to share with him when he made a visit. Aisha, fearing that it might lead to the Prophet spending more time with her rival, managed to persuade all his other wives to pretend that this honey made his breath sour, knowing full well that the Prophet Muhammad was a great stickler for cleanliness. The trick worked, though Aisha would later regret that her mischief-making had tricked Muhammad into avoiding all honey – which up until then had been one of his few favourite treats.

Aisha would also remember another round in her long sniping war against Umm Salamah. She had been waiting for her husband and was cross to find out that he had just been with Umm Salamah. She spoke out, 'Have you not had your fill of that woman?' and when she received just a smile by return she contin-ued with a parable of her own. She first asked, 'O Messenger of God, tell me something about yourself. If you were between two slopes of a valley, one which had been grazed whereas the other had been untouched, where would you pasture your herds?'

'On that which had not been grazed,' replied Muhammad.

'Ah,' exclaimed the triumphant Aisha, 'just so. I am the untouched one, not like your other wives. Every woman has had a husband before you, except myself.'

Once again Muhammad looked at her with a quiet smile but said nothing. On another occasion when she had been looking glum, Muhammad accosted her, declaring that 'It is not hidden from me when thou art angered against me, nor yet when you are happy.' Aisha was aghast at the idea that he could read her mind but he immediately assured her that it was no magical art that allowed him to divine her thoughts but simple observation: when she was happy she would swear, 'Nay by the Lord of Muhammad' but when she was cross with him, 'Nay by the Lord of Abraham.'

The Prophet was often asked whom he loved the most of all the believers. Among the men he would list his adopted son Zayd, his young cousin and son-in-law Ali, his oldest friend Abu Bakr, his young grandchildren and sometimes Zayd's son Usama. Among the women he would always mention his daughters and his granddaughter Umamah (the child of his daughter Zaynab), but it was noticed that only Aisha was ever mentioned from among his living wives. Aisha always knew that there was one woman who was even closer – as revealed one morning in her own room when there had been a casual knock on the door and a cry of greeting from Halah. Halah's voice sounded so like that of her sister, Khadijah (Muhammad's first wife), that Aisha watched as Muhammad grew pale and trembled with grief at this reminder of the woman who meant most to him in his life.

Decades later she would recall, 'I was not jealous of any other wife of the Prophet as I was jealous of Khadijah, for his constant mentioning of her and because God had bidden him give her good tidings of a mansion in Paradise of precious stones. And whenever he sacrificed a sheep, he would send a good portion of it unto those who were her intimate friends. Many a time I said unto him, "It is as if there had never been any other woman in the world, save only Khadijah."' The mention of 'precious stones' might have been an exaggerated addition by the embittered Aisha, for Muhammad, when he spoke about his hopes of paradise, talked simply of being alone with Khadijah in a hut built of reeds.

The jealousy that Aisha felt for the long-dead Khadijah (whom she sometimes derisively referred to as the old Qurayshite) was also felt against her by the other wives. They were not alone in noticing that Muhammad seemed at his most approachable after he had spent his turn with Aisha. Indeed that soon became the unofficially recognised 'day' in which to petition the Prophet, which was all too often accompanied by a present left at the door of Aisha's hut. The other wives grew irritated at this habit and the growing influence that Aisha was seen to have among the believers. First Umm Salamah and later Fatimah and finally the mischievous Zaynab approached Muhammad on this matter, though it was Aisha who finally cleared up the issue in direct conversation with her co-wives. The Prophet must be just and equal to his wives, and they all knew that his judgement would never be affected by outside considerations – but he could not dictate such even-mindness to others.

The Prophet's love for Khadijah was also wrapped up in the knowledge that this wealthy, clever and powerful woman had sacrificed everything to uphold the faith that he taught. Sometimes it seemed to him that the wives he had taken since he had moved to the safety of Medina were experiencing the exact opposite. After the conquest of Khaybar, followed by a number of successful expeditions, wealth flowed steadily into Medina oasis. The Prophet had set his share at a fifth but this was always speedily dissipated by his gifts to the poor, passing travellers, the ill of the community as well as his relations. On one such occasion his wives were vociferously arguing that his charity might also extend to his own home – and in particular they would not mind a fair choice from the bundle of garments that had just come into the household before he gave them all away to strangers. The Prophet hated to refuse a request but in the midst of these passionately articulated negotiations Omar walked in. His gruff, stern tones of greeting immediately silenced the women, who rushed behind a curtain to hide from this tough old puritan.

Years later Aisha remembered the dialogue of that day almost word for word. The Prophet, almost speechless with laughter at the rapid transformation in the conduct of his wives, spoke of how wondrous it was that they had hidden themselves at the first sound of his voice. Omar replied, with his normal gravity, 'It is rather thy right, not mine, that they should stand in awe of thee, not of me' and then turning to the quivering curtain declaimed, 'O enemies of yourselves, why fear me and not God's messenger?' Some nameless figure replied – could it be Aisha? – 'that it was so, for thou art rougher and harsher than God's Messenger.' Muhammad agreed, 'That is true, O son of Khattab [Omar], for I believe if Satan himself found that you were travelling on a certain path he would choose any other track other than thine.' Later when Omar persisted in questioning the wives independently he met – for once – with a united front. Even the normally pacific Umm Salamah took him to task for this effrontery: 'By all that is wonderful what has made you think to come between the Prophet and his wives? Yes, by God, we speak freely with him, and if he allows us to do that, that is surely his own affair.' One must also remember that up until this period the entire household had been living on what would now be considered well below the poverty line. By the standards of the twenty-first century they were all self-denying saints;

Aisha would later remember that it was not until after Khaybar had fallen that she had ever eaten her fill of dates, while Umm Salamah made her own wedding feast by grinding some barley seed into flour and baking a simple loaf of bread which she shared with her new husband.

However, the biggest domestic crisis within the household was yet to come. Muhammad had been sent a thousand measures of gold, twenty fine robes, a mule, a she-ass and a crown by a ruler of Egypt known as Muqawqis.* With this cavalcade of gifts came two ravishingly beautiful Coptic slave girls, Mariyah and Sirin. Muhammad with his customary generosity gave away all these gifts except for Mariyah, whom he kept for himself. He was clearly smitten by her, and lodged her in a separate house near the mosque enclosure where 'he would visit her by day and by night'. His wives were upset by this new love but the crisis came when Hafsah discovered the Prophet in her room with Mariyah on Aisha's day. She was beside herself with jealous fury, no doubt greatly aggravated by Mariyah's exotic otherness, her complete lack of Muslim faith and her youthful fecundity. Though Hafsah eventually calmed down, especially after the Prophet promised he would not see Mariyah again, the issue was reignited when Aisha was let into the tale.

This time the Prophet had had enough. He left his entire household and took lone refuge in a rooftop terrace which could only be reached by a ladder from the grounds of the mosque. This little terrace had not much in the way of luxury for the ruler of half Arabia, furnished as it was with only a rush mat and three dried skins, but it was the only place that Muhammad could call his own. While he lay there quite still, in fact so still that the woven

---

* This is not now considered a given name but probably the Arabic version of the Coptic description of the Byzantine viceroy Cyril – of whom we will learn more later.

pattern of the rush mat became imprinted on his side, rumours quickly spread throughout the oasis that he had divorced all his wives after the scene with Hafsah. Omar, Hafsah's father, was especially concerned at what effect this might have on the small community of the devoutly faithful, and indeed on his own position within the inner circle of believers. It was also an especially tense period, for at this time they feared an attack upon Medina from the well-armoured warriors of the Ghassanid Arab kingdom.

Omar went first to his daughter, asking her, 'Why are you weeping? Didn't I warn you? So the Prophet has divorced you at last,' but she replied, 'I do not know. He is in the upper room now.' Then Omar went towards the pulpit of the mosque and sat around with the disconsolate group of men who had gathered there, some of whom were weeping. Three times he enquired from the Abyssinian servant who was guarding the ladder up to the loft if the Prophet would see him, and three times he returned to the knot of supplicants around the pulpit, though at last he was called forward. When he climbed up, the Prophet was leaning on his elbow propped up on a tatty leather cushion stuffed with palm fibre. Omar asked him if he had put away his wives. Upon which the Prophet looked up and said, 'No.' Omar, still standing, then tried to soothe him with idle chatter. How the men of Mecca know how to control their women but had come among a people (the oasis of Medina) where it is the women who are in control. He continued chatting on, about his own problems with his wife – and with his daughter – until he got the Prophet to smile, whereupon he at last felt welcome enough to sit down. Then, looking around at the few very tatty possessions, he appealed to Muhammad to look after himself a bit better; after all, God had given great affluence to the Persians and Byzantines – why not to the Prophet's community as well? With this casual aside he had at last got the full attention of the Prophet, who looked Omar full in the face and asked, 'Do you doubt, O son of Khattab? Their good things hath been hastened on to them in this their earthly life' – and by inference believers must expect nothing from this world in order to concentrate on the next. Omar murmured back, 'Messenger of God, ask God to forgive me.'

To put a seal on the whole affair Muhammad decided to stay apart from his wives for a whole month. Mariyah was moved to a house in a more distant hamlet within the oasis – though her status would be much improved when it was found that she was pregnant, and even more so when she gave birth to a boy, named Ibrahim. After Ibrahim's birth Mariyah was welcomed back into the household, though it seems clear that she never converted to Islam, never lost her status as a concubine and would never be listed among the Mothers of the Believers.

After the month apart Muhammad went back to his wives, though he reminded them of their choice: this world or the next. 'If you desire this world's life and all its adornment, then come, I will give you a provision and allow you to depart a goodly departing,' but 'whoever of you is obedient to God and his Apostle and does good, We will give to her reward doubly; and We have prepared for her an honourable sustenance.' It was no more than the offer he made to all his followers. Aisha, like all of his wives, agreed that she desired 'God and his Messenger and the abode of the Hereafter'. Not to be outdone she also expressed surprise (perhaps with a certain ironic curl of her eyebrow) that the month was already passed. She had counted them and found that it was but twenty-nine nights he had lived apart. Most Muslim commentators add a pious little footnote explaining that the length of lunar months can vary from twenty-eight to thirty days. They seem to have wilfully ignored the charm and humour behind this exchange: of Aisha's unabashed delight in the company of her husband mixed with her understanding that Muhammad was now equally bored by his nights alone – but that he could also endure a little teasing first.

There would be yet one more wife to be added to this already bustling household. During the first Muslim pilgrimage to Mecca (in 629, as allowed by the truce of Hudaibiya) the Prophet met up with Abbas – his canny banker uncle – who proposed a marriage alliance. Muhammad accepted the hand of Abbas's wife's widowed sister, Maymunah, which would also make him uncle-by-marriage to Khalid, one of the most promising young commanders among the Arabs. They were not allowed to celebrate with a feast in the still-hostile pagan city of Mecca; indeed the Muslims were allowed just three days in the sanctuary. Just beyond the sacred precincts of the city, at the halt of Sarif, Muhammad waited with his disciplined force of 2000 Muslim pilgrims – women as well as battle-hardened warriors. Here the feast was held and the marriage consummated. It was acknowledged to be a highly political union and it soon brought forth exceptional fruit. Khalid, the man who had defeated the Muslims at the battle of Uhud – and who had even tried to intercept the Prophet when he led his barely armed men on the pilgrimage to Hudaibiya – deserted the pagan cause. Approaching Muhammad in Medina, Khalid recalled that 'his face shone with light as he returned my greeting of peace' and then Khalid made his Islam, 'I bear witness that there is no divinity but God, and thou art the Messenger of God.' If Christians can celebrate the conversion of Saul, the persecutor transformed into St Paul, so can Muslims delight in the turning of Khalid. Muhammad praised him: 'I ever saw in thee an intelligence which I hoped would not bring thee in the end to anything but good,' and he also assured him of a totally new beginning, for 'Islam cutteth away all that went before it'.

But it was also to be a year of sorrow in which the Prophet's eldest daughter, Zaynab, was to be buried beside her sister

Ruqayyah. Zaynab's story is tragic but also lit up by the innate chivalry and mutual respect that added such nobility to the casual suffering of the desert Arabs. She had been married to her maternal cousin, the well-connected Abd al-As bin Ar-Rabi, who was so much the favourite nephew of Khadijah that she virtually treated him as a son. Their children Umamah and Ali were the first of the Prophet's grandchildren. Abd al-As was not among those who embraced Islam in the early days, so that neither he nor Zaynab joined the migration to Medina. In fact he would be numbered among the pagan army that rode out to do battle in order to protect Mecca's trade caravan returning from Syria from being plundered by Muhammad's Muslim force. Abd al-As was to be captured at Badr but during the negotiations for his ransom a valuable necklace was offered for his redemption. Muhammad at once recognised it as one that had belonged to his beloved wife Khadijah, who had given it to Zaynab on her wedding day. His emotional reaction had been noticed by his followers, who immediately waived their ransom fee, returning both husband and necklace to Zaynab, who still lived in Mecca. Abd al-As for his part promised Muhammad that he would restore to him his daughter and grandchildren. The first attempt failed – but as Abu Sufyan privately explained, to leave in broad daylight was too much an affront to Meccan pride, though he guaranteed that no one would stop Zaynab if she left under the cover of night. Once safely welcomed into Medina, Zaynab became part of the household of her father.

She was to have a surprise reunion with her estranged husband when he stole into her room – having just escaped the fate of the rest of the Meccan caravan, which had been captured by a raiding party led by Zayd. That dawn, after the prayers were finished, she stood up from the rows of the women and announced that she had given her protection to Abd al-As (as was the right of any Muslim).

Later the goods he had been conveying in caravan were returned to him and he was allowed to pass in peace to Mecca. Having discharged all his obligations as an honourable Quraysh merchant, by conveying the goods back to their rightful owners, he made his protestation of faith to his surprised compatriots in Mecca. Only then did he feel free to ride back to Medina, make his formal confession of faith and win back the company of his wife and children after six years of painful separation. They had but a year together before Zaynab sickened and died. Muhammad asked that her body be carefully washed four times and then camphor mixed with the water for the fifth wash. He then gave them his own toga-like wrap to be her shroud and would descend into the very grave with her body and pray with especial fervour beside Zaynab's corpse.

Two of the Prophet's surviving children, Ruqayya and Umm Kulthum, would be buried beside their sister Zaynab in the cemetery of Medina. Not so his equally beloved – though adopted – son Zayd, who died in the hills of Syria (alongside the Prophet's young cousin Jafar) at the battle of Mutah. Muhammad could not pray over their distant graves though he did walk out to greet the warriors returning from this battle, holding the bridle of his favourite mule, Duldul, on which was seated Jafar's young son. The day before Aisha had peeped through the curtain and watched the Prophet share the grievous news with the household of Jafar. Although Jafar was Ali's full brother, and so might be reduced in Aisha's eyes, not a hint of that enters her description. The Prophet, once he had entered the house, had called for the boys so that he could tell them himself, but first he embraced them – and as he did so, his eyes filled with tears. When he returned to his own household (in which were gathered all the grieving family of Zayd) he gave instructions that food should also be cooked these next few days for the family of Jafar, 'for their grief doth busy them beyond caring for their own needs'. Just as he was about to reach his own door, he was seen by the little orphaned daughter of Zayd, who ran straight into Muhammad's arms. Perhaps his own childhood memories of loss also came to him at that moment, for as he hugged that child to him he wept unrestrainedly and his body shook with sobs. An awed believer stood aside in astonishment and asked, 'What is this?' The Prophet answered, 'This is one who loveth yearning for his beloved.' From these cherished memories of how the Prophet reacted to the death of his daughter and his adopted son come the practices of burial and bereavement still practised by Muslims today.

Despite the death of Zayd at the defeat of the Muslim army at Mutah in 629 the following twelve months would witness an enormous growth in the Prophet's authority, with the conquest of Mecca and the victory over the Bedouin at the battle of Hunayn in 630. Delegations from all the old powers of Arabia flocked to the Medina oasis to open negotiations with the growing power of Islam. One of these brought an offer of marriage from a princess of the Kinda dynasty – the family who had briefly ruled over all of central Arabia 150 years before. Aisha and Hafsah were alarmed at this potential threat to their status, especially when they saw that youth and beauty were combined with the impressive patronymic that stretched back through centuries of Arab heroism, which in this instance even outdid their own fiercely guarded pride in being of the Quraysh tribe of Mecca. But rather than show any outward hostility they instead took charge of the marriage preparations: the baths, the decoration with henna, the scenting and the dressing of this new candidate for the Prophet's love. They hinted that a certain royal gravitas mixed with some newfound piety would be most suitable on her first night and taught her to declare, 'I take refuge with God from thee!', which she should announce when she was left alone with Muhammad.

It was, of course, a disastrous phrase to use. Whether the Prophet suspected any trickery or not, he took the Kinda princess at her word. She was immediately returned, with every mark of honour, back to her father, Numan – but years later she would continue to bewail her fate and how she had been tricked out of happiness.

Later in that same year (630) the Prophet would lead into the Syrian borderlands a great Bedouin host numbering many tens of thousands of hardened warriors. Aisha, with her instinctive awareness of the way of the world, knew that her revered husband was day by day growing ever more powerful – and, to certain women of the world, ever more desirable. She worried over him; even to the extent of following him out on a night-time walk in case some beguiling adventuress might throw herself at him. One evening, somewhat to her shame, she followed the Prophet out into the oasis and watched over him for hours as he prayed over the dead. She slipped quietly away and left him to his duties, and he for his part pretended that he had not noticed – apart from slipping in a few days later some affectionate reference to her 'protective watchfulness'. These sessions at the cemetery praying for mercy over the dead were spiritually gruelling ordeals. After one such watch the Prophet found his own headache matched by Aisha's complaint of her own after she returned from a funeral at another cemetery. Half in jest, half in earnest, he told her that it would be not so bad if she died before him, so that he could wash and shroud his beloved wife, before burying and praying over her. Aisha was quick to reply in a jesting mood, accusing Muhammad of already making plans to fill her hut with another wife.

On other occasions she was content to reveal the depth of her admiration for the company of this remarkable man. Her feelings were more than shared. One day while she was busy at her tasks, spinning some woollen thread, she looked up to see Muhammad wreathed in a golden glow of contentment beside her – even when busy at such a lowly task as mending his sandals while seated on the floor. She praised him with a poetic quotation, and he, never to be outdone in gallantry, rose up and kissed her forehead, saying as he did so, 'O Aisha, may God reward you well. I am not the source of joy that you are to me.'

When Muhammad caught that fatal fever, once more praying over the dead, it was his turn to be with Maymunah. Here in Maymunah's hut he was visited by his anxious wives, and here in his delirium he tried to work out where he should sleep tomorrow, and where the day after. His women began to realise that he was trying to work out how long he had to wait until he could rest in Aisha's hut. This was confirmed when, as a special favour from them all, he asked if he could be allowed to stay with Aisha. This was the place where he spent the last ten days of his life, and it was in Aisha's arms that he would die on 11 June 632. When she was certain that his spirit had gone she gently placed his head on her pillow and herself joined the weeping women of the house united in their grief.

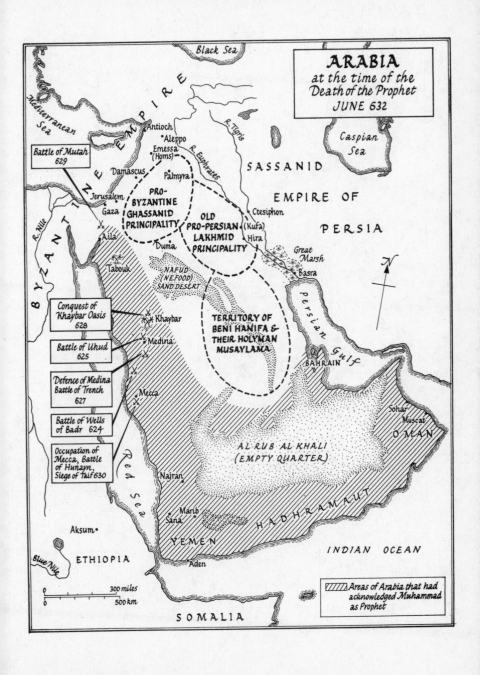

ARABIA
at the time of the Death of the Prophet
JUNE 632

Black Sea

Mediterranean Sea

BYZANTINE EMPIRE

Antioch
• Aleppo
Emessa
(Homs)

Caspian Sea

R. Tigris

SASSANID

Battle of Mutah
629

Damascus

Palmyra

R. Euphrates

EMPIRE OF

Jerusalem

PRO-
BYZANTINE
GHASSANID
PRINCIPALITY

Ctesiphon

PERSIA

Gaza

OLD
PRO-PERSIAN
LAKHMID
PRINCIPALITY

(Kufa)

Aila

Duma

Hira

R. Nile

Tabouk

Great
Marsh

NAFUD
(NEFOOD)
SAND DESERT

Basra

N

Conquest of
Khaybar Oasis
628

Khaybar

TERRITORY OF
BENI HANIFA &
THEIR HOLY MAN
MUSAYLAMA

Persian Gulf

Battle of Uhud
625

Medina

Defence of Medina
Battle of Trench
627

BAHRAIN

Battle of Wells
of Badr 624

Mecca

Sohar
Muscat

Occupation of
Mecca, Battle
of Hunayn,
Siege of Taif 630

OMAN

Red Sea

AL RUB AL KHALI
(EMPTY QUARTER)

Najran

HADHRAMAUT

Aksum •

Márib
Sana

ETHIOPIA

Blue Nile

YEMEN

INDIAN OCEAN

Aden

0   300 miles
0   500 km

////// Areas of Arabia that had
acknowledged Muhammad
as Prophet

SOMALIA

PART II

PART II

5

Caliph Abu Bakr and the Ridda Wars

Abu Bakr had been relieved to see the Prophet attend the dawn prayers that fateful last Monday. So much so that he felt that his personal vigil was now over, and left Muhammad's courtyard in order to visit one of his wives, Habiba bint Kharidja, who lived out in a farmhouse in the Medina hamlet of al-Sunh. By midday he – and everyone in the entire oasis – knew something had gone terribly wrong. The scattered hamlets of Medina were filled with the screams of men and the wails of the women (no matter that the Prophet had detested too public a display of emotion). By the time that Abu Bakr returned to the mosque courtyard the place was in total uproar. Abu Bakr slipped through the hysterical displays of grief and quietly entered his daughter Aisha's room. An embroidered cloak from the Yemen was draped over the still body of Muhammad. He raised the cloth to kiss the forehead of the dead Messenger of God and murmured, 'You are dearer to me than my father and mother. You have tasted death as God decreed: a second death will never overtake you.' Then he pushed his way through the crowd and tried to interrupt Omar, who was ranting at the crowd outside, threatening them with the most dire punishments if he heard any more rumours about the death of the Prophet. He promised to cut off both the hands and feet of any man who dared whisper that Muhammad was dead. Omar tried to explain to the crowd 'he has gone to his Lord as Moses went and was hidden from his people for forty days, returning to them after it was said that he died. By God, the apostle will return as Moses returned . . .' Perhaps he also imagined the reborn Prophet leading them to a triumphant military victory, just as the tribes of Israel had been allowed to enter the Promised Land only after the death of Moses. Much later he would confess to another hidden belief: that the Prophet would not die until he had prayed over the grave of the last of the believers.

Nothing that Abu Bakr could do, neither tugging at his clothes nor trying to whisper in his ear, could halt the passionate flow of Omar's rhetoric. Abu Bakr gave up this unequal struggle and moved away to another corner of the courtyard, where his calm, measured voice gradually summoned some of the people over to listen to him.

'O people. To those who used to worship Muhammad, Muhammad is dead. But for those who used to worship God, God is alive and can never die.' He reminded the crowd of the Prophet's own Koranic recitation of his mortality, 'Muhammad is but a messenger, messengers the like of whom have passed away before him. Will it be that, when he dies or is slain, you will turn back on your heels?'

Omar's passion dried up at this sound. In his own recollection, 'directly I heard Abu Bakr . . . my feet were cut beneath me and I fell to the ground.' If this was the reaction of Omar, most steadfast and iron-willed of believers, the panic that filled the hearts of other Muslims can be readily imagined. One contemporary recalled the mood of that day as being 'like sheep on a rainy night'.

It was ironic that old Abu Bakr, known to be a highly sensitive man, not strong of voice and given to tears when he recited the Koran, should have emerged as by far the strongest character at this critical moment. Then a messenger came hurrying to Abu Bakr and Omar to inform them that a meeting of some of the chieftains of the Medina clans had been called. Although many commentators like to give a whiff of treachery to this gathering, they had every right to assemble. The population of Medina had made a highly personal oath of loyalty to the Prophet Muhammad, who as their appointed judge and arbitrator had not only ended the recurrent civil wars of the oasis but had led them from victory to victory. They had no desire to sink back into civil war, and now that their chosen chief had gone, they were in need of another guide. Undoubtedly the man who had called them together, Saad ibn Ubadayah of the Beni Saidah clan, had political aspirations, but these might have only extended to a recognised position within oasis politics. Omar had by now recovered his poise and bravely insisted that he would lead a delegation of the Meccan Muslims – the Muhajirun – to this critically important meeting of the Ansar – the Muslims of Medina. They were politely met by 'two honest fellows' who advised Omar to call his own meeting of Muhajirun and leave the men of Medina to their own deliberations. Omar characteristically brushed this advice aside and forcibly declared, 'By God, we will go to them.' They arrived at a critical moment and were clearly impressed by the implicit Muslim faith that governed the actions of every speaker. Omar was incensed to hear the Muhajirun described as just another clan who had been welcomed into the Medina oasis, and was preparing a suitably proud and invective reply when Abu Bakr leant across, lightly touched his arm and whispered, 'Gently, Omar.' Abu Bakr was right: an aggressive speech from Omar at this juncture would have backfired. As Omar later described it when he ruled over a vast empire as

Caliph, 'He [Abu Bakr] was a man with more knowledge and dignity than I, and by God he did not omit a single word which I had thought of but he uttered in his inimitable way better than I could ever have done.'

So in a measured, calm and tactful speech Abu Bakr repeated the Prophet's praise for the men of Medina but insisted that now that Islam had become an Arabia-wide phenomenon they would have to choose a candidate from among the Prophet's own Quraysh tribe from the sacred city of Mecca if they wished to retain the respect of the great Bedouin tribes, the kings of Yemen and the borderland chiefs in Syria and Oman. Abu Bakr, who was of venerable age, finished by proposing two candidates for the assembly to choose from. He made no mention of himself. A clamour of excited voices soon filled the hall as Abu Bakr's ideas were debated by the rival clan chiefs of Medina. A respected old sheikh called out, 'I am the rubbing post and the fruitful propped-up palm,' a traditional oasis idiom which asserted that he was a greybeard whose good advice had proved fruitful over many a long year, and then suggested that the men of Medina elect one ruler and the men of Mecca another. This intriguing suggestion was broken by Omar, who roared out, 'Who will willingly take precedence over the man that the Prophet ordered to lead the prayer?' It was an unanswerable assertion. Omar made use of the brief silence to quickly seize the hand of Abu Bakr and pledge public allegiance to him. One by one his example was followed by the small delegation of Muhajirun that accompanied them. The solemnity of the occasion swept the clansmen of Medina along in a surge of emotion and they soon too plighted their troth. In the process Saad ibn Ubadayah (who seems to have been weakened by fever) was pushed aside and smothered.

The next day at the dawn prayers this accidental coup was formalised. As the worshippers filed into the mosque, Abu Bakr was *spencl*

already sitting in the pulpit and led the prayers. Immediately these were over, Omar got up an addressed the packed ranks of the assembled faithful. He repeated his oath of loyalty (the *bay'a*) and described Abu Bakr to the congregation by quoting from the Koran (Sura 9:40): 'the best of you, the Companion of God's Messenger, the second of two when they were both in the cave' (when they fled from the persecution at Mecca). With one voice the congregation acclaimed Abu Bakr as *Khalifat Rasul Allah*, the successor to the Messenger of God. The title *Khalifa* is derived from the Arabic 'to leave behind' or 'to succeed' and can also be translated as 'successor' or 'deputy'; by long-established usage it is customarily rendered 'Caliph' in English.

Thus was the Caliphate founded, by acclamation of the assembled faithful at the end of the morning prayer. Abu Bakr's reply to the congregation took the form of an oath in exchange, just as Muhammad had replied to that first midnight pledge of faith to the people of Medina at Aqaba. It should be engraved in stone on the gates of every presidential palace and in the public reception hall of every Muslim monarch. It should be stamped on the front of every identity card and passport so that the police and security forces of the Muslim world are daily reminded of this great and noble contract between the governed and the governor.

'I have been given the authority over you, although I am not the best of you. If I do well, help me; and if I do wrong, set me right. Truth consists in loyalty and disregard for truth is treachery. The weak among you shall be strong in my eyes until I have secured his rights, if God wills it: and the strong among you shall be weak with me until I have wrested from him the rights of others, if God wills it. Obey me for so long as I obey God and His Messenger. But if I disobey God and His Messenger, you owe me no obedience. Arise from your prayer, God have mercy upon you!'

Ali had clearly been too preoccupied by the burial of the

Prophet to take part in the discussions over the succession. As a thirty-year-old young father he may not have wished to be nominated as the political successor to Muhammad – indeed when encouraged to put forward his candidature by both his uncle Abbas and the old leader of Mecca, Abu Sufyan, he indignantly rejected the suggestion. He most certainly expected to have been part of an electoral committee or to have been consulted. He was certainly the most conspicuous of the Muslims to abstain from joining in the oath to Abu Bakr in the first few months of his Caliphate. During this period Ali had withdrawn to his house, where he heard with a leaden heart the last whispered conversation that had taken place between the Prophet and his daughter Fatimah. She had been seen to weep and then to laugh. She now explained to her husband that she had wept when her father had warned her that he was about to die. 'Then he told me that I would be the first of the people of his house to follow him and therefore I laughed.' This was to be Ali's heritage: the death of his beloved wife just a few months after the death of his adopted father, his cousin, his mentor, his father-in-law, Muhammad the Prophet of God.

To make things worse, an unpleasant row had developed between the ailing Fatimah and Abu Bakr. As Aisha would explain to later generations of Muslims, the Messenger of God died without leaving a dinar, a dirham, a sheep or a camel to his name while his battle armour was in pawn to a Jewish merchant for thirty measures of barley. His family did not expect anything other from a man who so passionately taught that every believer had a duty to care for the poor, the old, the sick, orphans and the needs of travellers. However, they did expect that his lands – especially those in the Khaybar and Fadak oasis estates – would pass on to them. Abu Bakr refused to allow this, quoting as his evidence a remembered saying of the Prophet: 'We do not have heirs, whatever we leave is alms.' The Prophet's portion of these conquered lands became part of the charitable trust lands that were administered by the Caliph. All that Abu Bakr allowed the surviving daughters and grandsons to directly inherit was a parcel of property in the oasis: seven small garden plots in Medina that had been left to the Prophet in the will of a childless Jewish convert to Islam from Medina's Beni Nadir clan who had died at the battle of Uhud. These little gardens were made into an endowment that was jointly administered by Abbas and Ali. Fatimah was furious and Ali quoted the Koran in her support, for Sura 26:16 gives a clear example of how the prophets of old had heirs: 'Solomon became David's heir and Zachariah said who will inherit from me?' It was to no avail.

When Aisha came down in doctrinal support of her father's position, the row grew even worse. There was also a suspicion that Abu Bakr had been exceptionally strict in this one case to discredit any notion that Ali and Fatimah were in any way the true heirs of the Prophet – and so give credence to the idea that they should also be his political and spiritual heirs. For in other matters of inheritance there were clear anomalies. For instance the Beni Hashim managed to keep hold of their claim to the Prophet's fifth of all war booty, which was distributed among all clan members. Despite this tough judgement Abu Bakr made certain that all the old stipends that the Prophet had been used to share with his family and his clan from out of the annual produce of the Khaybar and Fadak oasis estates continued to be paid out. Nor was Fatimah alone in her concern for the future. The wives of the Prophet were still housed in the huts that stood around the public mosque but desired a less public space in which to mourn. They asked Uthman to intercede with Abu Bakr on their behalf for some of the inheritance of the Prophet, but this embassy was withdrawn on the insistence of Aisha that Muhammad had wished that 'what he had left behind in this world should go to charity'. Later on Abu

Bakr would set Aisha up with some lands in the Aliyah quarter of the oasis and a useful portfolio of property in Bahrain.

While Fatimah was alive the row was impossible to heal. Only after her death was Ali able to explain his position in a face-to-face meeting with Abu Bakr. Ali declared, 'I know well your pre-eminence and what God hath bestowed upon you, and I am not jealous of any benefit that He hath caused to come unto you. But you did confront us with a thing accomplished, leaving us no say in the matter, and we felt that we had some claim as the nearest in kinship to the Messenger of God.' Abu Bakr had immediately replied that he would rather get on badly with his own family than suffer any disagreement with the family of Muhammad. They then made a public show of accord at the end of the noonday Friday prayers.

Some chroniclers try to indicate that for the rest of the Caliphate Abu Bakr worked in harmony with all the Companions of the Prophet as well as establishing the prototype Muslim division of administrative power between four ministries. In this amicable scenario Ali served as chief of the secretariat, Omar functioned as an embryo minister of justice, Abu Ubaydah as minister of finance, with Uthman in charge of information and communication. It seems unlikely, if only because the rush of circumstances allowed no time for such formal dispositions. What is known is that Abu Bakr did not give a military command to a single senior Companion but preferred to pick his men from the recently converted Muslims of proven ability. Abu Bakr knew that the fledgling Muslim state was surrounded by potential enemies, and he would have to use the most efficient and ambitious men if the community were to survive.

Islam owes a great deal to the modesty of Abu Bakr. He was determined to keep his leadership clean of the pomp and ritual of kingship and maintain the traditions of easy access and compassionate concern that had been established by the Prophet. To his undying credit he was also resolute that the era of prophecy had ended with the death of Muhammad. The 'successor', the Caliph, might collectively hold the political authority of the community, but Abu Bakr was adamant that the office conferred no spiritual powers. Nothing should be allowed to stand between God and man. Nothing should ever obscure the direct relationship between the believer at prayer and the single deity.

He was able to establish these lines of conduct thanks to the exceptional trust he had earned for himself within the Muslim community. Abu Bakr occupied a unique position: the first adult male to convert to Islam (although Ali was earlier: he had converted as a boy), one of the very few believers to be mentioned in a Koranic verse, Sura 9:40, chosen by the Prophet to lead the haj pilgrimage to the newly conquered Mecca in 631 and, most decisively, to lead the prayers during Muhammad's last illness.

He also had the advantage of age: he was just three years younger than Muhammad (exactly twice Ali's age) and commensurately rich in experience of the world. As a young man he had made a small fortune on the trans-Arabian caravan trade but had then spent it in middle age in the service of Islam, feeding the poor, helping those boycotted and liberating persecuted Muslims such as Bilal from oppressive slavery by outright purchase. From his fortune of 40,000 dirhams he had but 6000 left when he accompanied the Prophet on their daring escape from Mecca to the safety of Medina. Even this residual sum was immediately placed at the disposal of Muhammad when they arrived at Medina and was used to purchase the site of the house-mosque from the orphans who owned this plot of land. Abu Bakr's epithet 'as-Saddiq', which is translated as 'the truthful' or 'the sincere', had been truly won. Nor did old age make him any less generous, for having rebuilt some of his financial reserves by trading in Medina, he once again placed it all at the Prophet's disposal when Muhammad called upon his followers to help equip the Tabuk expedition. It was fairly said that no one had sacrificed more in the service of Islam. Abu Bakr was not renowned either as a warrior for Islam or as a military leader. The Prophet never gave him a separate military command and although we know he served alongside Omar in an expedition in 629 he is not associated with any epic tales of combat. He was numbered among that early band of the faithful that fought at the wells of Badr – for there is a celebrated tale from that day's fighting that reveals the depth of his zeal for Islam, even if it implicitly undermines his skill as a swordsman. Years after the event, one of Abu Bakr's sons who fought on the pagan side that day (but who later converted to Islam) confessed, 'Dear Father, I found you twice under my sword at Badr but I could not raise my hand because of my love for you.' To which Abu Bakr replied while gazing into the eyes of his oldest son, 'If I had had the chance I would have killed you.'

Modern Shiite leaders, including the late Ayatollah Khomeini, have gone to considerable lengths to repair the misunderstandings between the two paths of Islam and honour Abu Bakr's achievements. This was not the case among Shiites in the more distant past (such as the sixteenth-century Safavid Empire of Persia), who were encouraged to publicly curse the first three Caliphs. The partisans of Ali's right to succeed the Prophet were infuriated by the memory of the man who they thought had usurped the Caliphate. They looked carefully back over the narrative of events to reveal the conspiracy that had denied Ali his rightful role. They considered that much of Abu Bakr's authority rested on a secret political pact with Omar that was dependent on Aisha's (and to a lesser extent Hafsah's) skilful manipulation of events within the household of the Prophet.

There is clearly at least a grain of truth in this analysis. There was a strong understanding (though some might call it a friendship) between Abu Bakr and Omar and their position among the other close Companions was clearly greatly enhanced by their roles as fathers-in-law to the Prophet and the intimate access to his household that that entailed. Indeed Abu Bakr's very name is a reflection of the key role his daughter played within the imagination of the community. For Abu Bakr can be translated as 'Father of the Virgin' – and there was no doubt who that referred to, for Aisha let no one forget that she alone of all Muhammad's wives came to him as a virgin bride. Abu Bakr's name was Abdallah Abu Abdallah ibn Abi Quhafah but this was swept aside by a popular usage that wished to remember him above all as 'Aisha's father'. In this rare instance the usual Arabic honour of being remembered as the father of a male child and the son of your father was turned around in tribute to a daughter.*

Abu Bakr's new-found authority was to be immediately tested. In the last days of his life the Prophet had requested that his adopted grandson, the eighteen-year-old Usama, should lead an army into the Syrian borderlands. It had always been an unpopular decision – though as Arabs they all acknowledged that it was fitting that Usama should be given the opportunity to avenge his father Zayd's death at the battle of Mutah (629). Owing to the insistence of the Prophet, the army had to put aside its qualms about being led into battle against the well-trained Byzantine field army by an untried youth, and marched out of the oasis. They got as far as the first marching camp out of Medina before

---

* Although we can name Abu Bakr through his daughter, through his son (Abu Abdallah) and through his father (ibn Abu Quhafah), the name Abdallah is an epithet of all of the early Caliphs, and so we remain ignorant of the name he was given by his parents.

news of the Prophet's worsening illness brought them back home.

Once the community had found its feet again after their initial despair at the Prophet's death, Abu Bakr gave the order that it was now time that this expedition fulfilled its instructions. The clamour against it was now redoubled but as Abu Bakr patiently explained, 'How can I fold up the flag which was unfurled by the Prophet himself and yet pretend to be following the example which he set in all other things?' When the soldiers agreed but then asked for him to consider a change in command, Abu Bakr again asked them if they would 'want me to dismiss a man appointed by the Messenger of God'. The case was again clearly unanswerable, though Abu Bakr had listened to the complaints and already made certain that their fears were calmed by his other dispositions. Usama was left in formal command but he was equipped with experienced advisers and quietly instructed to make a 'parade in force' but not to make direct contact with a Byzantine or Ghassanid army. Nor was Abu Bakr ignorant of the gestures likely to win the approval of his fellow Arabs. So when this reluctant expedition finally left Medina it was led by Abu Bakr – their chief – walking humbly beside his mounted men on foot in order to bid them a formal farewell with his blessing. He had also kept enough soldiers in Medina to meet any outside threat and one such Bedouin raid was intercepted and soundly defeated at Dhu al-Kassa. When forty days later the expedition returned safely to Medina, having impressed the Bedouin tribes in the north with discipline, Abu Bakr's political stock had also risen.

It needed to. There was no Koranic justification for what he and Omar had claimed in that vital meeting with the sheikhs of Medina oasis after the Prophet had died. Theirs had been a purely political argument – that the rest of Arabia would respect only a leader drawn from the Quraysh of Mecca – and had absolutely nothing whatever to do with Muhammad's teaching, as Omar would later freely confess. The Prophet had been quite specific that there should be no hierarchy among true believers, while in two separate Koranic verses (8, 72–4 and 9, 100, 117) the Ansar – the believers from Medina oasis – are assured of their equality. Indeed the Muhajirun were not even a specifically Quraysh group at all – just the name given to all the Muslim emigrants that took refuge in Medina, composed of Bedouin tribesmen, Abyssinians and other outsiders just as much as the Meccans. The only indication of rank among the believers within the Koran is found in Sura 56:10–12, 'Those who preceded [in faith] are the ones who precede. They are the ones brought close in the gardens of bliss' – clearly not referring to the things of this world. For those who knew the Koran well enough there are three slight references to a khalifa (a Caliph) tucked among its many verses. In Sura 38:26 the Koran speaks to King David, 'we have made thee a khalifa on the earth; so judge between men with truth, and do not follow [personal] inclination so that it leads you astray from the way of God.' While in another verse the angels are warned by God that in Adam '"I am making in the earth a khalifa" and they said, "Wilt thou make in it one who will act corruptly and shed blood?"'

In both these Koranic verses the role of Caliph is clearly one that is liable to human frailty and has none of that semi-divine inviolability that would accrue in later ages when rulers were acclaimed as 'the shadow of God on earth'. If Abu Bakr dwelt long on these two references he is unlikely to have made much public use of the third reference (Sura 7:142), where 'Moses said to Aaron, "Deputise for me among my people and act well."' For the well-known public conversation between Muhammad and Ali when the Prophet likened the two of them to Moses and Aaron would, in combination with this Koranic verse, have clearly suggested that Muhammad intended Ali to succeed him. The passion and experience offered by Abu Bakr's leadership, backed up by the energetic support of Omar, must have been compellingly attractive to the bewildered Muslim community. One must always remember that there was never any doctrinal backing for their 'coup', that they had failed to consult with the other leading Companions, had failed to recognise Ali's special position and had consulted the larger community of the faithful only when it was a fait accompli. As I have already suggested, if Zayd (the adopted son of the Prophet and most militarily experienced of all the Companions) had not fallen in 629 at the battle of Mutah, the inheritance of the Prophet would have surely taken a different course. If the two men from the household of the Prophet, Zayd and Ali, had stood up together in the mosque even the brilliance of the Abu Bakr–Omar partnership would have been eclipsed.

Looking back over Muhammad's last years in Medina there were a number of precedents for Abu Bakr to follow on how a Muslim should rule over his brothers. The Prophet had appointed commanders of expeditions, sometimes specifying who should take over in the event of the death of a commander, but otherwise expecting that all Muslims (whatever their previous commands) should be content to serve as foot soldiers. When in the field himself the Prophet had always appointed a deputy to take care of Medina. He had also appointed men to supervise the booty seized in warfare and to take charge of prisoners of war. He had never imposed a governor on a free tribe that had converted to Islam but used the existing leadership whether he wished them to assemble their men for war or to call in the charitable tithe, though in the case of a conquered agricultural territory (such as Khaybar or a newly submitted tribe) an assessor might be initially sent out to estimate and receive the correct proportion of the harvest. After the conquest of Mecca Muhammad had appointed a governor over the city as well as confirming the need for such junior officials as the inspector of markets and custodians for the maintenance of sacred sites. From the booty taken in war, Muhammad took a fifth, with the rest shared out equally among the soldiers. The army commander had the old Arabic chieftain's right of the first pick of the *safi*, 'best qualities', be it a beautiful she-camel, horse, sword or slave girl. When it came to the division of a captive herd, roughly equal lots were prepared by assessing ten sheep as equal to one healthy camel. When it came to material goods these were also divided up into lots of equal value, though there was always some fierce trading after distribution of the lots as the goods were exchanged or sold for cash.

In the forty days that Usama and the main Muslim army were away on campaign in the northern desert, Abu Bakr had time to carefully consider his political options. Messengers to the tribes reminding them to deliver their tithe had been sent out just two months before the death of the Prophet, so the wheels of tribal politics had already begun to move.

Many of the great Bedouin tribes of Arabia had reacted to the death of the Prophet by quietly reclaiming their long-accustomed independence. Although this period is known as the *Ridda* – the apostasy – very few of the tribes actually renounced the Prophet's teachings or their newly adopted habit of daily prayer. What they rejected was the payment of the charitable tax, calculated on an annual tithe on their herds, while the more settled lands paid it in bundles of freshly worked leather, baskets of dates, sacks of barley or woven lengths of linen, all of which had to be laboriously taken across the deserts to the oasis of Medina.* Most of the tribes, in any case, felt their oath of loyalty had been a very personal contract

* The Arabic names for tax, *ushr* ('a tenth') or *khums* ('a fifth'), reflect the different tithes levied on livestock and the fields, though they were also called *zakat*: 'a purification'.

between them and the Prophet of God. Now that Muhammad was dead the motivation to collect the tithe and organise its transportation faded away, especially as the habit was not yet deeply ingrained, for the Muslims had been the power in central Arabia for just the past three years. Many of the tribes respectfully sent messengers back to Medina to recognise Abu Bakr as the 'successor' but tactfully refused to pay the tithe or asked for it to be cancelled. Omar and most of the other close Companions championed a lenient policy that would not insist on the payment of this charitable tax as the key definition of loyalty to Islam. It was an interesting reversal of roles, for at other testing times Omar had championed a very hard line indeed: it was he who had wanted the Meccan captives at the battle of Badr to be executed not ransomed, who had not wanted the Prophet to sign what he saw as a compromise truce at Hudaibiya and had not wanted Muhammad to grant a general amnesty to his old political enemies after the fall of Mecca – let alone award them with herds of camels.

Now it was Abu Bakr who took the hard line, declaring that 'if they withheld only the hobbling-rope of what they gave the Prophet [in camels], I would fight them for it'. In this, as in so much else, Abu Bakr was following the exact example of the Prophet, who had always been enough of a political realist to know that in dealing with the free tribes a line had to be drawn somewhere. And the physical transfer of livestock was a key indication of respect, even if, as the Prophet often practised it, the sum of tribute received would often be exceeded by the gifts that he offered in return. Abu Bakr was an expert in tribal politics and had often been called upon by his master to elucidate some complicated piece of tribal diplomacy, or unravel the genealogical alliances and ancient blood feuds. Although clan maps can be drawn that neatly divide the world of early Islamic Arabia into county-like divisions – each with its specific tribal label – the situation was

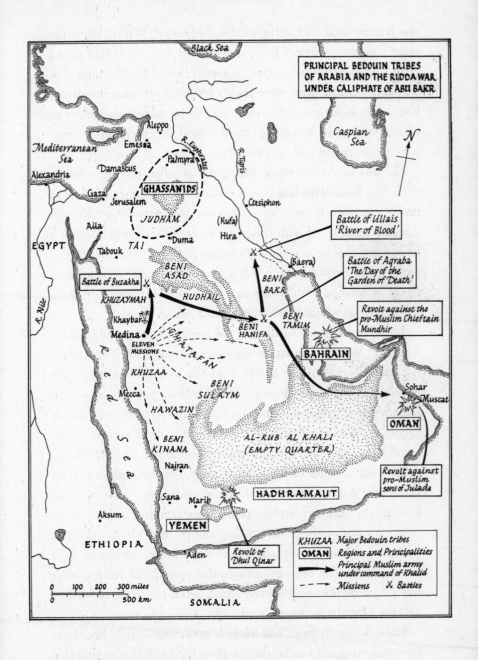

PRINCIPAL BEDOUIN TRIBES
OF ARABIA AND THE RIDDA WAR
UNDER CALIPHATE OF ABU BAKR

Black Sea

Caspian
Sea

N

Mediterranean
Sea

Aleppo

Emesa

R. Euphrates

Palmyra

GHASSANIDS

Damascus

R. Tigris

Alexandria

Gaza

Jerusalem

JUDHAM

Ctesiphon

Aila

(Kufa)

EGYPT

Duma

Hira

Battle of Ullais
'River of Blood'

Tabouk

TAI

BENI
ASAD

Battle of Buzakha

KHUZAYMAH

HUDHAIL

(Basra)

BENI
BAKR

Battle of Aqraba
'The Day of the
Garden of Death'

Khaybar

Medina

ELEVEN
MISSIONS

GHATAFAN

BENI
HANIFA

BENI
TAMIM

Revolt against the
pro-Muslim Chieftain
Mundhir

BAHRAIN

KHUZAA

Red Sea

BENI
SULAYM

Sohar

Muscat

Mecca

HAWAZIN

AL-RUB AL KHALI
(EMPTY QUARTER)

OMAN

BENI
KINANA

Najran

Revolt against
pro-Muslim
sons of Julada

R. Nile

Sana

Marib

HADHRAMAUT

Aksum

YEMEN

ETHIOPIA

Aden

Revolt of
Dhul Qinar

SOMALIA

KHUZAA   Major Bedouin tribes

OMAN   Regions and Principalities

Principal Muslim army
under command of Khalid

Missions   X Battles

0   100   200   300 miles

0   500 km

much more fluid and intriguing on the ground. Within the tribes there was always rivalry to be the leading clan, while within the clans there was always intrigue between the leading families – so that small erratic units were always breaking off from the parent body. Abu Bakr knew that there had to be some tangible act of obedience that included the whole tribe if the teachings of Islam were to be treated with any respect.

No one in Arabia knew this mesh of tribal identities better than Abu Bakr, who had been studying it – and learning how to profit from this knowledge – for some fifty years. For although Abu Bakr was faced with the entire reconquest of tribal Arabia if he insisted that he had the right to continue to collect the tithe – and he had probably only a few thousand totally reliable men based in Medina with which to do it – he also knew there were many ways in which to wage and win a war in Arabia.

Looking out from Medina to the western horizon, the Caliph Abu Bakr knew the situation was well under control. The Khuzaa tribe who occupied the desert from the west of Medina to the shores of the Red Sea (and guarded Medina's port of Jar) was to remain unswervingly loyal to Abu Bakr. This was especially true of the Aslam clan, which acted as the leadership of the Khuzaa. In the right hands the old Meccan connection could also be played upon – for another of the Khuzaa clans, the Kinanah, had once ruled over Mecca before the Quraysh took over. As a result of inviting the leading members of the Khuzaa to live in Medina, or to set up semi-permanent trading camps, the whole tribe had become gradually co-opted into the Muslim community. So if you looked at the Muslim army in this period, the Khuzaa were like a third division within early Islam, beside the Ansar of Medina and the Muhajirun from Mecca.

Looking north from the Medina oasis, the Caliph Abu Bakr knew the situation was far darker. Here the Asad, the leading clan of the large Khuzaymah tribal confederation, were a formidable enemy, determined to resist the expansion of Islam. North of the Asad were the lands of their age-old enemies the Tai (or Beni Tayyi). Given the right invitation, Abu Bakr knew that the Tai could be relied upon to join any assault that might weaken Asad power. The Tai tribe, despite early conflicts with the Muslims, had been won over by the spectacular generosity of Muhammad. So much so that Adi, the son of the famously generous sheikh Hatim al-Tai, had been coaxed out of his exile in Byzantine Syria and having converted to Islam now lived in Medina as an honoured sheikh. The Tai were also unusual in that although dwelling on the edge of Christian Syria they were within the Persian cultural sphere. All the other Christian Arab tribes of north and north-east Arabia could be relied upon to be enthusiastic allies of Islam if it came in the guise of a raid on Persian-ruled Iraq – especially one that promised rich pickings in captives and booty. The ancient rivalry between the Arabs of the Byzantine frontier and the Arabs of the Persian frontier was one that could be politically played upon again and again. It was said that even when they met as traders in distant Ceylon they would argue about the respective merits of the two antagonistic regimes as they loyally fingered the imperial effigies on their rival coinage.

Although the Judham tribe of the Syrian borderlands seems to have paid alms to two of the Prophet's commissioners, the Qudaah, Bali, Bahra and especially the proud Ghassan had not. At this period Abu Bakr would have considered these tribes part of the Byzantine state. It would be most unlikely that any of them could be drawn into a tribal war fought out in central Arabia. Even so there might be windows that the skilful diplomat could open. For instance the Hadas were a clan who had converted to Islam within the otherwise entirely Christian Lakhm tribe, while the Muslim general Amr ibn al-As's mother was from the Bali tribe. Such stout pillars of the Empire as the Arab lord Farwah ibn Amr of the Judham tribe, who then ruled as the Byzantine governor of the towns Amman and Maan, would in due course convert to Islam.

Elsewhere in the northern desert there were other potential threats. Abu Bakr knew that the Hudhail tribal confederation had to be handled very carefully. They had proved to be good allies of the old pagan leadership among the Quraysh when they had been strongly anti-Muslim, though since the fall of Mecca they had made their submission alongside their old allies. They could perhaps be won over by being asked to work beside some old friend among the lords of the Quraysh but had to be kept apart from any Muslim army dominated by the Khuzaa (especially the Kinana clan) with whom they had been locked into a blood feud for centuries.

Abu Bakr knew that the vast Ghatafan tribe, like the Asad, could not be trusted. The loss of such old Ghatafan territory as the rich oases of Khaybar and Fadak to the Muslims would not easily be forgiven by the Ghatafan sheikhs. They would surely be behind any rebellion against Islam. Two thousand Ghatafan warriors had helped attack Muslim Medina back in 627 at the time of the battle of the Trench. Later Muhammad had won over one of the key Ghatafan clans, the Ashja, who had provided 300 men for the conquest of Mecca. During the conquest of Khaybar, the Ghatafan tribe had been distracted from resisting Muhammad's army by their own inter-clan fighting, which was widely believed to have been stirred up by Muslim agents. So although Abu Bakr had to number them among his enemies, he also knew that in the past the deep divisions among the rival clans could be used to effectively neutralise this tribe.

If not, Abu Bakr knew that he could rely on the Beni Sulaym tribe to assist him in any attack on their old enemy, the Ghatafan – though a skilled diplomat would make certain that they were not invited to fight alongside their other great rivals, the Hawazin tribe. Abu Bakr also knew that he should not put too great a trust in the inner conversion of the Sulaym tribal sheikhs, men rather too greatly attracted to things of this world to think much upon the next. The presence of gold mines in their tribal territory – opened up with the assistance of the Quraysh – had placed great fortunes in the hands of their leading men. Although one clan had always favoured Muhammad, when it came to drawing up the battle lines, 700 Beni Sulaym warriors had fought on the pagan side at the battle of the Trench. Though later, when it was clear that the Muslims were in the ascendant, it was said that a thousand Sulaym rode behind the Prophet's banner for the conquest of Mecca.

When Abu Bakr turned his thoughts to the deserts south of Medina, he had first of all to consider how the Hawazin tribe would react. The Hawazin had not really figured in the early years of Muslim tribal diplomacy – perhaps because as old enemies of the Quraysh, Muhammad felt their alliance might prejudice the making of a final peace with Mecca. The Prophet's generous treatment of the tribe after his victory at Hunayn had won over many individuals – especially Malik, who was made chief of the section of his tribe, which had converted to Islam. But Abu Bakr suspected that the Hawazin were more likely to remain neutral than to actively serve as allies.

Looking much further south and south-east from the Hawazin territory one entered a different political world, that of southern Arabia and the ancient kingdoms of the Yemen and Oman. Until the fall of Mecca (630) there had been little direct contact between the Muslims and the people of southern Arabia. But by the time the first Muslim missionaries penetrated south into the Yemeni highlands there had, by fortunate coincidence, been an almost total collapse in Persian influence.

Before 628 the Persian protectorate of southern Arabia had been strong enough to have repelled all but the most determined army. The region had also been politically well handled, with a Persian governor (a junior marzaban) serving beside local leaders. In Bahrain, on the Persian Gulf, the local leader Mundhir ibn Saura had been 'advised' by a Persian governor, with a similar arrangement set up for Oman. In the Yemen, Sayf ibn Dhiu Yazan was the local ruler and was 'assisted' by a Persian governor whose garrison, initially set at 1800 men, had later been reinforced by an additional 4000 troops: a classic instance of an iron fist in a velvet glove. After the defeat of the Persian army at the battle of Nineveh in 627 by the Byzantine emperor, this iron fist had to be hurriedly withdrawn to defend the homeland, leaving just a few stranded velvet gloves among the mountains and deserts of southern Arabia. When the Muslim missionaries arrived in the Yemen these few Persian officials were supported by a handful of unpaid soldiers living among half-caste communities of Abna (the children of Persian fathers and Arab mothers). Rather than resisting the Muslim missionaries these groups were the first to convert, recognising that the new Muslim state, which already controlled such key trading cities as Khaybar, Medina, Mecca and Taif, was their only hope of a renewed central authority. Such was the case with the Persian governor of Sana and Badham, while the indigenous Yemeni rulers (that patchwork of princes, *Qayl*; kings, *Malik*; and lords, *Dhu*)* were all confirmed in their positions after conversion to Islam – so much so that the existing administrative units of Yemen, such as Sana, Hamdan, Marib, Najran and Hadramaut, passed seamlessly into the Islamic era.

The Yemeni cities had been used to paying taxes to a central

---

* *Dhu* can be translated as 'lord' or, more literally, 'the man'. The plural is *dhawa*, as *muluk* ('kings') is of *malik* and *aqyal* ('princes') is of *qayl*.

government for centuries and found Muhammad's poll tax (for the majority of town dwellers were either Jewish or Christian) and the charitable tithe a marked reduction and simplification of the dues that they were previously forced to pay. They also consented to his suggestion that they might feed and house his messengers for three days, and while not having to serve in an army (unless they converted to Islam) they also agreed to provide armour and mounts should they be called upon to do this. The Muslim expeditions led by Khalid and Ali had been genuine missionary journeys not military conquests. The same was true in Oman and along the Persian Gulf, where the sons of the previous Persian-backed ruler of Oman (Julanda) had become enthusiastic allies of the Muslims, as had the old Arab king of Bahrain, al Mundhir ibn Sawa.

So, looking over the political map of southern Arabia, Abu Bakr could be reasonably sure that the region would remain true to Islam if the Muslims continued to prove themselves the strong rulers of central Arabia. Conversely he knew that if a Muslim army was worsted in battle and began to lose control of the trade routes and oasis towns, his authority over the south would vanish like mist burnt up in the noonday sun.

If the tribes to the west of Medina were friendly, the tribes to the north hostile and the kingdoms on the southern periphery essentially neutral, Abu Bakr was in no doubt where the real threat lay. To the east of Medina the gently sloping desert plateau stretched all the way to Iraq and the fertile lands of Mesopotamia. This vast desert territory was known as the Yamamah (or the Najd) and was dominated by the Beni Hanifa tribe. Although this war a bleak and forbidding landscape to any inhabitant of the fertile crescent, the Yamamah could look rich from the perspective of the Bedouin of central Arabia. Within the Yamamah there was a string of large oases, filled with forests of palm orchards, while seasonal rains in a good year allowed large grain crops to be quickly grown on much of the arid steppe land. The Beni Hanifa were well organised and used to governing themselves. Their leader, Sheikh Hawdha ben Ali, had cooperated with the Persian Empire and seems to have given his support to a local holy man, Musaylama. After the old sheikh's death in 630 Musaylama became recognised as the prophet of the Beni Hanifa. At this time Musaylama attempted to correspond with the Prophet Muhammad in Medina and suggested a division of Arabia into two zones, an eastern and a western. His overtures were publicly rejected though in practice no Muslim expeditionary force was sent east into the Yamamah in the last two years of the lifetime of the Prophet. So although the Beni Hanifa could not exactly be accused of rebellion (since they had never submitted or paid any tithe-tribute) they were also the Muslims' only real adversaries for control over central Arabia. They alone had a political structure, a self-confidence, and in Musaylama a source of religious and political authority that could possibly prove to be a rival to the revelations of the Prophet Muhammad. Nothing of his teachings survives, though it seems he taught his followers to worship the One God, a ritual of daily prayers and received a body of divine revelations that synchronised with many of the doctrines of Mani and the Nestorian Church. Sura 6:93 of the Koran may refer to Musaylama: 'and who is a greater wrongdoer than he who forges lies about God, or who says: "I shall send down the like of what God has sent down"?'

By the time Usama and the Muslim army had returned safely to Medina, Abu Bakr had already made up his mind. His many enemies were to be confused, seemingly attacked on all fronts while beneath this dust screen of intense activity the small Muslim forces under his command were in fact to be concentrated, first to win over the northern tribes and then, reinforced with new allies, they would advance to do battle against the one enemy who really counted – Musaylama and the Beni Hanifa. Or as a traditional account would frame it, 'Our Lord strengthened the heart of Abu Bakr who gave the Faithful the resolve to give place not for one moment to the Apostates, giving answer to them but in these three words, Submission, Exile or the Sword.'

The first to be struck was a small subsection of the Ghatafan, by a Muslim army personally led by Abu Bakr, who defeated them at Dhu al-Kassa. Here Abu Bakr revealed the penalties of misguided opposition by confiscating some of their best grazing grounds and attaching them permanently to the state lands. Then, on his return to Medina, Abu Bakr gave out a dazzling succession of instructions, awarding each commander with a banner and a blessing. Eleven missions, all escorted by detachments of tribal cavalry, were sent out to all points of the compass – though you can be certain they were fully and minutely briefed as to which camp they should first stop at, to recruit allies, and to which they would come prepared as if for war. They bore formal messages from the Caliph: repent and submit and you will be pardoned and received back into Islam. Those who refused would be attacked, their crops trampled under the feet of the Muslim horsemen, their men cut to pieces and their women and children taken captive. As the Prophet had himself advised, the morning call to prayer was to be used as the test of faith. A Muslim raiding party should not give away the element of surprise but lie fully armed in watch over a camp as the dawn light breaks over the tents. If they heard the *Adhan*, the morning call to prayer, they were instructed to greet them as brothers; if not, they would fall down upon them as an enemy.

One such commander chosen by Abu Bakr was Ikrima ibn Abi Jahl. Some of the early Muslims must have shuddered at the idea that the son of the Prophet Muhammad's most ruthless pagan enemy was now a key emissary of the faith. But looked on as a tactical decision, Abu Bakr's judgement was faultless. Ikrima, a young nobleman of one of the leading Quraysh clans, was sent on a mission to the Hawazin tribe – in this case virtually on his own. This both flattered the Hawazin and delicately put the question of the tithe to one side as he was able to recruit the Hawazin horsemen for the next stage of his mission – which was on to Oman to give support to the beleaguered Muslim allies, the sons of Julanda. In one swift operation the Hawazin were turned from neutral onlookers to a Muslim war-party. A similar mission, entrusted to another respected young Quraysh nobleman of an old pagan family, Muhajir ibn Abi Umayya, did not waste any core troops on his escort. He was instructed to recruit Bajila tribesmen (in the region south of Mecca) and then pick up more supporters and munitions in the city of Najran for his mission in the Yemen.

Then, under this smokescreen of intense activity, which involved as many of the tribal allies as possible, Abu Bakr prepared his real campaign. The majority of the battle-hardened Muslim troops, especially those from Medina, had been held back from being employed as escorts for the eleven missions. This core group was placed under the command of the most efficient military commander, Khalid ibn al-Walid (despite the moral objections of many of the close Companions – including Omar). Their advertised task was to 'relieve' Khaybar from the petty raids of the Ghatafan. This was pure misinformation, for Khalid's real mission was to strike quickly against the confederation of northern tribes that was snowballing under the respected leadership of an Asad warlord, Ibn Khuwaylid. As Abu Bakr expected, the Asad clan and the Ghatafan tribe were at the heart of the rebel coalition but somewhat to everyone's surprise they had also attracted support from part of the Tai as well as from other fragments of the northern tribes.

Yet somehow, before the crucial battle at Buzakha, most of the Tai had defected back to the Muslim army, providing detailed local knowledge that allowed Khalid to win a quick and decisive victory. That day's fighting (for all that Abu Bakr's secret diplomacy with the Tai may have paved the way to victory) was one of the two turning points of the Ridda Wars. In order to give greater credibility to their resistance, this coalition of northern tribes had backed a prophet of their own. They had put up Tulayhah, a poetic soothsayer, as their religious leader. Tulayhah, however, must be understood more as a political puppet and a useful tithe-collecting device for his bosses – the sheikhs of the Asad – than as a religious authority. He would survive the battle, and, having fled to the safety of Syria with his wife, he would later be in a position to make his own submission to Islam. Years afterwards he was interviewed by Omar, who enquired if he had retained any of his oracular gifts. Tulayhah replied, 'It was but a puff or two as from a pair of bellows.' A modest but intriguing answer that yet suggests he sincerely felt he had been touched by some element of the divine. Khalid stayed in the region of the northern desert for a month after the victory of Buzakha, for a hard core of Ghatafan resistance remained under the leadership of Umm Siml, who led her men on her mother's sacred war camel. Once she and her famous mount were slain, Khalid was ready to move east.

Meanwhile Abu Bakr had been mixing much clemency with his otherwise hardline policy. Uyaynah, one of the captive sheikhs sent back to Medina by Khalid at the end of his campaign, was publicly mocked by the children of the oasis as a treacherous turncoat as he was led in chains to an audience with Abu Bakr. But once he had declared to the Caliph, 'I am no Apostate for I was never a believer . . . until now!' Abu Bakr at once forgave him and advanced to unshackle his chains. Even such real 'apostates' as the old Kinda dynasty (the ex-rulers of central and southern Arabia who had rejected not just tithe-paying but submission to Islam) were welcomed back into the Muslim fold once they had resubmitted. Abu

Bakr would invite the leading Kinda sheikh to take up residence in Medina, where he was given Abu Bakr's sister in marriage and skilfully co-opted within the Muslim power structure.

Similar tactics allowed the main Muslim army in the northern desert to win over many of its ex-adversaries as new allies for the great test ahead. Abu Bakr and his messengers had also been at work in the Yamamah region, testing out the local rivals of the Beni Hanifa, such as the Beni Tamim, as potential allies. The coastal-dwelling Beni Tamim were essentially Christian in culture and were then under the spiritual direction of Sajah, who though labelled a prophetess in the sources may well have been just a charismatic Christian mystical poet. The Muslim envoys had some minor success in finding allies among the clans of the Beni Tamim but most of the tribe decided to follow Sajah in her defensive alliance with Musaylama. It is said that jointly they could field an army of 40,000, though this probably refers to the total tribal population rather than the number of young fighting men.

This army was to prove the toughest adversary of the Ridda Wars. They fought as one people, united and determined to defend their independence, their lands, their prophet and especially their women. Two smaller Muslim expeditions had already been repulsed and so they had also acquired the confidence of victors. The two armies would clash on 12 May on the sandy plain of Aqraba. The Beni Hanifa, crying out, 'Fight for your loved ones,' rushed the Muslim camp at dawn and drove them off the field with the desperate bravura of their charge. Even Khalid's tent had its ropes cut, though later that morning he managed to rally his troops and organise a counter-attack. The Muslim army was arranged into three divisions, the soldiers of Medina in the centre flanked on either side by their Bedouin allies. The Muslim counter-attack was checked by a sudden sandstorm blowing from the south, after which the battle dissolved in vicious hand-to-hand fighting – a bitterly fought test between two spiritual visions. Eventually the Beni Hanifa were forced from the field of battle, and withdrew back into the protection of one of their walled palm orchards. By this stage in the day the Muslim cavalry had sealed off all escape routes and so these orchard gardens turned into a trap rather than a place of refuge. It would become the slaughterhouse of the Beni Hanifa, though there was also great loss of life among the Muslim warriors who fought their way into this dense palm grove.

The casualties at the end of the day were beyond anything that had yet been experienced in a tribal war in Arabia. Seven hundred Muslims died at Aqraba (of whom thirty-nine were Companions of the Prophet) plus another twelve hundred 'new Muslims' from among their Bedouin allies. When the even more numerous dead from the ranks of the Beni Hanifa were identified, the battle of Aqraba became known as 'the day of the garden of death'. With so many early believers killed that day, the Muslim community decided never again to risk the collective memory of the Koran and the traditions in such a manner. For these were the years before the Koran had been put down in writing, when it existed purely as an oral memory. It took a long time to identify the corpses strewn among the broken palm fronds in the garden of death. Musaylama's body was eventually identified – traditionally killed by Wahshi, that same Abyssinian marksman with the thrown spear who had killed the prophet's uncle Hamza all those years ago at Uhud. Years later as an old veteran (who maintained a very un-Islamic partiality for the millet beer of his old Ethiopian home-land) Wahshi liked to pass visitors his battle-worn javelin while declaring, 'With this I killed the best and the worst of men: Hamza and Musaylama.' Omar for his part was distraught that his brother Zayd had fallen that day, though his own son, Abdallah, had survived. That ultimately stern example of a father would address his son when he returned victoriously to Medina: 'Why have you returned home safe and sound while Zayd your uncle is among the fallen? Why were you not slain in his defence? Take your face away from here!' To which Abdallah replied, 'Father, he asked for martyrdom, and the Lord granted it. I strove after the same but it was not granted to me.'

In the aftermath of the battle it is said that Khalid celebrated his victory by marrying the virgin daughter of a captive chieftain of the Beni Hanifa, bedding this new concubine while the ground beneath their nuptial couch was still moist with the blood of thousands. He kept the army in the Yamamah to complete the subjugation of this new province of Muslim Arabia, though owing to the enormous casualties both sides were now disposed to come to easy terms. There were now enough troops in hand for Khalid to send out columns to assist the embattled Muslims along the Persian Gulf and in the mountains of Oman. He then led the army north towards the border with Iraq, sweeping through the farmland and marshes of southern Mesopotamia.

Khalid was much aided by support from the Beni Bekr tribal confederation, which had long dominated this region. Ever since the last Lakhmid king had been deposed by the Persian emperor back in 605, the Beni Bekr had been in a state of incipient rebellion. Their loyalty to the old Arab dynasty had been proven, for having been entrusted with the safe keeping of the harem and the treasury of the last of the Lakhmids they bravely fought off the Persian attempt to seize them. That day of fighting, the battle of Dhu Qar in 606, had a near-legendary significance throughout Arabia, for it was the first time that a mere Arab tribe had won a set-piece battle against a regular Persian army. Indeed ibn Harith, the chieftain who had persuaded his tribe to ally themselves with Khalid's Muslim army, had as a young man first won his spurs at the 'day of Dhu Qar'.

Jointly Khalid and ibn Harith now rode through the border-lands, sweeping aside a small Persian militia force at Kahdima (near the present site of Kuwait city) but allowing the port city of Ubulla (near where Basra would later be established) to buy them off with a 50,000-dirham payment of protection money. A short raid across the Euphrates into the rich agricultural province of the Sawad was quickly called off when Khalid received intelligence that a Persian field army was approaching them. At the battle of Ullais, fought on the edge of the desert, the campaign reached its bloody culmination when those Bedouin Arab tribes that were still loyal to the Persian Empire fought Khalid's force to a standstill. It was just the sort of army – composed of desert-hardened Arabs supported by the resources of the Empire and stiffened by experienced Persian officers – from which the Muslims had most to fear. This goes some way to explaining Khalid's utter ruthlessness. In the aftermath of this hard-fought cavalry battle, all enemy prisoners and wounded were methodically executed in a three-day massacre that was remembered as 'the River of Blood'. Their treatment was in graphic contrast to the respectable terms offered to the citizens within the walled city of Hira (the old Lakhmid capital), where Khalid accepted an annual payment of tribute in exchange for guaranteeing their Christian faith and their freedom to trade.

In Bahrain the local chieftain (al-Mundhir), who had embraced Islam during the life of the Prophet, was toppled by his rivals when the news of Muhammad's death came. In this period Bahrain refers to not just the present island-state of Bahrain but also the whole Arabic-speaking coastline of *bahr-ain* 'the two seas'* – the Persian Gulf. In the aftermath of Khalid's bloody victory at 'the

---

* Bahrain is 'the two seas' in Arabic, not by virtue of any division of the Persian Gulf into inner and outer waters but because submarine freshwater springs meant that there were both saltwater and freshwater areas.

day of the garden of death' the arrival of a victorious Muslim column decisively tipped the balance in the feud between the Beni Bekr and the Beni Abd al-Qays tribes for control of the region. The triumphant Muslims then pursued the defeated tribe to the island refuge of Darin, where they put all the men to the sword and seized a great fortune in spoil and captives. The material success of this expedition greatly stimulated other local tribes, who with or without formal 'Islamic' leadership, now began to press hard on the borders of the old Persian Empire.

When the news of the Prophet's death had first reached Oman the chief supporters of Islam in the region, the two sons of Julanda, were overthrown by their many enemies and had to take refuge with the hill tribes of the Hajar mountains. Two small Muslim expeditionary forces tried to give support, though it was not until after 'the day of the garden of death' that there were sufficient troops to break through the tribal resistance. Then, having penetrated the Hajar mountain chain, these Muslim columns reaped a material reward by sacking the trading ports along the Oman coast that had grown wealthy from the trade with India. So great were the eastward-leaning cultural links in this far corner of Arabia that the Muslim column under Ikrimah seized some 2000 Bactrian camels (the hairier two-humped camels of central Asia) before they continued their march on round the Arabian coast towards the Yemen.

In the Yemen the situation had become even more complicated. For just before the Prophet himself fell ill, the old Persian governor in Sana (who had become a Muslim) also died. His son Shahr tried to take over his father's position but was defeated by a local warlord, al-Aswad, who went on to earn the title Dhul Qina, the Man of the Veil, thanks to his enthusiastic support of traditional magical practices and occult divination which he championed in deliberate opposition to Islam. Support for this mysterious Dhul Qina mushroomed throughout the land when news of the Prophet's death reached the Yemen. Dhul Qina was also able to put himself at the head of the local backlash against the old pro-Persian regime. Once Abu Bakr had shown his true mettle as Caliph and Khalid had started winning military victories, Dhul Qina increasingly looked an embarrassment, not an asset, to the Yemen. He was assassinated and the local Muslims in Yemen succeeded in defeating his successor just before two Muslim military columns from central Arabia finally entered the country.

The suppression of the so-called Ridda rebellion had been an extraordinary and total triumph. Abu Bakr's diplomacy and Khalid's battlefield tactics had been so seamless that they had achieved the reconquest of tribal Arabia in less than two years. In the process Abu Bakr had doubled the size of the Muslim state. Yamamah, the eastern half of Arabia, which had never submitted to the Prophet Muhammad, was now part of the Islamic state. When Abu Bakr questioned some of the Beni Hanifa captives about the sayings of their prophet Musaylama he replied kindly, 'What kind of words are these? There is neither sense in them for good nor yet for evil, but a strange fatuity to have beguiled you thus.' With that he pardoned them and sent them back to their homes.

The Caliph did not rest on his laurels. Before the last operations against the Ridda were completed, he had already started preparing for the next phase of the new Islamic Arabia. He was aware that the total victory of Islam within Arabia would actually put intolerable pressure on the social dynamic of the tribes. Raids, tribal feuds, blood vengeance and the 'lifting' of each other's herds was in the lifeblood of practically every Bedouin Arab. It was that flash of intense excitement, the ever-present sense of having to be on your guard, that perfectly counteracted the gentle monotony of a herdsman's life in the desert. It would take time – a long time –

for the 'peace' which was at the heart of the Islamic message to enter the souls of these Bedouin and for them to realise that it was now a sin to make such wars on their Muslim neighbours. An external enemy was needed, a place where the furious energy of the Bedouin could be put to good cause. Fortunately such an enemy stood ready and waiting. The tribesmen could win honour and renown, and perhaps also some war booty, by attacking the Byzantine Empire's imperium over the Syrian Arabs, so as to allow all their Arab-speaking brethren the chance of embracing Islam. A new round of messengers were dispatched from Medina carrying letters from the Caliph Abu Bakr, who in the words of the chronicler Baladhuri 'wrote to the people of Mecca, Taif, the Yemen and all the Arabs in Najd [the Yamamah] and Hijaz summoning them to a "holy war" and arousing their desire for it and the booty to be got from the Greeks [the Byzantine Empire]'.

It was the season of destiny. The armies of the Byzantine Empire guarded the Holy Land while the whole strength of Muslim Arabia was being summoned to advance and give battle. The Conquest had begun.

6

The Invasion of the Holy Land and the Death of the First Caliph

The letters of the Caliph, small scraps of whitened parchment bearing the hieratic, almost stone-carved black calligraphy of early Arabic script were sent out to all the corners of Arabia. Folded to form their own envelope, they also bore the seal of the Prophet, stamped by a ring that bore a small cornelian inscribed 'God the best of potentates'. The ring was one of the few tangible possessions that Muhammad left behind on this earth. Since the successful conclusion of the Ridda Wars the heralds from Medina were now treated with a renewed respect and total attention. In the towns and the cities and weekly markets of southern Arabia Abu Bakr's letter would be delivered to the Muslim governor, men of such standing as old Abu Sufyan (once the first warlord of pagan Mecca), who now served as one of the delegated officials of the Caliph in the province of Yemen. Having been devoutly kissed, the seal of the letter would be publicly broken and the letter read out after prayers to reach the entire adult male Muslim population.

In the desert, news travelled almost as quickly. The heralds would be greeted by a distant herdsman and at once escorted to the grazing grounds currently occupied by the chief men of the tribe. Here they would be welcomed into the great black tents of the tribal chieftains and seated in the place of honour on the right-hand side of their host. After they had accepted the customary offering of a gourd cup filled to the brim with fresh milk, a feast would be hurriedly prepared by the slaughtering of a choice young calf, while outriders sped off to summon the other allied chieftains, so that all should equally share the news. This would be well attended, for the gossip of the desert had lost no time in recounting the bloody victory of the Muslims against the Beni Hanifa at 'the day of the garden of death' and the fortune in loot that had subsequently been won from the rich trading cities along the Persian Gulf and the coast of Oman – and was even now being earned by the army of Khalid as it raided the desert borderlands of the Persian Empire. Caliph Abu Bakr's invitation to join the armed struggle 'for your soul's good', to win renown in war and the opportunity to take home plunder, brought forth immediate results.

The young warriors of Arabia flocked to his standard, even though their knowledge of the teachings of Muhammad had probably not yet progressed beyond rote learning of the basic daily prayers. Those warriors who wished to fight under the banner of Islam had first to travel up to the oasis of Medina. They arrived in a steady but unpredictable stream, travelling along the old trade routes. In Medina they would be greeted and then slowly assembled in the camping grounds that were customarily used by the caravans in the dry wadi beds that stretched around Mount Uhud. Those who lacked equipment were generously supplied by gifts from the communal treasury that was under the control of the

Caliph, who no sooner had received his fifth of all that had been seized during the Ridda Wars than he at once started to give it all away as gifts to the poor and ill equipped. The treasury in this period was no more than an old date storage hut with a door. Abu Bakr was now entering the last year of his life, but not a flicker of the wealth that had already begun to pour into Medina had affected his bearing. He still proudly wore the simple cotton tunic and old woollen cloak that had been his habitual dress, and continued the Prophet's habit of making it his first duty to enquire after the well-being of the community after the morning prayers. He had also taken to patrolling the oasis alleys in the evening, personally checking that there were no poor widows or untended orphans who had failed to find a meal or a roof that night.

When Abu Bakr had escaped with the Prophet back in 622 he had to leave both his wives behind. His first wife Kutayla and her sons remained pagan and so stayed on in Mecca, though his Bedouin second wife Umm Ruman (the mother of Aisha) later joined him. Once established in Medina he would take two more wives. Asma bint Umays was from the desert-dwelling Bedouin tribe of the Beni Khatham. Habiba was a true daughter of Medina and followed the female-centred traditions of the oasis. She was known only through her matriarchal descent, the daughter of Kharidja from the al-Harith ibn Khazradj clan. There were children from both of these late marriages: Asma gave birth to a son, Muhammad ibn Abn Bakr (of whom we will hear much more), and Habiba to a daughter, Umm Kulthum.

Clearly there was life in his old body yet. Abu Bakr was also determined to personally lead the haj pilgrimage – which he had missed the previous year owing to his day-to-day supervision of the Ridda Wars.

It was said that nothing escaped his attention, so that when the number of young volunteer warriors had reached around 3000 they were formed up into a division, given a commander and sent on their way with a blessing. In this way Abu Bakr made certain that the oasis's water supplies and grazing were not exhausted, that the Bedouin youths did not grow bored with inaction and that the old scars of tribal vendettas were not reopened. As the arrival of Bedouin could never be accurately predicted, each of these field forces contained a chance cross-section of the tribes, which helped stress the unifying nature of Islam over the otherwise strong tribal and regional loyalties. A surviving tradition from the Beni Fazarah tribe recalls the arrival of Abu Bakr at their camp at Jarf. The young men stood up in his honour as he blessed them while they excitedly cried out, 'O Khalifa of the Prophet, we have brought healthy horses and mares, and we are very good riders. Please give us a big standard!'

Abu Bakr instructed each of the armies how they should behave if they wished to consider themselves Muslim soldiers. 'Do not betray; do not carry grudges; do not deceive; do not mutilate; do not kill children; do not kill the elderly; do not kill women. Do not destroy beehives or burn them, do not cut down fruit-bearing trees; do not slaughter sheep, cattle or camels except for food. You will come upon people who spend their lives in monasteries, leave them to what they have dedicated their lives. . . Now advance in the Name of God.'

The first three armies were placed under the leadership of charismatic young Arab commanders: the noble Yazid ibn Abu Sufyan (son of the old Meccan war-leader), and Amr ibn al-As and Shurahbil ibn Hasana with their proven military skills. Amr led his army on the westernmost route that would skirt the Red Sea coast and take them directly towards Gaza and southern Palestine. Yazid took the more central roadway that passed through Tabouk to approach the eastern shore of the Dead Sea. Shurahbil's force marched slightly further north towards Bostra and the broken

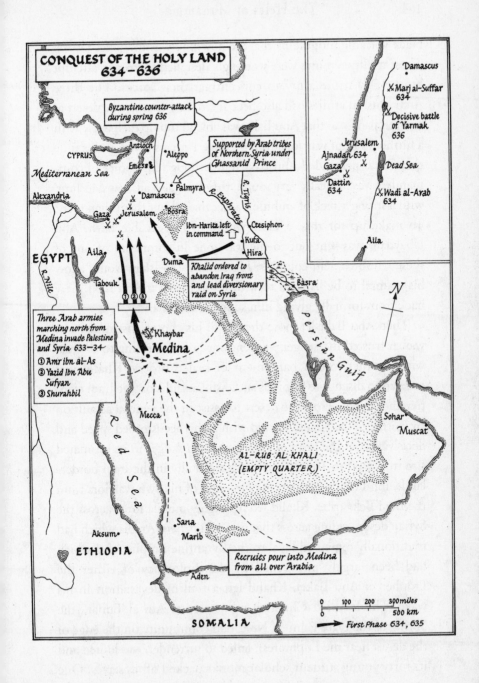

CONQUEST OF THE HOLY LAND 634–636

Byzantine counter-attack during spring 636

Supported by Arab tribes of Northern Syria under Ghassanid Prince

CYPRUS

Antioch

Aleppo

Emesa

Mediterranean Sea

Alexandria

Damascus

Palmyra

Gaza

Jerusalem

Bosra

Ibn-Harita left in command

Ctesiphon

Kufa

Hira

EGYPT

Aila

Tabouk

Duma

Khalid ordered to abandon Iraq front and lead diversionary raid on Syria

Basra

R. Euphrates

R. Tigris

R. Nile

① ② ③

Three Arab armies marching north from Medina invade Palestine and Syria 633–34
① Amr ibn al-As
② Yazid Ibn Abu Sufyan
③ Shurahbil

✗ Khaybar

Medina

Persian Gulf

Mecca

N

Red Sea

AL-RUB'AL KHALI
(EMPTY QUARTER)

Sohar

Muscat

Recruits pour into Medina from all over Arabia

Sana

Marib

Aksum

ETHIOPIA

Aden

SOMALIA

0   100   200   300 miles
0   500 km
→ First Phase 634, 635

Damascus

✗ Marj al-Suffar 634

✗ Decisive battle of Yarmak 636

Jerusalem

Ajnadan 634

Gaza ✗

Dattin 634

Dead Sea

✗ Wadi al-Arab 634

Aila

black volcanic mountains that we now know as the Jebel Druze. These multiple routes were seemingly designed to fox any attempt by the Byzantine army to concentrate their forces. The three Arab Muslim armies had also been instructed to cross the desert at an even pace – so that Abu Bakr was able to top up each army with a further draft of warriors from Medina. Perhaps it was at this time that Omar persuaded Abu Bakr that although his choice of commanders was tactically very sound, they were also all 'new Muslims' with a stronger reek of ambition and career about them than piety. To make up for this, a Companion of impeccable faith, Abu Ubaydah, was sent out to the war zone in command of one of these reinforcement columns. His seniority in Islam would allow his counsel to be listened to with respect even if Abu Bakr drew back from formally giving him supreme command.

Then Abu Bakr let loose the last of his chosen instruments of war. A trusted messenger was sent out in haste, riding to the east with another folded parchment of sealed orders. Khalid was ordered to disengage from his successful assaults on the Iraqi frontier and march across the desert to assist in the general assault on Byzantine Syria. Khalid moved with all his accustomed speed and decisiveness at the head of an army which ranges in its estimated size from 900 to 10,000 men. His tribal ally in the Iraqi borderlands, ibn Harith, was left in command of his own warriors from the Beni Bekr tribe. Khalid led his highly mobile force across the Syrian desert, riding across that part of northern Arabia which had traditionally remained loyal to the Byzantine Empire (and which had been largely untouched by the diplomacy of either the Prophet or Abu Bakr). Khalid left a trail of devastation in his wake. The fortified Christian monastery at Ain al Tamar, 'the Spring of the Date Palm' (a Nestorian community on the edge of the desert near the Euphrates), failed to surrender, was looted and its forty young student scholar monks packed off as slaves. One of these young captives, Nusayr, would convert to Islam and end up working as a clerk in Medina. His son Musa would later win undying fame as the conqueror of Spain and Morocco, the great Musa ibn Nusayr. Other captives were not so lucky, for Khalid slaughtered, and in one notorious case crucified, the pro-Byzantine chieftains of the Arabs on his epic ride through Duma and Palmyra as he approached the Syrian frontier. Khalid had taken the precaution of bringing three times as many camels as he would normally require, so that they could be slaughtered and their reservoir paunches removed and used to water the horses – who were kept unridden so that they remained fit for battle. In one section of this epic ride, his guide, a tribesman of the Tai, had become blinded by the sun and so could not lead them to a hidden water source. Fortunately the blind guide racked his memory and remembered the tell-tale presence of a large *awsaj*, a box thorn, near this secret source. Once the army outriders had spotted this tree, there was a frantic hour of digging before the first patch of life-giving damp soil revealed the presence of water.

Fifteen miles outside Damascus Khalid met a well-matched opponent: a force of desert Arabs led by a Ghassanid prince. After a cavalry skirmish fought at Marjal-Rahit, which may have been a deliberate attempt to mislead the Byzantines as to the direction of the Muslim attack, Khalid broke off hostilities and moved south to make contact with the other Arab armies. Abu Bakr had foreseen the possible rivalries that this flanking manoeuvre might cause and had informed the other commanders of his decision, sending to Amr this note of instruction: 'I have sent orders to Khalid ibn al-Walid to join you immediately. When he joins you give him due regard. Do not impose your superiority over him and do not try to solve your problems without consulting him, and do not oppose him.'

Khalid's ride across the desert and his skirmish outside

Damascus seem to have drawn the attention of the principal
Byzantine army to Syria. So the three armies sent out from Medina
could ride directly into Byzantine Palestine. The first engagement
to be fought was at Wadi al-Arabah, just south of the Dead Sea,
where Yazid led the attack on a force commanded by Sergios, the
Byzantine patrician of Palestine, whose troops were forced back
towards the coast. At Dattin,* just 12 miles outside the coastal city
of Gaza, Amr's army caught this retreating force in a second
pitched battle. Sergios, who here fought wearing the gorgeous
white ceremonial uniform of a Candidatos, a member of the
honorary bodyguard of the Emperor, was detested by the Arabs,
who remembered him of old. In an earlier stage of his career he
had closed the markets of Damascus to Arab traders in order to
extort a fortune of 20 pounds of gold. In the aftermath of battle
his corpse was identified and sewn up in a camel stomach as a last
testament to his greed.

The superiority of the Arab armies was then to be confirmed in
July by a third battle fought within Palestine, at Ajnadayn. Holy
Jerusalem was now cut off from the Mediterranean coast and the
great coastal city ports, such as Caesarea and Gaza, threatened by
the Arab armies encamped outside their walls. Bostra, once the
administrative capital of inner Syria, was now isolated and was
forced to sue for terms. These early successes of the Arabs were
secured when the Byzantine army in Syria was defeated in a
pitched battle fought on the plain of Marj al-Suffar (Scythopolis)
just 20 miles from the walls of Damascus. The victory belonged to
Khalid, who was entrusted with the command by all his brother
generals, who recognised his tactical brilliance and the very high
stakes for which they played.

In Medina Abu Bakr felt confident enough in his choice of

---

* Also spelled Dathin, and probably the same place as the biblical Dothan.

battlefield commanders to fulfil his most fervent wish, which was to lead the pilgrimage to Mecca. Sitting at the end of the week-long rituals in the shadow of the Kaaba in the great open courtyard that stands at the geographical centre of Islam, he summoned all the believers who had a grievance to come forth and receive justice at his hands – but none could be found.

When the old Caliph returned to Mecca after the ten-day ride across the desert he received messengers who brought him accounts of the triple victories that had been won in Palestine that summer: first Wadi al-Arabah, then Dattin and Ajnadayn. Even from the perilously weakened Iraqi frontier there were good tidings, for the Beni Bekr tribe under ibn Harith had beaten off a Persian attempt to recapture Hira. However, ibn Harith also heard some disquieting news. Ever since 628, when the Sassanid monarch Chosroes Anushirwan (Heraclius's old opponent) had been assassinated by one of his own sons, the Persian Empire had been in dynastic meltdown. For the subsequent massacre of eighteen princes of the royal family by their half-brother Shirnya (Siroes to the Byzantine Greek historians) had not cleared the way for a simple succession to the rule of Persia but had instead released mayhem as regional lords put forward various Sassanid pretenders and distant kinsmen as candidates to the throne of the king of kings. By the summer of 634 the young prince Yazdegird had at last succeeded in reuniting the empire and was now intending to concentrate all his resources in repelling the Arab Muslim incursion. To make certain that the Caliph fully understood the gravity of this threat, ibn Harith decided to be his own messenger and rode the whole way to Medina to directly plead with Abu Bakr for reinforcements. He arrived to find the Caliph confined to bed.

In that summer of victory the sixty-three-year-old Abu Bakr had caught a fever – just like his master before him. These fevers were a recurring feature of life in the well-watered oasis of Medina, and the Meccans (brought up in much drier conditions) were especially prone to them. This fever took such a grip on Abu Bakr that he decided to leave nothing to chance. He called together a group of the half-dozen leading Companions (who this time included Ali) and proposed that Omar be confirmed as his successor. This was based on no verse of the Koran nor on any remembered saying of the Prophet but was merely Abu Bakr's opinion. In later ages such decisions would become defined as *itjihad* by the legal codifiers.* The assembled Companions expressed their concerns about Omar's severity, his strictness and harshness of character. Abu Bakr was convinced that the burden of office would make Omar milder, just as it had made him tougher, so the proposal was agreed. Later it was put before an assembly of the faithful for their affirmation. The last days of Abu Bakr were spent among his wives and his daughter Aisha, who cared for him to the last. Recognising her strength of character, he asked her to take care of his family and share with them the private lands that he had given her. He was also concerned that any state property that he had made use of during his life be returned to the public weal.

Abu Bakr had also asked his daughter, 'Do not use new cloth for my shroud. Wash the sheet in my use and wrap my corpse in it.' After a fortnight of fever, Abu Bakr departed this world on 23 August 634. He was buried where he deserved to lie – his head close to his master's shoulder – in the marriage hut of his daughter. His reign had been short (just two years and three months) but after Muhammad himself there was none to whom the faith was more dear. Like his master he was possessed by an innate and continuous sense of the overwhelming presence of eternity. Like Keats he could sigh at a nightingale and express envy of a carefree bird

---

* *Itjihad* means 'exertion' or 'striving' and suggests that the intellect has been tested in a prolonged struggle to produce a clear judgement.

that he once watched in his garden in the oasis village of al-Sunh: 'O bird you are lucky indeed! You eat and drink as you like and fly but do not have to fear the reckoning of the Day of Judgement. I wish that I were just like you.' On another occasion he envied even the insensate: 'I wish I were a blade of grass whose life ended with the grazing of some beast; or a tree that would be cut and done away with.'

Aisha scrupulously obeyed her father's last instructions and even made certain that two milch cows that had been loaned to her father were promptly returned to the Bait al-Mal, the public treasury. While a small garden that he had acquired from the salary of 6000 dirhams a year he had been paid as Caliph was handed on to Omar. As Omar accepted the keys to this tiny walled garden for his use while serving as Caliph, he raised his hands, saying, 'May God bless him. He left no chance for anybody to open his lips against him.' When the public treasury was opened for inspection it was found to be empty – save for one gold coin that had slipped out of its bag and had become buried in the dust.

7

Omar and the Great Victories

Omar was to prove himself a remarkable leader, an inspired strategist and a brilliant administrator as well as setting an extraordinary personal example. There is no one quite like him in all in the centuries of Western history, though perhaps Giuseppe Garibaldi, Abraham Lincoln and Cato touch closest upon certain aspects of his character. Omar would consciously honour the role of his predecessor Abu Bakr by styling himself the successor to the successor to the Messenger of God. At other times he made use of the even more modest title *amir al-mu'minin*, 'commander of the faithful'.

For all this becoming personal modesty no one within the inner group of Muslims had any doubt that Omar had also been the power behind Abu Bakr's throne, had been his chief adviser and had also played the most decisive part in taking control of the community after the death of the Prophet. This was not court gossip but was directly acknowledged by Abu Bakr himself, who when some fellow Muslims complained about Omar to him, saying, 'He is behaving in such a way as though he is the Caliph instead of you,' replied, 'Of course, he is the fittest person to be Caliph. I am but a humble servant of the Almighty, who has been forced to take charge of this high office ... I swear by God, I never wished to be Caliph. I even never thought about it, nor desired it either secretly or openly ... The yoke of the Caliphate has been put on my head by force.' Omar could not have made that claim.

If Omar was a man one could not fail to respect he was also almost impossible to love. He could demand the highest standards from his subordinates because he asked nothing less of himself. As Caliph, the acknowledged leader of a rapidly expanding empire, he felt entitled to just two garments a year, one for the summer, one for the winter, and enough money to allow him to perform the annual haj and to feed his family and guests with the traditional hardy fare of a Bedouin. Like the Prophet and Abu Bakr before him he concluded that anything extra was likely to distract a man from a true relationship with God. Throughout his reign he remained a legendary puritan, a stern, austere man who came down hard on any public display of drunkenness, gambling, improper dress or the misuse of state property or delegated powers. He expected that those who had been entrusted with high office should have a morality to match their responsibilities. Like an overpowering uncle he warned his deputies, whether they were governors of vast provinces or generals in command of tens of thousands of warriors, not to be seduced into wearing fine clothes, eating delicate foods or to be ever found closing the doorways of their house (and by that he especially meant their kitchens) to the poor. When travelling, like the Prophet before him, Omar had no use for beds, tents or mattresses but would sleep on the desert floor under the cover of his well-patched cloak that had been stretched out, like a one-man bivouac, between some low shrubs. While Muhammad had been happy to confess his love for women and scent, there are no such images of cheerful humanity of Omar. Even in the lifetime of the Prophet it was said that the shadow of Omar before the doorway was enough to silence a room full of women and children, while if they recognised that it was Muhammad their laughter and chatter would continue undiminished. As a boy I was greatly impressed by the tale that Omar had shed tears only once in his life, when as a young pagan father he buried alive his unwanted newborn baby daughter in the sands. I was relieved to later discover that this is now considered a fabrication, created by a medieval historian attempting to blacken his character. Omar was also physically impressive, for as one of his contemporaries remembered, 'he towered above the crowd as if he were riding a horse', while his outspoken blunt honesty is backed up by a saying of the Prophet that attests, 'God hath placed truth upon the tongue of Omar ibn al-Khattab and upon his heart.'

When Omar took over the formal direction of affairs from Abu Bakr in August 634 one of his first actions was to demote Khalid from the supreme command, though he was allowed to remain in command of the army that he had led out of Iraq. That winter the four armies of the Arab Muslims spread out over Syria and Palestine, securing the submission of many of the minor walled cities (such as Pella, between the Dead Sea and Sea of Galilee) before reuniting outside the walls of Damascus in the spring. By March the Arab Muslim armies had entirely encircled the great Syrian city. Their knowledge of siege warfare had not much improved since the Prophet's failed siege of Taif, but they knew enough to realise that their greatest weapons in such engagements were the ability to completely cut off food and water supplies, patience, negotiation and to hold on to their reputation of honouring their word. After six months, the Damascus city fathers sued for terms to the commander-in-chief, Abu Ubaydah. At exactly the same time Khalid had stormed the East Gate (assisted by a traitor within) and broken his way by force into the city. Since the accession of Omar, Abu Ubaydah's authority had been confirmed as absolute and the city had its terms of capitulation honourably confirmed – even though it might technically have been considered to have fallen to assault and therefore be at the total mercy of the conquerors.

Following the example of how the Prophet had treated the Peoples of the Book in the Yemen, the Jews and the Christians of Damascus were to be confirmed in their houses and their place of worship but had to pay an annual poll tax of a dinar and a measure of wheat. After this great victory, the four armies broke apart and once again rode out against smaller local targets. Abu Ubaydah headed north, where he received the submission of such cities of northern Syria as Homs and Baalbek, while Yazid struck south to complete the subjugation of the old kingdoms of Moab and Edom (roughly speaking, southern Jordan). Shurahbil ibn Hasana enforced the surrender of Tiberias and the territories of northern Jordan while Amr advanced into the Judaean hills and started preparing the ground for a concerted siege of Jerusalem.

The Emperor Heraclius was thoroughly aware of this Arab invasion, for he was not locked behind the great triple walls of Constantinople and absorbed into the ritual life of a Byzantine monarch, but was instead residing in northern Syria, in Antioch – then the fourth-greatest city of the Mediterranean world. He was deeply embedded in the hideously complicated theological negotiations that would attempt to patch up a compromise doctrine on the vexed question of the nature of Christ (although the pragmatic compromise that he thrashed out would help give birth to yet another rival Church – the Maronites of modern-day Lebanon). Heraclius was also supervising the mutual evacuation of Byzantine and Persian garrisons as the two empires gradually sorted out the

frontier created by the peace of 629. The triple victories of the
Arab invasion of Palestine in 634 (Wadi al-Arabah, Dattin and
Ajnadayn) could possibly have been ignored as a temporary incur-
sion of barbarians (which the Byzantine Empire with all its many
endangered frontiers was all too well used to). The methodical
Muslim campaign strategy and especially the surrender of
Damascus at last forcibly seized Heraclius's undivided attention.
By the end of 635 the resources of the Empire were to be exclu-
sively focused on defeating the Muslim Arab invasion of Syria and
Palestine.

To do this Heraclius proceeded to assemble a formidable army.
This was the best of the best, the pick of the Byzantine Empire, the
soldiers recruited from Armenia and Anatolia that he had led to
victory against the Persians in 629. It was to be placed under the
command of Theodore, the Emperor's own brother, who was to be
assisted by Vahan (sometimes spelt Baanes), an experienced
Armenian general. Some authorities claim that the Emperor
Heraclius had summoned up an army of 80,000 over that winter.
This estimate may be excessive but what is certain is that by 636,
for the first time in this war, the Byzantine field army now sub-
stantially outnumbered the four Arab armies.

Throughout 634 and 635 the Arabs had enjoyed not only a
dazzling freedom of movement but also an overall numerical superiority which they had further emphasised with their accomplished
tactics. Now, in the spring of 636, the tide had changed as regiment after disciplined regiment poured down from the Anatolian
plateau, filing their way down through the valleys of the Taurus
Mountains to join the vast encampments that multiplied outside
the city of Antioch. Nor were they to lack a distinguished cavalry
wing, for the Ghassanid prince Jabala ibn al-Ayham, proud heir to
centuries of Arab leadership, personally commanded the squadrons
of Syrian Arab cavalry that also now flocked to the imperial stan-

dards. In the face of this massive military build-up the four Muslim Arab commanders decided to withdraw. All their hard-fought victories and long-drawn-out sieges were to be cast aside. The walled towns they had taken and the citadels they had occupied were now all speedily evacuated. Even that prize of prizes, Damascus, was to be abandoned without so much as a skirmish in its defence. Instead the Muslim forces retreated into the desert, back into the arid steppe land from which they had so suddenly appeared in the spring of 634.

By May 636 all the Muslim armies had completely evacuated the Holy Land and Byzantine officials once more took up the reins of authority over all the villages, towns and cities of Syria and Palestine. By the end of the month the imperial army had advanced as far east as it was safe to go. They possessed the Hauran, that strategic and fertile plateau of good farmland that watches over the approaches to both Syria and Palestine and was dotted with prosperous towns, olive orchards and ancient cities. To the immediate east, the volcanic terrain of the Jebel Druze marked the last frontier of arable land before the desert, while to the west rose the Golan heights. Here the imperial army pitched camp for the entire summer. Despite a vast superiority in manpower there was no aggressive move into the desert, either to threaten Medina or to seize control of some of the strategic oases. But there were good strategic reasons for sitting things out. The Empire had regained its lost provinces without losing a single soldier, while the overwhelming presence of such force would gradually break apart the carefully formed alliances that the Muslims had made with the desert frontier tribes. Heraclius might also have been aware that the Persian Empire would soon be applying similar pressure on the Iraq frontier, if not this year, surely next. In any case, the spring or winter months were the only time when an 'outsider army' could possibly contemplate an advance into central Arabia.

As the Muslim armies fell back into the safety of the desert, messengers were at once dispatched back to the Caliph Omar in Medina to inform him of this rapid turn of events. They also requested massive reinforcements if the Arabs were to have any hope of directly confronting the main army of the Byzantine Empire. And if they failed to engage this army, they realised that the whole impetus of loyalty to Islam among the only recently disciplined Bedouin tribes of Arabia would begin to unravel. While the Caliph sent out messenger after messenger calling upon all the tribes to send forth their young warriors, Khalid kept the Byzantine army busy that summer. Over the long, dry, hot months his small cavalry squadrons harried the much greater imperial Byzantine force but never allowed themselves to get caught in a pitched battle. So great was the need for more Arab reinforcements that Omar broke with Abu Bakr's earlier decision to exclude those tribes that had fought against the Muslims in the Ridda Wars. Instead he now summoned these recent apostates to join the Muslim armies being gathered together for this crucial test of strength.

By early August, Khalid had received these reinforcements. The Muslim army now numbered somewhere between 20,000 and 40,000 men. This force had been collected together by Caliph Omar, stretching all the resources of the young Islamic state to breaking point. So much so that it is said that even the half-blind, eighty-year-old Abu Sufyan and his hell-cat wife Hind could be found among the ranks. This army was irreplaceable, for if it was destroyed, so was the entire experienced fighting force of Muslim Arabia. Whatever their official ranking within Islam, there was now never any question among the senior commanders that Khalid should take over the day-to-day tactical command. After months of forced marches, raids and retreats Khalid and his army were also now thoroughly familiar with the terrain. On 19 August a vicious sandstorm blew out of the desert, one of those three-day affairs that can rise out of nowhere at this time of year. They are, even for those used to them, gruelling and debilitating. The storm-spat sand is often combined with an extraordinarily rapid increase in air temperature and an oppressive humidity, while the accompanying fine red dust gets everywhere. It becomes difficult to eat without swallowing mouthfuls of grit, while cooking, drawing water and lighting fires are made impossible. Even sleep can be taken only fitfully, for tents are either uprooted by the wind or flattened by the weight of the wind-blown sand. This storm was to be Khalid's opportunity. For the flat fertile farmland of the Hauran, so perfectly suited for the disciplined movement of the imperial army, had suddenly and briefly been transformed into the alien environment of the Arabian desert.

Khalid dispatched some of his most experienced raiders along the paths that they alone had got to know that led across the broken volcanic plateau, then, having outflanked the imperial camp, they cut across country to quietly seize such strategic sites as the bridge over the Wadi al Ruqqada. In mid-August all the wadi beds were as dry as the surrounding steppe land, but Khalid knew that as they ran west these harmless-looking gravel beds gradually deepened into cliff-edged ravines as they cut their way down through the Galilean hills. They were to become death traps.

Before dawn on 20 August Khalid called together all the old warriors of Islam, the men who had fought at the wells of Badr, at Uhud, and marched on that pilgrimage of grace that ended at Hudaibiya. They were formed into a spiritual corps, like the prophets of old in the Hebrew Testament, who were to pray all day for victory but were not actually to descend into the fighting. This very emphatic statement of the power of prayer might have been a reaction to the accusations of careerism that were always being levelled against him. Khalid knew that the very last Muslim fighter had been called up for this battle, which showed every promise of being exceptionally bloody. He deliberately wished to spare these veterans, for they were the collective memory of Islam, who knew the unwritten Koran and the unwritten sayings and deeds of the Prophet. When he had destroyed the Ridda rebellion, in the epic battle against the Beni Hanifa, he had also lost thirty-nine of these irreplaceable 'libraries'.

After the dawn prayer had been called, Khalid gave the order to attack. Accounts of the battle are confused but that was in the nature of this appalling two-day massacre. The Arabs had the decisive advantage of lifetime experience of these atrocious conditions, and they also had the wind at their backs, speeding their arrows, while the Byzantine army that faced them was confused and blinded by the harrowing wind. They had no hope of communicating with each other in the desert storm, no chance of calling upon their superior discipline and accomplished manoeuvres. Instead Yarmuk was a series of murderous hand-to-hand engagements which allowed the Arabs with their flexible command structure and passionate individualism to win. Before noon Khalid made certain that his troops had driven a wedge between the camps of the Byzantine infantry and the Ghassanid cavalry. Throughout the day and then over the next day the disciplined regiments of Byzantine infantry were slowly pushed back towards the network of wadi ravines. Even if the sandstorm had now miraculously halted, by this point in the fighting the imperial army had been broken up into dozens of separate units by the terrain, all unable to aid each other or communicate. Though they were trapped, confused and isolated it was never a rout, for the Byzantine regiments from Anatolia and Armenia didn't break, but fought on. They were destroyed piecemeal, cut down by virtually invisible Arab bowmen working their way through the ranks from the ravine heights. Then it was the turn of the broadswords. The dry river bed of the Yarmuk, its clay baked hard by the August sun, was abloom with oleander flowers. That night the Yarmuk poured a stream of blood flecked with pink petals into the Sea of Galilee. The Byzantine army was not defeated at Yarmuk: it was destroyed.

When the trickle of stragglers reached Antioch, the Emperor Heraclius knew at once that the Near East had been lost to the Empire. He had put everything into this army and now it had been totally destroyed. If he was fortunate, it might just be possible to save the rest of the Empire but even that was now in doubt. The entire strength of Byzantium had been destroyed at Yarmuk, he had no offensive army left, just a straggle of secondary troops tied to small garrisons scattered across North Africa, the Balkans and Anatolia. He gave orders for all of Syria to be stripped of mobile troops, declaring, 'Farewell, O Syria, and what an excellent country this is for the enemy.' A new defensive line would be drawn not in the sand but at the Taurus Mountains of Anatolia. This would remain the battleground of the two rival cultures, medieval Byzantium and the Muslim Caliphate, for the next four hundred years.

Yarmuk is one of the most decisive battles of world history, yet it revealed no new tactics and no new weaponry. There was, however, something about it, something about that desert wind, that sapped the confidence of the Emperor. The Arabs felt that on that day God had been fighting on their side, and the Byzantine Emperor began to fear that it was true. Heraclius was plunged into a paralysing depression by thoughts of Yarmuk as he completed the long march back across the Anatolian countryside to his capital. To his people he yet remained an awesome living hero: the man who had rescued them from the tyranny of Phocas, who had saved them from the Persians, who had repeated the conquests of

Alexander and returned the True Cross to Jerusalem. Heraclius the hero was also on the point of a nervous breakdown. His near-incestuous marriage to his niece began to haunt him and he became terrified at the idea of crossing water. He rested at the imperial villa at Hieram on the Asian side of the Bosporus but was incapable of giving the order to embark for the short row across the channel towards the two lions that looked out over the Porta Leonis – the gateway that guarded the entrance to the private harbour of the emperors and sat securely below the great sea walls of Constantinople's Bucoleon Palace. Eventually his courtiers managed to trick him into a cunningly camouflaged boat so that the broken Emperor could return to the palace built by Constantine the Great.

In Syria the struggle was over the day the sandstorm finally abated and the true extent of the Muslim victory was made clear among the ravines of the River Yarmuk. Even the Emperor's brother Theodorus was found among the slain. Damascus, Baalbek, Homs were speedily reoccupied by Arab armies and they have remained unconquered citadels of Islam ever since. It is recorded that at some of the Byzantine cities of Syria the Muslim army was welcomed back within the city walls with singing and dancing and formal eulogies that poetically stated their preference for Arab justice and honour rather than the 'arbitrary tyranny' of the Byzantine Empire. This was only to be expected, for the cities were everywhere determined to renew the often lenient first terms of surrender that had been negotiated with the Muslims – and wished to sweep away, out of memory, the way that the Byzantine army had been just as passionately welcomed as deliverers from the 'arbitrary tyranny' of the barbarian Arabs, just a few months earlier.

The Muslim army commanders for their part were content to acknowledge that they had themselves withdrawn their garrisons and the towns and cities would not be treated with the judicial severity with which Islam has always judged apostates.

The few cities that did resist, such as Chalchis (Qinnassin), fell to Khalid's assault and suffered the full devastation of war. Before autumn was over Khalid's cavalry had swarmed over the steppe land of northern Syria and established Marash, Urfa and Samsat as the northern outposts of the Caliphate. This line still marks the linguistic frontier of the Arabs. To the north of these cities began the foothills of Anatolia – a zone where the mobility of the Arab cavalry armies was frustrated by mountain passes, stone castles, forests and the bitter cold of the winter months.

A battle of sorts took place outside Antioch but the Byzantine garrison, having acquitted itself with some honour, abandoned the city for the protection of the mountains. This allowed the city fathers to sue for honourable terms of surrender with the venerable Abu Ubaydah – now once again everywhere saluted as supreme commander. Apart from a few well-protected coastal cities, such as Caesarea, there was only the walled city of Jerusalem, under the command of its redoubtable Patriarch, Sophronius, which continued to energetically resist the Muslim conquest. In the autumn (no one is quite sure whether this happened in 636 or 637) Patriarch Sophronius began to realise the full extent of his isolation and was forced to sue for peace. But the walls of Jerusalem were still well defended and he managed to insist that he would surrender only to the Caliph Omar himself. This may have been no more than a trick to play for more time while the Patriarch, known approvingly by the Greeks as 'the honey-tongued defender of the Church', fervently prayed for a revival of the Empire. The message was quickly dispatched by Abu Ubaydah to Medina and that winter the Caliph rode north across the desert, reaching the Judaean hills in February 638.

In advance of his arrival Omar had ordered all his principal army commanders to meet him at the campsite of Jabiyah. On his way along the old caravan trading route, which would have been familiar to him from many such journeys as a merchant of the Quraysh of Mecca, the now all-powerful Caliph was greeted by a delegation of Arabs from the Syrian steppe lands. They saluted him in their customary style with elaborate sung compliments, with sword jugglers, drums and lascivious dancing women playing enticingly on their tambourines. Omar was appalled at such a display and ordered his escort to stop them immediately – with their whips if necessary. Instead of being obeyed, Omar was politely cautioned that 'such is the custom' and that if the inhabitants were prevented from honouring the victor they would fear that he had not accepted their surrender and would soon order their massacre. Omar, no doubt in a furious temper, was forced to ride on surrounded by this jubilant melee of professional praise-singers. Later, when Omar approached closer to the Jabiyah military camp, the four great commanding generals respectfully rode out to greet the Caliph, who was still wrapped in the same tattered old cloak that he had possessed and diligently repaired over the past decade. Having utterly destroyed the army of the Byzantine Empire and conquered all of Syria and Palestine, with Jerusalem the Holy City on the cusp of surrender, they may have been expecting a word or two of praise. They had clearly forgotten Omar. He took one look at their gorgeous Syrian cloaks and the beautiful red and gilded leatherwork that now adorned their horses, and exploded in fury, 'Do you come to me dressed like that? Have you changed so much in just two years? You all deserve to be dismissed in disgrace!' It is said that in reply Khalid tore apart his parade cloak to reveal the armour that had been so dented and slashed with enemy blades in over four years of continuous fighting for the faith. It should have been eloquent enough testimony to his devoted service, but

Omar remained unforgiving of their corruption of the Prophet's example.

Once installed in the Jabiyah camp, the embassy from Christian Jerusalem waited upon the arrival of the Caliph, who agreed to the surrender terms. According to some accounts, the Caliph then discarded the soiled clothes of a traveller to approach the Holy City wearing not the armour of a conqueror but the white linen of a pilgrim. He approached the city gates on a milk-white camel, having ridden across the Jordan valley on the old roadstead that passed through Bansan. The scene at the gates, where the white-clothed Caliph receives the keys to Jerusalem from the black-clad Patriarch, has been immortalised in thousands of crude woodcuts, painted mirrors and posters. It is an icon, a symbol of power transferred, that has entered deeply into Arabic popular consciousness.

The Patriarch then took the barefooted pilgrim-conqueror on a guided tour of the city, pointing out its celebrated sites. As they were inspecting the Holy Sepulchre, Omar heard the muezzin call out the time for the noonday prayer. With great dignity he refused the Patriarch's request that he should pray where he stood and moved outside. There he unfolded a prayer rug and prayed in the porch of the church. He explained afterwards that he had only done this to spare the Holy Sepulchre, which would have otherwise been converted into a mosque by his followers. He was right. Within a few days his followers had converted the porch into a mosque. The example set by the Caliph and Patriarch would continue through the centuries. The ruling Muslim governor, the Pasha of Jerusalem, had the honour of escorting the Patriarch into the inner sanctum of the Holy Sepulchre every Easter Saturday. They would reappear to the crowds with a miraculously lit candle from which all the lights and fires of the city would be lit until they were doused before the next Easter.

At the end of the day, the Patriarch took Caliph Omar up to the ruined terraces of the old Temple of Solomon as rebuilt by Herod. Here Omar was shown the Sakhra rock, known as the 'navel of the earth' and believed to be both the site of the tomb of Adam, the place where King David sang his psalms of praise to God, and from where the Prophet Muhammad had set off on his mystical flight into heaven. Omar stood transfixed as he contemplated this extraordinary centre of spiritual power. Sixty years later, in 695, the rock would be covered by the Qubbat as-Sakhra, the serenely beautiful Dome of the Rock. It was a memorial building, not a mosque, the second-most holy shrine of Islam after the Kaaba at Mecca. As Omar stood in his simple but dignified robes looking out over the city, the Patriarch whispered in Greek to one of his aides beside him, 'Behold, the Abomination of Desolation spoken of by the Prophet Daniel that standeth in the Holy Place.'

This oft-quoted stage whisper, such a perennial favourite of Western historians and tour guides, has always seemed to me an extraordinary instance of doublethink. Leaving aside the ingratitude with which Sophronius repaid Omar's extraordinary respect for Jerusalem, for the Patriarch, for the city's Christian holy places and his own modest role as a pilgrim, Daniel's vision has itself always been taken to apply to the Roman invasion and its desecration of Jerusalem with graven images – which would ultimately be fulfilled with the destruction of both city and temple. As Omar had just vanquished the direct heirs of the Romans and brought an imageless worship of the One God back to the Holy Place raised up by Solomon, there seems little doubt whom Daniel would have considered to have been the Abomination of Desolation.

As dusk fell over the city the Caliph prayed at the southern end of the old temple enclosure. In the months that followed he and his warriors would clear this place of the heaps of garbage that had been symbolically dumped over the site of the fallen temple of the Jews by the Christians. This would be consecrated as the site of the Masjid al-Aqsa, the far-away sanctuary. For many years the mosque raised here remained an extensive but simple structure in keeping with the wishes of both Prophet and Caliph. Exactly thirty years later a visiting Christian pilgrim, Bishop Arculf, was able to sniff disapprovingly at its flimsy structure of palm beams, though 3000 worshippers could pray here together. The time for real regret was yet to come, when the Umayyad Caliphs swept away Islam's early pride in poverty and replaced it with a pride in stone. The mosque they constructed here has had a fateful history. It has been rebuilt seven times, though the present structure built by a Mameluke sultan in the mid-fourteenth century still stands.

It is often claimed that the various Christian churches of the Near East welcomed the Muslim conquest. Or that they formed some sort of Semitic fifth column. It was at best a very passive acquiescence in the status quo. It was impossible for any of the great cities of Syria and Palestine to stand against the victorious Muslim army. The whole basis of Byzantine military strategy had been that the walled cities should try to hold out until the imperial army could move up to their rescue. The imperial army had been destroyed: first the local legions stationed in the Near East had been defeated outside Gaza, at Ajnadayn and then outside Damascus over 634 and 635, but most decisively of all the entire Byzantine army had been wiped out at Yarmuk in 636. The Emperor had abandoned Antioch and returned to his capital. There was nothing to be done but to try to make good terms. As an Egyptian sage wrote many generations before, 'the art of towns is not to take sides'.

Much more alarming for the future of the Empire was the subsequent loss of the great walled cities on the coast which theoretically could have been replenished and supported by the navy for decades. The Empire was by then fighting a war on four fronts, and each one was potentially as desperate as that in the Near East. In the Balkans the Slavs and the Avars were overrunning Greece, the Lombards were overrunning the Byzantine strongholds in Italy, the rich cities of southern Spain fell back to the Visigoths, and the Luwata of the Sahara were raiding North Africa. There were barely enough troops at hand to protect Constantinople. Each province had to survive on its own resources: the rest of the Empire was left to stand or fall on its own. Caesarea did its best, and would hold out for four long years after Yarmuk against a continuous siege.

Khalid had been essential while the armies of the Byzantine Empire remained, but since the victory of Yarmuk it was one that Omar felt he could now live without. It may be that Omar suspected that the warriors of Islam felt greater confidence while under Khalid's command than merely trusting to their prayers. His fame as a commander must have then exceeded even that of the Caliph himself. Khalid was dismissed from his rank and Abu Ubaydah once again confirmed as commander-in-chief with Yazid as his deputy. Khalid's humble acceptance of his new position, a mere warrior among the thousands of other Arab horsemen, was the stoic action that would complete his identity among the pantheon of Arab heroes. In the following years he served with such distinction and loyalty on the northern frontier that Omar began to wonder if he had not made a mistake and publicly exclaimed, 'May God bless the soul of Abu Bakr, he knew men's character much better than I. He put Khalid in the right place.' Then news trickled through to Omar of Khalid's personal behaviour and how he was behaving just like a warlord of the pagan era and not at all like a principled warrior of Islam. Two stories especially infuriated the Caliph: the tale of an orgy in a Byzantine bathhouse whose basins were filled with heated wine and a more than princely gift of 1000 gold coins to a praise-singing poet who had sung an epic celebration of Khalid's deeds. He was summoned to Medina to stand trial before Omar, who demanded to know the means by which he had acquired such flamboyant wealth. Khalid would return to the Syrian front a humiliated and broken man and would die in obscurity two years later, swept away by one of the plagues that scythed their way through those first permanent Bedouin encampments. His tomb can still be found at Homs, where he lies beside his wife Fada. In later centuries his personality cult was revived, most especially by the thirteenth-century Mameluke sultan Baibars (who had a lot in common with Khalid), and he was appealed to as a miracle-working saint who could be fervently addressed in prayers by the title the Prophet first awarded him: the Sword of Islam. The current shrine-mosque that was raised above his tomb was added in the last decade of the Ottoman Caliphate in 1908, though his beautifully carved medieval catafalque has been moved to the Damascus Museum.

One of Khalid's old opponents on the battlefield was also to suffer justice at the impartial hands of Omar. Jabala ibn al-Ayham, the proud prince of the Ghassanid dynasty, had loyally fought for the Byzantine Empire right up until the catastrophic day of Yarmuk. In the aftermath he, along with an increasing number of Christian Arabs from the Syrian desert, was left with no choice but to make his submission to Islam. Prince Jabala rode to Medina to make his profession of faith to the Caliph himself, though he clearly understood nothing of the Prophet's teachings. Indeed far from considering himself a brother among brother believers he was so outraged when a Bedouin jostled him at the mosque that he struck that innocent so savagely that he put out his eye. The prince was summoned by his victim to appear before the Caliph in judgement, whereupon Omar ignored any diplomatic considerations and offered the simple Bedouin herdsman a chance to strike the prince a similar blow. The next day the indignant ex-monarch rode out from the oasis accompanied by several thousand of his relatives, tribesmen and faithful retainers. Omar was criticised for losing such a prestige 'convert', the representative of a family who had dominated Arabian politics, trade and poetic culture for nigh on four hundred years. Prince Jabala would lead his people out of Arabia into permanent exile within the frontiers of the Byzantine Empire. As an elderly refugee living on the periphery of the court in Constantinople he looked back in regret at his pride:

> 'Twas the rage in my heart made us Christians once more
> I resented that blow in the face.
> I felt that my honour I could not restore
> If I bowed to such shame and disgrace.
> Ah! Would that my mother no son ever bore
> Nor my name had in history found place.
> How I yearn for the land of my fathers of yore,
> Damascus the home of my race.

Three years after the occupation of Jerusalem, the Caliph Omar would once again ride north from Medina to revisit the Jabiyah camp. He had called together all his chief officers for a summit, the so-called 'day of al-Jabiyah', though it stretched over three days of meetings, concluded by a sworn covenant, the *ahd* of Omar. Although the actual clauses of the covenant are now lost to us the power of Omar's authority and the clarity of his vision established a political and military system that would endure for centuries – indeed arguably it shapes Arab and Muslim society to this day.

There were also some very pressing and immediate reasons behind Omar's return visit to Jabiyah. In 638 the Byzantine Empire had at last struck back, launching a seaborne assault which briefly reoccupied Antioch at the same time that a rebellion was raised among the Christian tribes of the Syrian desert. It was fought off and in the process the northern desert frontier was expanded, but it was a very worrying incident, one that threatened to cut communications and isolate the Muslim army. The following year, 639, was even worse. A savage drought pushed the subsistence diet of central Arabia down to the threshold of famine, a crisis further complicated by the absence of so many men and their camels and horses at the frontiers of war, so that there was no means to distribute emergency supplies. In Medina they long treasured the story of how Omar himself was seen carrying sacks of grain to the poor and how during the famine he refused to touch either of his two luxuries, butter and honey, in order to share some of the suffering of his people.

Also in 639 the dense, tightly packed encampment of the Bedouin Arab army outside Homs (which had been the central base for the recent military operations) became a crucible of pestilence. It incubated a plague which swept through the Arab garrisons, mocking the casualties of war by killing tens of thousands of warriors in a few months. Among the dead was Caliph Omar's lifelong confidant and trustee Abu Ubaydah, while his delegated second-in-command, Yazid, was also soon buried. Yazid's efficient younger brother, Muawiya, was a superb commander, every inch an Arab chieftain of the old school. Courteous, patient and understanding, he knew that his Arab troops had first to be consulted, then persuaded, before they could be successfully commanded. As he explained himself, 'I apply not my sword where my lash suffices, nor my lash where my tongue is enough. And even if there be but one hair binding me to my fellow men, I do not let it break. When they pull, loosen; and if they loosen, I pull.' He had his hands full. Not only had he to guard the new border with Byzantium but he had to arbitrate – and ultimately win over – the tribes involved in the 638 emergency. The long-established Bedouin tribes of the Syrian desert, such as the Judham and Kalb, were ferociously jealous of the Muslim army divisions that had moved into Syria. There was also a powerful Bedouin tribe, the Beni Taghlib, who refused to convert from Christianity to Islam and also refused to pay the demeaning poll tax which they rightly associated with a conquered people. Omar was all for refusing any special terms, but Muawiya, fully aware of the strategic position that the Beni Taghlib held (especially after the recent Byzantine counter-attack), pushed through a compromise that allowed them to keep their dignity by paying a double rate of the Muslim tithe. Omar was not alone in believing that Yazid's young brother had already proved himself an excellent commander, and so Muawiya took over Abu Ubaydah's position as supreme commander in Syria.

The recent fighting had also proved that the Jabiyah camp perched on the frontier between the sown and grazing lands (and which had been a historic base of the Ghassanid kings) was not so useful for defence. It remained in theory the central command centre, but four subsidiary garrison camps were to be strategically placed around the territories of Syria and Palestine. One camp was established beside Damascus to control southern Syria, another beside the city of Homs (ancient Emessa) to control northern Syria, with another at Tiberias (Tibarrayah) watching over Jordan (al-Urdun), while the fourth guarded Palestine (Filastin) from the site of ancient Lydda, though this was later abandoned in favour of Ramlah.

But above and beyond these immediate tactical dispositions, the Caliph wished to establish a blueprint for future conduct. Omar's first principle was of separation. The Muslim Arab army of conquest should be kept isolated from the conquered peoples of the Near East and neither by residence in a town or city, nor by the cultivation of land should they be allowed to integrate themselves with the provincials of Palestine, Syria and Jordan. They would remain uncorrupted by the wine-drinking, singing and dancing traditions of the locals. They would form a mobile military elite of devoted faith in Islam, sincere in their attachment to the traditions of the Arab Bedouin and ready to march at a moment's notice.

The inhabitants of Syria and Palestine, mostly Christians leavened by a few ancient Jewish communities, were to become demilitarised taxpayers. The *dhimmi*, the people protected by agreements with the Arabs, were to pay an annual tax. In later years this would be assessed as a tithe from lands (the *kharaj*) plus an annual poll tax (the *jizyah*), though this clear theoretical ideal had many local variants. The poll tax was usually assessed on a sliding scale, four gold coins (the golden denarius or dinar then weighed around 4 grams) for a rich merchant, two for a shopkeeper and one for a poor labourer. Despite the enduringly popular image of the Arab conquerors arriving with the sword in one hand and the Koran in the other, this was only true as a metaphor during the Ridda Wars. It was most emphatically not the case with the conquest of Syria and Palestine. There was no attempt to convert the Peoples of the Book, who right from the start were valued as a taxable resource and to be kept apart from the Muslims.*

Omar's second great principle was that all conquered land was to remain an inalienable resource of the Muslim state. Although

---

* This enduring image – a sword in one hand and the Koran in the other – can't ever have been literally true. The Koran had not yet been written down, and even when it had been there would not have been enough copies for each soldier to have one. There is also another hitch: the Koran could not have been held in the unclean left hand, but this is where it would have to be if the right hand was holding a sword – unless there was a large number of left-handed Arabic warriors.

portable property, humans and livestock could be – and had been – seized by the victorious warriors of Islam as the booty of war they had no such rights over land. The grain fields, the orchards and grazing lands belonged to the collective Muslim state and were never to be parcelled out to create a new landed aristocracy – in the manner of the Norman conquest of England or the English settlement of Virginia. Instead the wealth of this land, calculated in the monetary value of its annual tithes, rents and taxes, would be considered as a perpetual endowment (the *fay*) that belonged to the entire Muslim community: for the support of the poor, the aged, the widows – not just the armed warriors.

In practical terms all this meant that the Arab Muslim armies were to stay together, living together as an army of faith in a military camp and not scattered across the land like a bunch of *arriviste* squires. The new resources from the conquered lands would be paid into a central treasury and then distributed to support the Muslim community. As a corollary of this policy Omar was also determined to keep the Companions centred on Medina and not allow them to develop into a ruling class dissipated across the lands of the new conquests. He publicly explained that he 'did not employ such eminent persons to high office because of their virtues . . . lest for any lapse they lose the eminence that they had enjoyed'.

Muawiya soon proved his worth, so tightening the siege of the walled port of Caesarea (that had been dragging on for years) that it capitulated the next year, 640. His experience of this long siege, in which Caesarea had been constantly replenished from the sea, made him realise that the Byzantine Greeks could never be finally defeated unless the Arabs learned to fight them on the sea. The great seafaring traditions of the Arabs who lived along the coast of the Yemen and the Persian Gulf were emphatically not shared by the Quraysh of Mecca. In the words of one of

Muawiya's contemporaries, 'If a ship lies still it rends the heart: if it moves it terrifies the imagination. Upon it a man's power ever diminishes and calamity increases. Those within it are like worms in a log, and if it rolls over they are drowned.' Omar forbade his young governor in Syria to plan any conquests by sea, though Muawiya was permitted to gradually build up a defensive squadron, especially after the capture of Acre had given him possession of a fully equipped shipyard. For skilled shipwrights and artificers, Muawiya was dependent on the indigenous Christian workforce of Syria.

It was not just in naval matters that Muawiya made use of the skills of the highly sophisticated natives of Syria and Palestine. His personal physician and his court poet were Christians, as was the chief financial controller, one Mansur ibn Sarjun, who seemingly transferred his talents and his skilled staff of clerks from the service of Byzantium to that of the Islamic Caliphate without so much as the loss of a file. Muawiya also chose a Christian for his wife, and Maysun was to remain so to her dying day. His son Yazid would grow up in the company of this cosmopolitan court and so would number among his childhood friends St John Damascene, the grandson of Mansur, the chief financial controller. Although Muawiya looked longingly at the opportunities of naval raids into the eastern Mediterranean, he kept himself to the instructions of Omar and instead organised an annual attack against the Byzantine positions on the frontier of northern Syria – into the land of the Romans, the *bilad al-Rum*. Here on the northeastern frontier of Syria his armies brushed against the ancient frontier of the Persian and Byzantine empires. On the banks of the upper Euphrates a succession of ancient castles, ruined cities and crumbling curtain walls testified to one of the oldest battlegrounds of the world.

We must now turn our attention back to the eastern frontier of

Arabia, and look at how the armies of the Caliphs achieved a second miracle by conquering the Persian Empire. We leave Muawiya in command of the Near East in the year 640 and look back to the events in Iraq between 634 and 640.

The Prophet Muhammad, his Quraysh tribe and the city of Mecca had always been much more interested in the affairs of Byzantine Syria than in the Persian-held province of Iraq. Their historic trade routes and their ancient tribal alliances had led north to Bostra, Gaza and Damascus rather than east towards Mesopotamia. Iraq, with its dense black soil, its two great rivers, ancient pattern of peoples, its complicated patchwork of religious beliefs and superbly organised irrigation systems, always remained more of a mystery for the early Muslims. Khalid's successful raid of the Iraqi borderlands had been achieved at the victorious conclusion of the Ridda Wars in local alliance with the Beni Bekr tribe. Once the military situation in Syria and Palestine heated up in 634, Abu Bakr ordered that this war in Iraq be abandoned. In Khalid's absence the authority of the Caliph devolved almost by accident on the shoulders of Muthanna ibn Harith, a clan chieftain from the Beni Bekr tribe. Ibn Harith was one of those extraordinary characters who epitomise all the bravery and innate nobility that the world has come to expect from a Bedouin Arab. For all his heroic nature it must be remembered that ibn Harith, as a representative of Islam, was a very bizarre choice. Ibn Harith was a very late convert to Islam (some time after the Ridda Wars) and had joined only out of admiration for Khalid's generalship and his own historic enmity with the Persian Empire. As we have already heard, it was ibn Harith who had won his spurs as a young warrior when his tribe chivalrously defended the harem and treasure of the Lakhmid kings that had been entrusted to their protection. Although no more than a skirmish by the standards of Yarmuk, that 'day of Dhu Qar' back in 606* was recalled with glowing pride by all Arabs as the first time they had repelled a Persian imperial army. Despite this tradition, the Arab tribesmen who volunteered to fight for Islam were initially reluctant to be sent to the eastern, the Persian, front and preferred to volunteer for action in Syria.

After the departure of Khalid and his army to the Syrian front, in their epic desert-crossing ride of 634, it had been left to ibn Harith and his tribe to repel any Persian assault. This he achieved at a battle fought outside the ruins of Babylon, where, seeing the consternation that was being caused in the Bedouin ranks by a Persian war-elephant, ibn Harith himself led a squad of horsemen to bring down this fearsome beast with a javelin in the eye. The battle of Babylon allowed the Arabs to hold on to the citadel of Hira and control both banks of the Euphrates. In the aftermath of this small victory ibn Harith soon heard disquieting information from the Persian capital. The Persian Empire, weakened by a ten-year succession war, had at last been reunited under the rule of the boy-king Yazdegird and his regent Rustam, who planned to celebrate the new unity by attacking an external enemy – the Arabs. To show the urgency of the threat, ibn Harith chose to be his own messenger, riding into Medina to make a personal appeal to Abu Bakr. He was able to meet the Caliph, though by August 634 Abu Bakr was weakening fast and the news of the Muslim victories in the Holy Land dominated everyone's imagination. Omar invited ibn Harith to address the believers after prayer: the chieftain stressed the 'immense plunder available for those who followed the path of God and fought against the fireworshippers'. To reward those zealous in Islam, Omar gave the

---

* Dhu Qar is dated to 611 by some historians, and there is no unanimity among scholars past or present.

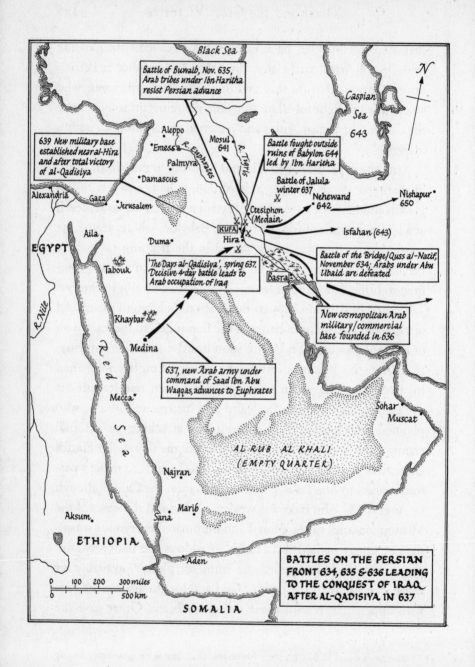

Black Sea

Battle of Buwaib, Nov. 635,
Arab tribes under Ibn Haritha
resist Persian advance

Caspian
Sea
643

N

Aleppo
Mosul
641
R. Euphrates
R. Tigris

Emessa

Palmyra

639 New military base
established near al-Hira
and after total victory
of al-Qadisiya

Battle fought outside
ruins of Babylon 644
led by Ibn Haritha

Nishapur

Battle of Jalula
winter 637
Nehewand
642

Damascus

Alexandria
Gaza
Jerusalem

Ctesiphon
(Medain

Isfahan (643)

KUFA

EGYPT

Aila

Hira

Duma

R. Nile

Tabouk

'The Days al-Qadisiya', spring 637.
Decisive 4-day battle leads to
Arab occupation of Iraq

Basra

Battle of the Bridge/Quss al-Natif,
November 634; Arabs under Abu
Ubaid are defeated

Khaybar

Red
Sea

Medina

New cosmopolitan Arab
military/commercial
base founded in 636

637, new Arab army under
command of Saad Ibn Abu
Waqqas, advances to Euphrates

Mecca

Sohar
Muscat

AL RUB. AL KHALI
(EMPTY QUARTER)

Najran

Aksum
Sana
Marib

ETHIOPIA

Aden

0   100   200   300 miles
0   500 km

BATTLES ON THE PERSIAN
FRONT 634, 635 & 636 LEADING
TO THE CONQUEST OF IRAQ
AFTER AL-QADISIYA IN 637

SOMALIA

command of this expedition to the first volunteer, Abu Ubayd from the Thaqif tribe of Taif.

Abu Ubayd proved strong in zeal and led the volunteer army east, arriving on the edge of the desert and the banks of the Euphrates in October 634. The Persian commander purposefully allowed Abu Ubayd to lead the Muslim army unopposed across the river over a bridge of boats. The two armies clashed in the well-watered farmland of central Iraq. Here the Arabs were at an important disadvantage, for their cavalry could not use the endless expanse of the desert steppe to freely manoeuvre, to fall back, to outflank the enemy. Instead they were bogged down in heavy ground that favoured the disciplined regiments of Persian infantry. Once again the Persians were also in possession of war-elephants, and once again the personal bravery of the Arab high command was displayed as Abu Ubayd led the attack on the magnificent, heavily armoured beasts. He had instructed his men that the trunk was their weak point and to prove it galloped swiftly behind an elephant and then rode close up to it to swipe at the trunk with his broadsword. Instead the gallant Abu Ubayd found himself plucked out of his saddle, lifted high in the air and then thrown on to the ground before being trampled lifeless into the black soil. Heartened by this, the Persian infantry began to push the Arab warriors back towards the marshland beside the Euphrates. The battle then centred on control of the bridge of boats across the river. At one stage this vital bridge was cut by the Persians, then recaptured by the Muslims and hurriedly repaired. It was only held against renewed Persian assaults by the determined last-ditch stand led by ibn Harith (once again left in command by default). This allowed the Arab army to withdraw safely back into the desert, though they lost a third of their force, some 3000 men, on the field of Quss al Natif – also known as the battle of the Bridge – on 26 November 634.

Despite this bloody reverse, ibn Harith was able to hold on to the desert frontier throughout the winter and the next spring. News from the Syrian front was so heartening (this was before Yarmuk but the year of the triple victories at Wadi al-Arabah, Dattin and Ajnadayn) that volunteers even began to pour into ibn Harith's camp. The summer was spent in fruitless manoeuvres as the Persian general tried to draw the Arabs once again across the Euphrates, while ibn Harith was equally determined that any battle should be fought in the desert. The old Lakhmid capital of al-Hira, off an eastern branch of the Euphrates, was the linchpin around which both armies pivoted. Finally in November 635 they met on the field of Buwaib ('the little gate') – where the Persian army had been lured east of the Euphrates and was advancing into the desert. The two armies were remarkably evenly matched but, unlike the mixed Muslim armies in Syria, here they fought as tribes under their traditional chieftains. At a critical point in the day when it seemed that the three advancing Persian columns might break his line ibn Harith placed himself at the head of the Beni Namir and the Beni Taghlib (two proudly Christian tribes of Bedouin) and calling upon them to prove themselves Arabs, even if they could not be numbered among the Muslims, led a desperate counterattack. During this charge ibn Harith's own brother and the chief of the Beni Namir were among the many Arabs cut down. Their deaths were not in vain, for ibn Harith achieved his objective, which was to briefly break through the Persian front and seize the bridge at their rear.

As ibn Harith had guessed, the Persians at first wavered, then began an orderly withdrawal to recapture the bridge, but in the process their line broke and panic breathed mayhem through their orderly ranks. By dusk the Persian dead that lay piled up before the bridge, along the river banks and scattered across the surrounding steppe proved a fitting revenge for the previous year's defeat at the battle of the Bridge.

The next morning ibn Harith, seated on a crude carpet that had been knotted by the women of his clan, received the congratulations of his allied chieftains on the field of battle. They had all, over the past years, complained bitterly about having to serve beside – let alone beneath – a mere chieftain of the Beni Bekr but now the proud lord of the Beni Bajeela, of the Beni Taghlib, of the Azd and the new chief of the Namir pressed forward to kiss his hand and bless his inspired leadership. During the night Selma, his Bedouin wife, had dressed his new scars and had noticed with alarm that the wounds he had received the year before – while defending the boat bridge over the Euphrates – had reopened. They would not heal. In the aftermath of the victory only ibn Harith recalled how closely matched the two opposing armies had been. On his deathbed ibn Harith sent another appeal to Omar for more troops. He also instructed one of his surviving brothers to hand over his battle standard and this advice to his successor, 'Fight the enemy only in the desert. There you will be victorious, or, even if you are defeated, you will have the friendly and familiar desert at your back. The Persians cannot follow you there and from there you can return again and again to the attack.' As an explanation of the astonishing success of the Muslim conquests of the seventh century ibn Harith's tactical summary has yet to be superseded.

By the winter of 636, after the decisive victory at Yarmuk, the Caliph could afford to start moving troops from newly conquered Syria and Palestine back to Iraq. Indeed for one heady moment Omar proposed that he should lead the next army out of Medina himself – though his advisers soon talked him out of this. Instead the forty-year-old Saad ibn Abu Waqqas was selected. He had been among the first to profess Islam, was a cousin of the Prophet

Muhammad and had been the first young Muslim warrior to draw blood. His precedence as a Companion would assure that none of the local chieftains felt dishonoured by serving beneath him. By the spring of 637 a Muslim army of around 30,000 men under Saad was slowly assembling in the diffuse grazing grounds in the desert south of the Euphrates (in the area occupied by modern Kuwait). This army had been predominantly recruited from the great tribes of the Yemen, which had assembled en masse at Medina under their traditional tribal chiefs. Omar had continued the Prophet's tradition of 'tipping' the great lords with gifts of silver, though in these inflationary days of victory, 2000 dirhams had become the accepted rate.

As the two armies once again skirmished, one could be forgiven for confusing the two campaigns of the Iraq war with each other. For once again the Euphrates remained the frontier, and once again the complicated manoeuvres of the rival generals were centred on the city of al-Hira – the Verdun of seventh-century Mesopotamia. But this time there was even more at stake, for by now the entire Persian field army was under the direct command of General Rustam. Exact figures are always contentious but both sides had put their all into this next round of fighting, which for the Persians probably meant around 30,000 front-line troops assisted by another 10,000 militia. The parallels with the Yarmuk campaign are concise, not least in that the imperial camp could win by merely holding ground. Old General Rustam fully understood this, though his young master, King Yazdegird, pushed endlessly for a decisive victory and offensive tactics. Rustam managed to stall over the entire spring campaign with a flurry of marches, countermarches and the sending of delegations, but against all his better judgement he at last gave way to his monarch's orders and crossed the Euphrates in June.

Saad had used this time well, getting his largely Yemeni army used to the different terrain of this part of Arabia and organising the tribes into units used to receiving orders. He was the model of a modern major-general, but on the day of battle he lost some of his personal dignity among the Arabs by taking up position in the old fort of Qadisiya. It had an excellent view over his chosen battlefield and was well placed as a communications centre, but this was not how ibn Harith had led his men. Saad later claimed that he was suffering from sciatica at the time but neither his men nor his new wife Selma, were convinced. The Bedouin soldiers sang a ditty that began

> *We fought patiently until God gave us victory,*
> *While Saad was safe inside the walls of Qadisiya.*

While Selma (ibn Harith's widow) infuriated her new husband by constantly exclaiming 'O for an hour of ibn Harith, Alas there is no al-Muthanna' until Saad slapped her face in his jealous fury and sent her away.

The battle of al-Qadisiya was a monumental and hard-fought engagement – the Borodino and the Waterloo of the Arab invasion of the East. Both Saad and Rustam proved themselves masterful in controlling the vast numbers under their command. The first day of fighting saw great casualties but no discernible weakness in either the Persian or the Arab lines. The following morning saw the two titanic armies clash again, after they had both first cleared away the debris of the dead, the wounded and the dying. In the middle of the second day of battle the Arabs were joined by a column of 6000 men, reinforcements from the Syrian front, who added fresh impetus to the assaults, but by nightfall it was once again clear that neither side would quit the field. This was repeated again on the third day, though with about 3000 fallen in each army over the three days' fighting, this war of attrition could not be permanently endured by the Arabs despite their reinforcements.

The decisive engagement was the so-called 'night of fury', though this was not planned or controlled by either of the commanders. It was a spontaneous assault launched by Bedouin warriors, who in the spirit of old pre-Islamic Arabia had called upon each other to offer up blood vengeance for their fallen brethren. In wave after murderous wave, they attacked the Persian camp throughout the hours of moonlight. They were inspired enough to repeat these attacks through the gathering light of dawn, even though it is thought that as many as 5000 Arabs had already perished. It was one of these reckless assaults, after nearly four days of continuous fighting in the terrible debilitating heat of the Arabian desert, which suddenly cracked open the Persian centre. Old General Rustam was identified and killed, and the Arabs then succeeded to break through to the river behind the Persian army. The two wings of the Persian force were able to withdraw in reasonably good order but the sustained losses over the 'days of al-Qadisiya' were crippling. But unlike the total destruction of the Byzantine imperial army at Yarmuk, the Persian army had been defeated but not destroyed. King Yazdegird had decided to move the bulk of his surviving army, and his family and as much of his treasure as could be carried, into the safety of the Persian homeland. A new defensive frontier was to be drawn at the foothills of the Zagros Mountains as they rise up to look over the flat alluvial plain of Mesopotamia (more or less following the modern frontier between Iraq and Iran). Iraq was to be evacuated.

It was not just the Persians who were shattered; the Arab victors were forced to rest for two months before Saad could order his army to advance even to occupy nearby al-Hira, which like a tattered battle standard once more changed hands.

Saad for his part seemed to proceed with almost exaggerated caution into the well-irrigated land of Iraq. Even at this distance of time one can feel the awe of the Arab conquerors as they progressed east over the densely populated farmland and its enormous forests of planted date palm and its tens of thousands of hard-working inhabitants. Their slow realisation that they, the poor Bedouin of the desert, were now the masters of this great agricultural breadbasket of the old world, the new heirs to the world's most distinguished litany of empires, to Sumer, Chaldea, Babylon, Assyria, Persia, Seleucia, Parthia and the Sassanians. They diffidently approached the walls of the immense, thousand-year-old city of Seleucia (the Greek- and Aramaic-speaking commercial city that stood on the other bank from the formal Sassanian Persian capital of Ctesiphon), which occupied the west bank of the Tigris and stood about 20 miles south-east of modern Baghdad. While still working out what on earth he should do about breaching these walls, Saad's scouts reported that the walls of Seleucia were suddenly being evacuated by ferry boats. A year later on the east bank of the Tigris, the Arabs, having effectively encircled the great imperial administrative capital of Ctesiphon, once again found the unbreached walls surrendered to them. The treasure from these two cities (usually known collectively by the Arabs of this period as 'Madain') exhausted the wildest possible imagination of the Arab army, and as province after province within Iraq submitted they found it impossible to impose the terms of conversion or death on the vast population of pagans. The once-despised Zoroastrian 'fire-worshippers' were recognised as another People of the Book (in principle rather than in practice, since they lacked Koranic chapter and verse) and were permitted to pay an annual tribute in exchange for maintaining their faith, alongside their Christian and Jewish neighbours.

That autumn the Persian army that had withdrawn to the

Zagros Mountains launched its counter-attack. Saad, following orders that he had received from Omar in Medina, dispatched a moderate-sized Muslim army of 12,000 men to repel them. They succeeded in stalling the Persian attack but the losses were high, so substantial reinforcements were sent to bolster the position. This Arab army won a decisive victory fought in the hills at Jalula and in the aftermath chased the Persian force back up the mountain passes into Persia itself. Jalula proved to be a second (if accidental) al-Qadisiya, which casually opened the way for the Muslim occupation of the central Persian plateau. The Arabs were not unopposed. There would be another twenty years of near-continuous fighting before the old Persian capital of Persepolis was occupied by a Muslim army. King Yazdegird would continue to resist all the days of his life.

The decisive twin victories against the two empires, first against Byzantium at Yarmuk in Syria, then against Persia at al-Qadisiya in Iraq, completely transformed Arabia. These were days of glory indeed. The two greatest empires of the old world had been defeated in battle. Islam had proved itself not only in the hearts of men but on the page of history. The doubters no longer doubted. It was a time of mass conversions when the last pagan Bedouin, half-convinced Arabs as well as previously hostile Christian tribes flocked to the banners of Islam. Even one of the guard regiments within the Persian army, numbering 4000 men, switched its allegiance en masse to the Caliph. While at the same time another division of 4000 warriors rode down from the hills of northern Iraq to pledge their loyalty. It is fitting that these men, the first Kurds to embrace Islam (who would later produce Muslim heroes such as Saladin), did so by their own will. These new allies were nicknamed the red people, al-Hamra, by the Arabs and were grafted into the Muslim army as clients of a sponsoring Arab tribe. It was still too early for any of the first believers to comprehend an

Islam that did not also have a completely Arabic identity. (Indeed this issue is arguably still unresolved today.)

At first Saad had converted the massive reception hall of the Sassanian monarchs at Ctesiphon into a public mosque and established his administration, and his army camp, in the half-despoiled Sassanian palaces that ranged all around this great hall (which still survives). Omar subsequently instructed Saad that the Muslim army of conquest must abandon Ctesiphon, in the centre of the wealthy, multi-ethnic distractions of Iraq. Omar wanted to establish a new Muslim army base on the old desert frontier of Arabia at Kufa, just 2½ miles outside the battle-scarred walls of the old Lakhmid capital of al-Hira. Near this lodestone of Arab history the official Muslim garrison city was to rise, the black-haired tents gradually replaced by reed huts that in their turn would be supplanted by houses of neat mud bricks in the millennial traditions of Mesopotamia.

Kufa was also to be a determinedly Islamic foundation in contrast with church-filled al-Hira. A mosque that could accommodate the whole army in prayer dominated the centre of Kufa. Its perimeters were fixed by a warrior who had thrown an arrow to each point of the compass. From these four points a perfect square was drawn and the land set aside for worship with an encircling moat. In subsequent years marble columns were taken from the palaces, churches and monasteries of al-Hira and hauled into the new enclosure. They were raised up again to support a roofed section along one side of the 200-cubit-wide mosque. This was to provide midday shade and a place for teaching, Koranic recitals and meetings. A worshipper was free to approach this place of prayer from any side, though the commanders' quarters, the Dar al-Imara, would soon rise on the south-east side of the mosque. This was in keeping with the established practice of the Prophet, who dwelt beside the mosque at Medina which had always served as a place for prayer, a place for meetings as well as a place of hospitality. After thieves stole from the state treasury in Kufa, the Caliph Omar decreed that the public treasuries should henceforth be protected by the watch of the faithful. In the first years of Islam the Bait al-Mal, the house of treasure, stood like a raised pavilion in the centre of the courtyard of the great public mosques.* It was a perfect symbol of the openness and public accountability of early Islamic society.

An alternative southern camp of Arab Muslims would also emerge at Basra. For along with the euphoria of the early victories came a great deal of confusion. Irregular tribes of Bedouin Arabs who were quite indifferent to Islam but passionate about booty continued raiding the farmland of Iraq. In other cases small armies of genuinely orthodox Muslim Arabs launched their own conquests, impatient at the delays inevitably caused by the Medina-based authority of the Caliph. Because the centre of Mesopotamia was occupied, warfare rippled out into the northern uplands and the southern marshlands. Basra was well suited as a base for the conquest of the latter as well as for raids along the Persian coast. It first emerged as a distinctively alternative centre of Islam but soon enough was included within the authority of Omar, even though its rivalry with Kufa remained vividly alive. Basra would prosper from war but also from its good trading connections with the Persian Gulf and the Indian Ocean, which helped to maintain its complex heterogeneous character. In the history of early Islam it would emerge as the fifth city of political and spiritual importance, alongside Medina, Mecca, Damascus and Kufa.

There would be another great urban centre founded in this period which would have a decisive role in the politics of early

---

* As it still does in the Umayyad Great Mosque of Damascus.

Islam. Fustat (from out of which modern Cairo would grow) is the sixth city of the Caliphs. Having witnessed the conquest of the Byzantine Near East, then of Persian Iraq, we must next turn our attention to the west and the Arab conquest of Egypt, returning once again to those dazzling first years of achievement all packed between 636 and 645.

In 636 the Byzantine governor of Egypt had sued with Caliph Omar for a three-year truce, in desperation at the fate of neighbouring Palestine and Syria, which had fallen to Arab rule after the battle of Yarmuk. He paid a rich tribute for this peace but at the time it must have seemed well worth the price, for he no doubt hoped that the Muslim Arab armies might yet dissolve into a tribal civil war or meet defeat at the hands of the Persians. Neither of those things happened, though the Byzantine counter-attack of 638 and the plague and famine of 639 were testing times for the Muslims. In 640 the bought time of the three-year truce was up. Omar gave the go-ahead for an exploratory raid against Egypt from the Muslim garrison in Palestine but then changed his mind in favour of a concerted attack on the northern frontier. He gave instructions for the advance of two separate Muslim armies against Byzantine Anatolia. One Arab army was to take the coastal province of Cilicia (south-eastern Turkey), the other was to invade the mountains of Armenia (north-eastern Turkey). The invasion of Egypt was no longer on the official agenda, though clearly there was now a slight muddle about Omar's precise intentions over the intended raid. Amr ibn al-As, in command of the Muslim army in Palestine, was determined to press forward with an attack. Amr feared that he was increasingly being passed over, in favour of the ever more popular commander in northern Syria, Muawiya. Amr also worried that Omar's disapproval of Khalid might extend to himself, for they were both late converts to Islam from within the traditional pagan leadership of Mecca. There was something irredeemably potent and pagan about Amr, who had the physique and charisma of an Achilles or an Alcibiades with a mysterious, exotic ancestry to match. Amr's mother had been a famously attractive girl of the Anaza Bedouin who had been enslaved and then bought for a fabulous price at the Ukaz fair by a leading merchant of the Quraysh. She had been set up as an expensive concubine with her own quarters, eventually gaining her freedom, though at the time that she conceived Amr it was rumoured that she was the lover of half a dozen of the leading noblemen of Mecca.

So Amr, before he could receive orders categorically forbidding him to advance into Egypt, rode west at the head of 3000 Bedouin warriors, the majority from the Akk tribe of the southern Hijaz. Even considering the previous string of Muslim victories it appears a mystery how this tiny force could have planned to seize control of the great land of Egypt with a population of millions and a standing garrison of 25,000. The capital of Egypt was the well-guarded city of Alexandria, sitting safe behind its walls and moats but also warded by inland lakes, the sea and a resident naval squadron. Through its fleet and three harbours Alexandria could freely communicate with the rest of the empire. It was also a passionately Christian land, the place that had co-invented monasticism.

The fall of Egypt is often depicted as some early version of the domino theory that US strategists concocted for Indo-China. First Syria and Palestine fell, then of course it was Egypt's turn. This is how a Westerner might think about Egypt's vulnerability from the Arabian desert. Not so Egypt. The ancient kingdom of the Nile knew all that it ever needed to know about Bedouins and desert raids. Indeed they had been one of the principal facts of Egyptian military life for thousands upon thousands of years.

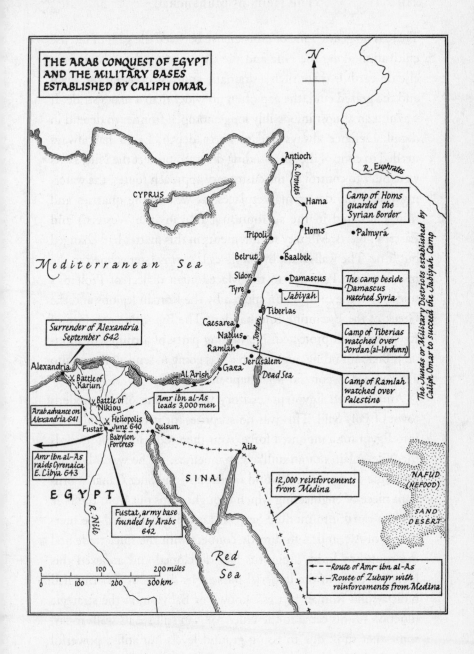

THE ARAB CONQUEST OF EGYPT
AND THE MILITARY BASES
ESTABLISHED BY CALIPH OMAR

N

Antioch

R. Orontes

CYPRUS

Hama

Camp of Homs
guarded the
Syrian Border

Tripoli

Homs

Palmyra

Mediterranean Sea

Beirut

Baalbek

Sidon

Damascus

The camp beside
Damascus
watched Syria

Tyre

Jabiyah

Tiberias

Caesarea

R. Jordan

Camp of Tiberias
watched over
Jordan (al-Urdunn)

Surrender of Alexandria
September 642

Nablus

Ramlah

Alexandria

Al Arish

Gaza

Jerusalem

Dead Sea

Camp of Ramlah
watched over
Palestine

X Battle of
Kariun

X Battle of
Nikiou

Amr ibn al-As
leads 3,000 men

Arab advance on
Alexandria 641

X Heliopolis
June 640

Fustat

Qulsum

Amr ibn al-As
raids Cyrenaica
E. Libya 643

Babylon
Fortress

Aila

12,000 reinforcements
from Medina

E G Y P T

R. Nile

S I N A I

NAFUD
(NEFOOD)

SAND
DESERT

Fustat, army base
founded by Arabs
642

Red
Sea

The Junds or Military Districts established by
Caliph Omar to succeed the Jabiyah Camp

0   100   200 miles
0   100   200   300 km

- - - Route of Amr ibn al-As
+ - + Route of Zubayr with
reinforcements from Medina

There is no gentle zone of transference between the gash of intense cultivation along the Nile and the surrounding desert. Nowhere else on earth is there such a dramatic contrast between the sown and the grazed land, the gap often no wider than a man's stride. It was also an almost impossibly long and open frontier to defend in detail. Defence always had to be in depth. Egypt has always needed to control the surrounding desert to protect the Nile. Forts were built to control all the customary approach routes, the watering holes, the desert marketplaces, as well as the quarries and mines situated in the surrounding Libyan (the Western) and Eastern deserts. Military requirements in this matter had changed but little. The walls built by Rameses II's army later echoed to the march of the Persians, to the Macedonian dialect of Ptolemy's soldiers, to the camp Latin spoken by the Roman legions and the Greek of the Byzantine commanders. The Byzantine province of Egypt was well protected. No raiding party of a couple of thousand Bedouin riding out of Arabia was going to send all Egypt into a frightened swoon. So what happened?

Amr entered Egyptian territory near the site of the modern town of Port Said. This was no surprise, for it was the only way into Egypt for a mounted force. Amr then rode due west towards the Nile. Again not an unlikely manoeuvre, for he was following the route of the ancient world's version of the Suez Canal, a brilliant piece of engineering which brought ships out from the Nile along a canal into the Red Sea. This canal had allowed the merchants of Alexandria to directly connect with the spice trade and the routes to India. Augustus had developed and annexed this lucrative trade to the imperial purse. His successor Tiberius had built a solid Roman fortress, known as Babylon, at the strategic junction of this canal to the Nile. You can still see its walls today, somewhat sunk due to rising ground levels but still a powerful enough architectural statement. The finely carved Roman gateway is easy to spot as one of the oldest Coptic churches of Old Cairo squats above it, like some ancient stork's nest of venerable stone. In Amr's day it towered 60 feet above the surrounding moat canal, a great 1000-feet-long rectangle formed from 8-foot-thick walls of mortared brick and stone.

At Babylon Amr received unexpected aid. Omar had acknowledged his subordinate's actions and dispatched a further draft of tribal warriors under the command of Zubayr which swelled the army to around 12,000 men. Amr swept past the secure walls of Babylon and struck out at the Byzantine field army which was advancing towards Heliopolis (now a smart western suburb of Cairo), which was less than a day's ride away. On 19 June 640 he led his army to victory at the battle of Heliopolis.

By September the Byzantine fortress of Babylon was isolated and blockaded by Amr's army. Though to say it was under siege would be an exaggeration, for this unsophisticated Arab Bedouin army had no siege weapons and no experience of the direct assault of fixed positions. None of this seems to have mattered, for that winter Cyrus, the Patriarch-governor of Egypt, began to negotiate a truce. In April 641 he handed over Babylon, which effectively surrendered all of central Egypt to the Arabs, in exchange for withdrawing the Byzantine garrison (including himself) safely back into Alexandria. Cyrus may have been playing for time in which to petition the Emperor Heraclius for reinforcements, but if this was so not even his contemporaries understood his tactics. Cyrus was summoned back to the capital of Constantinople to face a treason charge. However, events now escalated rapidly out of control in the court of the Caesars. The old warrior emperor Heraclius died on 11 February 641. His son, Constantine III, died shortly after his own accession, after which a young prince sponsored by Heraclius's second wife took the throne. They were both to be deposed by their dynastic rivals in the court, after which power rested with the regents of Heraclius's eleven-year-old grandson, Constans II, who was solemnly raised to the purple. In this confused environment, decisions about Egypt and Cyrus were simply not being made.

So in May Amr, having occupied the key stronghold to central Egypt, was free to ride north. When it came to dismantling the siege camp of the Arab army that had surrounded Babylon it was found that a dove had nested in Amr's tent and was sitting on a full hatch of eggs. Rather than disturb this bird which had sought his sanctuary, Amr left his tent standing.

His army crossed the Nile and rode through the imposing ruins of the ancient Pharaonic capital of Memphis, which was still a functioning city in this period. They were then free to ride up through the clean desert on the west side of the valley of the Nile, so avoiding the dangers of fighting in its densely farmed and populated delta. A week out of Babylon they broke through a force that opposed them at Tarrana before launching an assault on the fortress-city of Nikiou. The inhabitants, having resisted, were slaughtered, for such were the brutal customs of war, but this did not explain the harrowing of the Delta villages and the ruthless massacres of the poor Coptic farmers that followed the fall of Nikiou. It broke with the honourable reputation that elsewhere accompanied a Muslim Arab army which remained true to Abu Bakr's conditions for fighting a just war. Perhaps the unexpected immensity of Egypt and its teeming population of millions of farmers had made the small Bedouin Arab army feel isolated and nervous. State terrorism breeds from such fears.

As Amr advanced ever closer to Alexandria so the Byzantine resistance stiffened. The engagements of Kom Sharik and Damanhur in the Delta culminated in the ten-day running battle of Kariun before the Byzantine forces withdrew safely behind the walls of Alexandria that July. Amr's first precipitous assault was driven off with great dispatch as the ballistae mounted on the city walls found their targets. The Arabs were forced to withdraw out of range and make a fortified camp to the south-east of the city. From this camp the Arabs were able to harass the suburbs and keep control over the recently conquered Delta villages while Amr took the bulk of his army on a rapid ride south before the annual Nile flood swept across the land. When they reached their old campsite outside Babylon, Amr's tent still stood – though by now the dove had safely hatched her brood of chicks. Using this as a central marker, the Arab army once again spread its black tents.

Back in Alexandria the Patriarch Cyrus had returned. He had not only survived a charge of treason, and the murderous court politics of Constantinople, but also managed to get himself reinstated as viceroy. In a scene of the most bizarre irony, Cyrus then summoned the population of Alexandria to a morale-boosting sermon held in the city's enormous Caesarum theatre. He must have made a poor keynote speaker.

Among his personal, moral, tactical and strategic failings he was also the most hated man in Egypt. Cyrus had first landed in Alexandria in 631. Quite exceptionally he had been made both Orthodox Patriarch and Imperial Viceroy – though he disdained the manners of these two high offices in favour of the habits of a secret policeman. He had been instructed by the Emperor to try to end the theological row that had existed between the indigenous Egyptian Coptic Christians and the Orthodox. Cyrus unleashed a ten-year persecution against the native Egyptian clergy and the Coptic monks (already long since dispossessed of their revenues, estates and cathedrals) and even tried to assassinate the heroic Coptic Patriarch. He operated through his staff of Greek-speaking clergy, Greek-speaking imperial officials and their soldiers. Having failed to hunt down the Patriarch Benjamin,

Cyrus's thugs took it out on his brother Menas, who was kidnapped and tortured in an attempt to force him to publicly accept the official policy. This Menas would never do, but having so disfigured, burnt and maimed him by their investigations they began to feel ashamed of their work. So they took him out for one last attempt at 'reasoning', tied up in a weighted sack on a small boat. The martyrdom of St Menas is still honoured throughout Egypt.

So it was this very same Cyrus who now exhorted the population of Alexandria to resist Amr – which in his absence they had done with some success. A month later Cyrus began secret negotiations with Amr. He signed an accord on 8 November 641 which created a year of truce after which he planned to surrender the entire country and the city of Alexandria to the Arabs. As he patiently explained to his shocked officers, 'The Arabs are irresistible and God has willed to give the land of Egypt to them.' His actions are hard to fathom, though there is a traditional Arabic account that explains how greatly affected Cyrus was by the report of one of his envoys who had spent a couple of days in the Muslim camp during one of the negotiations. He had told his master, 'The Muslims are a people who love death more than we love life. They love humility better than pride. Greed is unknown to them. They do not think it is degrading to sit on the ground. They eat without sitting at a table. Their commander is just one of them. There is no special mark about him. The Muslims know no distinction between the high and the low or the master and the servant. When the time for prayer comes, they all wash and stand shoulder to shoulder, in all humility before the Lord.' To which tradition has it that Cyrus replied, 'Such a people will overcome any power, we had better make peace with them.'

Amr, true to his word, waited twelve months before he rode through Alexandria's gate of the sun on a white horse. Behind him rode 6000 horsemen. That morning in the name of the

Caliph, Amr solemnly took hold of the keys of the city founded by
Alexander and embellished by Cleopatra. In Medina, the Caliph
Omar greeted the messenger from Alexandria who brought the
news with a meal of dates and milk. As they sat down together
Omar read Amr's letter: 'I have taken a city of which I can only say
that it contains 4000 palaces, 4000 baths, 400 theatres, 1200
greengrocers and 40,000 Jews.'

The two great monuments, the Pharos lighthouse tower and
the mausoleum of Alexander, still dominated this city of a million
souls. The canopus, the great central avenue, stretched between
the great east and west gates: of the sun (Bab Shems) and of the
moon (Bab el Qamar). Henceforth the dignified canopus thor-
oughfare would be shaded from the sun by banners of green silk.
One early Muslim pilgrim goes so far as to claim (almost blas-
phemously) that 'I have made the Pilgrimage to Mecca sixty
times, but if Allah had suffered me to stay a month at
Alexandria . . . that month would be dearer to me.' To the great
standing marble monuments of the marble past the Muslims
would soon add the Mosque of the 1000 Columns, the Mosque
of Mercy and the Mosque of Daniel. Iskender (Muslim
Alexander) and the Pharos tower were both enthusiastically
adopted into the new Islamic culture and soon bred a whole sub-
stratum of additional tales. The ruin of the teeming city of
Alexandria is often blamed on the Arab conquest. An even greater
number bewail the burning down of its library (the greatest treasure of the Mediterranean world) which is still commonly blamed
on the Arabs. This had already been perpetrated by Christian
fundamentalists some 250 years before Amr rode unopposed
through the city gates. In 391 a rabble of cowled monks urged on
by Theophilus, the Patriarch of Alexandria, had sacked the Temple
of Serapis and made bonfires of the books of pagan learning that
were stored in the cloistered courtyards around the temple. A

monastery was raised over the smouldering ashes of antique learning and a decade later they progressed from books to blood,
lynching Hypatia, a middle-aged professor of mathematics who
was then editing her way through her father's philosophical work.
However, a propaganda story that the Arabs burned the library
has stuck, for even the scholar of Alexandria lore E. M. Forster
recalls this erroneous tale. Other commentators continue to quote
a fraudulent medieval account in which Omar is supposed to
have said of books, 'If they are in agreement with the Koran they
are unnecessary, and if they do not agree with it they are dangerous, so that in either case they should be destroyed.'

Earthquakes would progressively shatter another of Alexandria's
monuments, listed among the eight wonders of the world – the
monolithic Pharos lighthouse tower. From an island this rose on a
vast square foundation plinth and then up to an octagonal tower
which was capped by a round tower. The original circular lantern
fell in 700; the octagonal tower was thrown down in 1100, bringing down with it the Arab restoration work of 880 and 980. An
even greater quake in the fourteenth century left only the square
foundations standing, sweeping away the mosque that had been
lovingly included into the structure. The poetic fusion of a light to
guide the seaman and the light of true faith provided by a mosque
greatly pleased early Muslim travellers. Al-Derawi wrote how 'Its
lofty platform guides the voyager by night, guides him with its
light when the darkness of evening falls. Thither have I borne a
garment of perfect pleasure among my friends, a garment adorned
with the memory of my beloved companions. On its height a
dome enshadowed me, thence I saw my friends like stars. I
thought that the sea below me was a cloud, and that I had set up
my tent in the midst of the heavens.'

Amr must have been aware of the dangerous distractions that
the city presented to his troops, while the irrigated delta is not an

ideal place to stable the thousands of Arabian pure-bred horses and camels that the army required. The fodder is too rich and in the season of the flood, desert-bred camels and horses were susceptible to foot rot. Omar had also at the Jabiyah conference of 640 clearly stated the terms by which the armies of the faithful should occupy the conquered provinces. Amr decided to establish the new Muslim centre for Egypt in his favourite old campsite outside the Roman fortress of Babylon. His dove-favoured old campaign tent was to be the marker for the direction of prayer in a new mosque, laid out as a rectangle of 57 by 95 feet. Reused classical and Hellenistic columns would in due course be hewn out of the surrounding ruins to support a roof made of split palm trunks overlaid with branches. Dappled light trickled into the prayer hall and through the six doors that were cut through each of the side walls. Though now rebuilt dozens of times, this mosque still stands. The city that would emerge around it was to be known as Fustat, next door to which the various medieval and modern cities of Cairo would grow.

Omar refused Amr's request to be allowed to add a *minbar* (a preaching platform) to this new mosque at Fustat. Instead, having already heard rumours about the great wealth that attached itself to his commander in Egypt, he sent out his confidential agent to assess the situation on the spot. As Omar wrote in his blunt style, 'I have had enough experience of dishonest officials and my suspicion has been aroused against you, and I have sent Muhammad ibn Maslama to divide with you whatever you possess.'

Despite the surrender of Alexandria many of the smaller towns in the Delta obstinately refused to submit, so the Arab army spent all of the campaigning season in 642 in the wearisome subjugation of isolated Egyptian citadels. Just a year later, in 643, Amr was on the offensive once again. He rode west, initiating the drawn-out hundred-year Arab conquest of North Africa by capturing such fabled Libyan cities as mountain-top Cyrene, wall-guarded Apollonia with its wide harbour and the spreading mass of Ptolemais overlooking the sea. However, it was none of these still-cherished sites of Greek architecture but the Berber-populated highlands that caught his admiring eye. He wrote, 'If my own possessions were not in the Hijaz [central Arabia], I would live in Barca and never leave it, because I know no land more peaceful.' The sense of kinship with the Berbers was recognised in that Amr allowed them the privilege of assessing and delivering their own tribute, agreeing that no tax collector would be imposed on them. It also seems clear from his correspondence with the Caliph that there were a number of early converts. The province of eastern Libya (known as Cyrenaica or the Pentapolis) had for centuries been attached to the government of Egypt. So Amr could claim that he was merely 'rounding off' the subjugation of Egypt. This campaign had just whetted his appetite. The next year he launched an even more ambitious strike, riding right across the breadth of the Sirtic Desert to raid the rich olive groves of Tripolitania. Here Amr subjugated the walled cities of Tripoli, Sabratha and Leptis Magna, whose marble ruins from the golden age of Roman North Africa still dazzle our imagination.

Meanwhile one of Amr's deputies, his young cousin Oqba ibn Nafi, was commissioned to branch off from the main army and strike south, riding deep into the Sahara where no other conquerors, be they Carthaginian, Hellenistic, Roman or Byzantine, had yet dared to proceed. Oqba occupied such hitherto invulnerable settlements as the oasis of Zuwaya, which would later develop into such a boom town for the precious merchandise of the trans-Saharan trade that Cairo's principal gate would become known as the Bab Zuwaya. He even penetrated the hidden valleys of the old Garamantian kingdom in the Fezzan – though to do this he surely must have made local allies among the camel-riding Berber tribes of the Sahara such as the Luwata.

In 644 the victorious army columns of Amr and Oqba ibn Nafi were reunited at Barca and from there rode back into Egypt garlanded with spoils, slaves, a heroic store of adventure, tales of new lands and a legendary status. Part of the sermon Amr delivered that year to his soldiers in the Fustat mosque has survived: 'idleness and frivolity were the chief sources of sin and vice', but a softer note also crept into his address when he said, 'the Nile floods have fallen, the spring grazing is good for you. There is milk for the lambs and the kids. Go out with God's blessing and enjoy the land, its milk and its herds. And take good care of your neighbours the Copts, for the Messenger of God himself gave orders for us to do so.' On another occasion he evocatively described this land: 'At one season Egypt is a white pearl; then golden amber; then a green emerald; then an embroidery of colours.' In 645 a messenger from the Caliph waited for Amr, who was deprived of the governorship of Egypt and recalled to Medina.

Omar was determined to stay in absolute command of the Muslim state. Three years before sacking Amr, he had dismissed Saad from his position as commander of the army at Kufa and governor of Iraq. On that occasion Omar had been irritated to hear that Saad had set up a fence outside his house beside the central mosque in order to control the crowds that constantly interrupted his council meetings and badgered him with petitions and unsolicited advice. In his place Omar dispatched the aged but pious Ammar ibn Yasir, who had begun his life as a lowly slave in Mecca and had been among the first to recognise Muhammad as the Prophet of God. Abu Bakr had bought Ammar his freedom and he had remained one of the most modest of all the first Muslims, untouched by pride, envy and ambition. In the eyes of Caliph

Omar and all sincere Muslims he was a model believer. Over the thousands of squabbling Bedouin warriors packed into the garrison city of Kufa Ammar ibn Yasir proved to have absolutely no authority. Their knowledge of Islam was very slight and all too often buried under the pride of the victorious warrior and the booty and slaves they had won in the recent wars. Omar next turned to Mughira ibn Shuba, a tough, one-eyed, ruthless old warrior, and gave him the job. Rather than trust one man to do an impossible job, Omar also began to develop a coherent administration and to directly appoint a treasurer, a tax collector, a land surveyor and a judge to work beside the governor.

All these officials were to be housed in the central garrison camps: Kufa and Basra in Iraq, Fustat in Egypt, or the four that split out from the Jabiyah camp of Syria–Palestine – Damascus, Homs, Tiberias and Ramla. They became known as *misr*, from the Arabic for city, though collectively they are often referred to by the plural – *amsar*. Each of the *misr* was centred on a mosque where the soldiers could all pray together. In keeping with the example of the Prophet at Medina, the house of the Muslim commander was next door to this public prayer space. Later the treasury would be placed inside the mosque courtyard so that it could be watched over by the faithful. Later, as the conquest spread ever further west and east, this formulation would be consciously repeated with the foundation of such future *amsar* as Kairouan in central Tunisia, Sigilmassa on the frontiers of the Sahara in southern Morocco as well as such future capitals of Iraq as Baghdad, Raqqa and Samara.

As the annual tribute from the conquered provinces poured into the treasuries Omar was forced to work out how it should be spent. Even after the experience of the catastrophic year of plague and drought (when the need for a strategic reserve to cope with disasters could have been justified on practical grounds) he was emphatically against building up a reserve fund in the treasuries. As he answered the pragmatists among his advisers: 'We trust in God and his Prophet, they are our reserves.' At first the surplus was freely handed out to the serving warriors of the moment, or given to tribal chiefs to distribute to their men when they first arrived at Medina and offered themselves as volunteers for the wars. This remained adequate in those frantic first years of conquest, but after the decisive victories of Yarmuk and al-Qadisiya had placed a whole empire at his disposal, a more orderly and transparently fair distribution was increasingly required.

So Omar created an annual salary roll, the *divan*. It was graduated on the basis of priority of conversion and service within Islam and included the close relatives of the Prophet Muhammad as well as those who had performed exceptional military service. The table of precedence within the Muslim community that he created was to become known as *sabiqa*. Omar was determined that it remained totally unaffected by hereditary rank. So that a proud chieftain of ancient lineage from one of the great tribal confederations was likely to rank further down the scale than a humble ex-slave who had been an early convert to Islam. We still possess some of the annual salary figures. New Arab recruits into the army would be paid 200 dirhams a year, rising to 500 for experienced soldiers. Those who had fought at either Yarmuk or al-Qadisiya received 2000, while veterans from the Ridda Wars received 3000. For the 1500 early Muslims who had marched beside the Prophet on the pilgrimage of faith that had ended with the truce of Hudaibiya, the rate went up to 4000 while those survivors from the 300 or so who fought at the first battle of the wells of Badr received 5000. This put them on an equal rank with the cousins of the Prophet, though the most highly paid were the Mothers of the Faithful, the surviving wives of the Prophet, who received 10,000 except for Aisha, whose primacy was acknowledged by a salary of 12,000 dirhams a year.

Omar ruled this vast new empire from Medina. Though he proved himself quite ruthless with his army commanders, this was because he believed passionately in public honesty, the accessibility of rulers and the dignity of the people. Although undoubtedly severe, he was always approachable; and could be found either in the public mosque or shopping for his own household in the streets, markets and dusty public spaces of Medina. He was also an enthusiastic public speaker, addressing the faithful after prayers and in specially convened public meetings. Although this was far from a working democracy, for no votes were ever counted nor officials ever elected, the Caliph nevertheless invited free speech and encouraged criticism. Indeed once when the seated crowd tried to quieten down a known critic who had stood up to speak, Omar angrily insisted that he should be allowed to have his say, 'for he is free to give his opinion. If people do not give their opinions they are useless [here] and if we do not listen to them, we are useless.' Again and again he encouraged the believers to be actively involved, protesting that 'I am but an ordinary person like you. I can only request you to cooperate in the work which I have been entrusted with – by you.' In practice the most powerful objection was often the shortest, such as the lone cry by a veiled woman in the assembly of 'O Omar, fear God' which warned the Caliph that this believer feared that his new proposal on dowries was not in strict conformity with a well-known Koranic verse.

The women of Islam needed to be constantly on guard against the innovations of Omar, for he made many attempts to reduce their liberty from that which they had enjoyed under the Prophet. He halted the practice of temporary marriages on his own authority, tried to stop women from participating in the pilgrimage and tried to encourage women to pray at home and not attend the mosque – all against the very clear examples set by the Prophet. Omar's instinctive distrust of female sexuality extended to his own household. When a revered old Companion such as Abu Musa tried to give a small Persian carpet to one of Omar's wives (Atikah bint Zayd), Omar picked up the carpet and threw it back at Abu Musa's head as he castigated him for daring to make a present to one of his women. While Aisha had nothing but praise for Omar as a leader – 'He was a good manager and the only one of his kind, he was equal to every occasion' – one can still almost feel the bruises that he inflicted with his whip in her other, much quoted, character observation, 'When he spoke, he made one hear; when he walked, he was brisk and quick of step: and when he struck, he hurt.' Omar may have conscientiously travelled on the path set by the Prophet in many instances but he was the antithesis of his master in his treatment of women. He would provide textual ammunition and a clear example for later generations of clerical misogynists.

He was also instinctively conscious of the inevitable corruption of great wealth. After the fall of Ctesiphon, he was sent a fifth of all the spoils of the Persian court. His followers were astounded to find him in tears before the tottering piles of the world's most beautiful armour, golden regalia, jewel-emblazoned tunics and sumptuous silver tableware. He looked up towards their surprised faces and spoke: 'I weep because riches beget enmity and mutual bitterness.' On another famous occasion Omar, who had been personally cited in a court case, was infuriated on entering the court to find that the judge was treating him as a ruler (by standing up in his honour) rather than an ordinary citizen. Omar barked, 'That is your first unjust behaviour' before sitting down beside his legal opponent. It was probably difficult ever to get things exactly right with Omar, as he himself almost confesses in the prayer that he made when he first became Caliph, 'O God if I am strict, make me soft. If I am weak, give me strength.'

Omar certainly needed strength. For alongside the extraordinary changes caused by the conquest there was a constant need to adapt the Muslim society within central Arabia to fit the press of contemporary circumstances. Not all of his actions would have been immediately popular or understood. Every year Omar personally led the haj caravan from Medina to Mecca and watched the numbers of pilgrims grow year after year. He realised that the ritual space around the Kaaba had grown far too small and so he set about purchasing all the surrounding houses and merchant courtyards in the centre of Mecca, which were then summarily demolished to enlarge the space of the Haram. This holy space was then enclosed – for the first time – by a circuit wall pierced by gateways while the old Arabian cloth coverings that had been draped over the Kaaba were now replaced with Egyptian linen. Another innovation was the construction of a jail at Mecca, in a city that had never known such things. In Medina he likewise had to buy out all the immediate neighbours to the mosque in order to expand this central meeting place of all Arabia. Conditions in the *amsar* garrison citadels needed constant attention, especially as the Bedouin warriors were totally unused to being confined in any one place. It had been customary, since the days of the Prophet, to address the individual tribesmen through their clan chiefs and that was how the salaries were at first paid out. In armies formed from hundreds of different tribes on a distant frontier this was not always possible, so Omar created the middle rank of *Arif* to make for the easy distribution of pay to the soldiers. Bedouin families could migrate to the garrison towns to be near their kin, but if this was not possible, a warrior was permitted a leave of absence every four months.

Another far-reaching reform was Omar's creation of a distinct

Islamic calendar. This at first must have appeared very odd to the more ardent believers, who knew that Omar, like the Prophet Muhammad (and most of early Christianity), lived in an almost daily expectation that the end of the world was at hand. For such believers correct dating must have seemed totally irrelevant. But practical details needed to be settled. As Omar's *divan* roll of salaries grew in complexity, it became ever more important to establish the correct year of a Muslim warrior's conversion and work out his precedence in Islam. It was Omar's idea to take the migration to Medina in AD 622 as the start date (year 1 of the Islamic calendar), though theologically one might have thought he would have fixed upon Muhammad's first revelation as the starting date of the new era. There were good reasons. The migration of hundreds of individuals from Mecca to Medina (and the existence of a signed accord) was an event about which there could be no collective disagreement within the ranks of the Muslims. While for the proper sequence of events in Mecca there has never been a precise chronology. Not then, not now, even after 1400 years of obsessive scholarship. This confusion is also reflected in the memory of the first battles of the conquests. There is little real disagreement about their location but the exact dates or even the sequence for even such vitally important events as Yarmuk, al-Qadisiya and the conquest of Egypt flicker around a two-to-four-year margin of error. The sequence of twelve months, their names (with just one or two alterations) and the lunar basis of the Islamic calendar remained fixed on the pre-Islamic traditions of central Arabia that had been confirmed by the Prophet Muhammad.

Omar, while he delighted in the victory of Islam, was also aware of how prolonged military success could destroy the very soul of his master's religion. He was insistent that all his commanders make a full and formal invitation to their enemies to join Islam or submit to negotiated terms. There could be no just war without such a formal exchange. He was also against forcible proselytisation: no People of the Book should ever be forced to leave their faith from threat of violence, nor was there any need for empty-hearted missionaries. The superior attractions of Islam were to be demonstrated by the way of life of the believing Muslims and the sound of the Koran – or not at all. In the words of the Prophet, 'Will you dispute with us about God? When he is our Lord and he is your Lord! We have our words and you have your words but we are sincerely his.'

Later ages of Islam would look lovingly at his period of authority and would codify his achievements into the *awliat-i-Omar*, the forty-one initiatives of Omar, such as the foundation of the *amsar*, the *divan* salary roll, the dating of a new era and the other administrative improvements that we have already seen. For the Sunni majority within Islam these are like an additional law code of righteousness – though for the Shiites they can command no such reverence. Similarly the reported saying of the Prophet Muhammad 'If a prophet had to come after me, it would certainly have been Omar' is acknowledged to be true by the Sunni but not by the Shiites, who though they might now see him as an honourable man cannot but also see that he stood in the way of Ali.

What was especially astonishing about Omar was his personal integrity. He, almost alone, had been given the inner strength to disregard the importunities of his children, his wives, his cousins, his clan and his tribe. This one weakness has pulled down generation after generation after generation of Arab leaders, this complete inability to correct the faults of their own family, a weakness that if unchecked bleeds the most astute statesman into an empty shell. You have only to look around the world of contemporary Islam to see how exceptional Omar was. Half of Islam is ruled by hereditary monarchies, while the other half, the revolutionary Socialist republics of thirty years ago (such as Libya, Egypt and Syria), are turning themselves into family-dominated regimes.

This integrity came at a high price. When Omar's own son Abu Shahmah was found drunk in public, it was not hushed up to be dealt with privately. Abu Shahmah received the full force of the law: eighty lashes. It killed him.

Omar despised the trappings of kingship and wealth. He was used to being stopped in the streets and asked for his judgement. Foreign visitors were always amazed to find that there was no procedure of gatekeepers, court chancellors, audience halls and bodyguards and to be told that 'There is no door between him and the people. You can speak to him every day in the streets and the mosque.' One morning he was hailed by Abu Lulu Firuz, a Christian slave of Persian origin who wished to protest at the treatment he was currently receiving from his master, even though his master was Omar's recently appointed governor of Kufa. Abu Lulu had been made a captive during the war in Iraq but had in effect been given complete freedom of action, providing he stayed in Medina and paid his master two dirhams a day. Slavery in the Arab world should not be likened to the lot of plantation slaves in the Americas, having much more in common with the modern concept of the prisoner of war. Omar enquired what were Abu Lulu's skills and on being told that he was a skilled carpenter and painter, replied that those, if properly applied, were easily sufficient to pay his dues to his master and yet live quite comfortably in Medina. Despite the satisfaction of having aired his grievances before the Caliph of Islam, Abu Lulu remained furious. In truth he had had his full share of misfortunes: enslaved as a child during a Byzantine invasion and then again in later life by the Muslim Arab army – while the sight of a file of dejected prisoners from his Persian home town of Nehewand had reawakened these memories and reduced him to tears.

The next morning Abu Lulu made certain that he was among the first to enter the mosque. When the Caliph bent down to perform his prayers, Abu Lulu sprang upon him – a ferocious bundle of maddened energy who managed to stab Omar's sixty-three-year-old body half a dozen times before he was dragged off by the other worshippers. Even then no one could get a firm grip on Abu Lulu, who slashed at the surrounding crowd before he drove his blade deep within himself.

Omar's six wounds were too deep to be dressed but the dying Caliph was relieved to be told that his attacker was not an aggrieved Muslim and this was the act of a depressed captive. He was delicately questioned about who should succeed him, but Omar was reluctant to answer, for, as he said, he had two contra-dictory examples before him: the Prophet of God made no such testament while Abu Bakr had. Later he confessed that if Abu Ubaydah had survived (the man whom Omar had made the supreme commander in Syria but who had died during the plague of 639), he would have asked him to take on the burden of office. He angrily dismissed a sycophantic follower who recommended that Omar's own son Abdullah would make a good Caliph. Eventually he recalled that the Prophet had spoken highly of six of his fol-lowers who would enter the kingdom of heaven. He ordered that this group should meet after his death and agree on a successor from among themselves within three days. He advised his succes-sor to fear God and uphold the rights of the first Muslims, both those who had emigrated from Mecca and those from Medina oasis, that a Caliph should take from the rich and give to the poor, should treat the non-Muslims in the empire well and always keep his word.

Then he turned to his son Abdullah and requested that he be allowed to be buried beside the Prophet in Aisha's floor – which had survived in an isolated hut in the newly expanded mosque.

Aisha replied that she had reserved this spot for herself but 'I prefer Omar to Aisha.' When the end came, he asked his son Abdullah to help bend his exhausted frame in the attitude of prayer and with his last breath whispered, 'O God, cover me with your forgiveness.'

It is a commonly held belief within Islam that the dead on their first night in the grave are examined by the two recording angels and that no one escapes some censure and chastisement.

Omar had had a rich and rewarding life. He had been born some twelve years after Muhammad in 583. The Prophet often used to refer to him by his patronymic, 'the son of Khattab'; those in a less friendly mood would hiss out 'son of Khatamah [his mother]'. Omar's father was of the Adi clan of the Quraysh, who were renowned for their skill as negotiators, especially in setting up deals with the Bedouin tribes for the safe passage of the caravans across the desert. Omar had nothing of the diplomat about him. He was renowned in pagan Mecca as a champion wrestler and an orator. As a young man he became a violent opponent of Islam. At one point he was so incensed at the divisions that it was making within Meccan society that he determined to kill Muhammad himself. Filled with thoughts of noble self-sacrifice he made public his intentions, which were ridiculed by a wit in the street who suggested that first of all he had better make sure of his own household. When Omar arrived at his home he overheard his sister and brother-in-law quietly reciting the Koran. He entered the house in such a temper that he beat up his brother-in-law Said and even set upon his sister. When his fury had spent itself, he looked about himself in shame at his sister's disfigured face. She looked him in the eye and declared, 'Yes, we have become Muslims, do what you will.' He then sat down and asked to see for himself what noise they had been chanting. His sister made certain that Omar's hands were clean before offering him a precious sheet of parchment. Omar read aloud a verse and then found himself struck silent by its magic, before hurrying out to make his profession of faith to Muhammad. Omar never did anything by halves and soon this new convert was organising a public confession of faith to the tribal chiefs and then paired up with the Prophet's strongman, uncle Hamza, to guard the Muslims as they made a public demonstration of their prayer ritual. When it came time for the Muslims to move to Medina, Omar made the *hijira* – the migration – on his own terms. Not for him the quiet departure after dusk or camouflaged as a business trip, but fully armed, by day, and with a resounding challenge: 'If anyone wants to stop me, let me meet him across the valley. His mother shall then only have to weep for him.'

Omar left his second and third wives and a full brood of children (including five boys) behind him in pagan Mecca, though he would not formally divorce them until the Muslims had become a force to be reckoned with in 628. For this half of his family he would maintain only a distant scorn, though perhaps a great hurt had been buried beneath his fierce pride. His first wife, Zaynab, had died before the migration, and so it was only her three children who would accompany Omar to Medina. Omar was a strict parent to these three: Abdullah, Abdurrahman and of course Hafsah. They were the only members of his family that he cared about and they all appear as minor figures in the history of early Islam. They were also an exceptionally literate family, for not only is Omar listed among the seventeen early believers who could read and write but he encouraged his daughter Hafsah in this rare skill. Omar's sternness of character seems to have driven away both his two Muslim wives. Umm Hakim and Jamila bint Asim both left his household after they had given birth to a child. If the Prophet's famous saying 'If you would know a man's character look to the health of his wives' is to be applied to Omar, the great Caliph would not rate highly. However, towards the end of his life he requested from Ali the hand of his daughter, Umm Kulthum. Ali was very reluctant to allow his young daughter to pass into Omar's strictly controlled household but by this stage in his life (after the great victories of Yarmuk and al-Qadisiya) Omar had learnt some of the gentleness for which he had prayed. He was also the ruler of the entire Middle East, so that it was difficult for Ali to refuse Omar's formal request of a marriage alliance with the grand-daughter of the Prophet Muhammad. In their five years together, the young Umm Kulthum would bear two children, Ruqayyah and Zayd, so that the bloodline of the Prophet and the second Caliph mingled just as their bodies now lay side by side.

8

Uthman: Third Caliph of Islam

The close Companions of the Prophet carried the shrouded corpse of Omar to his place of burial. The earth floor in Aisha's old bedroom hut was once again dug up and they buried Omar close beside his master and Abu Bakr. His head, facing Mecca, was placed beside the shoulder of the Prophet. Then the surviving intimate disciples of Muhammad gathered together in solemn conclave. They had to choose from among them both a new leader to preside over the growing empire of the Arabs and the man who would also lead them in everyday prayer at the mosque and on the annual pilgrimage to Mecca. It was a tightly knit group, all early converts from the Quraysh tribe who had together endured a decade of persecution in Mecca, a decade of war against Mecca and had just emerged from a decade of victorious conquests under Omar's leadership. With the hindsight of history and in an attempt to explain the later schisms within Islam, commentators would try to divide this group into factions based on kinship. This doesn't really work, for by 644 the interconnections between these half-dozen men – Ali, Zubayr, Saad, Uthman,

Talha, Abder-Rahman – had become too intimate and intricate. Ali, Zubayr and Saad were all cousins of the Prophet and Talha was a cousin of Abu Bakr's while the practice of multiple marriages made for a further double-woven intimacy. Look for instance at the blood ties associated with the children of Asma. After the death of her first husband, Jafar (Ali's older brother), she then married Abu Bakr with whom she had a child, and then after the death of the first Caliph she passed into the household of Ali. Or consider the marital career of one of Uthman's sisters: first she married the Prophet's adopted son Zayd, then Zubayr, then Abder-Rahman before moving on to the conqueror of Egypt, Amr. Among the many other matrimonial links within this group, there was the marriage of Aisha's half-sister Asma to Zubayr, while Ali had become the father-in-law of Omar just as Omar had been the father-in-law of Muhammad . . . and so the intimate shuttle of marital alliances linked all the key figures of early Islam together.

In terms of military prestige within this group of six, Saad had won great fame from his victory of al-Qadisiya over the Persians, though Zubayr had shown much personal heroism in the recent conquest of Egypt, while Ali had been the most conspicuous individual warrior during the lifetime of the Prophet.

They had also all been called upon at various times to give advice to the Caliph and some had served as his appointed judges, governors and generals. When Omar had left Medina to visit Jerusalem and the army in Syria he had selected Ali to be his deputy – like the Prophet before him. In the intersection of all their talents, Ali was the natural and obvious successor. But perhaps there was still an underlying concern that if Ali became Caliph the office might henceforth become hereditary and pass down through Ali's children, the only male descendants of the Prophet Muhammad. As the debate among the electors continued over the three days it was clear that the choice was between Ali and Uthman, but none had a clear majority among the five (for the sixth elector, Talha, was on a mission that had taken him outside Medina and so he missed all of the electoral meetings). Ali was still young enough to wait for another chance to lead, unlike Uthman, who, aged seventy, stood at the apex of the traditional Arabic respect for a grey-bearded elder. The electors must also have borne in mind that Ali was considered to be the most ethically 'strict' of the candidates and that greater liberality was desired after ten years of Omar's puritanical rule. In a boisterous morning meeting held in the mosque on the third day, Abder-Rahman (who had emerged as a chairman by renouncing his own candidacy) put a single question to the two candidates: 'Do you pledge yourself to abide by the Covenant of God, to act according to God's word, to the practice of the Prophet and to the precedent set by his two successors?' The sting in the tail was in the artful addition of the last clause, which unexpectedly raised the political decisions of the first two Caliphs alongside the sacred texts. Ali replied with heartfelt sincerity and a humane diffidence, 'I hope that I should do so. I would act for the best, according to my knowledge and capability.' Uthman when questioned replied simply, 'Yes, I do.' Whereupon Abder-Rahman declared that Uthman's answer had been most satisfactory and asked him to 'Stretch forth your hand so that I may make the oath of allegiance to you.'

You don't have to be a Shiite partisan to feel a whiff of manipulation about these last-minute proceedings, which once again managed to deny Ali the leadership. However, Ali's personal behaviour was again impeccable and far from leading an opposition group or contesting the result, he was among the first to offer his hands in allegiance to Uthman. Ali would have remembered full well the Prophet's enormous regard for Uthman, whom he considered to have the countenance of an Abraham.

Uthman, after the ritual acknowledgement of all the faithful in the mosque that day, made a short address from the pulpit promising that his role was to follow what had already been laid down and to faithfully follow the Koran and the Sunna – the path of the Prophet. Then the emotion of the moment stifled him, so that he merely added, 'O people, it is not easy to manage a new horse. If God willing I live, there will be other occasions to talk to you. I cannot talk any more now but then you all know that I have never been good at making public speeches.' There must have been affectionate smiles among the congregation that day, as the venerable Uthman grew tongue-tied before the faithful. It was so refreshingly different from Omar, whose brilliance as an orator had never been questioned but who was also seldom seen without his whip.

Uthman had always remained slightly apart from the other close Companions of the Prophet. This had been even more pronounced when as a young man he stood out as an elegant, literate and cultivated merchant-prince among a community largely composed of passionate, pious paupers. This had even been acknowledged by the Prophet: Aisha vividly recalled the time when her husband had been reclining at his ease in her hut while he freely talked to Abu Bakr and Omar but gathered his clothes together neatly and sat up in a formal mood when the arrival of Uthman was announced. Later she asked Muhammad why he behaved differently to Uthman than to her father and Omar, to which the Prophet replied that 'Uthman is modest and shy and if I had been informal with him, he would not have said what he had come here to say.'

Uthman, for all his modesty, had always been good-looking. When he had first converted to Islam he had been a handsome broad-shouldered man of medium height, perhaps a bit fleshy in the thighs, but the pale golden skin of his face had been framed by a magnificent beard while the locks that cascaded down below his ears were much remarked upon: indeed it had been said of him that you were never likely to 'see a man of more beautiful face'. However, when you came up close to Uthman you would notice that his cheeks had been lightly scarred by smallpox caught as a child. When he smiled he was literally 'golden-mouthed', for his teeth had been bound by a jeweller-dentist with fine wires of gold.

Uthman was born into the Abd Shams, Mecca's most powerful clan, which customarily provided the Quraysh with its leadership. He was also one of the tiny minority of Meccans who had been well enough educated to be fully literate. What was even more important to his fellow Meccans was that he was also outstandingly able as a businessman and negotiator. For although he had, as an only son, inherited great wealth when aged twenty, this was but the seed from which he traded his way to even greater fortune. Nor was he just a cunning, sedentary banker. Uthman had been fully initiated into the hardships and dangers of the caravan routes, which as a young boy he had criss-crossed in the company of his father, Affan. Uthman's childhood was packed full of memories of buying cheap in the Yemen, selling well in Syria, but above all of the virtues of patience – whether in the marketplace or at the customs post – and of assessing a man by his actions rather than his words.

But even for such a fledgling merchant-prince of Mecca there had been times when decorum and dignity were not enough; such as the time when Uthman's father had been entrusted with the property of a colleague who had died on the journey. The caravan was intercepted by a war band of Bedouin who produced some spurious reason why they were the true heirs to this inheritance. Uthman's father refused to hand over so much as a bent copper coin – but such a principled stand meant that the caravan had to fight its way through the desert with much loss of life. The

Quraysh were appalled at such an insult and had immediately marshalled an army for a revenge assault on the Bedouin, though in the end the whole affair had been closed by the payment of blood money. But by and large, such adventures had been the spice which had animated an otherwise comfortable life.

Uthman was probably about six years younger than the Prophet, though his childhood shared none of Muhammad's intense experience of loss and austerity. Uthman was born in Taif not in Mecca, for his mother, Urwa (like her cousin-husband, from the clan of Abd Shams) preferred to escape from the summer heat and spend the dog days among the shaded gardens and palm orchards that they owned in that agreeable walled city – which in this period also acted as the summer hill station for the very wealthy among the Quraysh.

After the premature death of Uthman's father, she went on to marry Uqba, producing a second family of half-siblings and step-brothers whom Uthman would always cherish. Uthman was always a desirable catch in the marriage market. Not for him Muhammad's experience of an agonised contemplation of how many years it would take to accumulate a bride price or the loving looks at a girlfriend doomed to be offered to another better-connected hand. Uthman had married young and well, taking two aristocratic Meccan girls into his house, who would give birth to at least eight children that we know about. His wife Asma was the daughter of the Makhzum clan chief, while the quick arrival of a first-born boy allowed Uthman that title treasured by all Arab males, so that he could also be respectfully addressed as Abu Amr, the father of Amr.

Given Uthman's background, his conversion is all the more surprising. In terms of the things of this world, he had nothing to gain but everything to lose. But Uthman was in that first band of half a dozen converts who came to Islam when it yet remained a private matter restricted to the immediate household of Muhammad. In the matter of his conversion, Uthman had an extraordinarily direct experience that was dependent on neither the magical sound of the Koran nor the beguiling life example of the Prophet. It came to him one night when he was weeks out from Mecca, at a halt between the Zarqa and Maan stops on the Syrian caravan trail. Lying half-asleep on a bed of sand, he gazed up into the desert night with its breathtaking display of stars, bright constellations and the milky streak of the galaxy twisting into the black horizon like a roadway into heaven. Such a sight can be an awesome revelation of infinite space to those who have grown up in northern regions and slept shielded from eternity by roofs and clouds – but it can have had no such force for the desert-born Uthman – although he remembered thinking that even the stars must have a master before he dropped off to sleep. He was woken by a voice crying out in the stillness of the desert night, 'Sleepers awake, for Ahmad has come forth in Mecca.' Uthman knew not what to make of this until his caravan was joined by some other traders coming out of Syria, who included Talha, a cousin of Abu Bakr. When they finally reached Mecca, they both went to Abu Bakr, who at once took them to meet the Prophet, to whom they offered their profession of faith.

Later, when the hatred of the Meccans had turned against the Prophet and his family, the two Quraysh men who had been engaged to marry Muhammad's two daughters (Kulthum and Ruqayyah) publicly divorced their brides. This deliberate and damaging social insult was neatly reversed when Uthman, one of the darlings of Meccan society, took the rejected Ruqayyah's hand in marriage. In tribal Arabia to be a son-in-law was always the more honourable link than that made by a father-in-law giving away his daughter. At the wedding celebration the guests sang of this golden couple,

The sweetest couple seen by man
Is Ruqayyah and Uthman.

They would escape the persecution of Muslims in Mecca by lead-ing the vanguard, of eleven men and four women, who migrated to the safety of the Christian empire of Abyssinia. It is also possi-ble that Uthman was under instructions from the Prophet to continue as a merchant, for the wealth of the Muslim community in Mecca was rapidly being wasted because of the trade embargo that had been placed on them. In the security of the Abyssinian empire of Axsum, Uthman's wife gave birth to Abdullah, though this cheerful two-year-old boy would die from the wounds he received when he was pecked in the face by a cockerel. This grim domestic tragedy permanently affected Ruqayyah, who was never afterwards able to conceive another child. Around this period Uthman would take another woman to wife: the aristocratic Ramla, for whom he paid a dowry of 40,000 dirhams.

When Uthman heard that his father-in-law was now safely established and honoured in the oasis of Medina, he moved his household back to Arabia. At first they lodged with Aws, brother of the famous poet Hassan ibn Thabit, before Uthman acquired his own house. The Meccans were often susceptible to the fevers of well-watered agricultural lands at the oasis of Medina, and Ruqqayah was no exception. She was so ill that Muhammad gave Uthman permission to stay at home and nurse his wife while the rest of the Muslims set off for the wells of Badr. It was said that as the hurrahs of victory from the battle of Badr were being shouted to the sky, the moans of Ruqayyah at last released her spirit from her fever-tortured body. When the Prophet returned to his house at Medina one of his first tasks was to try to comfort Fatimah, who had been weeping over her sister's cold body. Muhammad drew the bent figure of his daughter up and carefully dried her tears with the hem of his shirt. At the cemetery, at the end of the prayers over the grave, he exclaimed, 'Praise be to God, burying a daughter is a heartbreaking act.'

The Prophet was conscious that Uthman had been an exceptionally considerate husband – and remained a useful asset to the small community. Muhammad betrothed his third-born daughter, Umm Kulthum, upon the son of Affan 'for the same dower and the same way of living'. As Umm Ayman – that almost indestructible presiding female genius within Muhammad's life* – recalled, 'He told me to beautify her and to lead her to her husband while beating on the tambourine.' On the third night of her marriage, Muhammad visited his daughter and asked her, 'How do you find your husband?' 'The best of all husbands,' she replied. Later Muhammad would remark that 'I married him to my two daughters and they now call him Dhun al-Nurayn [the owner of two lights].' To the penniless Meccan refugees in Medina, Uthman proved himself a continuous source of relief. He dug a well to provide them with free access to clean water, bought supplies for the oasis in a time of famine, sent fourteen camels laden with food to a military expedition that had run out of supplies, acquired the property next door to the Prophet's house so that the courtyard mosque could be expanded when the flood of new believers could no longer be received, and bought a shop that sold dates in the oasis and then set it up as a charity to feed Muslims. When the men of the Jewish Beni Qaynuqa clan were all executed and their women enslaved (in 627, after corresponding with the enemy during the siege of Medina), Uthman moved quickly to resolve the situation. He bought all the captive women, depositing his purchase price in the communal treasury. He was then in a position to

[handwritten margin note: Beni qaynuqa were exiled. Beni qarayzah were executed 700 men cf p 45]

---

* She had started out as his father's Abyssinian slave girl Barakah before marrying Muhammad's adopted son Zayd and producing his heir Usama.

be able to care for all the grieving widows and their children and joyfully freed those who converted to Islam but remained enough of a businessman to cover some of his costs with the sale of the rest.

Uthman was a living example of the best of Islam, endlessly compassionate and generous, and yet managing to combine business and administrative efficiency with charity, prayer, scholarship and a fulfilling and loving family life. However, there was an Achilles heel that makes his 'election' as Caliph in the great era of Muslim conquest a surprising choice. Humane, cultured, clever and devout he might have been, but he could never be mistaken for a heroic warlord – a Khalid, an Amr or an ibn Harith – who had led his warriors from the front and won their respect and loyalty. Instead he had avoided front-line action in practically all the early battles of Islam, and it was widely known that he had run away at the battle of Uhud, though he was formally forgiven by the Prophet soon afterwards.

Uthman must have known that he would never be loved by the hardened soldiers of Islam. However, he had his own agenda for winning the respect and consideration of his new subjects: mercy, generosity and an efficient administration. And for all his lack of military experience, he would prove himself adroit enough in the handling of the grand strategy of the Muslim Empire of the Arabs. He began with a popular gesture, adding a hundred dirhams to the annual stipends. At the same time he began to cautiously increase the central government control over the affairs of the garrison cities. He launched a diligent inspection of accounts, started to overhaul the *divan* salary rolls and asked for the accounts and the provincial surpluses to be forwarded to the treasury at Medina. He also continued Omar's practice of gradually splitting up the immense authority exercised by the provincial governors, who also doubled as the army commanders. He did this by creating a new breed of financial administrators who would look exclusively at the tax revenue. He had perforce to allow the existing clerks, mostly inherited from the Byzantine and Sassanian empires, to continue their work but whenever the skilled manpower allowed he began the long and slow process of converting the accounts into Arabic and making use of Arabic numerals.

The *zakat*, the charitable tithe paid by all Muslims, was reformed so that it included slaves and horses and was assessed at a flat 2½ per cent of capital value. Although it was enforceable, it was to be self-assessed by the individual Muslim but collected by the designated authorities. In terms of revenue it was of little significance compared with the vast sums levied from the annual tithe on agricultural lands and the annual poll tax (*jizya*) from all the protected non-Muslim People of the Book within the empire. As was to be expected, Uthman had to cope with passive opposition from the existing governors, officials and provincial treasurers who saw their old authority being weakened. Uthman had the charm, ability and persistent dedication to see this dull administrative chore through. As the old first generation of warriors died off, it was vitally important to clean the lists, determine the rights of widows and reward new recruits. Within a few years, by both streamlining the *divan* and increasing provincial tax revenue, the Caliph was able to increase the annual stipends across the board by 25 per cent, allow war widows to inherit 10 per cent of their husbands' salary and award a token child welfare payment to each new Arab boy born in the garrison cities. The maintenance of this system, paying around 100,000 annual salaries in the month of Moharrum, is an astonishing tribute to the financial acumen of the Quraysh traders of Mecca.

To achieve this Uthman started to create a permanent secretariat, employing a brilliantly talented young cousin of his,

Marwan, to oversee the paperwork. It is clear that he also developed an efficient filing system that allowed him to quote from previous written orders of Omar when entering into correspondence. As Medina and Mecca grew ever larger he instituted the office of a salaried 'inspector of markets', which would remain one of the key positions in any Islamic city and which would grow into a virtual mayoralty. Once again he recruited this official from his pool of talented young cousins.

Uthman also pushed through an ambitious schedule of public works funded by his efficient management of the central treasury. Embankments were constructed to protect the spreading mass of houses in Medina from being swept away by the periodic floods that once a decade might transform the empty gravel beds of a wadi into a raging torrent. He also began the systematic extension of clean water for the vastly increased population, digging new wells in Medina and Mecca as well as overseeing the strengthening and deepening of the old water sources with quarried stone. Ever since, it has been one of the greatest acts of public munificence for an Islamic ruler to provide free, clean water for his people – often enough accompanied by a poetic couplet that makes a literary link with the waters of Mecca's Zamzam spring.

Uthman also established other patterns of regal behaviour, by purchasing land and constructing purpose-built markets whose rents were then endowed for the feeding of the poor. As the needs of state increased, with more and more secretaries required and more and more messengers employed, Uthman once again used the resources of the central treasury to buy up additional land so that the state-owned herds of fine horses and quick-footed camels could be conveniently pastured. Uthman was always generous in these dealings, exchanging fine estates elsewhere in the large empire so that he could be sure of having enough land near the chief government centres. Later, when these grazing grounds were sufficiently extensive, he ordered that they be formally enclosed and set aside from casual tribal grazings. This was followed by the construction of state stables and guest houses for the use of travellers, messengers and poor pilgrims. He also continued Omar's example of extending the great public spaces of Islam: the great mosque at Medina and the shrine-mosque at the centre of Mecca. This was not achieved without opposition, for some citizens refused to sell, but with the example of Omar before him Uthman resolutely pressed ahead. He had become used to finding out that even the most determined opposition had its price. In any case the storm of controversy was silenced when the first worshippers entered the new mosque that he had made for them in Medina, the rotten old palm trunks now replaced by handsome pillars of hewn stone. He also turned his acute and ever practical mind to the sea. Uthman had long been dissatisfied with the traditional old Meccan anchorage of Shuaba and so began to construct a new port at al-Jeddah (the site of the tomb of Eve), which has ever afterwards remained the doorway into Mecca and Medina from the Red Sea.

Alongside Uthman's accomplished handling of the machinery of state he began to relax Omar's austerity measures. Omar had insisted that no man should ever possess more than four houses (one for each of his wives) and that no house should exceed the very modest dimensions established by the Prophet Muhammad, which restricted new building work to one storey. Omar had also restricted the number of foreign slaves allowed in Medina, had forbade any of the Companions to leave the oasis (unless on pilgrimage) without his explicit permission, and most crucially of all, had forbidden the sale of any of the conquered or state lands to the people. Uthman gradually lifted all these restrictions.

Omar's desire to keep the Muslim Arabs as a poor, highly mobile army of faith was shattered, as was his wish to keep the

Companions a studiously apolitical group kept in honourable confinement under his watchful eye in Medina. Instead Uthman's liberalisation had the effect of creating a new aristocracy, as the wealth received by the leading Muslim Arabs as their legitimate annual salary (not to mention the portions they had been awarded from the war booty of the early conquests) was directed to the acquisition of landed estates, especially in the long-coveted borderlands of Syria and Iraq. Such leading Companions as Zubayr and Abder-Rahman emerged as the new grandees of the Muslim Empire. Zubayr possessed as many slaves as he had horses (and he had 1000 of these) and would have palatial houses in all the key cities of the empire: Damascus, Medina, Mecca, Kufa and Basra. Indeed the latter was so finely built that it was still being pointed out as a landmark to visitors to the city four hundred years later. Abder-Rahman would leave behind a similar princely estate with landed property valued at 400,000 dinars and 1000 head of camel and 10,000 of sheep. In Medina Uthman led the way by building himself a palatial residence, the 'Zawar' on the edge of the growing agglomeration centred on the great mosque. This was a model of its age, with its enclosed gardens, multi-storeyed apartments, gatehouse, elegantly stuccoed walls and marble columns. Here there was room for all of Uthman's wives and children to live together plus a more public space for secretaries to work in and kitchens that could feed all who came to call upon the Caliph: visitors, messengers, ambassadors as well as the merely travel-worn and the poor. Omar's old furious injunctions against any of his followers riding a fancy foreign horse, or wearing fine clothes, eating sifted flour or keeping a porter at their doorway were swept away and quite forgotten.

The days of the simple food of the Khattab clan (as the plain meals preferred by the Prophet and enforced during the reign of Omar ibn Khattab were known) were soon to be past. Instead of

unleavened barley cakes Persian slaves and freedmen now prepared the most delicate wheat loaves flavoured with seeds, while
captive cooks from Armenia and Anatolia ground and rolled out
thin filo-like layers of flat-bread and pastries on their iron griddles.
Yogurt and cracked wheat had probably not yet been imported
into Arabia from Central Asia, nor couscous from North Africa,
nor the beloved aubergine from India, though the scented rice
dishes of Persia and a soup noodle of Byzantine origin and the
thick clotted milk dish known as laban were already well established. Meat was now blended, minced, seasoned and enriched
with flour, cinnamon, coriander, cloves, ginger, cumin, pepper
from Cochin, rock salt from Palmyra and basted, pan-fried or
stewed with raisins, currants, dried figs, almonds and walnuts.
Sugar had not yet appeared in the palace kitchens of early Islam
but it would not have been much missed, for honey and the thick,
sweet syrup produced by pressing dates were used in abundance,
enhanced by the dark blocks of rich, jelly-like rendered-down
grape juice or rummaniya (pomegranate juice). Black truffles from
the Arabian desert, the esteemed small, slightly bitter olives from
Palmyra oasis, *Zaytun Tadmuri*, asparagus (especially that from
Damascus), leeks (either Nabatean or just plain Syrian), sour
apples, white onions, carrots, mint, tarragon, lentils, beans, bitter
lemons and a cornucopia of vinegars, olive oils and salted cheeses
completed the Medina chef's list of basic ingredients. Fish had to
be salted to survive in the desert and so was usually fried and
sometimes served with a garam-like soya sauce later called 'blattes
de Bysance'. Despite the growing hierarchy of sweet and sour
courses, preserved vegetables, fried fish and soups that had to be
served to make an impressive banquet, the traditional *zarb* of
roasted meat (most especially lamb) slow-cooked over hot stones
in a pit was still given pride of place. Imported fruits were too
perishable to survive a desert crossing, though oasis-grown grapes,

melons, cucumbers and Medina's famous dates could be served alongside the traditional desert cake of the hungry traveller made from ground and pressed biscuit, dates, almonds and pistachio nuts.

In doctrine Uthman was an absolute conservative, so much so that his scholarly attempt to return to the first example of the Prophet by performing a further two sets of prayers in addition to the traditional two, during the pilgrimage rite of the standing at Mount Arafat, turned out to be the most controversial thing he ever proposed. Although this dispute may now seem a tiny, almost abstract detail of ritual, it does reveal how precisely the first Muslims observed the existing practices. Uthman's other administrative reforms within the practice of daily prayer were less contentious and entered the mainstream of Islamic practice and have been followed ever since. He instituted the second call to prayer at noon on Friday (to stress the importance of attending this great communal gathering of the week) and started the practice of providing charitable kitchens during the month of Ramadan as well as increasing the daily allowances. He used the state treasury for the upkeep and construction of mosques (an important innovation when compared with Muhammad's use of voluntary, communal labour of the faithful to build his house of prayer) and he also made the muezzin the first salaried 'religious' official. Previously the role of muezzin had been an unrewarded honour. Uthman was the first to establish a staff of four muezzin at the Medina mosque and pay them a regular salary. They had to be pious, trustworthy adult males, capable of calculating the prayer times and determinedly punctual. As the Muslim Empire grew in wealth their numbers increased and their status diminished, until it was not uncommon to have three muezzin to a balcony, calling out in all directions. The great medieval travel writer Ibn Batuta would record that there were seventy muezzin attached to the

Great Mosque of Damascus, while in the sixteenth century the great Ottoman mosques of Istanbul with their tapering pencil-thin minarets were built with multiple balconies. The Blue Mosque of Sultan Ahmet at Istanbul took this to its most extravagant heyday by providing sixteen balconies from six minarets. The high vantage point of a minaret balcony allowed the muezzin to look into private courtyards and forbidden quarters. In some mosques the muezzin were made to ascend blindfold or to swear an oath of secrecy, while others blended discretion with charity by employing the blind or partially sighted. Timekeeping would become the preserve of a new official, the *muwaqqit*, the mosque astronomer. Those of al-Azhar at Cairo would eventually have six sundials to consult and the privilege of making the first call to prayer, which would then be followed by the rest of the city. In the prayer hall the muezzin was often seated on a raised bench – usually resting on columns. Here at noon on Friday he could repeat the call within the prayer hall as well as recite the Koran on festivals and during Ramadan. Alone a muezzin was supposed to begin the call in the direction of Mecca, then turn to his right and then left. On his own initiative Bilal, the first muezzin at Medina, had introduced 'Benediction and peace be on you, O Apostle of God, and the mercy of God and his blessing' in his morning call. After the death of the Prophet, Bilal had not the heart to continue but volunteered to fight on the Syrian front before permanently settling in Damascus. There he was persuaded, on the occasion of the Caliph Omar's visit, to call the prayer one last time. The sound of that pure voice, back from the time of innocence when Islam ruled over just one oasis, reduced the distinguished congregation of generals, governors and conquerors to tears. In Medina the muezzin had addressed Abu Bakr as 'Khalifat Rasul Allah' – 'Caliph [successor] to the Prophet of God'. Omar and Uthman were also blessed in the morning call, but as *amir al-muʾminin* –

'commander of the faithful'. This morning blessing grew to be a vital recognition of sovereignty in a Muslim community. In later centuries it spread so that even governors of provinces were mentioned after their sultan, who was mentioned after the distant caliph in Baghdad. It awaited someone with the self-assurance of Saladin to halt this pretentious habit and return the call to Bilal's heartfelt blessing upon the Apostle of God. Although the muezzin is such a distinctive feature of Islam, especially to non-Muslims, it is important to remember that right from the days of Uthman they have never enjoyed any priestlike status. They have always remained just salaried staff.

Uthman's character was clearly quite different from those of both Abu Bakr and Omar. His influence on the future of Islam would be just as decisive. It is astonishing to remember that this was all to be achieved by a grey-bearded old man who came to the office of Caliph at the age of seventy. Uthman had been stricken with a chronic nosebleed during his first year, which was serious enough to stop him from leading the pilgrimage to Mecca, but seems to have been part of a widespread epidemic in Arabia that year. But his age and his infirmities were the least of it, for all these incremental reforms and building projects were to be achieved in the midst of ten years of continuous warfare on practically all the frontiers of the empire.

Uthman, when he helped carry Omar to his grave, had been heard to mutter, 'Out of us who can equal Omar?' This high opinion of Omar was one shared by the rest of the world. When the news of the great Caliph's death spread, it ignited spontaneous revolts as the conquered nations within the Muslim Empire saw an opportunity to recover their independence. Persia in particular was rocked by countless local rebellions, so that from 644 to 649 the two great Muslim armies based at Kufa and Basra were locked into a series of internal campaigns. The more distant principalities in the mountain territories of Armenia, Azerbaijan and the Caucasus quickly repossessed their accustomed self-dominion. They fought off the determined counter-attacks of the Arabs, destroying at least two armies. One of these, a 4000-strong column of Muslims, would achieve iconic status as martyrs, for having been isolated by the Turkic Khazars they fought on, all the time proudly testifying to their faith with the defiant cry of 'Allahu Akbar', until the last man was overwhelmed. Five years of campaign and counter-campaign at last re-established Muslim authority over the lands of the old Persian Empire. By 650 the Arab armies were once more on the offensive and had pushed the frontier into Central Asia as the ancient cities of Herat, Merv, Balkh and Kabul were occupied as Muslim outposts, to mirror the conquest-frontier of Alexander the Great. Two years later, Yazdegird, the last heir of the Sassanians, perished, murdered in a miller's hut for the value of the few jewels that this refugee prince still wore. This sad end to a great dynasty was long commemorated by the Nestorian Church (which had benefited from the enlightened tolerance of the Sassanids), while the Parsis, the remnant of the thousand-year-old Zoroastrian culture of Persia, begin their modern calendar with the death of Yazdegird.

Egypt was also to flare up in revolt in 644, the first year of Uthman's reign, supported by a bold counter-attack by the Byzantine Empire, which dispatched a fleet of 300 ships into Alexandria's great harbour. The Greek-speaking population of the city rose in support and massacred the 1000 soldiers of the Arab garrison. The Byzantine general Manuel then led a determined reoccupation of the Delta lands and seemed at one point to be capable of expelling all the Arabs from Egypt. The situation was doubly perilous for Uthman, who in order to improve the tax administration in Egypt had sacked the charismatic conquering general Amr and had promoted Abdullah, the chief financial officer, as governor in his place. Only when Amr had once again been entrusted with the military command by Uthman was the situation brought under control. Amr, with his long experience of fighting in Egypt, succeeded in drawing Manuel and his army ever further south, into the terrain that best suited the highly mobile Arab armies. Once again Nikiou, at the western edge of the Delta, was Amr's chosen battle ground. The surviving accounts suggest that the second battle of Nikiou was as hard fought as the first, but eventually the 15,000-strong Muslim Arab army of Amr prevailed. A series of running engagements pushed Manuel back into the safety of the walls of Alexandria, though the betrayal (or seizure) of a key gateway let Amr once again enter the city as a conqueror in 646. This time there was no quarter offered to the rebellious citizens, who were butchered or enslaved at the whim of their conquerors, who also devastated half of the great expanse of the city before Amr called a halt to the rapine. So that the city should never again be able to be used as a secure base by the Byzantine army, all the east-facing walls of Alexandria were levelled to the ground. In the aftermath of the fighting, Benjamin, the indigenous Patriarch of Egypt's Coptic Church, forcefully presented his people's case. He argued that, yes, they had bravely resisted Amr at the time of the first Arab invasion, but this rebellion had been a secret assault by the Greek Orthodox Byzantine Empire and had been none of their doing. So convincing was his case that Amr agreed that the Coptic community should not only keep hold of their property but that they should be paid back a year's worth of poll tax – for the Arab Muslim army had failed in its half of the contract, which was to protect them from external enemies.

After victory had been assured, Uthman once again showed the determination of which he was capable. The victorious hero of the second Arabic conquest of Egypt could remain as governor-general in Fustat but financial affairs would have to remain under the separate auspices of Abdullah. Amr protested, 'Am I to hold the cow's horns while another man draws off the milk?' He was once again sacked and Abdullah reinstated. Abdullah, praised by the historian Nawawi as 'the most intelligent of all the Quraysh', had great difficulty establishing his moral authority over the Muslim army, who were disgusted at the treatment of their heroic commander Amr. So it was perhaps as much for internal politics as for anything else that Uthman ordered an assault on North Africa for the next year, in which Abdullah could win his battle spurs.

A very considerable force was gathered, Uthman sending another 20,000 men to join the 20,000-strong army already in Egypt. In 647 Abdullah led this force into the west, across the breadth of Libya, which had been subdued by Amr just five years before. The Byzantine governor of Tunisia marched south from his walled capital of Carthage to make his stand at Sbeitla, the central city of the southern steppes. At Sbeitla the magnificent old triple Roman temple at the forum had been turned into a Byzantine fortress. Here Viceroy Gregory, accompanied by his elegant daughter, established his headquarters. The southern steppes were a classically favourable site for a mobile Arab cavalry army to operate in, but the Byzantine Viceroy Gregory had his own reasons for picking Sbeitla. For here on the southern edge of his province he had gathered together the horsemen from the fiercely independent Berber principalities of the mountains and pre-Saharan steppe to assist him in the defence of North Africa. To further encourage these proud Berber lords, he offered the hand of his daughter to whoever could bring him the head of Abdullah, the commander of the Arab Muslim army. The passionately Christian population of Byzantine Tunisia had been whipped up into a millenarian fervour by the preaching of Abbot Maximus. The resulting battle of Sbeitla was as hard fought as any, but the 40,000-strong Arab army once again prevailed. Gregory's wager had been reversed by Abdullah, so that the viceroy's daughter became the concubine of the man who beheaded her father. Abdullah dispatched Zubayr's son, who had fought with great élan, to take the news of victory back to the Caliph at Medina. Although the Byzantine army had been destroyed Abdullah was cautious of committing his battle-scarred troops to further operations against either the Berber tribes of the mountains or the walled port cities of the Tunisian coast. Instead Abdullah allowed himself to be bought off with a massive tribute, raised from Tunisia's vast olive orchards. He returned to Egypt from his raid laden with captives, spoil and a slightly better reputation among his soldiers. However, there was later to be a dispute over the fate of all this spoil; for Uthman had generously given his fifth to Abdullah and there were complaints that the Caliph's young secretary-cousin Marwan had also made too great a profit with a private speculative bid for the state portion of the war booty.

The campaign had, however, convinced Abdullah of the need for an Arab navy. For having ridden along the North African coast, which was then still dotted with walled harbours and fortress ports just a day's row apart from each other, he knew it would be impossible to permanently conquer this land without a navy. For otherwise the Byzantine forces in Crete, Sicily, Cyprus and southern Italy would always be able to counter-attack at will, raising rebellions among the Berbers the moment the Arab army had risen beyond the horizon. The Byzantine counter-attack on Egypt, with their rapid reoccupation of Alexandria, was a potent example of what they were capable of. Uthman, despite the precedent of Omar, who had clearly ordered that no Muslim army should ever allow itself to be isolated by sea from the sheltering arms of the desert, began to listen to the case for a navy – also energetically championed by Muawiya, the governor of Syria. Muawiya had written to his cousin the Caliph to assure him that the Byzantine-ruled island of Cyprus was so close to the Syrian shore that you could hear the barking of a dog. It is certainly true that on an exceptionally fine day you can just catch a glimpse of the Syrian mountains from the far end of Cyprus's Karpas peninsula but the only way you can hear a dog is to catch an echo from the roar of the sea. Uthman allowed himself to be convinced but set two provisions: the first Muslim naval assault was to consist of volunteers only, and if the commanders were so certain of victory they could prove it to him by taking their wives along on this expedition.

The joint assault of Abdullah and Muawiya, with Egyptian and Syrian sailors manning the ships that had been built in the harbours of Alexandria and Acre, but the decks packed with Arab warriors, proved a triumphant success. The island of Cyprus was occupied in 649 and agreed to pay to the Caliph the same tribute that it had been used to sending to the Emperor in Constantinople: 7000 dinars a year. There was little fighting and the only memorable casualty was Rumeysha bint Milhan: her mule stumbled on the shores of Lake Larnaca and in the words of the historian Ibn al-Athir she 'broke her pellucid neck and yielded up her victorious soul, and in that fragrant island was at once buried'. They laid her down beneath three prehistoric menhirs while her second husband, the chief judge in one of the garrisons in Palestine, intoned the prayers. It was a joyful burial, for Rumeysha, the brown-eyed lady from the oasis of Medina, had been one of the Companions of the Prophet (indeed her first husband, an important clan chieftain of Medina, had been one of the earliest martyrs) as well as the aunt of one of the Prophet's chief secretaries, Anas. Muhammad had once fallen asleep on the lap of Rumeysha (while she was combing his hair for lice) and had awoken with a revelatory dream and the assurance that she had a place in paradise as a bloodless martyr. Now the dream was at last understood. Her burial place is now covered by a lovely late-Ottoman domed mosque that sits on the edge of a salt lake dotted with flamingos. Surrounded by cypress, lemon and palm trees it remains an enchanting and still 'fragrant' shrine that is locally known as Umm Haram – the pious mother.

The new fleet would have a more testing trial three years later when the arrival of yet another Byzantine fleet, hovering threateningly off the coast of Alexandria, justified all of Abdullah's and Muawiya's strategic concern. The untried Arab squadron at once put to sea and recklessly grappled with the much more experienced Byzantine fleet. The fighting was indecisive, though the Arabs could celebrate the day as theirs when the Byzantine admiral hoisted a signal and led his fleet away to the safety of Syracuse. Here the disgrace of Byzantine arms had so infuriated the Sicilians that they broke into his palace and lynched the admiral in his bath – to encourage the others. Muawiya considered that the pacified island of Cyprus had, in defiance of the treaty terms, assisted this Byzantine operation and so the next year, 653, he ordered another landing on the island. The coastal cities were sacked, a pitiful stream of captives were marched back to the Arab fleet, and a permanent garrison of 12,000 was established on the island. These were but the opening manoeuvres for a great turning point in Mediterranean history when the Muslim fleet fought the Byzantine navy at Dhat al-Sawari – the battle of the Masts – off the Lycian coast of Turkey. What the Arabs lacked in seamanship they more than made up with their desperate courage, deliberately locking their ships into the rigging of their opponents and turning a sea war into a dogged battle on land. Even the presence of the Emperor Constans II's brother (a grandson of Heraclius) had no effect on this day which witnessed the birth of Arab sea power. In the aftermath of victory, one Abdullah ibn Qais emerged as the first corsair hero of the Muslims; the victor of fifty battles, 'who looked like a merchant but gave presents like a king' but would finally end his days on the scaffold, having been seized by his enemies as he spied upon yet another Byzantine port in disguise. Abdullah ibn Qais's epic career is touched with the shadow of Odysseus as well as presaging those infamous corsair captains Barbarossa, Dragut and Turgut Reis, who would emerge from these same waters a thousand years later. It was the exploits of such men as Abdullah ibn Qais on the war-ravaged frontiers that paved the way for that epic attempt to seize Constantinople (674–9) less than a generation after the first Arab warriors had been permitted to set sail.

Not all the military initiatives of the Caliphate were so successful. The first invasion of the Sudanese and Ethiopian shore (during Omar's Caliphate) ended with the wreck of an Arab squadron on the Red Sea shore, the same year that an old volcano outside Medina erupted. In Uthman's reign, the Sudan was once again attempted, though this time the army would march south down the Nile. The general who had ridden into the Sahara and conquered the Libyan Fezzan, Oqba ibn Nafi, was trusted with the command. Oqba, who would later make the epic conquest-ride right across Tunisia, Algeria and Morocco, was repelled by the silent archers of Nubia. A few years later the governor-general of Egypt, Abdullah mounted an even bigger expedition into the Sudan, but once again the Arabs found themselves powerless against the pitilessly accurate Nubian bowmen defending their steppe homeland. As the column withdrew back into upper Egypt it included such a large proportion of blinded warriors that the Nubians of Sudan were respectfully dubbed 'the Archers of the Eye'. A truce was then made and a frontier agreed. An official trade agreement was also signed that allowed for the purchase of 360 slaves a year – to be paid for in Egyptian grain. (The Sudan and its Coptic Christian faith would remain independent of

Muslim Egypt for another five hundred years until the Mameluke sultans extended the frontier of faith and dominion south in the early fourteenth century.)

Uthman's most glorious and enduring achievement was to be neither military, political or administrative. He had decided to create a definitive written edition of God's revelation – the Koran. At first the work seems to have been just the continuation of his own private practice, part of his lifetime of devotion in trying to fully comprehend the message that had been delivered by Muhammad. Once he became Caliph he began to see that those precious periods of his day that were devoted to private study and contemplation should be shared with the Muslim world. He also might have foreseen a period when the increasing competition between the various army camps, already active in their championing of rival Koranic reciters, might creep towards the development of rival versions.

First he appointed an inner editorial committee: headed by Muhammad's old secretary Zayd ibn Thabit and assisted by Abdullah ibn Zubayr, Said ibn al-As and Abd al-Rahman ibn al-Harith, who were helped by all the surviving Companions. Uthman then called in as many of the written drafts of verses from the provincial garrisons and the house libraries of Medina and Mecca as he could get hold of. Not all were surrendered, though he was trusted with many precious fragments, some inked on bone shoulder blades, some scratched on to stone tablets, others scribbled on the split stalks of palm branches. Zayd and the inner committee also recorded the great reciters of Islam at work.* In addition there was an invaluable proto-Koran in existence that belonged to Hafsah, Omar's daughter, one of the Prophet's wives

* There were either three, seven or ten of these celebrated reciters. In the list of seven are Nai, Ibn Kathir, Abu Amr, Ibn Amir, Asun, Hamza and Kisai.

and one of his most exacting literary critics. This copy is believed to have included some of the original drafts made by the Prophet's scribes and secretaries.

The collectors were extremely conservative and refused to edit out any small contradictions between some of the verses, or cut up chapters that appeared to have been an amalgamation of two or three historic revelations. For instance Sura 9 was known to have been delivered in Medina, except the last two verses, which were first recited in Mecca. They also incorporated some textual marks (perhaps from Hafsah's copy) whose meaning has never been discovered. Owing to the early Islamic practice of all-night recitations there was no editorial work to be done. For the proper reciting of the Koran had already been completed during the lifetime of the Prophet. There are references to this scattered throughout the Koran, such as in Sura 73:4, 'He put together and arranged well the component parts', in Sura 16:101–3, 'When we substitute one verse for another – God knoweth best what he revealed', in Sura 25:32, 'We have arranged in right order' and in Sura 23:32, 'We rehearse it gradually'. Uthman and his hand-picked team of scholars should not be seen as editors but meticulous copyists.

By 650 Uthman had overseen the creation of the first complete copy of the Koran. Seventy-seven thousand words had been gathered into 6211 verses and divided into 114 *suras* (derived from the Arabic word for 'rows'), as the chapters are known. The suras were arranged in order of their length and there was no attempt to order the chapters by the date of their first deliverance. This seemingly arbitrary ordering would prove extremely important in later ages. There can be no doctrinal seniority among the verses. No chapter can be seen to be more definitive than another, because it cannot be conclusively proven whether a revelation is late or early, and even if it can, all come from God and so must be equally valid. All of the Koran has equal authority, which makes the verses that apparently contradict each other of extraordinary interest. For instance a sincere Muslim would know that one of the most common words is 'salaam', peace, which occurs 129 times in the Koran. They would also know that Sura 2:86 reads that there is 'no compulsion in religion' and Sura 42:15 explicitly accepts the validity of other faiths, 'God is our Lord and your Lord. We have our words and you have yours. There is no argument between us and you. God will bring us together for the journey is to him.' As does Sura 109:6, 'to you your religion and to me mine'. But then what is the same believer to make of Sura 4:89? 'They long that you should disbelieve as they, so that you may be all alike, do not take friends from among them until they move to God's way; but if they turn back, seize them and slay them wherever you find them, and do not take any of them as friends or helpers.' There is no easy answer. Some have tried to remove any contradictions from the Koran by arguing that one verse 'abrogates' another, but then that clearly raises human interpretation above divine revelation.

For the various chapters of the Koran contain the divine answers but not the mortal questions. The Koran is a series of divine answers to a series of prayers, meditations and social problems to which the Prophet sought an answer. Many Muslim scholars from all ages have laboured to build up exhaustive commentaries that try to extract a definitive meaning from the exact context of a revelation but this, though immensely useful, can be deeply flawed as a theological tool, for once again it raises scholarship above divine revelation. A popular saying summarises some of the frustration with the endless caveats of the jurists and theologians: If all the rivers of the world were turned to ink and all the grains of sand to paper, there would still not be enough material to write down all the different meanings of the Koran,

Others have argued that because the Koran is an immensely complex divine document, a revelation to all mankind, for all time and for all the different human levels of spiritual under-standing, one should not fuss around with questions but concentrate on those truths that are clear and apparent. Some verses yet await their time to be fully understood, or await the human needs to which they are addressed. You have to trust your-self and let the spirit of the whole book enter your heart, in order to use it as a spiritual tool to approach God. In this reading the contradictions are not an embarrassment to be corrected with clever textual analysis but doorways to greater understanding. Uthman understood the absolutely vital importance of trusting in the Koran, not trying to tidy it up like a methodical editor or reduce it to a mere law code.

The sanctity of the text had already been preserved by the ritual of beginning every recited verse with 'In the name of God the merciful, the forgiving,' and concluding with 'God Almighty has spoken truly!' The small chapter of just seven verses that had become habitual by constant use in daily prayer was given promi-nence by being placed at the start of the Koran. It became known as the *fatiha*, the opening, and is also referred to as the quintes-sence of Islam and the 'mother of the book'.

In the Name of God, the Merciful and Compassionate
Praise belongs to God, the Lord of all Worlds,
The All-Merciful, the All-Compassionate,
Master of the day of judgement.
Thee only do we serve; to Thee alone we pray for succour.
Guide us on the straight path,
The path of those whom Thou hast blessed,
Not of those against whom Thou art wrathful,
Nor of those who are astray.

Unlike the traditional sacred texts of Judaism the Koran was not assembled on a series of papyrus scrolls but written on sheets of parchment that were bound together in a book – in the same manner that the Christians had preserved their gospels. There was an important difference: Arabic is written from right to left and so all Arabic texts start from the 'opposite' end to – for example – this book. For a people who assessed portable wealth in their flocks, the possession of any parchment book was an important status symbol: each page represents a prized animal because a page of parchment is the specially treated and bleached leather taken from the soft underbelly of a sheep or a goat. However, right from the start the Koran was treated as the book of books, which should always be stacked at a height above all others, wrapped up in cloth for any travels, always held above the waistline of a believer and opened only by those in a state of ritual cleanliness. While a believer would be content to sit on the floor, the Koran was always raised up from the ground on a small folding lectern – the *kursi* – the chair for the book. Although each verse and chapter is now numbered for ease of reference, this is a modern innovation. The chapter titles, 'The Bee', 'The Cow', were added a little later, as a mnemonic device already familiar to the poetry-loving Arabs. There is a reference to a similar memory device among the Jews when King David recites his famous verse known as 'The Bow' even though it was a panegyric that he had composed in honour of Saul and Jonathan.

The very first Korans had no punctuation marks and comparatively few of the additional dots and diacritical marks familiar from modern Arabic script. This allows for intriguing variations in some words as some Arabic letters are signified by these marks. Later generations of manuscript copyists would place the unchangeable heritage of Uthman's Koran in black and their textual suppositions about the right vowel choice, accents and verse breaks in a calligraphic coded hierarchy of authority, from gold down to red and yellow. These minor variations would eventually be codified into the seven different readings of the Koran that are sometimes associated with the accents of the tribes around Mecca and Medina or with the seven famous Koranic reciters in the garrison cities. None of these readings would be exploited by the doctrinal, theological or dynastic rivalries that would later divide Islam. Not even the celebrated schism between Sunni and Shia has created different editions of the Koran.

It is traditionally thought that over the next four months (the time a cautious copyist needs to create a new Koran) four copies were made from Uthman's original, one for each point of the compass, and these were the fathers of all the thousands upon tens of thousands of manuscript Korans that would be written in the centuries to come. No single physical fragment of Uthman's original edition has been positively identified, though some very early copies, perhaps from the end of the seventh century, certainly from the eighth and ninth centuries, have been preserved in the great mosque at Sana in the Yemen* and the great mosque at Damascus in Syria.

It had been a great and holy task that had been achieved with vital speed and authority but inevitably there were murmurs of objection. There were rumours that certain verses had been lost (especially a derogatory reference to Uthman's Umayyad clan) and that others had gone missing, eaten by an errant goat who had made his way into the scriptorium and chomped his way through a collection of inscribed palm stalks. However, these stories are a result of a confusion between the Koran and the Hadith – the lifetime sayings of the Prophet.

A few of the oldest believers even objected to the very idea of a

---

* Copies of the Koran worn out through use were tucked away from harm or chance defilement in the ceiling space above the wooden beams of the prayer hall.

written revelation, rather than the living sound. Some of the celebrated reciters of the Koran who had become attached to the great
mosques of the garrison cities were of course slightly scornful of
the process that now elevated a written book above their exacting
memory of the voice of the Prophet of God. But no one can deny
Uthman his greatest achievement: a single authoritative book that
unites all Muslims in common reverence to the word of God as
recited by the Prophet Muhammad. Years later when Ali heard
criticism of Uthman's work from among his supporters in Kufa he
silenced them with a decisive and heartfelt reply: 'Uthman acted
with the advice of all the leading men among us, and had I been
ruler at the time, I should myself have done the same.' Praise from
such a man (whom the world might have mistakenly considered
an enemy of Uthman's) is the finest testament.

The year 650 was to mark the halcyon peak of Uthman's reign.
He had then reigned for six remarkable years, each one full of
achievement and a joyful avuncular generosity of spirit. The following year, a small accident would reverse this flow of fortune; so
that the next six years of Uthman's Caliphate would bring the
young Islamic state to the brink of civil war. The old Caliph was
once again concerned about the safe supply of water for the people
of the oasis and was directing a team of workmen who were deepening the Arees well in Medina. Uthman leant over the wall,
peering down into the recently scoured depths with his fingers
gripping the stone wall. He adjusted his grip slightly and then
moved his right hand to point out some stone that needed further
reinforcing. At just that moment, an old ring slipped from his
finger and spiralled down into the depths. Uthman stood up
aghast. The signet ring of the Prophet had fallen from the hand of
the Caliph. Over the weeks to come the well was methodically
emptied, all the mud cleaned out and every handful sieved and
sieved again in an increasingly desperate attempt to locate the lost

ring. The more fervently they searched, the more ominous the loss began to feel. The seal of Muhammad, the seal of the Prophets, had gone. Despite this superstitious dread, the messengers who came galloping into the oasis of Medina brought nothing but good news from the Persian front. Every month, every year, glory was added to glory as the armies of the Caliphate pushed the frontiers of Arab rule and Islam ever further east. It was only much later that the incident would grow in the telling and the Caliphate of Uthman would be divided into two: the six good years followed by the six bad years after he had lost the signet ring of the Prophet inscribed 'God, the best of potentates'.

The last years of Uthman's rule (651–6) were six years of trouble. He had failed to follow the wise example of Omar, who in the last years of his rule had been accustomed to regularly sacking his governor-generals in order to maintain the central government's control over these ever-larger garrison cities and to stop any Khalid-like figure emerging as the hero of the soldiery. One of his last replacements, the fascinatingly wicked Mughira, was a distinctly unusual appointment for Omar to have made, but then governing the Arabs was an art of its own which was rarely to be found among the holy, the simple and the pious. Omar was not alone in this opinion, for everyone in Arabia knew that politics was a dirty business. Indeed Omar managed to make a principle out of this and publicly refused to employ the Companions of the Prophet, lest they diminish the high spiritual status that they had acquired. This attitude is still widely shared among many Muslims and Arabs to this day, that you should keep out of politics if you wish to keep your honour and stay true to your religion. This healthy pessimism, combined with an exact understanding that those who rise by the sword shall surely perish by the sword, helps give Arab politics its peculiarly mercurial intensity. The best of men tend to stay out of the political arena, leaving it in the hands of ambitious young colonels, police chiefs and colourful opportunists. For alongside the bare handful of moral political heroes of the Arabs, men of the nature to rank beside Saladin, Nasser, Abu Bakr and Omar, there are thousands upon thousands of leaders who look to an alternative tradition followed by men such as Mughira. Uthman, who was perhaps just as aware as Omar of the brutal realities of power, fell into the other great cul-de-sac of Arab political activity, which is to trust only in your immediate family and clan.

Mughira was an opportunist of the first water. His shrewd careerism, tied to a rackety lifestyle and an endearingly unabashed sexuality, reads like a scarcely credible historical fiction – he is the Flashman of early Islam. William Muir describes him as 'of rude and repulsive aspect, whose harem of four wives and a score of concubines failed to satisfy his vagrant passion'. Mughira makes his first appearance in the lifetime of the Prophet as a modest refugee sheltering in Medina, having fled from his home city of Taif, where he was wanted for the killing of thirteen tribesmen and had a blood price of 1300 camels on his head. Mughira's profession of Islam proved itself highly opportune. For not only was he personally assured by the Prophet that 'conversion cuts off what was before it' but Taif (back in 630) remained a bastion of paganism and Mughira's sage advice about the clan divisions within the Thaqif tribe of Taif proved very useful to Muhammad's diplomacy. When Taif surrendered the next year, the errant Mughira was able to return to his home town, not discreetly through the back door, but riding high as one of the three ambassador-governors of Islam. It was Mughira who organised the destruction of the revered pagan shrine of The Lady al-Lat of Taif – and who was rumoured to have greatly profited from melting down the votive objects that had been buried in her sanctuary over the centuries.

The opportunist Mughira always had a deft political touch, and we later find him helping the Prophet draft treaties for the Yemen and Syria while the peace he had brokered at Taif allowed the city to safely weather all the potential storms of the Ridda Wars. Nor could his valour be doubted, for one had only to look at his face. After the key battle of 'the day of the garden of death' in 633 it wore a permanent decoration of scars that left him sightless in one eye. His appointment as governor-general of Basra in 638 came at a critical time in the Persian Wars, for the victorious commander Utba had just died, and Omar needed a safe pair of hands. Mughira quickly proved himself an acute administrator even if his uninhibited sensuality shocked the pious. For despite having acquired forty of the most desirable concubines and four elegant wives (the latest batch from out of the eighty that he would wed, bed and divorce) he conceived a passion for Umm Jamil, a notoriously independent-minded Bedouin of whom it was said that she alone was more promiscuous than Mughira. Their flirtatious courtship was spied upon by his prim adversaries, who staged a highly dramatic incident in the great mosque where Mughira was publicly shouted down from the pulpit as an adulterer. This charge quickly reached Omar, who at once called Mughira back to face trial in Medina. Three of the legally required four witnesses swore that they had directly observed the adulterous pair but the fourth witness (of whom we will hear more later) made a subtle shift to his testimony, declaring that although he had seen a black-veiled woman he could not now swear to her being Umm Jamil. On this technicality the case collapsed, and Omar was forced to follow the example of the Prophet and not only acquit Mughira but order the scourging of the unsuccessful prosecution witnesses with eighty lashes of the whip. Mughira, recovering his poise with admirable speed and now crowing with unabashed delight, bade the executioner 'to strike hard', 'strike hard with your whip and comfort my heart'. This was more than Omar could tolerate and he gruffly ordered Mughira to 'Hold thy peace, it had wanted little to convict thee; and but for that you would now be about to be stoned to death as an adulterer.' In the aftermath of the scandal Mughira was deprived of his governorship, though he was too clever a political analyst not to remain a valued counsellor of the Caliph. A few years later, as was his wont, Omar removed the Victorians Saad ibn Abu Waqqas from his governorship of Kufa, but the sincerely pious man sent out in his stead (who ranked among the first of the converts to Islam) had not the authority to exercise power over tens of thousands of battle-hardened victorious veterans. So once again, almost despite himself, Omar had need of a strong hand to master the turbulent warriors who populated Kufa, and Mughira was appointed governor.

Uthman when he took over the Caliphate allowed Mughira to remain at Kufa for a year but then replaced him with Saad ibu Abu Waqqas. Malicious tongues remembered that Saad had been on the council of Companions that had elected Uthman. If it was a reward it was not to last for long. Saad had a row with the austere treasury official of the region, who could not tolerate the governor's habit of taking unsecured loans from the regional treasury. So in the second year of his authority, Uthman appointed Walid ibn Uqba to the post. It was not a good choice.

Walid was Uthman's half-brother and though he, like most of the talented Umayyad cousins of Uthman, was intelligent and confident, he was an even more deeply flawed Muslim than Mughira. Walid's powerful father had been one of the most notorious persecutors of the Muslims back in the old days of Mecca, and when he was made captive at the battle of Badr, the Prophet had ordered his execution. There he had begged for his life. 'Who will care for my children after I am dead?' he had pleaded, to which in a grim mood the Prophet had answered him that all his pagan children would be destined for hell. Nor had Walid proved himself forward with his Islam, for he had converted at the last possible moment, after the conquest of Mecca. Notwithstanding the bad blood between them, the Prophet had later proved generous, trusting Walid to lead a delegation to the Beni Mustaliq tribe. However, even in this he proved unworthy, for he was found to have unjustly accused them of rebellion.

Walid came to Kufa therefore with a marked card and his friendship with such talented, free-thinking and free-drinking poets as the Christian Abu Zubayd of the Tai tribe did not endear him to the pious. In one notorious incident Walid seems to have left an all-night symposium and turned up to lead the dawn prayers still smelling of drink. Other accounts accused him of vomiting on his way back home, though the story that he was sick over a lectern and then passed out while giving the Friday sermon in the great mosque was surely exaggerated by his enemies. On another occasion he was found unconscious, either from drink or just tired and emotional from overwork, which enabled his opponents to remove his signet ring and send it back to Medina to his half-brother the Caliph. Walid was recalled from office, judged and quickly pardoned – for it was publicly declared that no one could be found who was prepared to execute the punishment of eighty lashes for drunkenness. The contrast with Omar's impartial justice could not have been more acute.

In the meantime the Basra garrison had deposed one governor and elected another. Uthman's response was not to select a tough old politician of the Mughira school or a respectable old Companion but to look once again to his own immediate family. Two of Uthman's twenty-five-year-old cousins, Abdallah ibn Amir and Said ibn al-As, were appointed as commanders of Basra and Kufa. These young men (who proved themselves excellent generals) would be further incorporated into the Caliph's close-knit family by their marriage to Uthman's daughters. In Uthman's eyes he had at last achieved an efficient team of provincial governors who were personally responsive to his instructions. To those outside his immediate court, the situation looked completely different.

For where Uthman saw a group defined by its efficiency, speed and ability, the rest of Arabia saw only the total triumph of Uthman's family, the Umayyad clan of the Quraysh. The Umayyads now controlled all the top posts in the empire. The secretary of state in Medina, Marwan, was an Umayyad; the inspector of markets in Medina, Harith ibn al-Hakim, was an Umayyad; Abdullah in Egypt was an Umayyad; Muawiya in Syria was an Umayyad and now the two commanders of Kufa and Basra were Umayyads. The intermarriages arranged within this ruling clique only made matters worse, especially as Uthman's family could afford bigger dowries and more magnificent celebrations than any other clan. They also used their wealth to finance the acquisition of landed estates in the conquered territories. Unkind tongues began to insinuate that these had been paid for by the state treasury, which was in all fairness strictly untrue.

The actual fiscal reality that these were official loans granted by the Caliph from the surplus in the state treasury, or generous gifts from Uthman's own personal resources, hardly seemed to make a difference to the gathering storm of suspicion – and envy – directed against the Umayyad clan. It was this worry about the monopolisation of power that had almost certainly encouraged the chief Companions to deny the leadership to Ali – lest the Hashimite cousins of the Prophet acquire control of the Islamic state. How much worse, they now thought, was the domination of the Umayyads, who for all their intelligence and quick wits could also be seen as basically un-Islamic. For there was hardly a single

Umayyad who had not in some way acquired a reputation that put Mughira's in the shade.

Marwan, the secretary of state, had like Walid converted only at the last possible opportunity, at the Prophet's conquest of Mecca. Indeed his family was so directly connected with the heart of the pagan opposition to Islam that his father, Hakim, had been exiled to Taif on the instructions of the Prophet himself. This ban had been upheld by both Abu Bakr and Omar, so that Marwan had to grow used to the nickname 'Ibn Tarid', 'son of the exiled one'. Uthman's pardoning of Hakim, who was released from internal exile, had at first been accepted as the dutiful act of a nephew (for Hakim was Uthman's paternal uncle) but later, once suspicion of the Umayyads had grown, it could also be seen as breaking the Sunna – the example of the Prophet and the first Caliphs.

Abdullah, the governor of Egypt, could (in a hostile light) be seen as another living testimony to the evil genius of the Umayyads. Abdullah ibn Abu Sarh was the same foster-brother of Uthman who had been an early convert to Islam. His undoubted intellectual talents had been put to work by Muhammad, who trusted him enough to allow him to record some of the early Koranic verses. Abdullah, however, would desert the Muslims, return to pagan Mecca and denounce the Prophet as a fraud. Abdullah's black propaganda may have been behind all the most ridiculous stories of Muhammad's prophecy such as the bird that was trained to eat grain from his ear and that his messenger was not the Archangel Gabriel but a defrocked Jewish rabbi or Christian hermit. Abdullah's treachery so rankled with the Prophet that he was specifically excluded from the amnesty that was freely granted after the conquest of Mecca – though by waiting for a propitious time and making an emotional appeal (that he was forced to repeat three times) Uthman had finally been able to get the treacherous Abdullah forgiven by Muhammad. This was the man whom Uthman had imposed on the Egyptian army even to the extent of twice sacking the heroic conquering commander, Amr. The dismissal of Amr from his governorship of Egypt had also added an implacable, and able, enemy to those who already opposed the Umayyads.

Muawiya, the experienced governor of Syria, was the most admired of all the Umayyads – and though he was the child of the Prophet's leading enemy, Abu Sufyan, and his witchlike wife Hind (who had once saked her vengeance by chewing on her dead opponent's liver), that was never much held against him. For in his own lifetime had not the Prophet married a daughter of Abu Sufyan, freely employed Abu Sufyan's two young sons (Muawiya and his elder brother Yazid), and so accepted Abu Sufyan's conversion that he had sent him to Yemen as a missionary? However, while a sincere Muslim might find it easy to tolerate the presence of one sincerely converted Umayyad as governor of Syria, this clearly did not extend to allowing the clan to monopolise the command of all the armies of Islam. If ammunition for further disapproval of the Umayyads was required it was not forgotten that the father of the new Umayyad governor of Kufa had fought against the Muslims at the battle of Badr.

It was on this one issue that Uthman, who was otherwise so clever and astute, appears to have been completely blind. He was warned privately and sympathetically by the Companions as well as the Mothers of the Faithful that he must not allow his clan and his immediate kinsmen to be seen to be dominating the Islamic state. One can only guess that Uthman's personal weakness, his failure as a young warrior, or never having been chosen by the Prophet to be a commander of any expedition or raid, exacerbated by his lack of involvement in the spectacular battles of the Ridda and then the conquest, made him over-conscious about his control of the armies. His lack of the slightest flicker of the charisma of military glory might well have made Uthman desire to have totally dependable surrogates to fulfil this role.

Whatever his motivation, he found himself incapable of responding to the gathering clouds of criticism – even by removing just one man from his appointments. The personal histories of so many of his inner court (or their fathers), especially those of Walid, Abdullah and Marwan, made it easy for their rivals to see them as a threat to the whole nature of the Islamic state. The casual comments of one of the Umayyad governors, who had in passing referred to the great agricultural lands of Iraq as 'the garden of the Quraysh' and remarked he had been surprised to find that in Kufa 'noble birth passed as if for nothing', were repeated and embellished by their enemies as if they had become official policy. But the Umayyads were also proving themselves irritatingly talented, and there was no room to complain about their generalship as the empire continued to expand on all its frontiers – into the Aegean, along the North African coast, into Central Asia and to the very frontiers of India. When the criticisms came from families already rich and powerful beyond their wildest dreams, Uthman could afford to bide his time. They might argue that no one who was not an Umayyad or a close relative of Uthman could hope for high office. Uthman could reply, with some accuracy, that many of the appointments, such as those of Muawiya in Syria and Abdullah in Egypt, had been first made by the great Omar.

There were, however, other critics, who though poor and virtually powerless were a much greater threat. The most distinctive of these was Abu Dharr al-Ghafari, an early convert who had remained true to the Prophet's emphatic example of personal poverty, simplicity and reckless generosity. On a visit to Syria, the elderly saint could not refrain from preaching against the extraordinary transformation of the Arabs, now dwelling in palaces, waited on by hundreds of slaves and surrounded by every instance of luxury. Abu Dharr promised that, 'This gold and silver of yours shall one day be heated red-hot in the fire of hell: and therewith you shall be seared upon your foreheads, sides and backs, you ungodly spendthrifts. Spend now the same in alms, leaving yourself enough for your daily bread; or else woe betide you on that day of judgement.' Those with any knowledge of the example of the Prophet, or the habits of Omar, must have thrilled to hear the new lords of Syria so chastised for their pride. Muawiya for his part put the zealot to a small test of corruption, sending Abu Dharr a purse filled with a thousand coins and then a few days later pretending that he had made a mistake and asking for its return. He was impressed to find that the preacher had lived up to his own rhetoric and had given away this entire fortune the very same night that he had acquired it. Muawiya realised that such a man could not be silenced with gold as swiftly as all the others. He sent him onwards to his cousin Uthman at Medina, privately warning the Caliph that he was honest but misguided. In Medina Abu Dharr warned the people: 'You have departed from the ways of the Holy Prophet. You are after amassing wealth, you have raised palatial buildings and have become the victims of luxury. I give you the tidings of troubled times that lie ahead, for the Holy Prophet said that when the city [of Medina] expanded to the Salaa hill there would be trouble for the people.'

In a reception at the Caliph's palace, the preacher and the ruler soon fell out, for Uthman argued back, 'When once men have fulfilled their sacred obligations what power remains with me to compel any further sacrifice?' And when Uthman then turned to his court scholar, Kaab, a famously learned Jewish convert, for further proofs of the tolerance of justly earned wealth from the holy books of the Jews and Christians, Abu Dharr exploded into anger, striking Kaab in the stomach and shouting, 'Out with thee, son of a Jew. What has this debate to do with thee?' As a result of this public disagreement, Abu Dharr was banished from Medina and sent to live in internal exile, to Rabada in the desert, there to practise his austerities. It was a mild enough persecution, though the death of Abu Dharr just two years later created a powerful new martyr for all those who opposed the self-satisfied wealth proudly displayed by the new ruling class. In the process Uthman's own generous valediction, 'May God have mercy on Abu Dharr. He was a great soul, who was more of a citizen of the next world than of this world,' would be forgotten. But there were now others who took up his voice, such as Ammar, who spoke bluntly to the Caliph about his evil innovation which allowed for the sale of state lands and the creation of a new ruling class. The manner in which Ammar had addressed the venerable old Caliph greatly angered the court of young Umayyad cousins who surrounded him. Ammar was dragged out of sight and beaten unconscious for his effrontery. These actions, regrettable enough in their own right, fed the Arab soldiers in the garrisons with fear that the Umayyads were constructing a princely court for themselves in Medina.

Within the garrison cities themselves, a new generation was emerging. As the revered old Companions and warlords passed away so did the passionate zeal of the first believers. The new generation of young Arab warriors knew nothing of the years of persecution and adversity that had tempered the first Muslims into a collective body. Old tribal identities gradually reasserted themselves, which curiously enough had been reinforced by the creation of the garrison cities, in which whole quarters (even if they were at first no more than tents and huts) were occupied by distinct tribes.

Further, there was a vast explosion in the population of Arabia as the victorious warriors enthusiastically collected a household of four legitimate wives and any number of concubines and slave girls from the spoils of war. The Koran gave explicit permission for a master to have sexual relations with the women of his household but also provided an automatic mechanism for their freedom once they had become Umm Walad – the mother of a child. From the surviving genealogies it seems commonplace for Arab men of this second generation within Islam to father twenty children. The more energetic and powerful who collected larger harems, such as Mughira, would leave behind eighty descendants. The garrison cities were the breeding factories for a vastly expanding population – which might already have tripled in their first thirty years. In the process the Arab Bedouin warriors of the desert had lost some of their old anarchic freedom, for families of this size could not be supported by grazing the arid steppes. It was no longer a question of simply riding back into the desert when you had had enough of war or the Caliph, for these large garrison families were dependent on the annual salary and stipends for their existence and their higher standards of living. At the same time the ethnic identity of the tribes was also being changed by the babble of new voices. The sounds of Berber, Persian, Turkic, Aramaic, Caucasian, Greek, Egyptian, Syriac and Armenian were now heard in the Arab garrison cities from the tens of thousands of concubine mothers and slave girls who teemed in the camps, the well-heads, the markets and the bakeries. Would the mixed-race children of the Arab fighters be able to inherit their position in the army and the *divan* salary? Would the widows have any rights to a pension? These questions became ever more urgent to this rising class of professional, salaried warriors. The garrison cities of the Islamic Empire were beginning to worry about their fiscal future, to be watchfully jealous of their rival cities and envious of the regime established in Medina.

So much so that a revolutionary ferment of disaffection was brewing up, especially in the garrison camps of Kufa and Fustat, where the Umayyad governors were publicly reviled. The practice of the annual pilgrimage also allowed the many disaffected elements to meet and share their common concerns. A group of ten dissidents was singled out from the Kufa garrison and sent into internal exile in Syria on the direct orders of Uthman, but stronger action was needed and the worried commander Saeed rode directly to Medina to consult with his Caliph. In his absence one of the exiles, Malik al Ashtar, slipped back into Kufa and whipped up the population by eloquently reciting all their common grievances and the collective crimes of the Umayyad family. When Saeed rode back from his pep talk he was faced by 1000-strong force which had symbolically assembled on the old battlefield of al-Qadisiya and threatened him with death should he try to return to Kufa. When the news was brought to Medina, the eighty-two-year-old Uthman began to waver in his determination, not helped, no doubt, by the simultaneous arrival of a deputation from Fustat requesting him to replace their unpopular governor Abdullah. Uthman permitted the rebels in Kufa the legality of their action, confirming the dismissal of Saeed and appointing a veteran (Abu Musa) in his stead, but did not accept the petition from Fustat.

The pilgrimage to Mecca of 655 was once again to be led by the old Caliph. He also used it to have an informal conference with all his key governors and advisers to discuss the troubled times. Some counselled a great new offensive to distract the dissidents with war, others recommended that they should be won round with money, others argued that it was simply a matter of efficient administration. When it was Amr's turn to address the conference he gave brutally frank advice when he addressed Uthman thus: 'O Prince of the faithful, you have subjected the whole nation to the Beni Umayya. You have gone astray and so have the people. Either make up your mind to be just or give up the job.' He had thrown down a public challenge – which would all too soon be taken up.

For at the same pilgrimage of 655 delegates from the disaffected Arab armies at Fustat, Kufa and Basra were making their own meetings. They agreed on a plan to march upon Medina some three months before the next haj and petition the Caliph to sack his unpopular kinsmen or step down from the high office he occupied. Perhaps Muawiya had received some whiff of information about this conspiracy (though none of his Syrian garrison were involved) for he privately pressed the old Caliph to either move to the safety of Damascus or allow him to post a reliably loyal Syrian garrison in Medina. Uthman was aghast at the suggestion – which would indeed have assured him some protection but would also have completed the Umayyad grip over the empire.

In 656 the dissidents fulfilled their plans with admirable speed and efficiency. Three columns of men, ostensibly on their way to Mecca for the pilgrimage, left the three garrison cities. In Egypt their action revealed how desperately fragile the governorship of Abdullah had become, for he hurriedly decided to desert his post and cross the Syrian frontier to seek safety in a garrison camp in Palestine which was safely under Muawiya's authority. Once they reached Medina the three rebel forces made separate bases in the accustomed camping grounds on the dry river beds that surrounded the oasis. The men from Kufa camped at Awas, the Basrans at Dhu Khushub and those from Fustat at Dhu l-Marwah. There was no violence but the arrival of the armed bands shocked the population into a renewed support for the old Caliph. The rebels sent deputations to the three most respected members of the old inner council of Companions: Ali, Talha and Zubayr – for Abder-Rahman had since died. At first the Companions rebuked the rebels for coming armed and unsolicited to the holy city and refused to have anything to do with them. Later, as the deadlock intensified, Ali agreed to act as go-between and counselled

Uthman that it was time that the unpopular Abdullah was sacked from the governorship of Egypt – which would be a sufficiently generous compromise with which to send the rebels back to their own camps. This policy was also, by chance, energetically championed by Aisha, who had forcibly argued that if Amr was given back his old job, the political situation would be instantly transformed. The rebels of the Egyptian garrison now put forward another demand: they wanted one of their own number, the young Muhammad, the last-born child of Abu Bakr (and stepson of Ali), to be given the job. Uthman reluctantly conceded and the rebels, for their part, struck their tents and prepared to march home. A collective sigh of relief spread over the entire oasis and many individuals took the opportunity to depart for Mecca, before the crowds packed into the city.

Three days into their march back to Fustat the rebel column from Egypt was overtaken by an African slave, riding post-haste for the frontier. He was pursued and brought back and a single letter was found in his leather pouch closed with Uthman's new seal. The letter was torn open: it requested Abdullah (who was assumed to be governor of Egypt still, though in fact he had fled to the safety of Ramlah) to arrest the rebel ring leaders and put them to death on their return. The rebels were incensed at this double-cross and at once turned around and rode hard for Medina. They were joined by their brethren from Basra and Kufa, who resumed their old campsites. Once again, Ali consented to act as an arbitrator, though he perspicaciously enquired of them that if the intercepted letter was authentic, how had they been able to communicate so quickly with the rebels from Kufa and Basra, who had set off in completely the opposite direction? This was never satisfactorily answered. When a delegation of rebels directly confronted the old Caliph, Uthman denied all knowledge of the letter but freely admitted that the slave was indeed from his household and 'Yes, the letter does appear to have been sealed with my seal.' The mystery surrounding the letter has never been solved, though it has been common to attribute responsibility to either a rebel forgery or his young secretary of state, Marwan, making decisions behind the Caliph's back or one of Amr's machinations.

Whatever the intended result, it helped stiffen the battle lines, for the rebel mutineers now feared for their lives if they left Medina with Uthman still on the throne. They shouted him down as a liar, an incompetent old man who was ruled by his treacherous family rather than by the dictates of Islam. His promised reforms had proved to be lies behind which further villainies were concealed. He was no longer their Caliph: he must resign and if he refused to resign they would come back and kill him.

Uthman behaved with all the dignity of his years. He promised to listen to their grievances but he could not 'take off a dress in which God had dressed him'. As for fighting other Muslims, that was something he would never do, for if he had wished to he could have summoned an army to Medina but he preferred to accept his own death rather than spill the blood of his fellow believers. At length the rebels departed from his house but they refused to quit the city and camped in the al-Aswaf quarter of the oasis, with a good number now picketed directly around the Caliph's house as well as close to the great mosque. The following Friday the dispute broke out again when in his weekly noonday sermon the Caliph called upon the people of Medina not to be cowed by the mutineers, as well as reminding these rebels that they were sinning when they attacked the successor to the Apostle of God. The sermon was never to be finished, for the rebels within the congregation began pelting Uthman and his close supporters with stones. The old Caliph was knocked unconscious and had to be carried home through a jeering mob. Henceforth the rebels barred him from ever returning to the mosque or leaving his house.

Faced with the impossibility of leading the haj, Uthman appointed a cousin of Ali, Abdullah ibn Abbas, to be the official commander of the pilgrimage to Mecca that year. The rebels sought to force the Caliph's resignation or at the very least the expulsion of Marwan. The house had no well of its own, and was therefore vulnerable to a determined siege. Ali could not bear to think of the distress of Uthman's household and dispatched three goatskins of water. Another kindly intervention was later attempted by Umm Habiba, one of the Prophet's widows, who personally led a water-bag-laden mule to Uthman's door; but so bitter were party feelings now that even one of the revered Mothers of the Faithful was prohibited from performing her act of mercy.

Ali, Zubayr and Talha sent their own sons to guard Uthman's door from any direct assault but otherwise stood aside from actively opposing the siege. They had fulfilled to the letter the Koranic instruction of Sura 48:9, 'If two parties of the faithful fight, conciliate between them, but if one transgresses on the other, fight the one that transgresses.' Politically they stood on a narrow path, for though they had emphatically opposed the rebellion and sought to physically protect the Caliph by posting their own sons at his door, they would also no doubt have been delighted to have watched Uthman dismiss his Umayyad family from their monopoly of power. Whatever the truth behind the sealed letter, at this point most people believed that Marwan was behind it and at the very least wished the old Caliph to make some form of public renunciation of his young cousin.

The time for a satisfactory compromise was rapidly passing. For the rebels had received news that Muawiya had dispatched an elite force of Syrian cavalry that was rushing in a series of forced marches to the relief of the old Caliph. They also had reliable reports that a similar 'loyalist' column had been sent out from Basra. By mid-June it was known that the relief column from

Damascus was just 120 miles away, having crossed the Wadi al Qura. If the rebels failed to strike now they would be caught in a trap. Their first assault on the Caliph's house, made as archers cleared the surrounding rooftops, was a failure, for Ali's son Hasan and Talha's son Muhammad bravely defended Uthman's door. The rebels now feared that they might have alienated the two most powerful men in Medina, who might now rally their kinsmen and their clans to avenge the wounds inflicted on Hasan ibn Ali and Muhammad ibn Talha. However, the death of Niyar ibn Iyad, who had been calling upon Uthman to resign until a freed slave of the household dropped a rock on him, once again inflamed their passions. That night of 16 June, fires were lit all around Uthman's palace to summon the rebels. In the morning a concerted attack was launched. Some pressed at the gateway while others swarmed over the palace roofs using ladders let down from the neighbouring house of Ibn Hazm. Others then followed with lighted torches in hand and rolling barrels of naphtha, which was poured over the wooden gates and high roof beams and then ignited.

Uthman proved majestically imperturbable in his last hours. He ordered all the defenders in his household not to resist – for he alone was the target of the rebels' venom – and instructed them to look after their own families. Most of his followers meekly complied and laid down their arms, but some preferred to follow Marwan, who organised an armed resistance. Indeed at one point in the morning's fighting Marwan and his troops managed to push one band of intruders back out through the gate they had entered, seal it and then sally out from a side door to launch a spirited counter-attack on the rebels. They were hopelessly outnumbered. Marwan was felled by a sword blow to his neck and left for dead. In the confusion his old wet-nurse, Fatima bint Aws, a humble Bedouin from the desert, threw herself over his body, believing him dead but wishing to protect her old charge from any ritual mutilation. Later she was able to drag Marwan's body off to her house, where she patiently nursed him back to life.

There could be no such escape for Uthman, whom the rebels located just as the noonday Friday prayer was being called out. He was alone in the room of his wife Naila calmly reading his Koran. Muhammad ibn Abu Bakr grabbed the old patriarch by the beard and called out, 'May God disgrace you, besotted old man.' 'I am not besotted but the servant of God,' answered Uthman, to which Muhammad replied, 'Marwan and his like can be of no avail to you now.' Uthman called out, 'Son of my brother, leave my beard, for your father would not have touched what you have grabbed hold of.' To which his assailant answered, 'My father, if he had seen your acts, would have censured you for them . . . but I want stronger medicine for you than just tugging at your beard.' As Muhammad pierced Uthman's forehead with his sword blade, the old Caliph cried out, 'I seek God's support.' Another sword was thrust in behind his ear so that its point emerged through his throat. Uthman's great pride, his personal copy of the first Koran, which had remained undisturbed but opened on a raised stool, was drenched with the blood of the Caliph.

As his body lay prone on the ground one of the assassins sat on the dead man's chest and pierced his shirt nine times, but then his young wife Naila (from a Christian Bedouin tribe of northern Syria) threw herself over his body to protect Uthman's corpse from any further indignity. Even after a blade had sliced off two of her fingers, Naila would not desert her dead husband. The rebels would not allow Uthman to be buried in the Baqi Gharqad cemetery, which had been used by all the Companions and the family of the Prophet. Instead the sorrowful file of twelve loyal friends that carried his bier were forced to make use of a neglected Jewish burial ground, the Habsh Kawkab. The entire Umayyad clan and its clients had gone to ground, hiding from the rebel mob. The house of Umm Habiba bint Sufyan, the Umayyad widow among the Prophet's wives, was so packed with refugees that she was forced to house some of her relatives in her granary. It might have been here that one of the half-understood sayings of the Prophet was remembered, 'Verily the Lord has a sword sheathed in a scabbard as long as Uthman lives, and when Uthman is slain that sword shall be drawn and it will not be sheathed until the day of resurrection.' Islam has been at war with itself ever since Uthman's lifeblood stained the pure white parchment pages of the first written Koran.

Uthman had proved true to himself and his own ideal of Islam. Despite the opposition that he had provoked, it was later to be recalled with pride that he had ordered no Muslim killed during his long rule. He had never been drawn to violence and bloodshed and this was how he had preferred to die. At peace with himself, having rejected any thought of being protected by regiments of guards and having bravely dismissed his own household servants, so that at the end he was protected only by his faith and his wives.

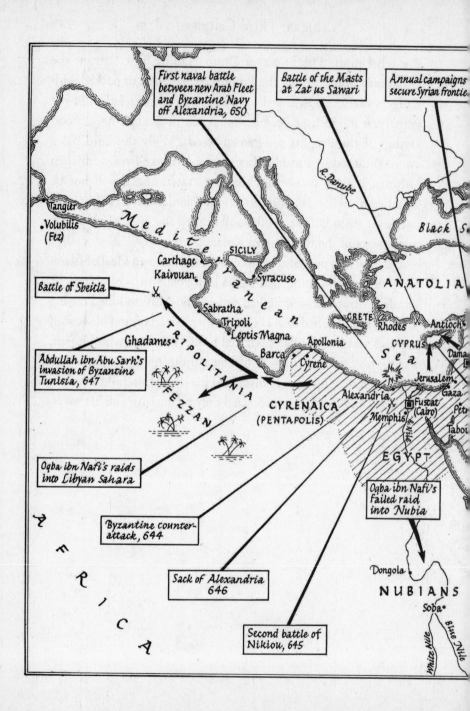

First naval battle between new Arab Fleet and Byzantine Navy off Alexandria, 650

Battle of the Masts at Zat us Sawari

Annual campaigns secure Syrian frontie[r]

Tangier

Volubilis (Fez)

Mediterranean

Black S[ea]

SICILY

Carthage
Kairouan

Syracuse

ANATOLIA

Battle of Sheitla

Sabratha
Tripoli
Leptis Magna

CRETE

Rhodes

Antioch

TRIPOLITANIA

Ghadames

Barca

Apollonia

Cyrene

CYPRUS

Dama[scus]

Sea

Abdullah ibn Abu Sarh's invasion of Byzantine Tunisia, 647

Jerusalem

Gaza

FEZZAN

Alexandria

Memphis

Fustat (Cairo)

Pit[?]

Tabo[?]

CYRENAICA
(PENTAPOLIS)

EGYPT

Oqba ibn Nafi's raids into Libyan Sahara

Oqba ibn Nafi's failed raid into Nubia

AFRICA

Byzantine counter-attack, 644

Sack of Alexandria
646

Dongola

NUBIANS

Soba

Second battle of Nikiou, 645

White Nile

Blue Nile

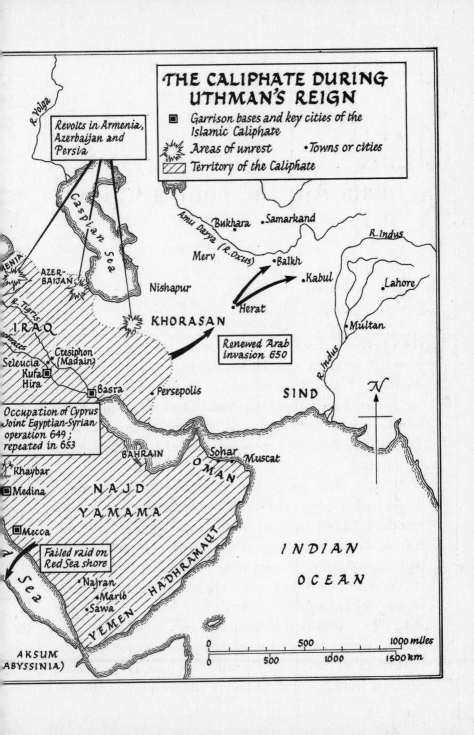

THE CALIPHATE DURING UTHMAN'S REIGN

▣ Garrison bases and key cities of the Islamic Caliphate

✺ Areas of unrest   • Towns or cities

▨ Territory of the Caliphate

R. Volga

Revolts in Armenia, Azerbaijan and Persia

Caspian Sea

Amu Darya (R. Oxus)

Bukhara   • Samarkand

Merv   • Balkh   R. Indus

ARMENIA

AZER-BAIJAN

R. Tigris

Nishapur

• Kabul   • Lahore

KHORASAN

• Herat

IRAQ

R. Euphrates

Ctesiphon (Madain)

Seleucia

Kufa

Hira

Basra

Renewed Arab invasion 650

• Persepolis

• Multan

R. Indus

SIND

N

Occupation of Cyprus Joint Egyptian-Syrian operation 649; repeated in 653

BAHRAIN   Sohar

OMAN   Muscat

Khaybar

▣ Medina

NAJD

YAMAMA

HADHRAMAUT

INDIAN

OCEAN

▣ Mecca

Failed raid on Red Sea shore

Red Sea

• Najran

• Marib

• Sawa

YEMEN

AKSUM (ABYSSINIA)

0   500   1000 miles

0   500   1000   1500 km

9

Imam Ali: the Fourth Caliph

The next morning Ali was acclaimed Caliph by the massed crowds in the marketplace. He was now nominally commander of an Arabian Empire that stretched east across Iraq and Persia into the borderlands of Afghanistan and Central Asia, while to the west his writ ran across Egypt and Libya, and to the north all of Syria, Jordan, Palestine, Cyprus and much of Armenia was under his direction.

Ali was a cornucopia of the virtues: now the only surviving son-in-law of the Prophet, the father of the Prophet's only beloved grandsons, his first cousin, his adopted son, his first male follower, his closest disciple, the youthful hero-warrior of Islam who in the past decade had also emerged as the principal expert on law and the understanding of the Koran. As he had pledged his obedience to men who had arguably a lesser claim to the office, first to Abu Bakr, then to Omar and to Uthman, there was now no question that he deserved the leadership of the Islamic community.

He was also, at this point, the man of the hour. The only figure who was trusted by the mutineers camped in the oasis, the

Quraysh of Mecca, the distant garrison armies as well as the indigenous population of Medina. Indeed the Ansar, the men of Medina who had been so conspicuous and decisive in providing support for the refugee Prophet Muhammad, saw Ali as their especial champion. Abu Bakr, Omar and Uthman had chosen their generals and governors from their own Quraysh or allied Bedouin tribes and seldom had they promoted one of the people of Medina. Indeed the coup that first placed Abu Bakr in power can be seen as an instinctive reaction to the threat of any self-assertion from among the Medina clans.

The public ceremony took place the next day (18 June 656) in the greatly expanded mosque of Medina, the faithful personally pledging their loyalty to Ali in a ceremony that directly mirrored the oath made to the Prophet under the thorn tree twenty-eight years earlier at Hudaibiya. Both Talha and Zubayr, the surviving members of the six-man electoral committee that had met after Omar's death in 644, were among the men who swore obedience to Ali that day. Abdullah, the son of Omar, ominously declared that he would hold back from his oath until he had seen 'the people' give theirs – by which Abdullah meant the powerful men within the Quraysh who had not yet returned from the haj. Ali would not allow his militant supporters to coerce such a man into any act of hypocrisy. 'Leave him be, I will be his guardian. By God, I have never known him other than ill-natured as a child and as an adult.'

There was bad blood between Ali and the children of Omar. For some twelve years before Ali had publicly come forth and protested against the murders of Ubaydallah, one of Omar's sons. Ubaydallah had slaughtered five innocent Persian Muslims as an act of blood vengeance after the assassination of his father, the Caliph Omar, by Abu Lulu the Persian carpenter. Ali had pressed that the full rigour of Islamic law be exercised lest the petulant demands of tribal honour supersede respect for the law of the Koran – a stance that Omar himself would have respected. In the event, Ali's principled stance had been rejected by Uthman, who had characteristically decided to be merciful by ordering Ubaydallah to settle his crimes with the payment of blood money – and then personally generous by paying this fine out of his own pocket.

Ali had always attracted his share of enemies because of his forthright regard for the truth. There was something in his saintly nature that either kindled passionate support or an almost equal fear. For Ali had always remained a radical and an idealist who shared the Prophet's sense of the all-pervading immanence of God and the ever-present threat of divine punishment. He championed a militant role for the Caliphate, as an instrument for inspiring deeper belief in Islam and guiding the conduct of believers on the right path. Perhaps some of his opponents were also fearful that he might try to assume some of the religious authority of the Prophet. For there is an enduring tradition within Islam that the Prophet had privately imparted to Ali and Fatimah various prayers, practices and concepts that he judged to be too demanding for normal believers. These beliefs would later be codified by the Shia into the belief that Ali was the designated Imam who had the sole authority to interpret and explain the Koran. In a similar way, the various Sufi brotherhoods all look back to Ali as the fountainhead authority for their tradition of esoteric teaching. Whatever it was about him, Ali faced determined opposition right from the very first days of his authority.

The core of this opposition can be located around a single individual. Aisha first heard of the accession of Ali, her old rival, to the Caliphate at the caravan halt of Sarif, just 12 miles north of Mecca. She had been returning to her home in Medina after the conclusion of the formal farewells at the end of that year's haj, but rather

than continue with her journey and face the reality of Ali's leadership she immediately ordered that her caravan turn back on its
tracks and ride back to Mecca. There she put herself at the head of
the vocal opposition to Ali. Without her impassioned stance, it is
quite probable that there would have been no united opposition to
Ali's accession among the Meccans. But once the chief wife of the
Prophet Muhammad, the senior Mother of the Faithful, had publicly raised her standard, the doubters and the disappointed had a
very public and revered figure around which to collect.

Aisha's first task was to distance herself from the opposition to
Uthman's last six years of authority (of which she had been a very
vocal part). She began to rewrite the record by declaring, 'We had
reproached Uthman for some matters which we stated and pointed
out to him. He recanted and asked his Lord for forgiveness. The
Muslims accepted his repentance as they had no other choice.' She
then accused Ali of manipulating the political strife so that it had
inexorably led to the murder of Uthman, 'a single finger of whom
was better than the whole of Ali' – in her highly personal estima-
tion. It was clever, artful propaganda that carefully ignored Ali's
own reluctant role as an arbitrator and his evident disdain for the
mutineers. It also ignored the fact that Ali had remained behind in
Medina in order to protect Uthman through an arbitrated peace
and his son Hasan had been wounded defending the Caliph's
doorway. Aisha, despite the appeals of Marwan and Uthman, had
absented herself.

Once Aisha had entered the fray, the battle lines were rapidly
drawn. Talha and Zubayr slipped out of Medina to join Aisha's
camp in Mecca. They now renounced their earlier oath of loyalty,
which they claimed had been offered out of fear of the mutineers.
Some have seen their actions as merely disappointed ambition, for
if Ali could be deposed or an electoral council convened, they would
surely stand in the first rank as the two most favoured candidates. It

has long been argued that Aisha secretly favoured and conspired for the candidacy of her cousin Talha, though in truth the ties of kinship in this period had become so inextricably confused that it was no longer possible to talk in terms of clan units. For instance, Aisha's own half-brother Muhammad (the last child to be conceived by Aisha's adored father, Abu Bakr) was himself passionately loyal to his stepfather Ali – but as the principal assassin of Uthman, Muhammad was also a potential embarrassment to both sides.

In Aisha's house at Mecca the conspirators held a council of war. There seemed to be but three options open to them: to strike quickly against Ali at Medina, to join Muawiya's army in Syria, or to seek support from one of the other garrison cities. They were not strong enough to attempt the first (and were rightly hesitant to be seen to strike the first blow of a civil war), while they were even more reluctant to become too dependent on Muawiya (the ambitious cousin of the murdered Uthman). Only the third option seemed feasible. Because Ali's supporters were known to be strong and vociferous in both Fustat (Egypt) and Kufa (mid-Iraq), the conspirators' only real option was to move quickly towards Basra (southern Iraq) and seize the leadership of the army there. They were speeded on their way by an ex-governor of Uthman's who stumped up a 400,000-dirham contribution to the war chest.

The numbers involved in this first schism within Islam were small. The vast majority of Muslims were appalled by the prospect of fighting their brethren and preferred to take no sides. So that instead of the 40,000-strong armies which the Muslim state had now become accustomed to marshalling for simultaneous wars on three frontiers, perhaps only 900 men rode out from Mecca under the triumvirate of Aisha, Talha and Zubayr. Umm Salamah, the most politically astute of all the Prophet's wives, had refused to be drawn into the affair and had instead insisted on riding back

from Mecca to give her oath of loyalty to Ali at Medina. Likewise
Hafsah refused to allow her name to be used in any plot to imply
that Ali was responsible for the death of Uthman, and seems to
have persuaded her less gifted brother, Abdallah ibn Omar, to
remain neutral. There were rumours that Muawiya had already
sent agents to make overtures in support of Zubayr's candidacy for
the Caliphate (if Ali were to be deposed), though both Talha and
Zubayr refused to be drawn into the sort of dangerous speculation
that would divide their party. They publicly called for a *shura*, a
council, so that the Caliphate would 'go to one of us, whoever will
be chosen by the people'.

Caliph Ali for his part behaved with the sincerity that was to be
expected of him. Uthman's carefully hoarded reserves were at once
distributed to the poor and the state pensioners so that there was
not one silver coin left on the treasury floor. Ali intended to return
the Muslim community to faith in God's bounty rather than the
dependence of a salaried man upon the efficiency of the imperial
administration. His first official sermon to the assembled faithful,
delivered just two days after the oath of allegiance, was no honey-
tongued exercise by a man with an eye for the creation of broad
consensus politics. Instead Ali delivered a harsh warning about the
dangers of complacency, slackness, disloyalty and lack of sincerity
in religion. It was noticed that the first two Caliphs not only
escaped any censure but were praised by Ali as fitting examples of
a true Muslim. Ali did not attempt to either justify the violent
death of Uthman or condemn his killers but confirmed his opinion that the late Caliph had provoked the people by his unjust
acts.

The new officials that he appointed marked the birth of a new
order, one that would embrace all Arab Muslims irrespective of
their place within the noble clans of the Quraysh. The new
governor-general of Basra was from the Ansar of Medina, a man of

such proven integrity that he had been employed by Omar as a land surveyor. For the governor of Egypt and the garrison city of Fustat he overlooked the claims of the rebel mutineers (all strong partisans for Ali) and appointed another man from Medina, Qays from the Khazraj clan. At this critical period there was a privy meeting held between Ali and that canny old reprobate with one roving eye, Mughira. One of Ali's young cousins, Abdallah (the son of the Prophet's banking uncle Abbas), would remember years later how that private conference had gone. Mughira, the Machiavelli (as well as the Casanova) of early Islamic realpolitik, tried to advise Ali how to become an effective political operator. Send messengers to immediately confirm the existing governors, he counselled; write to them, flatter them, appeal to their greed and their pride, make promises for the future – even if you have no intention of fulfilling them. In the same letter that confirms and strengthens their position instruct them to administer the new loyalty oath to Caliph Ali to the soldiers of their command – and they will be as meek as lambs. Ali had admitted that this policy might be effective but 'By God, this will never be.' For he was obliged to act according to what was right and in conformity with his religious mission to uphold the teaching of the Koran. Mughira listened with silent respect to this uncompromising man of principle but soon afterwards slipped out of the oasis and rode north towards Syria, where he knew Muawiya might be more prepared to appreciate his advice.

Meanwhile the 900-strong party from Mecca, having avoided the caravan routes that passed close to Medina, were about to reach the frontier of Iraq. They were met by a cautious delegation from the garrison of Basra, who respectfully asked if Aisha had come on her own judgement or in fulfilment of a hadith (a saying of the Prophet). Aisha declared that she had decided on her course of action only after she had heard the story of the death of

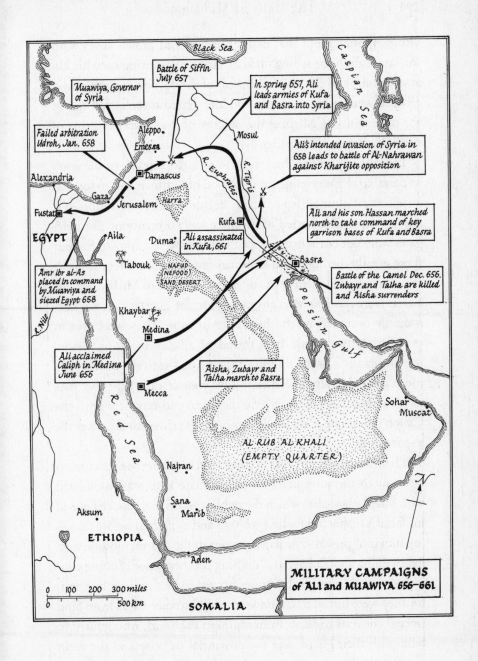

Black Sea

Muawiya, Governor of Syria

Battle of Siffin July 657

In spring 657, Ali leads armies of Kufa and Basra into Syria

Caspian Sea

Failed arbitration Udroh, Jan. 658

Aleppo
Emessa
Mosul

R. Euphrates
R. Tigris

Ali's intended invasion of Syria in 658 leads to battle of Al-Nahrawan against Kharijite opposition

Alexandria
Damascus

Gaza
Jerusalem
Harra

Fustat

Kufa

Ali and his son Hassan marched north to take command of key garrison bases of Kufa and Basra

EGYPT

Aila

Duma
Ali assassinated in Kufa, 661

Basra

Amr ibr al-As placed in command by Muawiya and siezed Egypt 658

Tabouk

NAFUD (NEFOOD) SAND DESERT

R. Nile

Khaybar

Persian Gulf

Battle of the Camel Dec. 656. Zubayr and Talha are killed and Aisha surrenders

Medina

Ali acclaimed Caliph in Medina June 656

Mecca

Aisha, Zubayr and Talha march to Basra

Sohar
Muscat

Red Sea

AL RUB AL KHALI (EMPTY QUARTER)

Najran

N

Sana
Marib

Aksum

ETHIOPIA

Aden

0   100   200   300 miles

0   500 km

SOMALIA

MILITARY CAMPAIGNS of ALI and MUAWIYA 656-661

Uthman. She agreed that many Muslims had grown angry with the late Caliph for selling off state lands, appointing only his kin as governors and for his punishment of the devout, but those who rebelled against his authority had 'desecrated three sacred rights: the sovereignty of Medina, the sanctity of the Caliph and that of the holy month of Ramadan'.

For that reason they had come to seek the support of the army at Basra 'to claim revenge for the blood of Uthman and to see that an electoral council is set up to decide on the succession'. Of Aisha's implacable hatred of Ali there was no mention. The delegates were not entirely convinced but they were happy to honour these greatly distinguished Companions by asking them to pitch their tents beside them at the open marketplace of Mirbad outside Basra. Here the 900 Meccans camped in the quarter that was customarily occupied by the Beni Sulaym tribe. They were able to proselytise their cause in a round of all-day meetings before moving camp – in the middle of the night – into the quarter of a more amenable ally, the Beni Tahiya clan of the Azd tribe. Ali's newly appointed governor gave them leave to stay here until the Caliph (whom he had already summoned) arrived to take over the negotiations.

The following night Aisha's party struck, seizing the governor as he went to the mosque. This unfortunate man was humiliated with forty lashes, after which the public executioner plucked out all his facial hair (including his eyebrows and eyelashes) before throwing him into prison. The dawn prayers in the central mosque were led by Talha and Zubayr as if nothing had happened. Seizing control of the other public buildings proved to be a messier business, for they were forced to cut down the loyal soldier slaves from Sind (recent converts to Islam from southern Pakistan), who refused to relinquish their guard over the provincial treasury and the grain stores.

If the triumphant Meccans now succeeded in extending their control over both the Basra garrison and that of Kufa, Ali's new authority as Caliph was doomed. Letters and messengers criss-crossed each other as Ali in Medina and Aisha, Talha and Zubayr in Basra communicated with their key supporters in Kufa. The acting governor of Kufa, the stern and independently minded Abu Musa (who had served all three previous Caliphs), counselled his warriors to stand aside from any political activity that would weaken the unity of Islam. Another key figure, the chieftain of the Beni Saad, declared that he would fight against neither the Mother of the Faithful nor the cousin of the Prophet and led his 6000 tribesmen back into the neutrality of the desert.

It must again be stressed how small the politically active groups were in this epic but confusing first schism within Islam. For when Caliph Ali left Medina his force was not much larger than that of Aisha and her confederates and the bulk of it, some 700 men, was composed of such key components of the old clan society of Medina oasis as the Najjer and the Khazraj. While Ali made straight for a camping ground halfway between between the two garrison cities he had instructed his son Hasan to ride straight into Kufa, where the moral authority of the grandson of the Prophet allowed him to eclipse the governor. Hasan was then able to lead 7000 men (recruited from a whole range of Bedouin tribes) into his father's encampment.

By the winter of 656, the two opposing forces had reluctantly advanced to confront each other meeting on the waste ground where the castle of Ziyad would later stand. For three days the three male principals – Ali, Zubayr and Talha – sat to negotiate a settlement. They met within a round tent.

On the morning of Thursday 8 December 656 Ali left the tent and pinned up the wall of his side, for the talking was now over. At noon the two armies advanced to give battle, but from the fragmentary stories that have filtered down from this extraordinary day, it seems very few of the warriors had any real heart for the conflict. For everyone still secretly expected a settlement to be agreed at the very last moment. Only this desire for a last-minute peace explains the story of how Ali's otherwise heroic standard-bearing son, Muhammad ibn al-Hanafiyya, faltered before the line of enemy lances, or how Zubayr abandoned the field of the battle and was killed by three Bedouin from his own army. It seems impossible that Zubayr, one of the bravest and most resolute of all the Prophet's Companions, could have turned coward – though it is quite plausible that at the last possible instant he refused to draw the blood of his fellow Muslims. When his head and his sword were brought to Ali, the Caliph sorrowfully remarked that he knew it well, for many a time had he fought beside it in the front rank as they both protected the Messenger of God. The death of Talha, who bled to death from an arrow that severed his sciatic vein, also reads as if it was an incident in a duel rather than a full-scale battle. So too the chivalric conclusion to the day, when in the late afternoon light the fighting concentrated around the camel litter in which Aisha sat, protected by armoured panels. Champion after champion from her ranks came forth to take the place of honour – and near-certain death – by advancing to hold the camel halter of the Mother of the Faithful and serve as her protective knight. One by one they were felled by the surrounding archers, as if an ode from some old pre-Islamic battle verse were being brought back to life. Kab with a Koran around his neck was slain, then it was the turn of ibn Attab, known by his followers as 'the lord of the Quraysh', to fall, later to be followed by one of Talha's own sons, and then Aisha's own nephew, Abdullah, son of Zubayr, was laid low and left for dead. These proud leaders of the Quraysh were to be followed by the simple but desperately proud warriors of the

Beni Dabba tribe, who were garrisoned in Basra. It was said that forty of the young men of the Dabba took their death-pride in turn by guarding Aisha's camel before Ali gave the decisive order that the beast be hamstrung. When it fell to the ground, one of Ali's keenest warriors, Muhammad ibn Abu Bakr, leapt forward so that none but he should touch his eldest sister, whose army he had so relentlessly fought against all day. The howdah in which Aisha had presided over the battle had been so often hit by Ali's archers that it now looked like a hedgehog. Her younger brother whispered through the leather armour of the howdah, 'Has anything hit you?' to which Aisha quietly replied, 'Yes, an arrow in the upper arm.' Muhammad put his arm through the screen into the litter, felt for the shaft of the arrow and having drawn his elder sister towards him deftly extracted the barb – without so much as a whimper emerging from within the howdah.

Ali then approached and banged on the leather walls, and declaimed, 'Surely this is the Humayra of Iram, who wanted to kill me as she killed Uthman ibn Affan.' Ali's forceful greeting was full of carefully graded references: Iram was the name of a garden oasis of one of the pre-Islamic peoples of Arabia that had been destroyed due to the misguided actions of just one of its members, Humayra (the little red one) was one of the favourite pet names which the Prophet Muhammad had used to address his beloved Aisha, while in conclusion Ali had neatly turned around Aisha's most public grievance (the killing of Uthman) upon her own head. In reply Aisha meekly surrendered: 'You have won the reign, son of Abu Talib, so pardon now with goodness.'

Ali gave orders that Aisha was to be escorted by her own young half-brother to a house in Basra, after which she was to be taken back to her home in Medina. Then he ordered his heralds to cry out,

No one turning his back shall be pursued;
No one wounded shall be killed;
Whoever throws away his arms is safe.

Ali had pardoned with goodness. The dead were buried, only captured arms and animals could be held as war booty, for Ali would not permit any Muslims (even his adversaries) to be enslaved, while the heirs of the killed were assured that they would suffer no penalties. To compensate his own men for his generosity to a defeated enemy he awarded them 500 dirhams each from the Basran treasury. The only enemy to be executed lost his life because he used the phrase 'the religion of Ali', something that because of its implied deviation from the Prophet's message never failed to infuriate Ali.

Ali rode on to Kufa. Once there he refused to be put up in the governor's sprawling palace, which he dismissed as the Qasr al-Khabath (castle of corruption) and instead selected a modest courtyard. Uthman's kinsmen and children had already been removed from their public positions but they too were now guaranteed their freedom and immunity. In their place the devout kinsmen of the Prophet, Muhammad's cousin Abdallah ibn Abbas and his stepson Umar, were appointed governors of Basra and al-Bahrain. Much more contentious was his choice of his stepson Muhammad ibn Abu Bakr to be the new governor of Egypt, for he had been one of the killers of Uthman. However, Ali felt for certain that Muhammad totally shared his vision of returning the Muslim Empire to the purity, simplicity and poverty of its first years.

There remained one more important issue to be settled before Ali would be free to leave his temporary headquarters in the garrison city of Kufa and return to Medina. He had to settle the fate of Muawiya, the man who had ruled Syria for almost two decades.

Mughira's advice, which Ali had indignantly rejected, was to temporise and make an ally of the powerful governor-general. In the six months that had passed between Ali's accession in June and the battle of the Camel in December, neither side had made any move to settle this tense situation. Ali was too preoccupied with the immediate threat, while Muawiya still hoped for a peaceful understanding that would confirm him as ruler of Syria.

Muawiya had good reason to believe that he could survive the fall of Uthman. For although he was a cousin of Uthman he had specifically been excluded from the general tide of popular opposition to the Caliph's kinsmen. For Muawiya had not been brought to power on the coat-tails of his cousin but had climbed there through his own abilities. By the year 656 there were very few Muslims who could look back over such a long and distinguished career in the service of Islam as Muawiya. He was not, however, to be numbered among the Muhajirun, the early converts to Islam. He had made his submission only when his home town of Mecca had finally surrendered to the Prophet. It was also undeniably true that he was the son of the two great early opponents of the Prophet (his father was the pagan leader Abu Sufyan and his mother the liver-chewing Hind), though throughout this period he had been but a child in his father's household. When Muawiya grew into manhood, the Prophet trusted him well enough to have employed him as an occasional secretary in Medina. Muawiya would participate in all the early battles of the Caliphate, fighting alongside his elder brother Yazid, who had been entrusted by Abu Bakr with high command in the conquest of the Holy Land. The great Omar subsequently raised Muawiya up to become one of the four governor-generals of Syria. Such were his organisational talents, revealed annually in the energetic prosecution of the war against Byzantium (and the speedy suppression of two major counter-attacks), that he gradually assumed control over the other three garrison commands within Syria and Palestine. Under Uthman's reign he had expanded the frontiers of the Muslim Empire into the Mediterranean and Armenia, while his governorship was the only one not touched by the unrest that characterised the last six years. If offered the chance to continue working under Ali as he had served the first three Caliphs, he would undoubtedly have been content to do so. It was only Ali's determination to replace him and sweep aside the panoply of wealth and power that underpinned Muawiya's authority that would gradually turn him into an opponent.

The arrival in Damascus of the first refugees from Uthman's discredited court of kinsmen at Medina must have been an embarrassment to Muawiya. Certainly Uthman's brother, Walid (the man who had been sacked from the governorship of Kufa for public drunkenness), must have seemed more of a burden than anything else. Walid publicly taunted Muawiya to take up the burden of blood vengeance:

> *By God, Hind will not be your mother if the day passes*
> *Without the avenger taking revenge for Uthman.*
> *Can the slave of the people kill the lord of his household*
> *And you do not kill him? Would your mother were barren!*
> *Surely if we kill them no one can retaliate*
> *For them; the wheels of fortune have turned on you.*

This verse must have been especially irritating. Walid was the closest male relative of Uthman but in this reference he was clearly trying to pass on the burden of vengeance to a cousin. The language that he used looked straight back to the habits of pre-Islamic Arabia, with not so much as a nod in the direction of the new moral order of Islam. In the six-month period between June and December 656, Muawiya wished to remain a loyal friend to all the principal candidates in order that he might remain the de facto ruler of Syria. Walid in this period was also trying to cause a public breach with Amr (the conqueror of Egypt), who Muawiya instinctively knew might yet prove to be a useful ally in the future. In the immediate period after the death of Uthman, Amr was widely considered to be one of the chief culprits. Not only had he publicly split with Uthman the year before, and then gone on to reinforce this by repudiating his marriage to Uthman's sister, but the old soldiers of the Egyptian garrison (most of them still fanatically loyal to their old commander Amr) had been at the forefront of the peculiar chain of actions that had quickly turned petitioners from protesters into assassins.

However, by late December it became clear to Muawiya that Ali was now the unopposed leader of the Muslim Empire. Aisha had been defeated in battle and had kept true to her peace, while Talha and Zubayr were dead. Ali had not only emerged as the victor but had rejected all his overtures for an 'understanding' and was preparing to invade Syria in the spring of 657 in order to appoint a governor of his own choice. So if Muawiya wished to resist him, he was forced to build up his own political position so that he had a chance of withstanding the otherwise unassailable legitimacy of Ali. The only course open to him was to pose as the avenger of Uthman. The previously embarrassing kinsmen of Uthman were now publicly honoured at Damascus. His sister in Medina, Umm Habiba (one of the wives of the Prophet), had in the meanwhile sent a bundle of family relics for safe keeping in Damascus. The bloodstained shirt of Uthman with its multiple stab wounds was sent around Syria on an emotional tour of the provincial garrisons before being nailed to the pulpit in the Great Mosque of Damascus. The severed fingers of Uthman's young Syrian wife Naila, cut off as she protected her husband's body from desecration, heightened the emotional charge. Verse 33 of Sura 17 of the Koran became the linchpin of Muawiya's campaign: 'If anyone is killed wrongly, we give the next of kin authority [to avenge him], but let him not be excessive in killing.'

Ali's appointment of Muhammad ibn Abu Bakr as the governor of Egypt unwittingly played straight into Muawiya's new diplomatic offensive. For although he would not dare to claim directly that Ali had been involved in Uthman's death, the known regicide Muhammad was now an honoured member of Ali's new administration. This opened the door to a campaign of whispered innuendo and defamatory public poetry and provided Muawiya with a certain political security. He could now publicly call for justice to be served upon the murderers of Uthman knowing that Ali would find it virtually impossible to comply. Muawiya now had a cast-iron cause with which to justify his refusal to vacate the governorship of Syria at the command of the new Caliph. In his words, 'the people of Syria will accept nothing until you surrender to them the killers of Uthman'.

Muawiya was nothing if not a pragmatist. He knew that Ali was still revered by the Muslim warriors and junior officers under his command and was canny enough to appear otherwise loyal: 'As for your nobility in Islam and your close kinship with the Messenger of God and your place among the Quraysh, I do not deny them.' At this period, far from aspiring to become Caliph himself, Muawiya was content to try to persuade potential candidates to his cause. He sent messengers from Damascus to privately win over a few Companions by promising them the earth, as with his well-honed phrase to Omar's son Abdullah, 'he did not want to reign over him but wanted the reign for him'. But the envoys were sent back home with their ears ringing with rebukes. What had Muawiya, a mere *taliq* (a convert to Islam made after the testing period of persecution and struggle) and the son of the man who waged war on the Prophet, got to do with any process by which a

virtuous Companion might be chosen to become Caliph? It is as
well to bear in mind that the leaders of Islam in this period were
still exclusively resident in Medina. Indeed in Omar's reign they
had been forbidden to leave the oasis without his express permission. Uthman had of course released them from this obligation
and allowed them to buy lands elsewhere, though the vast majority of the Companions would always be wedded to this oasis,
filled with poignant, deeply cherished memories of Muhammad
and the many locations where the Koran had been revealed.
Medina's cemetery had now grown into a pantheon filled with
most of the heroes of early Islam. There was still also within the
community a tangible belief that the day of reckoning – which fea-
tures so largely in the Koran – was years, not decades or centuries,
away. Given this fearful understanding of the imminence of the
end of the world and the terrifying Day of Judgement, Yaum al-
Din, there was enormous comfort to be had in physical proximity
to the Prophet. When Muawiya mentioned that Syria should have
a voice in the next shura, the council that elected the Caliph, Ali
witheringly replied that there was not in Syria one man eligible to
sit in such a shura. He was also able to remind Muawiya that back
in 632, Muawiya's own father, Abu Sufyan, had come privately to
Ali to pledge him his support at the time that Abu Bakr was
assuming the Caliphate 'but I declined because the people were
close to infidelity and I feared division among the people of Islam.
Thus your father was more ready to recognise my right than you.'
Other partisans of Ali, less respectful of diplomatic niceties,
recalled that their hero at the battle of the wells of Badr (in 624)
had killed three close kinsmen of Muawiya: his elder brother
Hansala as well as his maternal uncle and maternal grandfather,
and that perhaps Muawiya was also fated to fall one day beneath
Ali's sword like the rest of his family.

In an open council meeting of the leaders of Islam, the chief men of Medina as well as the Quraysh of Mecca, Ali asked for their public advice. They were all in favour of attacking their enemies in Syria, 'who had become entirely motivated by worldly greed'; one old fighter declared that war against 'these people was dearer to him than against the heathen Turks and the Byzantines'. Other wiser heads declared that they were for Ali 'equally in peace and war' but advised him to be careful to win over the whole support of the people of Kufa, 'which would be crucial for him'.

In Syria Muawiya had been making his own, more tactically minded decisions. He had patched up a truce with the Byzantine Emperor (even agreeing to pay tribute) so that he could free up as many troops as could be spared for the coming test with Ali. He then dispatched all the soldiers who were well disposed towards Ali (especially those of Yemeni origin) to guard this Byzantine frontier. Next he further secured his already excellent relationship with the chieftains of the tribes of Syria, pardoning one such ruler for his seizure of a provincial treasury and promoting the son of another, so that he could be assured of the support of the key tribes of the desert frontier between Syria and Iraq. These manoeuvres also helped strengthen the already tangible rivalry between the Iraqi and Syrian Muslim garrisons by evoking the age-old rivalry of the Byzantine Arab kingdom of Ghassan with the pro-Persian Arab Lakhmid kingdom. All the old boasting poetry between the two dynasties (several centuries of rivalry buried beneath just twenty years of Islam) could be excavated to stir on the coming conflict.

> *I see Syria loathing the region of Iraq*
> *and the people of Iraq loathing her.*
> *Each one hates his partner.*

Muawiya had also begun to woo Amr to his cause, even though

Amr was popularly considered to have had some role in Uthman's death. This unpalatable rumour was put to one side, so that they could both concentrate on the more agreeable subject of the fate of Egypt. Muawiya promised Amr that he would assist him in recovering possession of the governorship of Egypt, which Amr had twice conquered for Islam. To prove his good intentions Muawiya began to quietly arrest Ali's various messengers and agents when they passed through Palestine on their way between Medina and Egypt. Ali's appointment of the young Muhammad ibn Abu Bakr as governor of Egypt made the pact between the two old experienced generals even more likely. There was another, scarcely credible, ingredient to their secret understanding. Amr's patronymic and place in Mecca's clan system came through his legal father, Sahmi al-As ibn Wail, who had been one of the six lovers of Amr's notoriously attractive mother at the time of his conception. Those who wished to publicly insult Amr liked to remind him of his indeterminate paternity by referring to him not as the son of any man, but as the child of a prostitute, 'the son of al-Nabigha', for his mother came to Mecca as a slave and had to work as a prostitute before she acquired her freedom and could choose her own lovers. It was said that Amr's mother had only chosen Sahmi al-As ibn Wail to be the legal father of her child because he was the kindest and most generous of her six lovers. By the time Amr had grown into manhood, his looks, commanding stature and martial ability were uncannily similar to those of Abu Sufyan, who was well known to be one of those six men. Muawiya and Amr might well have been blood brothers. Whatever their family links, they were most certainly brothers in ambition, united in their old age by an absolute determination to remain the rulers of one of the two great kingdoms of the ancient Middle East that each had separately conquered in the name of Islam.

*

In May 657 Ali led his army out of the garrison city of Kufa and marched up through the fertile farmland of central Iraq beside the River Tigris. Once they reached Mosul his column, numbered in tens of thousands of men, swung west and reached the Euphrates at Raqqa. Here the fertile black soils of the Sawad have given way to arid steppe land that stretches across low gravel-strewn desert hills. It is good grazing country. The Euphrates valley, now just a gash of green a few hundred yards wide, was even then no serious impediment to the movement of thousands of cavalrymen. Nevertheless, Ali made his supply line secure by ordering a bridge of boats to be laid across the Euphrates so that he could advance, if need be, into central Syria. At Siffin, an old flood plain on the west side of the river, the two vast armies of the Caliphate came face to face. Ali's army drove Muawiya's advance guard off from the river – but then chivalrously allowed them access to water their mounts.

Ali and Muawiya both offered to negotiate but there was no longer any room for compromise. Ali then challenged Muawiya to settle their differences in single combat, so that the blood of innocent Muslims might be spared. Muawiya sidestepped this lethal invitation. Instead over the following days a tournament developed as champion after champion rode out from the rival camps and challenged a named adversary to single combat. In one such duel, Ubaydallah ibn Omar challenged Ali's son Muhammad to bring forth a small retinue and fight. As Ubaydallah rode out from Muawiya's army he was saluted with the cry 'With us is the good one, son of the good, the son of Omar.' His opponents took up the challenge and cried back, 'With you is the abominable one, son of the good.' Ubaydallah fell that day. In the evening light a veiled young woman riding a mule and accompanied by her servants left Muawiya's camp and rode fearlessly towards Ali's. She was Bahriyya, a daughter of the Rabia tribe, whose warriors had distinguished themselves in the duel against Ubaydallah and his hand-picked retinue of heavily armoured Syrian knights. She had come to praise her Rabia kinsmen for their bravery that day. Only after she had fulfilled this duty did she ask for the body of her husband Ubaydallah to be given back to her – like Paris begging Achilles for the body of Hector. As she washed the blood and dust of the battle from her husband's corpse, her servants were quietly digging a grave. As Ubaydallah was placed in the ground, Bahriyya recited two lines of an elegy before mounting her mule and riding back to the opposing campsite in the night.

When the new moon first lit up the desert night (on 19 June) the period of courtly duels came to an abrupt end with the month of Muharram. It had been kept as one of the months of truce and free trade in the years before the arrival of Islam and though this no longer held validity, both armies avoided a full-scale battle over Muharram. The first week of the month of Safar (19–25 July) can be read like an Arabic *Iliad*, as day after day the leading warriors rode up to the enemy lines to curse their opponents, boast over their future victory and order them to 'fear God and to respond to the summons of what is right'.

According to the traditional accounts, the battle of Siffin began on the eighth day of Safar, Wednesday 26 July. Ali led his army from the centre, surrounded by the men from Medina, with the army of Kufa forming one wing and the army of Basra the other. The fighting raged over 'three days and three nights and one morning', the first day favouring the Syrians while the second pushed them back almost into their camp. The third day's fighting, 'the day of the sword', was the most bloody and indecisive of all. The confused hand-to-hand fighting continued into the 'night of the rumble' – *laylat al-harir*. By the dawn of the fourth morning of battle, in something of the same manner in which al-Qadisiya had been won, the passionate champions of the cause of Ali alone seemed to possess the hidden reserves of strength to launch attack after aggressive attack. By mid-morning it seemed entirely possible that the army of Ali would prove victorious.

At this critical point, when an Empire of Faith was to be decided one way or the other by another hour of pitiless slaughter, something totally unexpected happened. A body of Syrian cavalry rode out between the battle lines with open copies of the Holy Koran tied to the heads of their lances. They cried out, 'The word of God. Let the word of God decide between us and you. Who will protect the border towns of Syria if we are slain and who will protect the people of Iraq after you are gone? Let the book of God judge between you and us.' It must have echoed the secret wishes of the soldiers of Ali's army, for they at once took up this refrain, this new battle cry of peace. Ali and his key commanders feared it was a ruse of Muawiya's, a trick to delay his imminent defeat, and urged their men on into battle. But it seems possible that it was a spontaneous decision that captivated both armies – though some historians see the hand of Amr behind this potent gesture. The semi-professional Koranic readers and reciters, who formed a sort of guard regiment in both armies, were especially vociferous in favour of the trial by book. Ali and his chief confederates raged at their men but there was no turning them now. A messenger was sent to Muawiya, who was delighted to accept a truce just when his army was on the brink of defeat. Now the men of Ali's army, the majority of them from Kufa and Basra, shouted out the name of one of their old commanders, Abu Musa, to be their arbitrator. Ali protested that Abu Musa was a neutral and was not to be numbered among his supporters. He would never have chosen such a man for his ambassador. Muawiya for his part was quick to nominate Amr as his delegate. Amr in the minds of the Muslim rank and file was, just like Abu Musa, a heroic figure from the early days of the conquest, and a respected governor-general. He was very far from neutral, for he had skilfully commanded one of Muawiya's divisions throughout the four-day battle of Siffin. We also know that he had already made a secret pact with Muawiya to support his cause to the utmost in return for being given back his command over Egypt – though this was not then common knowledge. In those few unpredictable hours around the noonday sun, among a rabble of exhausted troops, confused beyond their mettle by the chain of events that led them to fight their Muslim brothers, Ali's long-awaited reign as Caliph began to rapidly unravel. It was just a year since he had been acclaimed by the ecstatic crowd in the marketplace of Medina and accepted their pledges of obedience.

Two days later Amr rode across the battlefield and entered the camp of Ali's army. Armed with his new-found authority as one of the two delegates, trusted by both armies with the arbitration of God's word, he set about drawing up the protocol for negotiations. When the secretaries began their first draft with 'This is what has been agreed between the Commander of the Faithful and Muawiya . . .' Amr at once interrupted with a burst of well-framed indignation. Ali was the commander of his own army just as Muawiya was of his, but by God, if he was to be acknowledged as Commander of the Faithful in the very first line there was neither reason nor purpose for this arbitration. In such a manner did Amr skilfully manage to get the protocol agreement to gradually drop Ali's title and range Ali and Muawiya as two seemingly equal candidates for the arbitration. By the end of the session, on 2 August 657, Amr's text stated that 'both parties agreed to bind themselves by God's word, and where the Koran was silent, by Muslim precedent. All should accept the decision of the two arbitrators who bound themselves to judge righteously.' A military truce was to be upheld until the two arbitrators could meet at a place equidistant from Damascus and Kufa.

For Ali's cause, Amr's skilful finessing of the truce was an unmitigated disaster. As the army of Kufa and the army of Basra marched south back down through the farmland of Iraq, the extent of the casualties that they had bravely endured during the battle of Siffin became ever more conspicuous. Nor were they returning as victors proudly bearing their scars, nor even as the heroic army of God under the command of their Caliph. More and more the clauses of the truce led them to look upon themselves as but just one faction in a civil war. Ali had led them north as undisputed and rightful Commander of the Faithful, taking them on a war to suppress the ambition of the over-mighty and disobedient governor of Syria. As the long columns trailed back past the fertile black soil of the Sawad, they realised that Ali had somehow become demoted to one of two petitioners awaiting the decision of the arbitrators.

By the time they had reached the outskirts of Kufa that September, at least a third of the army felt disgusted by the outcome of the truce. They were the most ardent supporters of Ali's right to rule as well as those who had been most disgusted by the wealthy oligarchy imposed on them in the last six years of Uthman's rule. They refused to pitch camp with the majority back in the old garrison-base of Kufa but instead established a rival camp across the Tigris at Harura. Later they would be joined by like-minded soldiers from the Basra force. They would become known as the 'seceders', the *khawarij*.* They were bitterly opposed to the idea of arbitration and argued for 'No judgement but God's' and talked about electing their own leader. Ali treated them with compassion, sending his most eloquent supporter, Abdullah ibn Abbas, to talk to them before riding across himself. He reminded them of that day in Siffin, of how he had stormed

* Anglicised in the plural as 'Kharijites'.

and pleaded with his soldiers to continue the fight, but to no avail. And how it had been their own desire to heed the cries of the cavalrymen of Syria with the Koran suspended from their lances that had frustrated his leadership. Most of the seceders returned to their homes.

To confirm the new accord it was decided to repeat the oath that had been first made to Ali as a young man. This was the famous oath of Ghadir Khumm composed by the Prophet in the last year of his life. On 16 March 632, at the caravan halt of Ghadir Khumm on Muhammad's return from the last pilgrimage, he had asked his followers to swear to Ali to 'be a friend to whomever he befriends, and an enemy of whomever he takes as an enemy'. From among the crowd of believers milling in the dusty square outside Kufa's central mosque Ali publicly asked for any surviving witness from that day to come forward and testify. Twelve Companions made their solemn witness, after which the twenty-five-year-old oath of personal allegiance to Ali was once again renewed by the soldiers of Kufa and Basra.

In January 658 the two arbitrators formally met at Udruh in Jordan. Amr and Abu Musa were each accompanied by 400 followers as well as a host of Companions and Koranic reciters who gathered to witness the great peacemaking. This solemn conclave started on an auspicious note: Abu Musa gravely declaring that all Muslims should aspire to end the civil war and work towards unity – to which Amr piously joined his prayers. Abu Musa hoped to create a framework in which Uthman's death would be treated as murder, after which a shura could be formed which would allow Muawiya to be confirmed in his office and Ali (or a compromise candidate) acclaimed Caliph. Amr pretended agreement, but one by one the various compromise candidates were rejected, so that all they could agree on was that both Ali and Muawiya should retire and leave the choice up to the people.

Amr tactfully indicated that as the senior in years, it was Abu Musa's right to make the public announcement on behalf of them both. Abu Musa did so. Then, as he had agreed with Abu Musa, Amr stood up to confirm their joint decision. But instead he made his own announcement. 'You have heard the decision of Abu Musa,' he gleefully cried, 'for he has decreed the deposition of his candidate Ali, and I confirm this decision. As for my candidate Muawiya, I confirm him as the true Caliph, the heir of Uthman and the avenger of his blood.'

It was larceny on a grand scale and the peace conference at once broke up in violent rebukes, curses and bitter reproaches. Abu Musa, now despised as a gullible fool by Muawiya and Amr and reviled as a traitor by the partisans of Ali, took the lone road to Mecca, where he lived out his last days in piety, privacy and prayer. Amr's trickery was at once denounced as a marketplace fraud, though Muawiya now at last felt confident enough to announce himself Caliph. That May of 658 he received an oath of loyalty from his obedient troops in the Great Mosque of Damascus. Ali, who had never stopped being considered Caliph by his supporters, responded by adding a formal curse on Muawiya and his associates into the practice of the morning prayer. However, the disastrous, near-comical chicanery of the arbitration had deeply upset the seceders, the Kharijites. Although most of them had made their peace with Ali, once they heard the farcical result of the arbitration they abandoned their homes in the streets of Basra and Kufa and made an exodus, trying to establish a community among the Persian ruins before moving north to a promising site on the banks of the Tigris at Nahrawan – near to the present site of the City of Peace – Baghdad. Although they shared Ali's passionate desire for a community of true Muslims, they felt so appalled by the chicanery of the political turn of events that they decided to create their own self-governing and independent settlement. A council of godly men was elected to look after the day-to-day administration and an imam to lead them in prayers – and if need be in war.

By March 658 Ali had determined once again to lead the army of Kufa and Basra north to make a decisive test of strength against Muawiya's usurpation. He had tried once more to persuade the Kharijites to rejoin his army, for in the past they had been among his boldest supporters and in the heroic vanguard of his army. His peace missions, sermons and envoys, combined with the promise of forgiveness and safe conduct, managed to whittle down the number of Kharijites from around 4000 to 2000. However this inner core, deprived of all their more moderate members, became increasingly militant and began to send out raiding parties into the surrounding countryside. This Ali could not afford to ignore, especially as he would be leaving the people defenceless when he led the armies out of Iraq.

In mid-May (though some other chroniclers would have it mid-July) the two armies clashed outside Nahrawan, the remaining 1800 Kharijites falling with near-suicidal bravery upon the army of Ali, which was at least ten times the size. Most of them perished with the battle cry 'Paradise, paradise' on their lips.

With their deaths, so too died something of the spirit of Ali's army. Among the dead that day, fathers found sons, brothers found brothers, but all could join in the mourning for the loss of many of the most passionate, zealous and ethically pure of the Muslims. Many of the men who had led the charges at Siffin, or fought most ardently for Ali at the battle of the Camel, or suffered most under the proud kinsmen of Uthman, were to be found dead on the field of Nahrawan. It was the civil war within the civil war, waged not so much against Ali but in desperation against the political corruption that was quickly overwhelming Muhammad's pure dream of Islam, in which every man was free to equally address God and where their leader could honestly boast that poverty is my pride.

The Kharijites are condemned by both Shia and Sunni historians as the first, and the most violent, of the schismatics. Their beliefs also straddle the dividing line between the two main sects, for their leaders would declare that 'we associate with the two sheikhs' (by which they meant Abu Bakr and Omar), but 'we disassociate ourselves with the evil-doers' (by which they meant both Uthman and Ali). They also largely came out of the nomadic culture of the Bedouin tribes, where the decision to move off, or exclude dissenting groups, came naturally (like the movement to a different pasture or the breaking away of a clan from the main tribe); but it was less relevant to the increasingly urban nature of the great Islamic garrison cities. Unlike both Shia and Sunni, the Kharijites would never agree to raise up the Hadith (the sayings of the Prophet) as a basis for Islamic law and culture. They trusted only in the Koran, and continued to delight in the traditional oral culture of the nomad Arabs, excelling in oratory and poetry.

For Ali it was a second accidental disaster to put beside his soldiers' decision to agree to an arbitration just as they had nearly achieved victory at Siffin. Now they insisted to Ali that they must first return to their garrison cities before they could contemplate the invasion of Syria. For 'their arrows were used up, their swords dulled, their spearheads had fallen off their lances'. These were poignant metaphors for an inner reality, for their zeal and spirit had also been blunted by memories of Nahrawan. When Ali issued the summons for war later in the season, the response was so muted that he had to abandon any thought of an offensive campaign that year.

Muawiya for his part was determined to play it safe. His army in Syria was allowed to indulge in a few hit-and-run raids on Iraq's upper Euphrates valley, but no campaign was launched that could result in a decisive battle. These manoeuvres were in any case no more than a smokescreen for his real objective that year – which was to seize control of Egypt. One of Ali's most accomplished subordinates, al-Ashtar, had foreseen this. He had ridden quickly across the Arabian desert and taken a ship across the Red Sea (to avoid Muawiya's agents in Palestine and Syria) in order to assist Ali's garrison in Egypt. Upon his safe landing into Egypt he was greeted by a friendly customs officer who served him with a welcoming drink of cool honey-sweetened water. It was poisoned.

Meanwhile Muawiya's other confidential agents had been identifying useful allies among the old supporters of Amr in Egypt – as well as those few who looked back to the reign of Uthman with affection. Amr had also been given his reward, the command of 6000 men with whom he now advanced through Palestine in order to approach Egypt. Muhammad ibn Abu Bakr felt his support among the Muslim Arab soldiers in the garrison city of Fustat to be dwindling and so he determined on an early test of strength. However, in pushing for an early battle he allowed his vanguard to become isolated, then trapped and ruthlessly annihilated by Amr. After this early reverse the rest of Muhammad's army promptly deserted and noisily welcomed Amr back, as he once more marched back into 'his' Fustat in triumph. Amr had given orders that Muhammad should be captured alive but the troops who found him sheltering in an old ruin had other ideas. First they blockaded Muhammad so that he was weakened by lack of water, then, having accepted his surrender, provoked him into a fight so that he could be done to death while resisting arrest. His corpse was wrapped within the carcass of a donkey and buried. When the news reached Amr he was angry, though back in Medina Aisha was prostrate with grief at the death and dishonour done to her youngest half-brother. She cursed Amr and Muawiya, plunged herself into violent mourning but also made certain that she took safe charge of her brother's surviving family and dependants. (Muhammad's young son, Qasim, was to grow up under the protection of Aisha's roof at Medina to become one of the great early scholars of Islam.) Amr for his part avoided any mention of his role as an avenger of the murder of Uthman in his victorious Egyptian campaign. Those with an inconvenient memory might recall that he was still one of the principal suspects. Ali had scraped together a relief force of 2000 men for Egypt. This was recalled just five days after the column had set off, when the news of the death of both Muhammad and al-Ashtar reached Ali.

The ever-harsher political landscape did not change Ali's total commitment to good government. His demand to see all the figures, accounts, exact sources of revenue and expenditure from his cousin's government of Basra led him to dismiss Abdallah ibn Abbas (one of his few remaining political allies and advisers) from this post. Ali asserted that neither he, the Caliph, nor Abbas the governor was due more reward than was paid out to any other Muslim. Though as long as the family of the Prophet could prove themselves worthy by their knowledge of the Koran and the example set by Muhammad they had the best right to serve the community as Imam. When questioned closely by his followers about his true feelings for Abu Bakr, he confirmed that he had willingly 'put the cause of Islam before his own interest and had pledged allegiance to Abu Bakr, assisted him in overcoming the apostates and backed him with sincere advice'. About the second Caliph he declared that 'Omar's conduct was pleasing and blessed with good success.' Years later he would write in confidence to Ali's son, 'You know that the people turned away from your father Ali and went over to Muawiya only because he made equal the share from the endowments among them and treated them all the same in regard to their stipends.' Such was the purity of his government that his own brother Aqil, infuriated by Ali's refusal to reward his own family with pensions, loans or positions, would be won over to Muawiya's court.

Muawiya preferred to slowly bite away at Ali's authority by offering jobs to the discontented, a doubling of the stipend for the garrison soldiers and tactful explanations of how his rule would be 'beneficial to all concerned'. Muawiya's Damascus-based realm now stretched over Egypt (where Amr ruled as his governor), Syria, Palestine, Cyprus and Armenia, while Ali's legitimist Caliphate remained in control of Arabia, Iraq, Persia and the newly conquered lands in Central Asia and Afghanistan. Of all the regions, the situation in Arabia was the most complex. The enormous growth in the populations of both Medina and Mecca had by now far exceeded their capacity to feed themselves. In practice both cities had become heavily dependent on the import of foodstuffs from Egypt – which was now under the authority of Amr, the sworn ally of Muawiya.

From his bases in the eastern Syrian desert, Muawiya continued the practice of raiding northern Iraq but also made certain that his army commanders would not risk battle by threatening either Kufa or Basra. Throughout the years 658 and 659, Ali was in any case distracted by his eastern front. So much so, that Kufa and Basra had now become the effective centres of his government, even if he yearned to return to Medina once the civil war with Muawiya had been resolved. One of the surviving bands of Kharijites had raised the standard of rebellion in Persia: first in Fars and then later in Kerman. The Kharijites attracted considerable local support, in part because the proud Persians were interested in backing any rebellion against their conquerors but also because the Kharijites' doctrine of an elective imam assisted by a council of the just had its own innate appeal. Eventually both revolts would be suppressed by Zayyad, Ali's tough-minded and ambitious governor. Zayyad had to make his own way in society with the support of neither clan nor tribe, for he was the bastard son of Sumaiya, a local prostitute from Taif who was supposedly married to a freed Greek slave. He had first made his name when his evidence (or sudden lack of it) had been decisive in acquitting Mughira of the charge of adultery before Omar. Zayyad also found himself a patron that day. With Mughira he could also share childhood memories of their home town of Taif – of which they had both been outlaws – and an interest in realpolitik. These two sons of Taif would be listed by later historians as among the four political geniuses of the Arabs alongside Muawiya and Amr.

660 was the year of two oaths. First a Muslim Arab army from the Syrian garrison toured the Arabian peninsula, forcing the inhabitants of the two Holy Cities of Medina and Mecca and the people of Yemen to swear loyalty to Muawiya at the point of the sword. This was speedily succeeded by a counter-march by the men from the garrison at Kufa, which, though it failed to intercept Muawiya's army, did at least supervise another oath of allegiance back to the legitimate Caliph, Ali. However, both sides saw that this sort of rivalry undermined the patterns of trust and true belief. By the end of the year a guarded exchange of letters had established an informal truce. Muawiya would administrate Egypt, Syria and Palestine, while Ali held Iraq, Persia, Central Asia and Arabia. Unwittingly the old frontier that had for centuries divided the Middle East between the Byzantine Empire and the Persian Empire was once more imposed.

The incident of two contradictory oaths of loyalty being imposed upon the Muslims of Arabia by rival armies had disgusted many of the old believers. It also rekindled the righteous anger of three Kharijites – who even on the holy pilgrimage to Mecca found themselves caught up in the messy world of political compromise and doublespeak. At the conclusion of the haj they met and vowed themselves that they would act. They drew lots and promised that on the fortieth anniversary of the Prophet Muhammad's migration from the persecution of Mecca to the safety of Medina they would strike, and once again free Islam from persecution by removing Ali, Amr and Muawiya.

Their attacks would take place during Friday prayers in the second week of Ramadan in the three great mosques of Fustat, Damascus and Kufa, where they could be assured that Amr, Muawiya and Ali would be personally leading the prayers. In Fustat the white-veiled imam who was lying prostrate in prayer before the front rank of the worshippers was felled like a bull at the altar by one powerful blow of the assassin's blade. However, Amr had chosen not to lead the prayers that morning and was able to execute his executioner before the day was out. In Damascus Muawiya was bent in prayer at the head of the massed ranks of Muslims, but a quick-moving bodyguard, observing an unusual movement from among the crowd, managed to save his master from all but a glancing blow. In Kufa, the Kharijite assassin Ibn Muljam loitered in the shade beside Ali's modest doorway alongside the other petitioners. His attack, a broadsword swung at the head of Ali, was neither expected nor intercepted. The fourth Caliph of Islam, Imam Ali, had suffered a mortal blow, and though he would remain conscious for another two days, his fate was never in doubt. He died aged sixty-three, the same age at which his revered master Muhammad, the Prophet of God, the first Caliph Abu Bakr and the successor to the successor, Omar, had all been carried to their graves. His body was washed by his three sons, Hasan, Husayn and Muhammad, and his nephew Abdallah ibn Jafa, but fearing that his grave might be desecrated by his enemies, they never disclosed its exact location. So although Ali's tomb is nowhere it is also everywhere, for his shrines are scattered at sites across the length and breadth of the Muslim world, such as

Mazar-i-Sharif in Afghanistan and Hyderabad in the Indian sub-continent, though most specially beneath the golden dome and minarets of the great shrine mosque at Najaf, just a half-day's ride from Kufa.

The murderer of Ali, although reviled as a schismatic assassin by the vast majority of Muslims, both Sunni and Shia, would yet be sung about as a hero within the small community of Kharijites – which in three distinct geographical enclaves still survives within Islam. So much so that a romantic myth was woven into the story of Ibn Muljam that his mission had been wished upon him by Qatam, his Kharijite bride. Qatam had lost both father and brother on the field of Nahrawan. Like an Islamic Salome she had demanded three thousand dirhams, two slaves and the head of Ali as her dowry before she would consent to join Ibn Muljam upon the marriage couch. So that in the secret fastnesses of their deserts, the Kharijite poets would sing,

Ne'er have I seen so fine a dowry paid
As that of Qatam, as the world has heard.
Three thousand dirhams, a black slave and a maid,
And Ali's head, cleft by a flashing sword.

But the rest of the Islamic world soon realised that they had succeeded in murdering the perfect Muslim man. With every passing day his personal virtues became ever more blindingly obvious: his complete honesty, his unbending devotion to the true practice of Islam, his innate fairness, compassion and generosity. He could honestly claim to know the message and practice of the Prophet better than any other man. Muhammad was remembered to have declared that 'I am the town of knowledge and its gate is Ali, whoever seeks knowledge should first pass through its gate.' Ali would sometimes be referred to by future generations as the

Bab – the gateway through which mystics, poets and religious thinkers would aspire to connect with the experience of the Prophet Muhammad. He stands at the head of the complicated diagrams kept by the Sufi masters, which document the descent of mystical knowledge and spiritual practices through every genera-tion of Islam, just as he is the genealogical fountainhead of all the dynasties of the descendants of the Prophet. He is also the guild master par excellence, the revered patron and exponent of practi-cally every craft and profession: humble basket-weavers or the esteemed masters of Arabic calligraphy, teachers or soldier cadets. They all march in the shadow of Ali.

Ali possessed a profound nobility that could also be considered foolishness. His refusal to play the dirty game of tribal power pol-itics would always have frustrated him from becoming an effective political leader of the Arabs. This is part of the real beauty of the man, for Ali is testimony to the fact that the most beautiful ideals must perish in the sordid world of human politics. Ali chose the road of suffering rather then compromise. He is the paragon of chivalry, the very perfect first knight of Islam. The man who would pursue the noble cause wherever and against whomever it led him. The man who was not afraid to fight alone in the front line, to labour long hours at the building sites and at the well-heads, to speak the truth rather than win an argument through flattery and bribery, to share his meagre daily wage with his neigh-bours and his master and who never aspired to more money than was required to maintain a roof over his head, for clothes to shield his body and food enough to share with whomever was in need.

Ali is also a role model of Islamic romance. His love for Fatimah was the ideal of perfect marriage, for she was his true companion, a childhood friend, a cousin and a spiritual equal. They were human, so they had their trials and disagreements like any couple, but Ali always remained true to the contract that he had agreed with her father: 'Fatimah is yours, Ali, on condition that you live with her on good terms.'

When Fatimah asked for a gift for her sons her father gave them not horses or precious swords but blessed Hasan with forbearance, good looks and a loving nature, Husayn with courage and generosity. On another occasion she asked her father for a gift to relieve herself and Ali from their poverty. Muhammad offered her the choice of five goats or five blessings. Despite her physical hunger she and Ali chose the latter and were given the blessing for the poor, 'O God the first before all, the last after all, owner of power, the most strong, merciful towards the poor, most merciful of those who show mercy.' And when Ali was setting out on a long journey, Fatimah asked for something to alleviate her husband's travels. Again the Prophet gave neither dates nor a new goatskin but a blessing for travellers: 'Go guarded by God, may he forgive your sins and guide you to goodness wherever you are.' In the last year of Muhammad's life, Ali's eye had strayed towards the attractive form of Juwayryah but he knew it would not be a popular choice because her father Abu Jahl had been among the most malicious of the persecutors of early Islam. The Prophet did not forbid the match but warned Ali that he might first have to divorce Fatimah. In fact Ali would never take another wife while Fatimah was alive, though like his master before him he also loved the comfort and company of women. At the end of his life, Ali had exchanged the lean frame of his warrior youth for that of a white-bearded patriarch with a slightly rounded stomach. His noble forehead wore a bruise from frequent prayer but nothing could change the clarity of his piercingly true and intelligent eyes. On his deathbed Ali was mourned by four wives (among them Umamah – the Prophet's granddaughter through his daughter Zaynab), eleven sons, sixteen concubines and fifteen daughters. They knew that his proudest title was not Caliph or Commander of the Faithful but

Abu Turab, 'the father of dust'. It was the nickname the Prophet had awarded Ali when he found his young cousin praying in the mosque after work with his cloak carelessly dropped on the dirty floor. Muhammad had quietly picked up the cloak, dusted it down a little and then stayed until his young disciple had finished his prayers. Then he greeted Ali ibn Abu Talib ibn Abdul Muttalib as Abu Turab, for he like Muhammad could pray with a genuine heart: 'O Lord, keep me alive a poor man, and let me die poor; and raise me among the poor.'

Ali had the immense good fortune to have been brought up in the household of the Prophet of God, to know him as a friend, a cousin, a son-in-law and as a disciple. He recalled, 'The Messenger of God was cheerful, of bright countenance and good-natured, modest, of humble appearance, merciful, and possessed of a superior morality. He neither had a violent temper, nor was he stone-hearted. He never spoke an unkind word, never pried after people's faults, never confronted them with their defects . . . refraining from saying hurtful things. Those who knew his morality could divine what he wanted from his attitude.'

Ali, the linchpin of the whole tale of the Heirs of the Prophet, is a figure crafted from the purest principles of honour, truth, bravery and faith. Like all such men, he was not fated to prosper in our venal world, ridden with secret ambitions, private fears and covert jealousies. All Muslims revere Ali as the most enlightened spiritual figure after the Prophet Muhammad. All acknowledge him as a Caliph. All Muslims agree that with the assassination of Ali in 661, the era of holiness within the Islamic community is over. So just a generation after the death of the Prophet Muhammad in 632, the rule of the enlightened Heirs of the Prophet is finished. So after just thirty years, the tough-minded generals, the scheming politicians, the police chiefs and the old clan chiefs are once again back in power. By 661 men of the ilk of Muawiya, Amr and Mughira have triumphed over the Muslim Empire of the Arabs. No one doubts this, whether they are Sunni Muslims or Shia Muslims. This concept, of how speedily the example of the Prophet Muhammad was betrayed by mankind, lies at the very heart of all disputes over the nature of Islam. This is the principal difference between the two streams of Islam. For while the orthodox Sunni majority list four Rightly Guided Caliphs, Abu Bakr, Omar, Uthman and Ali, the Shia historians argue that there was just one true heir.

For the Shia the betrayal of the inheritance of the Prophet begins within a few hours of Muhammad's death, while the Sunni consider that despite the slow creeping decay in spiritual values, this first generation of the Heirs of the Prophet set an example that can be usefully studied by mankind. So that the collective example of Abu Bakr, Omar, Uthman and Ali (and other Companions of the Prophet) forms a heroic role model, a secondary source of inspiration for the Muslim community.

The Shia concentrate their spiritual energy on a sense of immediate loss, of a divine vision so quickly betrayed by mankind. They argue that only Ali was qualified to uphold the spiritual values that underpinned the whole essence of Islam. This is a melancholic vision, though on another level it allows the Shia to aspire to create a holy state such as Ali might have instituted on this earth. The price that they pay for this inspiring vision of the future is, however, a heavy one, for they have to turn their back on many of the heroic achievements of this first generation of the Heirs of the Prophet. They also have to embrace a testing declaration of faith, which is to believe that the true succession of the rule of Islam passes through the direct male descendants of Ali. The Shia, like the Jews awaiting their long-postponed Messiah and those Christians who watch out for the terrifying fulfilment of the world predicted in St John's Book of Revelation, also patiently await the arrival of a just society with the coming to power of their true Imam.

To understand the true grief of the Shia, we cannot end the story of the Heirs of the Prophet with the death of Ali in 661. For there is a further tragic twist to the tale of suffering which will engulf the house of God in fire and spill the bloodline of the Prophet's heirs once again into the soil of Iraq.

10

Muawiya the Umayyad, Imam Hasan and Imam Husayn

There are two things with which men gain a kingdom,
One steel blue and one of saffron colour.
One is gold, stamped with the King's name,
The other is blue, tempered in the Yemen.
Whoever aspires to kingship
Must have an eloquent tongue, a liberal hand,
A heart both vengeful and loving . . .

Daqiqi

Hasan bent down to kiss his father's wounded brow. He then went out from the house to announce the death of their Imam to the people of Kufa. It was still Ramadan and so the streets around the great central mosque, and the aisles within, were packed with Muslims listening to the all-night recitations of the Koran that were such a feature of the holy month of fasting. Hasan had been born with a slight speech defect but he had conquered this disability to become a slow but deliberate speaker, whose measured pace was in effective contrast to his quick-tongued and fiery contemporaries. That night he described his father as a man whose acts were unrivalled and would for ever remain so. He reminded the congregation of his father's bravery and how in battle he had often protected the Prophet with his own life. As his legal legatee, Hasan also formally reported to the people that Ali held no government loans, no treasury hoard of bullion that now needed to be returned, just a purse of 700 dirhams that he had been saving up from his salary in order to be able to acquire a servant for his family. At the memory of the man they had now lost, fit to stand beside Abu Bakr and Omar for the absolute moral rectitude of his administration, the thirty-seven-year-old Hasan found himself too moved to continue his speech. The congregation wept for him, and at the end of his father's elegy Ubaydallah ibn Abbas stood up and called the people to pledge their loyalty to the grandson of the bringer of good tidings, the son of the warner, the son of the summoner to God (powerful and exalted) and with his permission, the shining lamp. The congregation needed no such prompting. Hasan was adored by all.

He was also, by all accounts, the spitting image of his grandfather, and a charming conversationalist, who never spoke evil of any man. He was also a genuine ascetic, who had already performed the pilgrimage twenty-five times, travelling the whole 250 miles between Medina and Mecca on foot. He is one of the great unsung heroes of Islam, a pacifist and a scholar with a totally independent mind that looked to the true nature of a cause. Typically it was Hasan who had stood guard over Uthman's door until rendered unconscious by the assaults of the mutineers. For despite his own father's opposition to Uthman's last six years of rule, Hasan had always looked beyond the day-to-day disagreements over policy and appointments. He had appreciated Uthman's brilliant achievements and also had a personal sympathy for this gentle, clever, scholarly man and could empathise with the personal reticence of his aristocratic and uxorious uncle. Above all, Hasan shared with Uthman an innate understanding that mercy, forgiveness and compassion were at the root of Islam. His Islam was such that 'he desired neither evil nor harm to anyone' and enormously admired Uthman for being prepared to die for his beliefs but not to cause the death of any man. When he preached he summoned up, out of the teachings of the Koran, not a cause for war but the call for peace. Again and again he stressed that the lesser jihad, the armed struggle, should be just a preparation for the greater jihad, which was the lifelong struggle to master oneself. He quoted Sura 2, verse 216, 'God has prescribed the jihad for you though it is a *loathsome* duty.'

Hasan was ahead of his time in his vision of Islam as a religion of peace – perhaps he would still be if he were with us now. The soldiers of the Kufa garrison, the same men who had refused to fight for his father on the fourth day of Siffin and after that tragic day at Nahrawan, now angrily demanded he lead them to war. Those two decades of endless victories when the Arab armies had conquered half the known world had introduced a very dangerous imbalance into early Islam. For far too many young Muslims had grown used to the idea that their faith would be reflected in military victory. They erroneously saw glorious triumphs in this world, fame, glory and wealth as proofs of the rightness of Islam. They could no longer understand that Muhammad's message was entirely about the individual's relationship to God and was not a charmed banner under which they were destined to conquer the world.

In vain did Hasan preach that like all true Muslims they should aspire to abandon worldly ambition, that 'shame is better than hellfire' and that he sought not a worldly dominion but to 'seek the favour of God, and to spare the blood of the people'. Instead the soldiers began to publicly abuse their prince until they had worked up their passions into a riot. Hasan's house was looted, his prayer mat was ripped from underneath him and his tunic pulled from his shoulders. Only the protection of the mounted warriors of the Rabia tribe, devoted partisans of Ali and his family, stopped Hasan from being martyred that day. The violence only made Hasan absolutely determined to end the schism within Islam and halt any further bloodshed between Muslims.

Muawiya for his part moved with speed and tact, once he began to fully appreciate that Hasan was not indulging in some pre-fight propaganda but was genuinely seeking a lasting peace. He led his army out of Syria, but showed a gracious forbearance to his opponents as he advanced ever closer to Kufa and Basra. He responded to Hasan's pious modesty by dropping all his own claims to imposing titles of power, so that the correspondence between the two over the peace was simply addressed between Hasan ibn Ali and Muawiya ibn Abu Sufyan. Another chronicler recorded that Muawiya sent his seal already attached to a completely blank draft of the proposed treaty – so that Hasan could fill in whatever terms he desired. These charming gestures may well have occurred, a public duel in chivalry, even if no one was in any doubt of the true issues at hand. Hasan agreed to relinquish all authority to Muawiya in exchange for an agreement not to harm any of the supporters of Ali, and to govern by the book of God and the example of the Prophet. This he would do by letter and by word, explaining to the congregation in the Kufa mosque that he had ceded his right to rule 'for the best interest of the community and for the sake of sparing blood'. Muawiya acknowledged that 'the reign would belong to Hasan after him' (though this would soon be quietly forgotten) and that to avoid all future strife the next Caliph was to be decided by a formal electoral council. Hasan was assured of an annual salary of a million dirhams, with which he could generously support his companions, all the Beni Hashim and the old clients of his father.

In July 661 Hasan and his younger brother Husayn rode out of Kufa and took the road back to Medina. Hasan had ruled for just six months 'with the skills of the Arabs in my hand, for they were ready to make war on whomever I declared war, yet I abandoned it, seeking instead the face of God'. His enemies would later attempt to blacken his saintly pacific nature by naming Hasan 'al-Mitlaq', 'the great divorcer'. Tales of his extravagant wedding parties, his boundless generosity and the hundred wives that he took in Medina, some for no more than a night, read like episodes from *The Thousand and One Nights*. Though the details of these fantasies are a still relished element of popular culture they must also be recognised as the traces of black propaganda designed to discredit this man of peace. Hasan's seven marriages and descendants are exceptionally well chronicled, for practically all of the thousands of families of Shareefs that claim descent from the Prophet Muhammad trace their descent through one of Hasan's two surviving sons, Zayd and Hasan.*

Muawiya entered Kufa as the sole recognised Caliph of the Arab Empire. He promised forgiveness to all those in the Kufa garrison who immediately came forth to pledge allegiance, though he warned that after three days the season for pardon and protection would be at an end. He also promised the assembled soldiers a vast new horizon for their ambitions: an ever-expanding Arab Empire to be forged from their future conquests. Salaries would be paid punctually from now on, wars would always be fought in the territory of the enemy, with campaigning seasons for border raids set at six months, while for more ambitious conquests the Arab

---

* The families who trace their descent from his brother Husayn are customarily known as Sayyid.

warriors should be prepared for a whole year's absence from their base camps and their families.

The armies of the Caliphate were soon to be on the march again, further extending the frontiers of the empire. Muawiya had always believed that the way to keep an army of Arabs obedient was to keep it well occupied. At the head of these Arab armies stood a man whom Omar had prophetically described as 'the Caesar of the Arabs'. Muawiya was indeed a prince among the Quraysh, tall, tanned and handsome. He also had the common touch of Caesar, the ability to charm, persuade and delegate rather than to merely command. Muawiya had grown up in the political heart of Mecca with an instinctive grasp of Arabic political culture: when it was expedient to listen, when it was time to consult and when to be patient. His most consistent military opponent, the Greek-speaking Byzantine Empire, got to know the measure of the man through the constant shuffle of ambassadorial diplomacy. It is therefore especially intriguing that the Byzantine historian Theophanes chose to describe Muawiya as neither the king of the Arabs nor their emperor but as their first counsellor. For as long as Muawiya could lead and direct the Arab armies to victory there was no doubt that they would accept his counsel. As a commander-in-chief, Muawiya was a near-genius, and the range of his strategic vision is astonishing to behold.

On the western front, the battle-hardened nephew of Amr, Oqba ibn Nafi, was dispatched to complete the conquest of North Africa. In 670, to facilitate this, an advance base would be established some 1500 miles west of Fustat in central Tunisia. This *kairouan*, a 'temporary halting place' of the Arab cavalry army, was well sited: it not only dominated the good grazing grounds of the steppe but it allowed Oqba to drive a strategic wedge between his two opponents, the walled Byzantine cities of the coast and the fierce Berber principalities of the mountains. Oqba's halting place

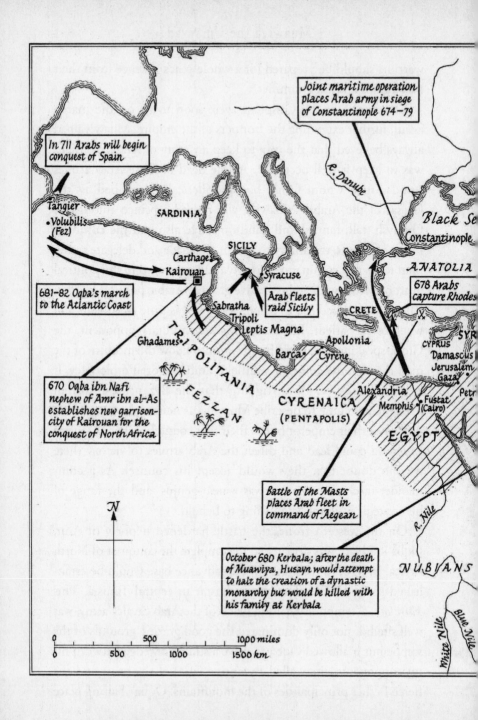

Joint maritime operation places Arab army in siege of Constantinople 674–79

In 711 Arabs will begin conquest of Spain

681–82 Oqba's march to the Atlantic Coast

678 Arabs capture Rhodes

Arab fleets raid Sicily

670 Oqba ibn Nafi nephew of Amr ibn al-As establishes new garrison-city of Kairouan for the conquest of North Africa

Battle of the Masts places Arab fleet in command of Aegean

October 680 Kerbala; after the death of Muawiya, Husayn would attempt to halt the creation of a dynastic monarchy but would be killed with his family at Kerbala

Tangier
Volubilis (Fez)
SARDINIA
Carthage
Kairouan
SICILY
Syracuse
Sabratha
Tripoli
Leptis Magna
Ghadames
TRIPOLITANIA
FEZZAN
Apollonia
Barca
Cyrene
CYRENAICA
(PENTAPOLIS)
Alexandria
Memphis
Fustat (Cairo)
EGYPT
R. Nile
NUBIANS
White Nile
Blue Nile
R. Danube
Black Sea
Constantinople
ANATOLIA
CRETE
CYPRUS
SYR
Damascus
Jerusalem
Gaza
Petra

N

0   500   1000 miles
0   500   1000   1500 km

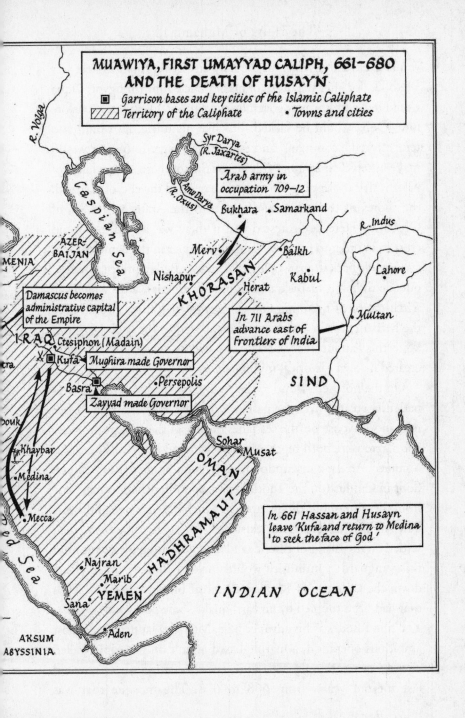

MUAWIYA, FIRST UMAYYAD CALIPH, 661–680 AND THE DEATH OF HUSAYN

■ Garrison bases and key cities of the Islamic Caliphate
▨ Territory of the Caliphate • Towns and cities

R. Volga

Caspian Sea

Syr Darya (R. Jaxartes)

Amu Darya (R. Oxus)

Arab army in occupation 709–12

Bukhara • Samarkand

AZER-BAIJAN

MENIA

Merv • Balkh •

R. Indus

Nishapur •

KHORASAN

Herat •

Kabul •

Lahore •

Damascus becomes administrative capital of the Empire

In 711 Arabs advance east of frontiers of India

Multan •

IRAQ Ctesiphon (Madain)

X ■ Kufa Mughira made Governor

SIND

tra

■ Basra •

• Persepolis

Zayyad made Governor

bouk

Sohar •
Musat

• Khaybar

OMAN

• Medina

In 661 Hassan and Husayn leave Kufa and return to Medina 'to seek the face of God'

• Mecca

HADHRAMAUT

Red Sea

• Najran

Marib

• Sana

YEMEN

INDIAN OCEAN

• Aden

AKSUM
ABYSSINIA

would eventually grow into the holy city of Kairouan. There was a setback, for after the death of his old uncle Amr (in Egypt) Oqba would row with the new governor-general and, like his uncle before him, Oqba would be sacked. But like his uncle, he would also return to take command and exact his revenge. In 681 he would make his epic exploratory ride across the southern steppe lands of North Africa, stopping only when he reached the end of the road, the shores of the Atlantic – known to the Arabs as the Sea of Obscurity. Here he protested that if there was a ford, he would cross it, in order to find new lands to conquer in the name of God. On his ride back Oqba would be killed by a Berber prince, Kusayla, outside the oasis of Biskra (in southern Algeria), after which the witch-queen of the mountains, the priestess Kahina, would raise the Berber tribes in a widespread revolt against the Arab Muslims. With this extraordinary narrative of events, North African Islam created its own historical mythology.

On the northern frontier, the Arab navy that Muawiya had so patiently created over the past two decades was at last given free rein and let loose on the sea lanes of the southern Aegean. Sicily and Crete were both repeatedly attacked and in 672 Rhodes was occupied. An Arab inscription recently found carved into a church floor in Cnidus (on the Turkish coast opposite Rhodes) may date from these swashbuckling years – in which case it is one of the earliest Arabic inscriptions in existence. An Arab colony was then settled on the island of Rhodes and an enterprising merchant from this vanguard community would make a fortune by smelting down the Colossus of Rhodes, the great brazen statue of Helios that had been toppled by an earthquake some 300 years before.

Using Rhodes as his advance base, Muawiya launched his most ambitious operation, a marine-based assault on the triple-walled city of Constantinople. This siege, a series of attacks by sea, would last for ten years, from 668 to 678. The mosque that was established at Eyup, the base camp just outside the land walls of Constantinople, would be rediscovered by Ottoman archaeologists in the fifteenth century and restored in magnificent style to become the oldest Muslim prayer hall in Europe. It was an extraordinary achievement to have kept an army in the field for that length of time so far from their homeland. They were entirely dependent on control of the sea route, so that when an Arab fleet was defeated by a Byzantine squadron, at the battle of Syllaeum in 678, Muawiya wisely called off the siege which had been commanded by his first-born son, Yazid. In the process of this orderly withdrawal, a truce was agreed with Byzantium that would last for a whole generation. The Muslim world would have to wait another 800 years before it had a leader who could breach the walls of the city of the Caesars. The Byzantine land frontier, embedded with the dozens of stout castles that guarded all the important passes through the Taurus Mountains, had remained firmly in place throughout the ten-year siege. On this frontier Muawiya had raised up one of Khalid's surviving sons, Abdal Rahman, to become governor of Homs and to lead the summer raids of the Arab armies against these mountain redoubts.

In the troublesome east Muawiya would leave nothing to chance. He chose the most resilient power-politicians of the day to govern the two potential trouble spots: the Iraqi cities of Kufa and Basra. So once again that one-eyed rogue Mughira was promoted to rule over Kufa, while his fellow Taif-born protégé, Zayyad, watched over Basra. Trusting in no one's good faith, they established the infrastucture of state power complete with a police force (the dreaded *shurta*), law courts, prisons, treasury officials and curfews as well as covert agents to report on the mood of the markets and the gossip at the doors of the mosque. Under these two political bosses the two garrison cities of Iraq were made to concentrate their energies on the coordinated conquest of the far eastern frontiers of Persia. Muawiya had skilfully bound Zayyad into a position of personal loyalty by settling the delicate matter of his social origins (for he was literally the bastard son of a whore), by officially recognising Zayyad as one of his father's lost sons. Zayyad was no longer to be referred to by the tongue-in-cheek patronymic ibn Abihi, 'the son of his father', but as the son of the great warlord of Mecca, Abu Sufyan. Later Muawiya would heap further rewards on this 'new brother' by making Zayyad's son Ubaydallah the governor of the new 50,000-strong garrison city in Khurasan, while Caliph Uthman's son Saeed was given command of the newly conquered forward post of Bukhara.

Throughout Muawiya's nineteen-year reign (661–80) the centre of administrative power was firmly located upon Damascus. No longer did foreign ambassadors, confidential agents, officials and delegations make the long and arduous journey across central Arabia to Medina. Instead they once again made their way to the old commercial capital of Byzantine Syria, now doubly glorious as the new political centre of a worldwide empire. There was, however, no attempt to coordinate the vast conquests into a coherent Arabic-speaking empire. Each conquered province continued to use its own language, its own indigenous class of state officials and units of measurement as well as retaining the exact units and shapes of the traditional coinages, the gold dinar of Byzantium and the silver dirham of Persia. The simplicity of the Prophet's life and rule had now been totally transformed, so that even one of Muawiya's deputy governors was now surrounded by the panoply of power consciously modelled on the Byzantine and Sassanid courts, and a visiting foreign ambassador could observe 'a crowd of silver-sticks and lectors, and at his gate 500 soldiers mounted guard'.

At the beginning of his rule as Caliph, Muawiya had made the journey from Damascus to the oasis of Medina in order to accept the oath of allegiance from all the old revered Companions of the Prophet who dwelt there. Few came to the mosque to pledge their obedience, for though they might reluctantly accept the efficiency of his administration and the continued success of his armies, they could manage only a passive tolerance of his usurpation and would not give him their active support or blessing. It is remembered that Muawiya tried to take them to task over this indifference. He asked, 'How come all the people have come to swear allegiance except those from Medina?' To which the laconic reply was, 'We have no riding camels.' Muawiya, knowing full well that all the Companions now possessed sizeable herds, replied in the same offhand spirit, 'But what became of all those camels you used to use for fetching water?' 'They were lamed when we chased after you and your father after the battle of Badr' was the derisive reply. To drive the point home further they proceeded to inform Muawiya that the Prophet had warned them of a state of calamity after his death, to which 'he commanded us to be resigned'. That was to be the extent of the loyalty he could expect from all the chief men of Islam – patient resignation. Others in the oasis remembered that Muhammad had predicted that the succession to his prophethood would last for thirty years, to be followed by a 'biting kingship'. These beliefs were to be codified, with the pleasing prospect of eternal damnation for the usurper Caliph, by a poet of Medina who sang at this time:

> The Prince of the Faithful, Muawiya, we greet him
> In this message from the Prophet's own city:
> We will be resigned till the Day when we meet him,
> The last Day of Judgement, the Day without pity.

Towards the end of his reign Muawiya would once again try to win over the chief men of Islam to his rule. The empire had been ceaselessly expanded in every direction, their annual stipends had been paid with relentless punctuality and efficiency, but when the leading Muslims of the second generation of Islam heard that the Caliph Muawiya was coming again to Medina they voted with their feet. Husayn ibn Ali, Abdur Rahman ibn Abu Bakr, Abdullah ibn Zubayr and Abdullah ibn Omar waited until the old ruler was within a few days' ride of the oasis before they saddled their camels and rode out of town. They feared that he had come to force them into accepting his son Yazid as a suitable candidate for the Caliphate. It was not just that Yazid was debauched and addicted to hunting that horrified them, for like his father he was also an experienced administrator and a proven army commander as well as being a poet and a patron of learning. What was even more insulting to them was that Yazid was being imposed upon them like a crown prince who had first been hailed by Muawiya's generals and governors at the sycophantic court of Damascus. The shura, the Council of Companions at Medina, had been brushed aside and with it all their claims to an honoured place in the new society. All the first four Rightly Guided Caliphs had first been acclaimed by the people of Medina but this right and duty had now been brushed aside in favour of the courtiers at Damascus. Muawiya had also broken his solemn pledge to hold a shura, which had been part of the peace agreement with Hasan. None of the previous Caliphs had thought to impose their own sons on the community, and had looked beyond the narrow loyalties of a family, towards their brothers in faith. Muawiya was turning a community of believers into a hereditary kingdom to be based on the military power of distant Syria. Rather than accept this ultimate degradation, these young men, the heirs of all the chief Companions of Muhammad and the first four Rightly Guided Caliphs, would each in his own way be prepared to die. This would form the last bitter act in the long-drawn-out tragedy of the Heirs of the Prophet.

In 680 the seventy-seven-year-old Muawiya was buried, his body decorated with a carefully hoarded treasury of relics, for the nail clippings and hairs from Muhammad's head and beard had already acquired a totem-like reverence that would have appalled the Prophet.* In Damascus Yazid was acclaimed as the 'successor to the Prophet of God' by all his father's loyal placemen, that court of governors, generals, police chiefs and treasury officials that Muawiya had commanded for half a lifetime.

In Medina the mosque was filled with groans and silent tears at the decisive emergence of a dynastic monarchy triumphing over the religion of God. From Kufa streamed a series of messengers, calling upon Husayn in Medina to ride north and lead them against the usurpation of the Islamic world by the thirty-seven-year-old Yazid and to reclaim his rightful place at the head of the community. Husayn, urged on by the chief men of Medina, decided to respond and follow in his father's footsteps by riding out of the oasis to assume the leadership of the true armies of Islam. Having summoned the last grandson of the Prophet to lead them out of slavery, they now failed to honour their own appointment. Watched over by the police and the secret agents of their implacable governor, not a man, not a youth left the teeming garrison city to join Husayn on the desert trail. Instead, Husayn's young cousin, Muslim, who had secretly journeyed up to Kufa and gone to ground in a safe house to await Husayn, was betrayed. He was arrested with his host Hani by the *shurta* and led away to his death.

---

* Though this treasury would be destroyed eighty years later by his dynastic rivals, his tomb can still be found in Damascus's old cemetery.

The governor Ubaydallah (who had succeeded his father Zayyad to both Basra and Kufa) now felt secure enough to order his own army out into the desert. Husayn and his small body of devoted followers and family, numbering around thirty horsemen and forty warriors on foot, would not be deterred from their mission. The Bedouin tribes, through whose territory he rode, looked longingly at their potential young Caliph, though none of the chiefs (having heard of the silence at Kufa) would commit to rallying their men to the true cause. A fervent supporter, the poet Farazdaq, rode out to warn Husayn of the treachery of Kufa, 'for though the heart of City is with thee, its sword is against thee'. Still Husayn rode on.

A detatchment of cavalrymen under the command of Hurr from the Kufa garrison now emerged to bar the direct path to Kufa but also to stop Husayn's small caravan from turning back to Mecca. Then a few weeks later, a much larger force of 4000 cavalrymen issued out from Kufa to surround Husayn and his men. They were now forced to make camp at Kerbala,* just above the bank of the Euphrates about 25 miles from Kufa. The commander of this new cavalry force was Amr, one of the sons of Saad ibn Abu Waqqas, the victor of al-Qadisiya. He had been ordered by Ubaydallah to deprive Husayn and his supporters of any access to water until they had all pledged unconditional submission. Husayn for his part asked only to be allowed to meet Yazid face to face; or if that was impossible to be allowed to join the jihad on some forgotten frontier against the enemies of Islam. Despite the crippling thirst imposed upon his young family and his few faithful followers, Husayn refused to submit to the unconditional pledge demanded of him. The dignity with which he conducted himself had by now so impressed Amr ibn

* Also spelled 'Karbala'.

Saad that he began to waver in his mission. However, the arrival
of Shamir, a confidential agent of Ubaydallah who demanded to
take over the command if Amr proved himself incapable of
acting, stiffened the resolve of the army. That evening Husayn's
little camp at Kerbala, a cluster of tents reinforced by a small
fence formed out of brushwood and thorns, was placed under
close siege.

Husayn now feared the worst, and on the evening of the 9th of
the month of Muharram (9 October 680) he ordered his close
kinsmen and young family to leave the camp and seek refuge with
the enemy. This they would not do, even though Husayn's young
son Ali now lay delirious with fever and there was no longer so
much as a drop of water with which to relieve the parched lips of
the Prophet's infant great-grandson. That night the muffled cries
of the children mingled with the sobs of the women and the soft
screech of the whetstone as the small band of desiccated warriors
carefully sharpened their swords and their lances for their last
battle. In the morning they drew up their battle line, 70 men
ranged against over 4000, and again Husayn proudly offered his
terms. As the small band advanced they were cut down by the
massed ranks of archers, who fired shower upon pitiless shower, so
that the arrows fell like a hailstorm upon them. Neither Husayn's
ten-year-old nephew Kasim, nor even his infant son, was spared, as
one by one the family of Muhammad fell writhing to the ground.
Then the members of this mortally wounded clan were trampled
into the dust by a cavalry charge, after which their heads were
hacked off by swordsmen. Before dusk had settled over the fields
of Kerbala, seventy heads had been rolled out from bloodied
leather sacks on to the palace floor of the governor of Kufa. As
Ubaydallah carefully turned these grim relics over with his staff, the
better to make a positive identification, one of the old judges
attached to his court cried out, 'Gently, it is the Prophet's grandson

and by God I have seen those very lips kissed by the blessed Apostle himself.'

It is the memory of this fearful day* that unleashes the annual passion of regret and self-recrimination which is the Ashura (the 'tenth') on the 10th day of Muharram. Acknowledged by both Shia and Sunni as a day of mourning, the passionate commemoration of Ashura is perceived to be one of the distinctive signs of a Shiite community.

The news of Kerbala sent a ripple of horror around the entire Islamic world. In Medina and Mecca, Abdallah ibn Zubayr now openly led the defiance against those officials of Muawiya who sought to enforce the rule of his son Yazid. To complete the mortal tragedy perpetuated at Kerbala, there was now to be a physical defilement of the Holy Cities. Three years after Kerbala, in 688, an army sent out from Damascus, bolstered by regiments of Christians from Syria, first slaughtered the defenders of Medina in a battle fought out in the volcanic landscape of the Harran hills and then sacked, looted and raped its way through the capital of Islam for three days. Then holy Mecca itself was besieged. Two months into this offensive, the Kaaba was burned down to the ground when it was accidentally hit by the naphtha-treated arrows launched by the besiegers. The sacred black stone that had been set into the Kaaba wall during the manhood of the Prophet Muhammad was fractured into three pieces by the heat of the blaze, 'like the torn bosoms of mourning women'. This stone, believed to be the altar of Abraham, would henceforth be held together only by rivets of silver. At about the same time, the forty-year-old Caliph who had ordered this conflict expired in his isolated hunting palace in the Syrian

---

* The only survivor among the men was Husayn's son Ali Zayn al-Abidin, who lay transfixed by fever in his tent but would later recover his health.

desert. A creative Persian poet commemorated his death with the immortal lines

the dead body of Yazid
lying in his pleasure palace at Hawwarin
with a cup next to his pillow
and a wineskin whose nose was still bleeding.

When the news was brought to his army, they halted the siege and prepared to return to Damascus.

It was just over fifty years since the death of Muhammad. A vast empire had been conquered from out of which poured an annual tribute of millions upon millions of gold and silver coins, which first filed into the coffers of the Caliph's treasury in Damascus and from there flowed out to support a salaried ruling class. A hundred thousand Arab warriors now dwelt in half a dozen garrison cities, housed in comfort, equipped with the finest weapons, armour and horses and cared for by the labour of slaves in a manner beyond the wildest dreams of their grandfathers. In Mecca the house of God was a burned-out ruin and in a neglected field at Kerbala the headless corpses of the murdered family of the Prophet of God lay buried. It was as if the things of this earth had been won but in the process the kingdom of heaven had been forgotten.

All Muslims feel the horror of this transformation, the gradual corruption of the moral rule of God as established by the Prophet Muhammad to a mere temporal empire ruled over by Muawiya's heirs, the Umayyad dynasty. This forbidding example helps explain the political fatalism that is so often encountered among Muslim communities. If it was just fifty years after they had buried the Prophet of God that the godly rule of the 'saintly Companions' was so decisively overthrown, what hope have we in this even more corrupt and less religious age? Did not the Prophet himself declare, 'No time cometh upon you but it is followed by a worse' and that 'The best of my people are my generation; then they that come after them; then they that come after them'? Is it not true that this world is for the likes of Muawiya, Mughira, Amr and Zayyad rather than the saints?

To make a safe haven of the brief period of true Islam on earth, the majority of Muslims continue to look back upon the rule of the first four Caliphs (Abu Bakr, Omar, Uthman and Ali, 632–61) as the Eden of good government before the fall from grace. This is the Sunni position. Others see even this period as a flawed and corrupted version of true Islam, and instead like to imagine the shape of a Muslim state if the true spiritual heroes, Ali and his sons, had been the leaders of this community of faith. That is the difference between how the Sunni and the Shia regard the story of the Heirs of the Prophet. From this small but passionately important detail, two distinct paths of Islam would develop, each with its own history of who is the true heir of the Prophet. There is no group within the vast body of Muslims, either now or back in the seventh century, who see the triumph of Muawiya and his brilliant team of political operators, Mughira, Amr and Zayyad, as other than a profound tragedy.

Those who have been born outside the Muslim heritage of faith are free to honour both pathways and to remember that two rival narratives can yet become one. For while the Sunni version tells of how the Prophet Muhammad died on the lap of Aisha, and while the Shia tell of how the Prophet Muhammad died leaning on the shoulder of Ali, we know that both versions may be literally as well as figuratively true.

Ten days before he died the Prophet Muhammad had prayed over the tombs of the dead, 'Peace be upon you, O people of the graves. Rejoice in your state, how much better is it than the state of men now living. Dissensions come like waves of darkest night,

the one following hard upon the other, each worse than the last.'
It is a dispiriting testimony from a brilliantly successful leader at
what is otherwise considered to have been the triumphant conclusion of his life. But then the future leadership and political
organisation of mankind was never his purpose. As the Koran so
clearly states (Sura 42:15), 'God is our Lord and your Lord. We
have our words and you have yours. There is no argument between
us and you. God will bring us together, for the journey is to him.'

If one looks to find a true Heir to the Prophet Muhammad,
look not for thrones, or through the dynastic lists of kings, look not
to the triumphant progress of a great conqueror or at the beaming
smiles and promises of a popular politician. Look out for one who
journeys towards God.

APPENDIX A

The Political Heirs of the Prophet after the Death of Husayn

After the murder of Ali in 661 and the killing of Husayn in 680 political authority was anchored into the firm grasp of the Umayyads. This dynasty would rule the Islamic world from Damascus for another hundred years, but apart from the brief and saintly rule of Caliph Omar II (717–20), the ruling family would be continually threatened by the revolts of the godly, be they the true heirs of the Companions of the Prophet (in Medina and Mecca), the implacable desert-dwelling Kharijites (who would also convert the Berbers of North Africa to their cause), or those who championed the right of Ali and his family to the Caliphate (usually based in the Iraqi cities of Basra and Kufa or in Persia). The Umayyads remained in power because of their military and administrative ability but in the end they were toppled by a revolt that came out of Persia led by the still mysterious figure of Abu Muslim. This rebellion, led by the warriors recruited from the city of Merv and also from out of the province of Khorassan,* was to be led by the black banners that indicated their support for the 'cause' and family of Ali. They won a decisive victory in January 750 on the banks of the Zab, a tributary of Iraq's Tigris. However, once victorious, Abu Muslim would support the Abbasids – the descendants of the family of Abbas, the Prophet Muhammad's canny banking uncle – not the Alids (the descendants of Ali). This historic swindle (the conspiratorial details of which are still far from clear) would see the Abbasid caliphs ruling over a vast Islamic Empire from such celebrated capital cities as Baghdad, Raqqa and Samarra – all located in central Iraq.

Although truly a golden age of Islamic culture, especially in terms of architecture, agriculture, trade, literature and an effervescent spirit of intellectual inquiry, the Abbasid regime also had a nervy paranoid quality at its doctrinal core. For though outwardly devoted to the cause of the lineal descendants of Ali in sympathy and public politics, the Abbasid caliphs (who include such world-famous figures as Caliph al-Mansur, the Vizier Jafar and Haroun al-Rashid) also managed to quietly arrange for the assassination of the very men that they so publicly championed. So that none of the lineal heirs of the Prophet Muhammad through his daughter Fatimah and his cousin Ali (the Alids) actually exercised any political authority throughout the long period of Abbasid rule, from 750 to 1258.

Nevertheless, the Shiite community would later venerate these men, the powerless descendants of Ali, as the 'true Imams' who should have ruled in this period. In this world-view Abu Bakr, Omar and Uthman do not figure in the list of true Imams, let alone the criminal Umayyads of Damascus, nor the scheming Abbasid caliphs of Baghdad. The list of true Imams begins with

* Also spelled 'Khurasan'.

Ali, then passes to his eldest son Hasan (the second Imam), followed by his martyred younger brother Husayn (the third Imam), then on down through Husayn's son Ali Zayn al-Abidin (the fourth Imam). All Shiites of whatever creed and persuasion follow this heritage but thereafter the paths of belief diverge so that there are half a dozen traditions of loyalty. The mainstream tradition reveres the next-generation Alid heir, Muhammad al-Baqir, as the fifth Imam. Others would back the claims of his brother Zaydi, and become known as Fivers, or Zaydis. They would later accept that the Imamate, the divinely ordained leadership of true Islam, might not necessarily be restricted to the descendants of the Prophet. They would always remain a politically militant group within Islam and the vortex out of which a number of independent states would claim their legitimacy, such as the Zaydi Imam of Yemen.

In mainstream Shia Islam, the next descendant of Ali to be honoured as Imam (the sixth) is Jafar as-Sadiq: a scholarly mystic who disappeared into an Abbasid state prison where he was murdered around 763. After his death there is another great diverging of the ways between Shiites: some see the line descending though Jafar's eldest son Ismail (who had predeceased him), others argue that it must have passed to his surviving son Musa al-Kazim. This is the origin of the split between Sevener and Twelver Shia, between the Ismaili and the mainstream Shiites. The latter tradition, which follows the Alid line through Musa, continues honouring its true Imams through another four generations, though Ali al-Rida, Muhammad al-Jawad, Ali al-Naqi and Hasan al-Askari were no more than private citizens within the Abbasid state. Like their ancestors before them they tended to be publicly honoured but privately murdered. For instance, the Abbasid Caliph Mamun married off his sister to Muhammad al-Jawad (the ninth Imam) but would also later arrange for him to 'die from eating a surfeit of grapes'. The unexplained death of Hasan al-Askari (the eleventh Imam) on 1 January 874 was widely considered to be yet another successful Abbasid assassination, this time on the direct orders of the Abbasid Caliph Mutamid. He left no public heir, though the mainstream Shia believe that through his secret marriage with a Byzantine princess, Narjis Khatun, he produced their final heir, the twelfth Imam: Muhammad al-Muntazar al-Mahdi. In order to frustrate Abbasid secret agents, this last true Imam spent his life in hiding and is known as the 'hidden Imam'. At first he continued to instruct the faithful through his deputies (*naib*), but after four generations of these officials had passed away in 939 the 'hidden Imam' passed into 'occultation' and remains beyond the vision of mortal mankind.

This period, between the death of Hasan in 874 and the occultation of 939, was to be decisive in creating the full theological and historical position behind mainstream Shiite belief. In this same period the Islamic-wide intellectual ferment of the eighth and ninth centuries, centred on the great Abbasid capital city of Baghdad, would also produce the literary cornerstones of Islamic thought. This period had begun in the 760s with Ibn Ishaq's biography of the Prophet Muhammad and would be followed by the great multi-volume collections of hadith (the sayings of the Prophet). It was also the time in which Arabic grammars were compiled and Koranic commentaries were written (the better to understand the meaning of the Koran) as well as vast, ambitious historical narratives.

The return of the hidden Imam as the Mahdi is patiently awaited by the Shiite faithful as the dawn of a New Age of purity, right action and correct belief – the final manifestation of true Islam before the end of the world.

In support of this belief many hadith have been collected and cited, such as this reported statement of the Prophet: 'If there were to remain in the life of the world but one day, God would prolong that day until He sends in it a man from my community and my household. His name will be the same as my name. He will fill the earth with equity and justice as it was filled with oppression and tyranny.' Another much quoted hadith has Ali asking Muhammad, 'O Prophet of God, when will the *qaim* ['support'] who is from our family appear?' The Prophet replied, 'His case is like that of the Hour [of the resurrection],' to which there is a reference in the Koran, Sura 7:187, 'He alone will manifest it at its proper time. It is heavy in the heavens and the earth. It cometh not to you save unawares.' There is also another tradition that warns that the coming of the 'Hour' will be ushered in by a time when 'religious ignorance will become widespread, knowledge will vanish and there will be much killing'.

The belief in the Mahdi, which is based on Hadith sayings but is not explicitly spelled out in the Koran, is a central aspect of mainstream Shia faith. Indeed the historical logic of their veneration for the missing rule of the pure Imams, from Ali onwards, requires the imposition of a just rule as the long-delayed reward for their forbearance. This belief would also be gradually absorbed into the Sunni imagination, for they too have had to endure unworthy caliphs and ungodly rulers ever since the death of their fourth Caliph, Ali, in 661. While within the world of the most spiritually elevated of the Sufi mystics – who recognise no doctrinal boundaries between the Sunni and Shia communities (any more than they acknowledge the confessional boundaries of Judaism, Hinduism or Christianity) and would indeed open the arms of Islam to embrace all the people of the world – it was also a highly popular doctrine.

From out of this scholarly background the Twelver Shia tradition took firm root in eastern Arabia, southern Iraq and most especially Persia. Though it was not until the emergence of the Safavid dynasty of Persian shahs in the fifteenth century that the beliefs of the Twelver Shia emerged as the 'state religion' of Persia. The scholars who protected the truth of this tradition would later be ranked from *mujtjahid* ('striving to make a true legal judgement'), up through *hajjatalIslam* ('proof of Islam'), to *ayatollah* ('sign of God'), capped by the pre-eminent *ayatollah al-uzma*. Though often accused by their Sunni rivals of being no more than a priestly class of intellectuals imposed on the people, it would be the Ayatollah Khomeini (1902–89) who led the popular revolution which deposed the Shah of Iran in 1979 and established an Islamic Republic. Some of the enthusiasm for Khomeini's rule came from the widespread belief that as a true descendant of the Prophet Muhammad it was possible that he might also be the long-awaited Mahdi.

Returning to the eighth century and the split between the Twelver and Sevener Shia as to who was the true Imam, we can now focus on the latter. They are also known as the Ismailis because of their support for the candidature of Ismail to be the seventh Imam rather than his brother Musa. This might be an academic issue were it not that this line of descent survived after the disappearance, or occultation, of the twelfth Imam. It is still a focus of intense loyalty today. Led by their Imams, the Ismailis have remained relentlessly active, though they too look for a historical resolution with the arrival of a Mahdi/messiah.

Indeed the Ismaili cause would burst into dramatic fruition with the creation of the Fatamid Caliphate at just the same time that the Twelver theologians were perfecting their concept of the Hidden Imam. The Fatamid state explodes out of the history books in 909 when they create a 'living Shiite Empire' from their base in the North African mountains. Indeed throughout much of the tenth century they seemed on the point of taking over the

Islamic world, though they were to be opposed by a remnant Umayyad state in Spain (the Caliphate of Córdoba) and the Abbasid Caliphate based in Iraq and Persia. Ultimately the Fatimid Empire would be centred on the great new city of Cairo, which at its height governed all of North Africa, Egypt and Syria and most of Arabia.

The Fatimid Caliphate would be extinguished in 1171 by the great Sunni hero Saladin (of Kurdish descent), who united Egypt and Syria to create a state strong enough to expel the Crusaders from the Holy Land. Saladin reaffirmed the right of the Abbasid caliphs, who lingered on in Baghdad, to be considered the legitimate source of political authority, even though their real power seldom strayed beyond the walls of their palace-prisons.

From the glory days of the Shiite Fatimid Empire (910–1171) three distinct spiritual traditions would develop. The Druze of southern Syria emerged in the early eleventh century and still revere the memory of the sixth Fatimid caliph, al-Hakim, as a future Mahdi-like figure of redemption. While in 1090 a succession dispute between two sons of the ruling Fatimid caliph (al-Mustali and Nizar) would polarise the Ismaili community. The ruling Mustali majority was thought to have disappeared after Saladin formally disbanded the Fatimid state, though they would re-emerge many centuries later allied to the Bohra sect in India. The more militantly political and activist Nizari wing of the faith had already moved away from the lands of the Fatimid Empire before it fell to Saladin. Though they were few in number, the determination of the Nizari faithful was never in doubt. The Nizari fortresses, the so-called castles of the Assassins scattered across the mountains of Lebanon, Syria and Persia, have since passed into world history alongside such other peoples of passionate faith as the Cathars and the Zealots.

Although their fortresses would fall, the Nizari Ismaili Shia faith survives, still under the leadership of its hereditary Imams. They are still devoted to improving the world, though now known for their championing of Islamic architecture, Muslim female rights, social housing and educational reform. Their Imam has been popularly known in the West as the Aga Khan, from a title bestowed by a nineteenth-century Qajar shah. A nineteenth-century court case in Bombay, then under British judicial administration, confirmed their dynastic claims to be descended from the Prophet Muhammad through his daughter Fatima and Imam Ali.

When you examine the religious practice of a Sunni and a Shia Muslim for differences, the variations are small. They acknowledge the same Koran, the same practice of five daily prayers, the same calendar, the same practice of fasts and the same rituals of the haj pilgrimage. The fractional differences are basically these: the Shia break their fast a few minutes after the Sunni (a tiny technical difference over what constitutes sunset) and often combine the noon and afternoon prayers as well as the evening and night prayers to make just three visits to a mosque a day rather than five. The Shia are also given to visiting the tomb-shrines of their martyred Imams and the descendants of the Prophet, but then anyone with any experience of Sunni religious life in North Africa, India, West Africa, Sudan and Egypt will realise that this habit of praying beside the tombs of the great heroes of Islam is very widely shared. The most distinctively separate Shiite practice is the *rawdah-khani*, which in the words of Seyyed Hossein Nasr combines 'sermon, recitation of poems and Koranic verses and drama which depicts the tragic life of the different Imams, particularly Imam Husayn'. These are often held in specially constructed 'mourning halls', which may be found in Persia, India, southern Iraq and eastern Arabia. They are often held on a Thursday evening throughout the year but reach their annual emotional zenith in the months of Muharram and Safar, when the tragic death of Husayn at Kerbala is commemorated. This is the time of the year when the annual *ta'ziyah* passion play once again inflames the sense of historical regret and foredoomed tragedy and of endless political disappointment which lies at the emotional heart of a Shia. The public street processions, the impassioned chants, the cries and occasional scenes of self-mutilation by young Shia men once more bring the betrayal of the Alids to the present.

The Sunni tradition is the belief of the majority of the world's Muslims. No one should make the mistake of dismissing the Sunni as a conformist alternative to the Shia, for they have their own traditions of dissent from unjust rulers, their own martyrs and fiercely debated idealism. The guardian of Sunni orthodoxy is not a hereditary or a delegated imam, nor is it a ruling caliph. The Sunni look to a council drawn from all the leading Muslim scholars of the day to make an opinion, a fatwa, as to what is or is not correct belief. Sometimes these scholars emerged from a revered university, such as Cairo's al-Azhar; sometimes they were confirmed in their position as a member of the council of the learned, the ulema, by the accepted ruler of the time.

Until 1258 the Abbasid caliph residing in one of the old palaces in Baghdad was acknowledged as the titular ruler of the worldwide Muslim Sunni community, even if actual power was exercised by provincial dynasties such as the Seljuk sultans. In 1258 this old order was swept away when the Mongols obliterated Baghdad and left behind towers of skulls, formed from hundreds of thousands of slaughtered Muslims. It was a holocaust of ancient skills and learning, fully equal in emotional intensity to how the Western world had reacted to the fall of Rome. According to popular tradition the last caliph was placed in a velvet bag and trampled to death by the

Mongol cavalry, or rolled up in a carpet and beaten to death with clubs so that none of his blood would spill on the ground. A cadet branch of the Abbasid line would continue in Cairo (under the protection of the Mamelukes) from 1259 until the Ottoman sultan Selim the Grim conquered Egypt and Syria and deposed al-Mutawakkil, the last titular Abbasid, in 1517. Later generations of Ottoman sultans would be acknowledged as the greatest rulers of the Muslim world, though their claim to the Caliphate emerged only in 1774 from the chance wording of a treaty with Russia. As an exclusively Turkish dynasty without a drop of Arab blood, let alone that of the Prophet Muhammad, the Ottomans' claim to the Caliphate was not always accepted outside their own wide domains. The last Ottoman caliph was deposed by Kemal Ataturk in 1924, after which the Khedive of Egypt, the Nizam of Hyderabad and the leader of the Hashemite family of Mecca all showed some interest in reviving the title, though no agreement was ever formally concluded. Many Sunni Muslims still yearn for the return of the caliphate as an emotional centre for their aspirations to political and cultural unity. Though ever since the death of Ali in 661, the last of the four Rightly Guided Caliphs, they have never looked to any of their sovereigns for religious guidance. The Sunni, like all Muslims, believe in the primacy of the Koran assisted by the sayings and traditions of the Prophet Muhammad. They also believe that the example of the first four Heirs of the Prophet, Abu Bakr, Omar, Uthman and Ali, is useful as a secondary stream of religious example and authority. A Sunni Muslim might continue to honour the Umayyad Caliphs of Damascus, the Abbasid Caliphs of Baghdad and the Ottoman sultans of Istanbul as 'Commanders of the Faithful', they might venerate them as great inspiring examples of historical leadership of the Muslim peoples, but they do not consider them to have any spiritual or ethical authority.

The leading figures of the Sunni tradition are not the rulers but the scholars, historians and judges of Islam, especially those from the first two centuries. They helped preserve and codify the purity of the Muslim tradition in that critically important period when the first biography of the Prophet was being written down in Baghdad by Ibn Ishaq and when the first collections of hadith were being put together from the precious bank of Medina's collective oral memory. It was also the period when biographies of the pious early Muslims and the first Companions were assembled and the traditions of the early judges, teachers and lawyers were sifted together into the four canonical law schools or traditions that still run concurrently within the world of Sunni Islam. The early decisions of a revered old judge from Medina, Malik ibn Anas (who died in 795), were the basis around which the Maliki legal tradition was formed. From the slightly different traditions of the Kufa garrison city, Abu Hanifa (a gentleman scholar from a Persian mercantile background who lived from 699 to 767) would compile the basis of the Hanafi law code. Egypt and the traditions of the old garrison city of Fustat was the geographical source for the Shafi law code. This would be assembled by Shafi (an orphaned boy from Palestine who grew into the scholar-genius of his age). Shafi was an enormously beneficial influence on Islamic thought. He attempted to create a unanimously accepted Islamic law. He established the definitive hierarchy of sources within Sunni Islam, insisting on the absolute primacy of the Koran followed by the hadith. In a like manner he also insisted on the primacy of the life example of the Prophet, which could be illuminated but not contradicted by any of the carefully kept traditions and examples of the Companions and first four Rightly Guided Caliphs.

In Baghdad itself a fourth school developed from the controversial teachings of Ahmad ibn Hanbal, who suffered persecution at the hands of the Abbasid authorities and who would die around 855. He argued throughout his life against the creation of any law code or any government-supported system of clerical or theological authority. Ibn Hanbal argued that true Islam must always refer back to the prime sources of inspiration, the Koran and the example set by the Prophet. This attractively dynamic message could, however, betray its own simplicity when later generations of Hanbali scholars got bogged down in textual arguments. For among the recurring problems of all the Sunni law schools are that there are inherent contradictions even within the Koran and that there are many problems about which is and which is not a pure hadith. There is also always an ever-present danger that the body of 'learned scholars of religion', which includes the *muhaddithun* (experts in hadith), would gradually evolve into something very close to a self-serving and self-defining priesthood. This is of course the very antithesis of Muhammad's teaching and against the whole ethos of Islam, which is to connect mankind in spiritual communion with the deity.

Despite these inherent tensions, two of the most influential Sunni reformers would come out of the Hanbali tradition. Ibn Taymiyyah (1263–1328), a refugee who fled to Damascus to escape the Mongol destruction of his Iraqi homeland, tried to cut back to the true egalitarian spirit of Islam but his teachings led to his being persecuted by the rulers of both Syria and Egypt. Four hundred years later, a similar-minded scholar who came out of the Hanbali legal tradition, Abd al-Wahhab (1703–92), would emerge into prominence in central Arabia. However well intentioned, Abd al-Wahhab's reforms lacked the compassion of Ibn Taymiyyah (who instead of insisting on the stoning of unrepentant adulterers had campaigned for the return of dowries to divorced Muslim women). Worse was to follow when the Wahhabi movement was grafted on to the ambitions of such local power-brokers as the Saudi and Rachidi emirs of central Arabia. A Wahhabi-inspired state emerged from this union of reforming Islam and political ambition but was to be crushed by the military power of the new Egyptian kingdom of Muhammad Ali, whose son, Ibrahim Pasha, conquered Mecca and Medina in 1813.

The Wahhabi re-emerged as a force to be reckoned with a hundred years later when a Saudi emir completed his conquest of central Arabia with the seizure of the two Holy Cities from the Hashemites in 1926. This was also the period when the influential Muslim Brotherhood was being established in Egypt by Hasan al-Banna. It was a grass-roots educational reform movement which aspired to educate the humble people, the workers and students, back on to the path of the Prophet. Like all such Sunni reforms it looked back to the era of the Heirs of the Prophet, the first four Rightly Guided Caliphs, as a cherished oasis of Islamic unity and right thinking. It also borrowed from the organisational traditions of the Sufi brotherhoods as well as from the intellectual discipline exercised by the Communist and Marxist parties. The Muslim Brotherhood, with the various offshoots that it has inspired, has been one of the most enduring forces within late-twentieth-century Islamic politics, though time and time again, in separate incidents in Syria, Egypt and Algeria, it has been crushed in vicious civil wars just when it seemed on the point of achieving power. Its time may yet come, especially if democratic habits continue to slowly take root, though already there are new currents of reform afoot, a return to the root and branch of the very earliest days of Islam, a complete return to Koranic authority and a dismantling of all the law codes based merely on the authority of hadith.

APPENDIX B

How Can We Know?
Aisha's Legacy among the
Storytellers of Medina

The triumph of Muawiya in 661 had removed political authority from the oasis capital of Medina. Though deprived of its key role at the centre of the Caliphate's political, financial and administrative life, Medina would yet survive as an alternative capital of the mind. Very few of the families descended from the cousins and Companions of the Prophet would leave Medina and the heartland of Arabia to take up residence with the Umayyads in Syria. They preferred to stay on in the oasis, a place perfumed by innumerable associations with Muhammad and sanctified as one of the only two sites in which God had chosen to communicate with his Prophet. To the pious, Medina positively glowed with cherished associations, not only the tombs of all those great in faith but the actual spots where the verses of the Holy Koran were delivered to earth. They preferred to dwell upon this holy past rather than lower themselves by jostling among the *arriviste* court of tax collectors, police chiefs, Christian secretaries and generals that had assembled around the Umayyads. Assured of salaries commensurate with their seniority within Islam, the descendants of the Companions formed an intellectual and spiritual elite locked into residency within the oasis.

They also preferred to marry among their equals, so that the already close bonds of faith, ancestry and language were bound ever tighter by intermarriage. To take but one example: when Hasan retired to Medina having resigned from the office of Caliph, he took as one of his wives Umm Ishaq, who was not only 'extremely beautiful' but of distinguished Islamic blood, for she was both the daughter of Talha and a granddaughter of Abu Bakr. After the death of Hasan she would marry his younger brother Husayn and bear a daughter, Fatima, who in her turn would be betrothed to one of Abu Bakr's great-grandsons. When we look at the marriages of Hasan's daughters – such as Umm Abdallah, who married her first cousin, Ali ibn al-Husayn, or Umm Salamah, who was married to a grandson of Zubayr – the same picture emerges of a tight web of interconnections, binding the leading families together. Deprived of power but not of wealth, it is not surprising to find that they dwelt on the incidents of the past in which their fathers, grandfathers and great-aunts had played the leading parts. These stories became the lifeblood of the oasis, and would be recalled by witnesses, by professional singers and also by some of the participants themselves. We know that Aisha and Umm Salamah would live on in the oasis some forty-six years after the death of the Prophet, telling and retelling their favourite stories to the ever-eager band of new converts or proud old believers who met or were given audiences with the revered old 'Mothers of the Faithful'. The men could not hope to compete with the women's intimate details of Muhammad's life. They preferred to dwell on the epic tales of the early campaigns, military expeditions and missionary journeys of the Prophet. The oasis was packed so full of these stories that there was no need for them to be ordered, let alone written down, for they were the conversational lifeblood of the place.

After her defeat by Ali at the Battle of the Camel in 656, Aisha had totally withdrawn from any expression of a political opinion but nevertheless remained a very active figure in the oasis. Dressed in patched rags, she devoted her life to alms-giving, the care of her kinsmen, especially her nephew Muhammad ibn Abu Bakr's two orphaned boys (Qasim and Quraibah), and was a vocal self-critic. She raked over every detail of her involvement in the highly controversial events around Uthman's death, to the extent that she could even quote Marwan's personal appeal for her to stay behind and patch together a peace, for it was she who had 'set the country afire against me and then, when it was ablaze ran away'. But beyond her remorse for the tragic stream of events that she had helped unleash there was also a very real delight in the craft of storytelling. Aisha even made herself into a great expert on the battle of al-Qadisiya, which had been fought far away from Medina in Iraq. Her rivalry with Ali, most especially after the triumph of Muawiya in 661, was buried under a real and abject contrition. But she had lost none of her old precedence as the first lady of Islam, nor had her status in the eyes of others been diminished. For instance when Sawdah died aged fifty-four in 674, during the reign of Muawiya, she left her old marriage hut that she had shared with the Prophet to Aisha in her will. For all her patched clothes and public grief, Aisha remained a fascinating mixture of pride and piety to her very last days. She made a list of the ten unique privileges of her life: things such as being the only virgin wife of the Prophet, that Muhammad had received revelations in her presence, had died in her arms, in her house, on her night, and had been buried there. Yet on her own deathbed in the summer of 678, aged sixty-four, Aisha was heard to express a heartfelt wish that she had never existed or that she could sink into complete oblivion. She felt no sense of celebration for a life fully lived, or that her faith would be rewarded, and did not consider herself worthy of being buried in her own hut floor, beside the body of her father Abu Bakr and her beloved husband, Muhammad.

Whether directly fostered by Aisha or not, the old rivalry between Aisha and Ali would continue into the next generation. For Aisha's niece and namesake (the daughter of her young half-sister and her kinsman Talha) was one of the two acknowledged 'Pearls of the Quraysh', locked into a lifelong rivalry with Sukainah, Ali's granddaughter, for the first position within the oasis society of Medina. They fought over the patronage of the most esteemed singers, poets and storytellers within the two holy cities by the power of their purse, their influence and the bounty of their tables. Nor was this just an oasis-centred event, for Medina had evolved into an open university for the whole Islamic Empire where male Koranic reciters as well as song-singing slave girls were sent to learn their thousands upon thousands of lines before they were dispersed throughout every province and garrison city of the Caliphate to seek their fame and fortune.

It was in this period that about a dozen individuals within the oasis society of Medina became recognised for the quality and discernment of their knowledge of historical events. We know some of these individuals by name: men such as Urwa, one of Zubayr's sons, and Aban, one of the sons of Caliph Uthman, as well as the ex-slave Shurahbil, an intimate of Ali's household, who lived on beyond his hundredth birthday. Urwa could boast that 'My mother is Asma the daughter of Abu Bakr, my grandmother Safiya was an aunt of the Prophet, Aisha was my aunt on my mother's side and Khadijah my aunt on my father's side.' It became his practice to meet, after the prayers and his evening meal were over, in the mosque of Medina with his friends and talk over the golden days of the past. One of these friends remembered how Urwa denounced a young visitor, just arrived from the court of Damascus with the gossip of all the new promotions, favours and rewards that had been awarded by the Umayyad court. Urwa declared, 'I want none of these things that you want. My wish is piety in this world and a portion of paradise in the next, and to belong to those by whom knowledge is transmitted to future generations.' Urwa would grow into an institution among the Arabs, visited by ruling Caliphs on their way to make the pilgrimage at Mecca. Indeed his public question-and-answer session with Caliph Abdel Malik would be recorded by court scribes and so by this chance accident would become the oldest written 'history' in Arabic. Urwa would later privately advise two of his sons, Hisham and al-Zuhri, that they would become indispensable if they carried forward his knowledge into the next generation. Urwa was never in any doubt about the veracity of his stories, which had come directly to him from Aisha. When praised by a visitor, 'I never saw anyone who recited more verses than Urwa,' he was quick to deny his own primacy by replying, 'What is what I recite, compared with what Aisha could tell? Nothing came in touch with her on which she did not recite an ode.'

It was only when this generation started dying off (that is to say, the children of the main participants of the tale of the Heirs of the Prophet Muhammad) that we begin to find the first serious collectors of stories at work; men such as Jabir al-Jufi, who had also spent time in Kufa, collecting stories about Ali, and who died around 730. More typical of the Medina oasis social structure was Saad ibn Ibrahim, who, as one of the grandsons of the leading Companions (Abder-Rahman ibn Awf), was in a perfect position to collect the old stories. A more unusual figure was the ascetic-scholar Wahb ibn Munabbih, who came from southern Arabia, from that pre-Islamic half-Persian, half-Yemeni caste of administrative officials known as the Abna. Fluent in many languages and scripts, he brought his own considerable knowledge of Jewish, Christian, Persian and Yemeni historical traditions into the Islamic mainstream. By this period the oral stories had settled into two basic forms: the male-orientated accounts of *al-maghazi*, the campaigns of the Prophet, and the *ashab al-nuzul*, the occasions of a Koranic revelation, which came out of the cherished memories of Aisha and Umm Salamah.

The next generation of scholars and story collectors to come out of the old Medina families of Islam includes Abdallah ibn Abi Bakr (whose great-grandfather had been one of the missionary ambassadors sent by the Prophet to the Yemen) and Asim (whose grandfather had been one of the standard-bearers at the battle of Hunayn). Though they would be revered as prime sources, it was their contemporary Muhammad al-Zuhri (of the Beni Zuhra clan) who stands at the crux point where the living oral traditions of Medina would be transformed into written history. Al-Zuhri worked on creating a collection of the sayings of the Prophet, a formal biography of him and a definitive genealogy of the clans of north and central Arabia. These vast and ambitious projects would never be fulfilled, though the young men who worked with him would in their own way complete their master's work.

None of these young men (Musa ibn Oqba, Mamar ibn Rashid and Muhammad ibn Ishaq) who worked for al-Zuhri came from the inner circle of Medina-based descendants of the Companions of the Prophet. They were all descendants of ex-slaves, bondsmen or subservient clients. For instance Ibn Ishaq's grandfather Yasar was a Christian Arab from Iraq who had been made a slave during the very first Muslim raids into the Persian Empire. Yasar was sent to Medina but, having been freed upon his conversion to Islam, decided to stay on in the rapidly expanding oasis city that was growing up at this time. So his three sons were all born into the Muslim faith and grew up in Medina. The most scholarly of Yasar's three boys, Ishaq, was a collector of the Prophet's sayings, and so his son Muhammad grew up within a literate and scholarly household. It also seems clear that Muhammad ibn Ishaq's low caste earned him some resentment from the better-born 'sources' within Medina's society. On one occasion he was shaved and scourged on the order of the city governor because of his too assiduous questioning of women at the back part of the mosque. Having learned all he could from the three great storymen of his day – Abdallah, Asim and of course his master al-Zuhri – he later cross-checked these revered sources with a hundred other lesser chains of authority within the oasis. Later he would travel to Alexandria, Fustat and Kufa to listen to and interview other scholars, before leaving Medina (probably due to academic jealousy) and setting up house in the newly established Abbasid capital of Baghdad. There before his death (in AD 761/150 AH) he wrote a biography of the Prophet that survives to this day and remains our prime written source. Though published in the princely, cosmopolitan city of Baghdad, ibn Ishaq's great work was formed from the unique oral culture of Medina. Such was also the background out of which the other famous younger contemporaries of ibn Ishaq, such as al-Sindi and al-Waqidi (the most impartial and professional of all the first historians), would emerge. They would be the last: Waqidi's own secretary (and literary heir) had been born in Basra, while of the fifteen young scholars who collected around ibn Ishaq in Baghdad, only one of them came from Medina.

With the creation of these first biographies and histories Medina had fulfilled its historic destiny. The 'shadow capital' of the oasis of Medina had, because of its exclusive population of depoliticised but eminent families, preserved the story of the Prophet and early Islam for the future of humankind. The collective memory would prove remarkably consistent for all the events that had occurred within the oasis of Medina. As you read this last paragraph, you have become part of this chain of story-telling that leads directly back to ibn Ishaq and from him back through that crowd of men who liked to meet in the evenings in the mosque of Medina. The greatest of these, Urwa, would decline all praise and demand of his listeners, 'What is what I recite, compared with what Aisha could tell?'

KEY DATES

in political and military history for the fifty years after
the death of the Prophet Muhammad, 632–83

(Please note that the dates of all the key battles of the conquest cannot
be definitive and may vary by as much as four years.)

632   Death of the Prophet Muhammad as an army under the command of Zayd's young son Usama is mustered for a raid to avenge the defeat at Mutah in Syria in 629.

      Accession as Caliph of Abu Bakr, who decides that the paying of the charitable tithe will remain the defining test of which tribes have accepted Islam. Widespread opposition.

      Death of Fatimah, leaving Ali to care for their two children, Husayn and Hasan.

633   The Ridda Wars – the so-called War against Apostasy.

      Abu Bakr appoints Khalid army commander, who wins three victories.

      Battle of Buzakha: defeat of Ghatafan tribe and allies.

      Battle of Aqraba, 'day of the garden of death': defeat of Beni Hanifa tribe and death of their prophet Musaylama.

      Battle of Ullais, 'river of blood' (against Arab tribes loyal to Persian Empire).

634   Invasion of the Holy Land by four Arab armies, three advancing from Medina, one from the Iraq front under the command of Khalid. Three military victories in Palestine, Wadi al-Arabah, Ajnadayn and Dattin, and one in Syria, Marj al-Suffar.

Death of Abu Bakr in August; accession of Omar to Caliphate.

On Iraq front Persian army defeats Muslim force at battle of al-Jisr just outside Hira.

635　　Muslim armies occupy chief cities of Syria and Palestine.

On Iraq frontier, ibn Harith manages to repel Persian counter-attack at battle of Buwayb.

636　　Arab armies evacuate all of their territorial gains in Syria and Palestine as full force of Byzantine Empire sent into battle.

In mid-August, Khalid destroys the Byzantine field army at the decisive battle of Yarmuk and speedily reoccupies all of the Near East.

637　　Counter-offensive by imperial army of Sassanid Persia. Yazdegird's (last Sassanian emperor) experienced commander Rustam drawn into four-day battle of al-Qadisiya.

In aftermath of victory Muslims occupy all of Iraq, while Sassanian forces withdraw into Persian mountains.

Surrender of Jerusalem by Patriarch Sophronius to Caliph Omar.

638　　Muslim Arab armies push into northern Iraq and advance into Persia and northern Syria.

639　　Year of plague and famine.

640　　Caliph Omar presides over conference of army commanders at Jabiyah.

Amr ibn al-As leads raid into Byzantine Egypt while bulk of Muslim forces engaged in advance on Anatolia and Persia.

Victory against Byzantine army in Egypt at battle of Heliopolis.

Amr advances north into Nile Delta, fights battle of Nikiou and attempts siege of Alexandria.

641　　Emperor Heraclius dies in February.

Byzantine counter-attack into Syria and rebellion among Arab tribes of Syrian desert.

642　　Surrender of Alexandria to Amr by Cyril. Amr establishes Fustat as new garrison/administrative centre for Egypt.

Muslim victory at battle of Nehawand in Persia.

644 Assassination of Omar by Abu Lulu Firoz, a disgruntled prisoner of war/slave.

Election of Uthman by council of six leading Companions.

Amr and his nephew Oqba ibn Nafi return in triumph to Fustat having raided and conquered parts of Libya and the Sahara.

645 Widespread revolts against the Muslim Empire throughout Persia, Armenia, Azerbaijan and in Egypt, aided by the arrival of the Byzantine navy. General Manuel reoccupies the Nile Delta.

646 Amr (briefly reappointed as commander) leads reconquest of Egypt with second battle of Nikiou and siege and sack of Alexandria.

647 Uthman's governor of Egypt leads a 40,000-strong army out of Egypt into the west, defeating army of Byzantine governor of Tunisia at battle of Sbeitla.

648 Arab fleet skirmishes successfully with Byzantine fleet found off Alexandria.

649 Muslim occupation of Cyprus in combined operation organised by the Arab garrisons in Egypt and Syria.

650 Definitive edition of the Koran completed in Medina.

Arab armies establish advance bases in the Central Asian cities of Herat, Merv, Balkh and Kabul.

651 Uthman loses the seal of the Prophet.

652 Death of Yazdegird.

653 After renewed threat from Byzantine fleet, Cyprus is reconquered in second invasion the same year that an Arab army secures Armenia.

654 Rhodes raided by Arab fleet.

655 Battle of the Masts: Arab fleet wins command of the Aegean in naval battle fought off the coast of Lycia.

656 Assassination of Uthman in Medina by dissidents from army garrisons in Fustat, Kufa and Basra.

Ali acclaimed fourth Caliph in Medina.

Aisha plots rebellion in Mecca backed by Talha and Zubayr.

Aisha and her confederates seize control of army garrison in Basra. Ali's son Hasan takes command of garrison at Kufa.

Battle of the Camel outside Basra. Talha and Zubayr are killed and Aisha is returned to Medina having recognised Ali as Caliph.

657   Ali's candidate, Muhammad ibn Abu Bakr, becomes governor of Egypt.

Ali marches on Syria to depose Muawiya from the governorship of Syria.

Four-day battle of Siffin culminates in a surprise decision to seek arbitration.

Schism as Kharijites attempt to secede from Ali's Caliphate in fury at the decision to arbitrate.

658   Farcical chicanery at arbitration conference in Jordan as Amr outwits Abu Musa.

Muawiya is proclaimed Caliph by his supporters in Damascus.

Ali forced to fight militant Kharijites at battle of Nahrawan.

659   Amr, supported by Muawiya, takes command of Egypt for the third time in his life. Death of Muhammad ibn Abu Bakr.

660   Muawiya renews assault on Byzantine Empire.

661   Ali is assassinated in Kufa.

Ali's son Hasan acclaimed as Caliph but in order to halt bloodshed surrenders his title in Muawiya's favour.

662   Zayyad and Mughira rule over Basra and Kufa as tough-minded governors of Muawiya.

663   First Arab raid on Sicily.

669   Muslim siege of Constantinople supported by command of the sea route.

670   Foundation of Kairouan as the advance base for the conquest of North Africa by Amr's nephew Oqba ibn Nafi.

Merv established as the new advance base for the conquest of Central Asia and Khorassan by drafts from Basra and Kufa. Hasan dies in Medina.

671   Kharijite revolt in Iraq suppressed by Zayyad.

678   Defeat of Arab fleet at battle of Syllaeum requires that the Arab siege of Constantinople be lifted.

       Thirty-year peace is made between the two empires.

680   Muawiya dies and is succeeded to the Caliphate by his son Yazid.

       Husayn responds to calls of soldiers of Kufa garrison to lead them in revolt against this new hereditary monarchy. Abandoned by those whom he had come to aid, he and his band of followers are killed at Kerbala.

       In Medina and Mecca, Abdallah, son of Zubayr, leads revolt against Yazid.

681   Oqba ibn Nafi reaches the Atlantic coast of Morocco at the end of his legendary ride across North Africa.

683   An Umayyad army marches from Damascus to Medina. It wins the battle of Harran, sacks Medina, then advances and places Mecca under siege. The city's Kaaba is accidentally burned to the ground. Yazid dies.

KEY CHARACTERS

in the life of the Prophet Muhammad

Arabic names usually indicate both whose child you are and who are your children. *Abu* translates as 'father of', *ibn* or *ben* as 'son of', *bint* as 'daughter of', *Umm* as 'mother of'. A clan or tribe can be described as the Beni (or Banu), as they are 'children of' their common ancestor – for instance, the Beni Hashim or the Beni Umayya, who are also referred to as the Hashemites or the Umayyads.

Al-Abbas – wealthy and influential paternal uncle of the Prophet Muhammad, half-brother to Abu Talib and from whom the Abbasid dynasty claims its descent.

Abdallah ibn al-Abbas – the son of Al-Abbas and so a first cousin of Ali. Abdallah was a key supporter and adviser to Ali during his Caliphate but was ultimately dismissed from the post of governor of Basra.

Abd al-Muttalib – beloved grandfather of the Prophet Muhammad, successful merchant and sheikh of the Beni Hashim clan of the Quraysh tribe.

Abder-Rahman ibn Awf – early convert to Islam and one of the Companions who formed the inner committee of six that elected Uthman Caliph in 644.

Abdullah ibn Ubbay – one of the principal chieftains of Medina before the arrival of the Prophet Muhammad.

Abu Bakr – father of Aisha; acclaimed first Caliph after the Prophet's death. Arguably the first adult male convert to Islam, and a close colleague and devout disciple of the Prophet Muhammad. The only man to accompany Muhammad when he escaped from Mecca. He was chosen to lead the prayers by the Prophet in the last week of his life, which gave him a critical edge to become his acknowledged successor.

Abu Jahl – 'Father of Ignorance', important figure in pagan Mecca and key early opponent of Muhammad.

Abu Lahab – 'Father of Flames', one of Muhammad's half-uncles, but the one least well disposed to him.

Abu Musa al-Ashari – revered and pious commander of Arab armies on the Persian front and sometime governor of both Basra and Kufa. Chosen by the army to be the representative for Ali after the battle of Siffin in 657, when he was outwitted by Amr ibn al-As.

Abu Sufyan – nobleman of Mecca who for ten years commanded the pagan opposition to early Islam after Muhammad's migration to Medina. After his acceptance of Islam, prepared for by the marriage of his daugher Umm Habiba to Muhammad, he would become a loyal ally of the Prophet. He would serve as a provincial governor in the Yemen for the first two Caliphs and is traditionally considered to have fought at Yarmuk. Legitimate father of Yazid and Muawiya and possibly to others, such as Amr and Zayyad.

Abu Talib – father of Ali and the uncle of Muhammad who cared for and protected his young orphan nephew until his last dying breath, though he never accepted Islam.

Abu Ubaydah – chosen to be supreme commander in Syria by Omar, and would have been trusted with the Caliphate by Omar if he had not died during the plague of 639.

Aisha – beautiful young daughter of Abu Bakr and Umm Ruman who married Muhammad three years after the death of his beloved first wife, Khadijah. The most passionate, jealous and wonderfully animated of the Prophet's many wives, a vital oral source and a key political figure.

Ali – young cousin of Muhammad (the younger son of Abu Talib) who was brought up in the Prophet's household. The first man to publicly accept Islam, a hero of the early Muslim community both as a warrior and as an inquiring champion of a living faith. The Prophet's son-in-law through his marriage to Fatimah, father of Hasan and Husayn, fourth Caliph in the Sunni hierarchy, sole Imam and only true Heir of the Prophet according to the Shia tradition.

Aminah – daughter of Wahb of the Zuhrah clan of the Quraysh and mother of Muhammad.

Amr ibn al-As – influential Meccan nobleman who fought against the Muslims in Medina but would later embrace Islam and rise quickly through its ranks. He was appointed by Abu Bakr one of the three commanders that led the first Muslim armies out of Medina for the conquest of the Holy Land. In 640 he led a raid that would lead to the conquest of Egypt, which he would conquer and rule over on three separate occasions. Dismissed by Uthman, he would regain his old position by a political alliance with Muawiya.

Barakah (also known as Umm Ayman) – slave girl whom Muhammad inherited from his father. Cherished figure of Muhammad's childhood to whom he gave freedom on the day of his marriage to Khadijah. Many years later she became one of the wives of Zayd ibn Haritha and although she must have been around twenty years older than her husband, they would have a child, Usama.

Bilal – Abyssinian slave and early Muslim convert. Much abused by his pagan master until Abu Bakr bought his freedom. Selected as the first muezzin (prayer caller) of Islam.

Cyrus – catastrophically incapable Byzantine official who ruled over the province of Egypt as both civil governor and Greek Orthodox patriarch.

Dhul Qina – 'the Man of the Veil', charismatic Yemeni warlord who led the pagan resistance to Islam in the immediate aftermath of the death of the Prophet Muhammad.

Fatimah (often spelled Fatima) – one of the four daughters of Muhammad and Khadijah. Wife of Ali, mother of Hasan and Husayn, and a key early believer. Her patience, modesty and devotional practice provide an alternative Muslim female role model to Aisha.

Hafsah – fourth wife of the Prophet and daughter of Umar. Hafsah's first husband died at the battle of the wells of Badr, leaving her an eighteen-year-old widow. Known to be fiery-tempered, literate and independent-minded. She possessed the first written prototype of the Koran, the basis for the great compilation later achieved by Uthman.

Halimah – foster mother of Muhammad, of the Hawazin clan of the Beni Saad tribe of Bedouin.

Hamza – Muhammad's boisterous uncle. A great fighter, hunter and wine drinker, around whom in later centuries the Persians would collect a whole cycle of legends.

Hasan (sometimes spelled Hassan) – first son of Ali and Fatima, grandson of Muhammad, fifth Caliph of Islam. A heroic practitioner of Islam as the true religion of peace.

Hashim – Muhammad's great-grandfather, whose numerous descendants would form the Beni Hashim clan – hereditary guardians of the Kaaba in Mecca for centuries and from whom the Hashemite dynasty would emerge.

Husayn (sometimes spelled Hussein) – second son of Ali and Fatima, grandson of Muhammad. After the death of his elder brother Hasan, he took on the mantle of the Alid cause and would respond to the call of the people of Kufa to lead them back into freedom. Abandoned by his own supporters, he chose martyrdom at Kerbala rather than dishonour.

Ibn Harith, Muthana – chief of the Beni Bekr who had fought against the Persians as a young man and became military ally of Khalid in the first raids on Iraq. Fought at battles of Ullais, Al-Jisr and Buwayba.

Jabala ibn al-Ayham – last prince of the Ghassanid dynasty who loyally fought for the Byzantine Empire at the battle of Yarmuk in 636.

Jafar – young cousin of Muhammad, son of Abu Talib and one of the early believers who took refuge in Christian Abyssinia and who would be killed alongside Zayd at the battle of Mutah in 629.

Juwayriya – wife of the Prophet and daughter of the chief of the Beni Mustaliq Bedouin tribe.

Khadijah – first wife of Muhammad, his senior in wealth and years. Mother of four daughters (Zaynab, Ruqayyah, Umm Kulthum and Fatimah) and two boys (both of whom died in their infancy). Chief confidante and colleague in Muhammad's early search for religion and the first person to recognise him as a Prophet of God.

Khalid ibn al-Walid – pagan Meccan nobleman who fought against Muslims in Medina before converting and taking his place as the most talented general of early Islam, saluted and promoted by even the Prophet himself. A succession of three victories during the Ridda Wars culminated in his inspired manoeuvres during the conquest of the Holy Land which led to his ultimate achievement, the decisive victory at Yarmuk. He would later be reduced to the ranks by Omar and prosecuted into disgrace.

Mariyah or Marya or Meriem – Coptic concubine sent to Medina as a gift to the Prophet from Muqawqis, a ruler of Egypt. She was given her freedom after she gave birth to Muhammad's son Ibrahim, though she was never given the honour of being addressed like the Prophet's other wives as a 'Mother of the Faithful'.

Maymunah – wife of the Prophet and widowed sister-in-law to Muhammad's clever banking uncle Abbas.

Muawiya – founder of the Umayyad dynasty, brilliant politican and army commander. The Caesar of the Arabs. The second son of Abu Sufyan and Hind, he may have briefly served Muhammad as a secretary after his submission to Islam in the last two years of the Prophet's life. He rose to prominence when he assisted his elder brother Yazid in the conquest of the Holy Land, and would take over his command after Yazid's death from plague. His outstanding military and organisational talents were recog-

nised by Omar and Uthman, who both left him in command
of Syria. Ali's refusal to renew Muawiya's command was one of
the key motivations behind the civil war that would conclude
with Muawiya's triumph.

Mughira ibn Shuba – renegade from the Thaqif tribe of Taif who
greatly benefited from a timely early conversion to Islam.
Despite his moral failings his political insights made him an
indispensable adviser who served both the Prophet and Omar
and would seek to serve Ali before defecting to Muawiya's
camp during the civil war. He would die in office as Muawiya's
feared governor of Kufa.

Muhammad ibn Abu Bakr – last-born child of Abu Bakr who
would grow up in the household of his beloved stepfather Ali.
One of the assassins of Caliph Uthman; appointed governor of
Egypt by Ali.

Musaylama – prophet of the Beni Hanifa tribe of eastern Arabia
who would be killed during the battle of Aqraba during the
Ridda Wars.

Omar ibn al-Khattab (often spelled 'Umar) – second Caliph of
Islam is a major figure in the development of Muslim civilisa-
tion who supervised the installation of Abu Bakr as the first
Caliph as well as the victories over both the Byzantine and
Persian empires. He was the father of the Prophet's wife
Hafsah, an implacable puritan and the architect of the whole
political shape of the Islamic Empire.

Oqba ibn Nafi – nephew of Amr and an almost legendary figure of
conquest and exploration from the annals of the first Muslim
conquests. He participated in the conquest of Egypt, commanded the raids that would penetrate the Libyan Sahara, and
was repelled from the Sudan before founding the city of
Kairouan as an advance base for the conquest of North Africa.

Ruqayyah – daughter of the Prophet Muhammad and Khadijah,
wife of Uthman; died in Medina the day that the battle of
Badr was won.

Saad ibn Abu Waqqas – early convert to Islam who was among the first seventy believers to migrate to Medina and the first to draw blood in the subsequent ten-year war against the pagans of Mecca. He commanded the vast Arab army that achieved the decisive victory over the Persian Empire at the battle of al-Qadisiya, and would be among the group of six close Companions chosen by Omar to elect the next Caliph.

Saad ibn Ubadayah – chieftain of Medina's Saidah clan who was a passionate early supporter of the Prophet and who called the meeting of the men of Medina after the Prophet's death.

Safiyah – wife of the Prophet. She was the daughter of Sheikh Huayy, leader of the Jewish–Arab Bani Nadir clan of Medina, and the widow of another great Jewish sheikh who was executed during the siege of Khaybar.

Sawdah – second wife of the Prophet who came into his household after the death of Khadijah as a thirty-year-old widow and a stepmother to his daughters. She had been one of the first Muslims to escape persecution by pagan Mecca and emigrate to Ethiopia.

Shurahbil ibn Hasana – one of the three army commanders appointed at Medina by Abu Bakr for the conquest of the Holy Land, alongside Yazid, son of Abu Sufyan and Amr ibn al-As.

Sophronius – Greek Orthodox Patriarch of Jerusalem who would organise the surrender of the Holy City to Caliph Omar.

Talha ibn Ubaydallah – cousin of Abu Bakr, one of the early believers who would be chosen by Omar to sit in the committee of six that elected the next Caliph and who would with Zubayr join Aisha in her revolt against Ali.

Umamah – Muhammad's granddaughter, the child of his daughter Zaynab and Abu al-As, the son of Rabi.

Umm Habiba – wife of the Prophet and daughter of Abu Sufyan, great sheikh of the Quraysh tribe that dominated pre-Islamic Mecca.

Umm Salamah – wife of the Prophet. She was the widow of Muhammad's first cousin, Abu Salama, who had died of wounds received at the battle of Uhud. She had been in exile in Ethiopia and brought her young children into the protection of the Prophet's household. It was her sage advice that broke the brief spell of disobedience at Hudaibiya.

Usama – Muhammad's grandson through his adopted son Zayd. He won Aisha's friendship by supporting her in her hour of need and would (somewhat controversially) be placed in command of the Muslim army by the Prophet Muhammad in the last month of his life.

Uthman ibn Affan – third Caliph of Islam and the man who supervised the editing of the first written edition of the Koran. A wealthy, clever, scholarly early convert to Islam who was descended from one of the most important noble clans of Mecca. He would be trusted to marry two of the Prophet's daughters and would be chosen as third Caliph in 644 owing to his skill as an administrator. His great failing was too great a dependence on his own family and clan, which may have been due to his personal failing as a warrior; he would yet redeem himself in the manner of his death.

Yazdegird – last Sassanian to rule over the Empire of Persia and its Zoroastrian faith.

Zayd ibn Harithah – captured in a Bedouin raid as a boy and brought to Mecca's annual fair of Ukaz as a slave boy. He was bought at auction and given to Khadijah by one of her wealthy nephews. She in turn gave Zayd to Muhammad as a wedding gift. Muhammad later offered Zayd his freedom and formally adopted him as a son and would give him Barakah as his first wife, from whom he had a son, Usama. Zayd was one of the most devoted followers of Muhammad and later rose to become one of the key military commanders of early Islam until his death at the battle of Mutah.

Zaynab – daughter of Muhammad, married to one of her mother's favourite nephews, the handsome Abu al-As, who remained a pagan in Mecca until almost the last. Mother of Umamah.

Zaynab – daughter of Khuzaymah, the fifth wife of the Prophet was the daughter of an influential Bedouin chieftain of the Amir tribe. She was widowed after her first husband died at the battle of the wells of Badr. Famously generous to the poor; died eight months after her marriage to the Prophet. Zaynab – Jewish sorceress at Khaybar who attempted to avenge her community by trying to poison the Prophet.

Zaynab bint Jaysh – cousin and sixth wife of the Prophet, first married to Muhammad's adopted son Zayd. This marriage was ended and she was given (as recorded in a Koranic verse) to the Prophet as an additional wife to bring his household in Medina up to five women.

Zayyad – shrewd political operator who, like Mughira, was from the Thaqif tribe of the city of Taif. As the bastard of a prostitute owned by a foreign merchant, he had no social status or clan allies to help him through life but he would nevertheless rise to become a trusted secretary, then governor, and finally governor of both Basra and Kufa and all Persia for Muawiya. Zayyad was officially adopted into Muawiya's family and his sons were awarded lesser governorships within the regime, which helped bind his family into total loyalty to the Umayyads. It was one of Zayyad's sons, Ubaydallah ibn Zayyad, governor of Kufa, who masterminded the chain of events that led to the tragedy of Kerbala.

Zubayr ibn al-Awwam – early believer who would be placed in charge of an army of reinforcements sent by Omar to support Amr ibn al-As's raid into Egypt. He would win renown among his men by leading an assault on the Byzantine fortress of Babylon. One of the committee of six chosen to select a Caliph after the death of Omar, he joined Aisha in her revolt against Ali.

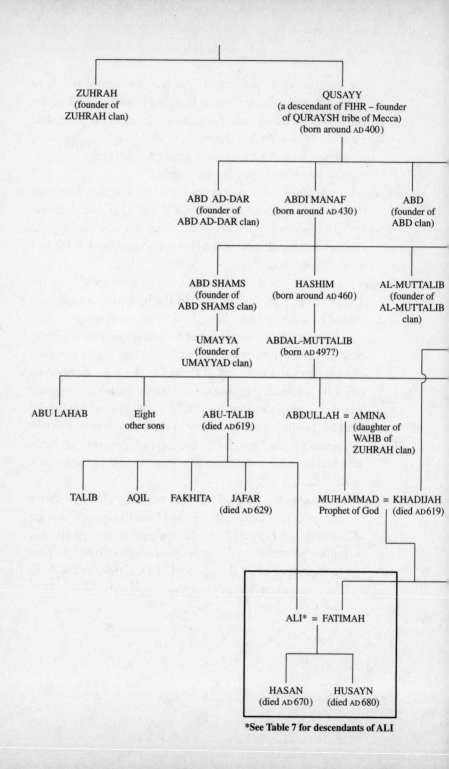

ZUHRAH
(founder of
ZUHRAH clan)

QUSAYY
(a descendant of FIHR – founder
of QURAYSH tribe of Mecca)
(born around AD 400)

ABD AD-DAR
(founder of
ABD AD-DAR clan)

ABDI MANAF
(born around AD 430)

ABD
(founder of
ABD clan)

ABD SHAMS
(founder of
ABD SHAMS clan)

HASHIM
(born around AD 460)

AL-MUTTALIB
(founder of
AL-MUTTALIB
clan)

UMAYYA
(founder of
UMAYYAD clan)

ABDAL-MUTTALIB
(born AD 497?)

ABU LAHAB

Eight
other sons

ABU-TALIB
(died AD 619)

ABDULLAH = AMINA
(daughter of
WAHB of
ZUHRAH clan)

TALIB   AQIL   FAKHITA   JAFAR
(died AD 629)

MUHAMMAD = KHADIJAH
Prophet of God (died AD 619)

ALI* = FATIMAH

HASAN
(died AD 670)

HUSAYN
(died AD 680)

*See Table 7 for descendants of ALI

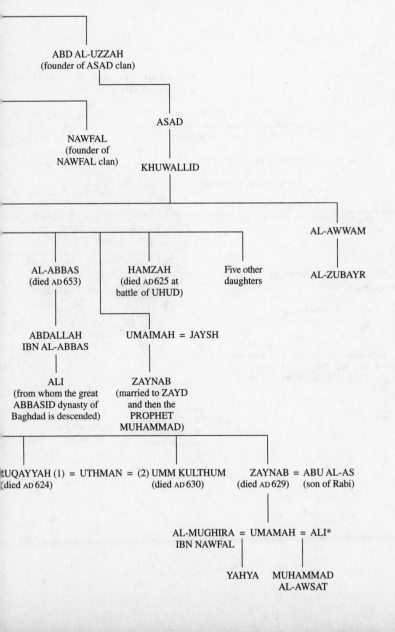

TABLE 1

The family of THE PROPHET MUHAMMAD
and the clan chieftains of Mecca's Quraysh tribe

ABD AL-UZZAH
(founder of ASAD clan)

NAWFAL
(founder of
NAWFAL clan)

ASAD

KHUWALLID

AL-AWWAM

AL-ABBAS
(died AD 653)

HAMZAH
(died AD 625 at
battle of UHUD)

Five other
daughters

AL-ZUBAYR

ABDALLAH
IBN AL-ABBAS

UMAIMAH = JAYSH

ALI
(from whom the great
ABBASID dynasty of
Baghdad is descended)

ZAYNAB
(married to ZAYD
and then the
PROPHET
MUHAMMAD)

RUQAYYAH (1) = UTHMAN = (2) UMM KULTHUM
(died AD 624)   (died AD 630)

ZAYNAB = ABU AL-AS
(died AD 629)   (son of Rabi)

AL-MUGHIRA = UMAMAH = ALI*
IBN NAWFAL

YAHYA   MUHAMMAD
          AL-AWSAT

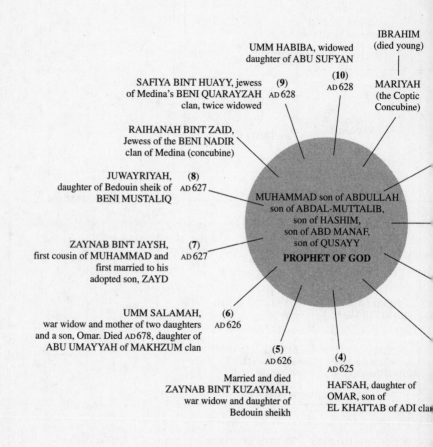

IBRAHIM
(died young)

UMM HABIBA, widowed
daughter of ABU SUFYAN

MARIYAH
(the Coptic
Concubine)

SAFIYA BINT HUAYY, jewess   **(9)**   **(10)**
of Medina's BENI QUARAYZAH   AD 628   AD 628
clan, twice widowed

RAIHANAH BINT ZAID,
Jewess of the BENI NADIR
clan of Medina (concubine)

JUWAYRIYAH,   **(8)**
daughter of Bedouin sheik of   AD 627
BENI MUSTALIQ

MUHAMMAD son of ABDULLAH
son of ABDAL-MUTTALIB,
son of HASHIM,
son of ABD MANAF,
son of QUSAYY
PROPHET OF GOD

ZAYNAB BINT JAYSH,   **(7)**
first cousin of MUHAMMAD and   AD 627
first married to his
adopted son, ZAYD

UMM SALAMAH,   **(6)**
war widow and mother of two daughters   AD 626
and a son, Omar. Died AD 678, daughter of
ABU UMAYYAH of MAKHZUM clan

(5)
AD 626

(4)
AD 625

Married and died
ZAYNAB BINT KUZAYMAH,
war widow and daughter of
Bedouin sheikh

HAFSAH, daughter of
OMAR, son of
EL KHATTAB of ADI clan

TABLE 2
The marriages, concubines and children of THE PROPHET MUHAMMAD

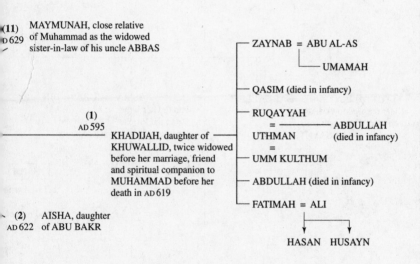

(11)
D 629   MAYMUNAH, close relative of Muhammad as the widowed sister-in-law of his uncle ABBAS

(1)
AD 595

KHADIJAH, daughter of KHUWALLID, twice widowed before her marriage, friend and spiritual companion to MUHAMMAD before her death in AD 619

ZAYNAB = ABU AL-AS

UMAMAH

QASIM (died in infancy)

RUQAYYAH
=   ABDULLAH
UTHMAN   (died in infancy)
=
UMM KULTHUM

ABDULLAH (died in infancy)

FATIMAH = ALI

HASAN   HUSAYN

(2)
AD 622   AISHA, daughter of ABU BAKR

(3)
AD 622

SAWDAH, widowed 'housekeeper'

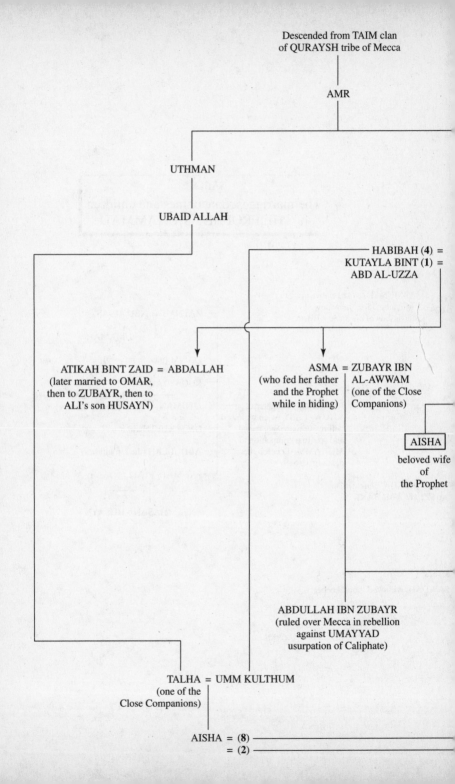

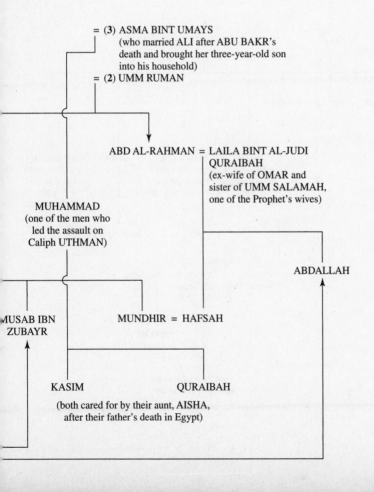

TABLE 3
The family of ABU BAKR, first Caliph of Islam, and its close links with the family of TALHA and ZUBAYR

AAMIR

ABU QUHAFA

ABU BAKR

= **(3)** ASMA BINT UMAYS
(who married ALI after ABU BAKR's
death and brought her three-year-old son
into his household)

= **(2)** UMM RUMAN

ABD AL-RAHMAN = LAILA BINT AL-JUDI
QURAIBAH
(ex-wife of OMAR and
sister of UMM SALAMAH,
one of the Prophet's wives)

MUHAMMAD
(one of the men who
led the assault on
Caliph UTHMAN)

ABDALLAH

MUSAB IBN
ZUBAYR

MUNDHIR = HAFSAH

KASIM   QURAIBAH

(both cared for by their aunt, AISHA,
after their father's death in Egypt)

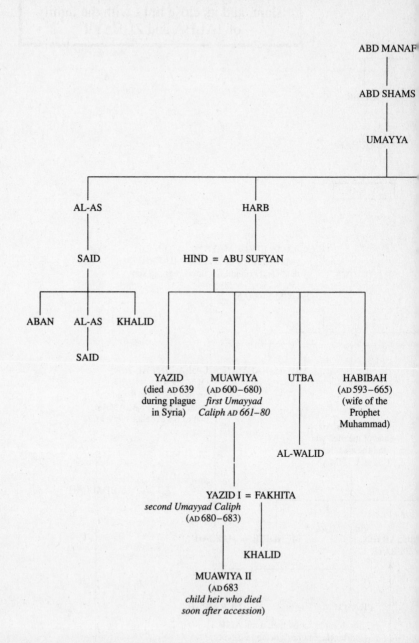

TABLE 4

Family tree of UTHMAN IBN AFFAN (third Caliph of Islam) and his relatives from the ABD SHAMS clan of the QURAYSH tribe of Mecca

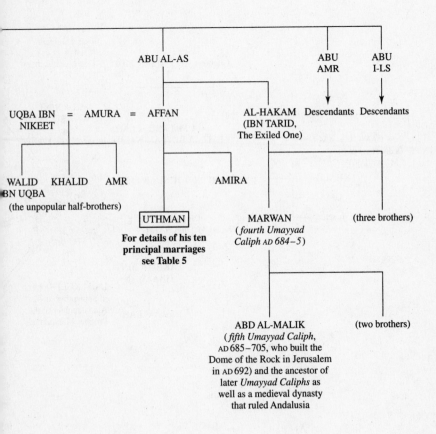

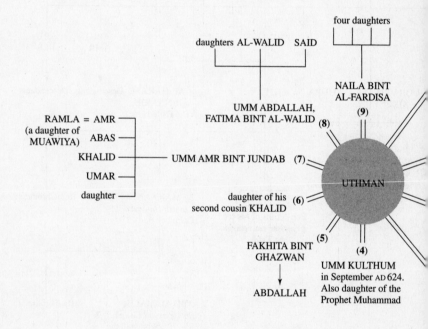

four daughters

daughters AL-WALID   SAID

NAILA BINT
AL-FARDISA

(9)

RAMLA = AMR
(a daughter of
MUAWIYA)   ABAS

KHALID

UMAR

daughter

UMM ABDALLAH,
FATIMA BINT AL-WALID   **(8)**

UMM AMR BINT JUNDAB   **(7)**

daughter of his   **(6)**
second cousin KHALID

UTHMAN

(5)

(4)

FAKHITA BINT
GHAZWAN

ABDALLAH

UMM KULTHUM
in September AD 624.
Also daughter of the
Prophet Muhammad

TABLE 5
The marriages and children of
UTHMAN, third Caliph of Islam

(10) the daughter of the cheif
of the FAZARA tribe

(1) UMM HAKIM ASMA, daughter of ABU JAHL ⟶ AL MUGHIRA
who would then marry AL-WALID of the
ABD SHAMS clan

(2) RUQAYYAH, daughter of the ⟶ ABDALLAH
Prophet Muhammad   (died aged six in exile
in Abyssinia)

(3) RAMLA, daughter of
SHAYBA IBN RABIA ⟶ three daughters ⟶
UMM ABAS = MARWAN
UMM AMR = SAID IBN AL-AS
AISHA = (1) AL HARITH
(2) ABDALLAH IBN
AL-ZUBAYR

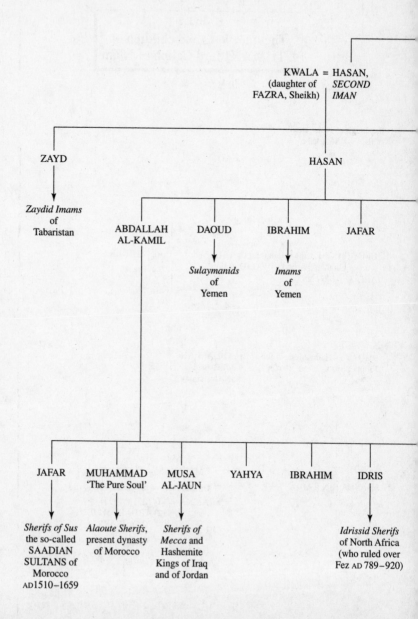

TABLE 6

Descendants of ALI and FATIMA

KWALA = HASAN,
(daughter of   *SECOND*
FAZRA, Sheikh) | *IMAN*

ZAYD   HASAN

Zaydid Imams
of   ABDALLAH   DAOUD   IBRAHIM   JAFAR
Tabaristan   AL-KAMIL

                                Sulaymanids   *Imams*
                                    of   of
                                  Yemen   Yemen

JAFAR   MUHAMMAD   MUSA   YAHYA   IBRAHIM   IDRIS
              'The Pure Soul'   AL-JAUN

Sherifs of Sus   *Alaoute Sherifs,*   *Sherifs of*   *Idrissid Sherifs*
the so-called   present dynasty   *Mecca* and   of North Africa
SAADIAN   of Morocco   Hashemite   (who ruled over
SULTANS of   Kings of Iraq   Fez AD 789–920)
Morocco   and of Jordan
AD1510–1659

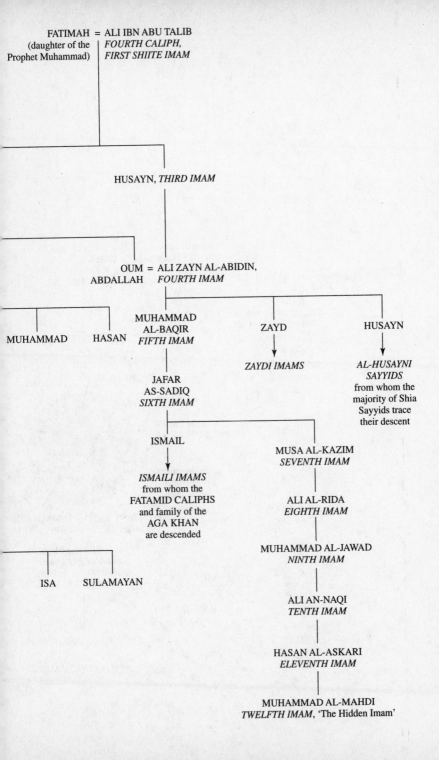

FATIMAH = ALI IBN ABU TALIB
(daughter of the   *FOURTH CALIPH,*
Prophet Muhammad)   *FIRST SHIITE IMAM*

HUSAYN, *THIRD IMAM*

OUM = ALI ZAYN AL-ABIDIN,
ABDALLAH   *FOURTH IMAM*

MUHAMMAD

HASAN

MUHAMMAD
AL-BAQIR
FIFTH IMAM

ZAYD

HUSAYN

JAFAR
AS-SADIQ
SIXTH IMAM

ZAYDI IMAMS

*AL-HUSAYNI
SAYYIDS*
from whom the
majority of Shia
Sayyids trace
their descent

ISMAIL

ISMAILI IMAMS
from whom the
FATAMID CALIPHS
and family of the
AGA KHAN
are descended

MUSA AL-KAZIM
SEVENTH IMAM

ALI AL-RIDA
EIGHTH IMAM

ISA

SULAMAYAN

MUHAMMAD AL-JAWAD
NINTH IMAM

ALI AN-NAQI
TENTH IMAM

HASAN AL-ASKARI
ELEVENTH IMAM

MUHAMMAD AL-MAHDI
TWELFTH IMAM, 'The Hidden Imam'

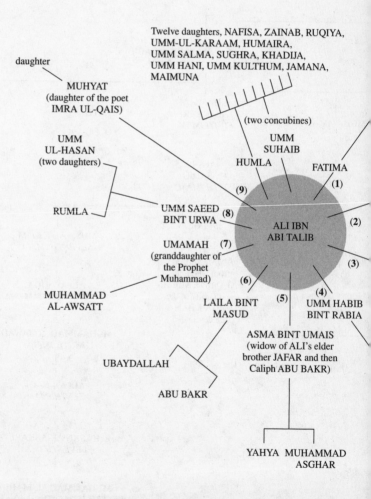

daughter

MUHYAT
(daughter of the poet
IMRA UL-QAIS)

Twelve daughters, NAFISA, ZAINAB, RUQIYA,
UMM-UL-KARAAM, HUMAIRA,
UMM SALMA, SUGHRA, KHADIJA,
UMM HANI, UMM KULTHUM, JAMANA,
MAIMUNA

UMM
UL-HASAN
(two daughters)

(two concubines)

UMM
SUHAIB

HUMLA

(9)

FATIMA

(1)

RUMLA

UMM SAEED **(8)**
BINT URWA

UMAMAH **(7)**
(granddaughter of
the Prophet
Muhammad)

(2)

ALI IBN
ABI TALIB

(3)

MUHAMMAD
AL-AWSATT

(6)

LAILA BINT
MASUD

(5)

(4)

UMM HABIB
BINT RABIA

ASMA BINT UMAIS
(widow of ALI's elder
brother JAFAR and then
Caliph ABU BAKR)

UBAYDALLAH

ABU BAKR

YAHYA MUHAMMAD
ASGHAR

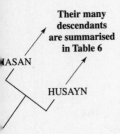

TABLE 7

The descendants of ALI
(fifteen sons and eighteen daughters)
from FATIMAH and the various wives
and concubines he took after her death

Their many
descendants
are summarised
in Table 6

HASAN

HUSAYN

five sons; four, excepting
ABBAS, died at Kerbala

UMM UL-BUNIAN
BINT KHALID

KHUALA BINT JAFAR,
known as AL-HANIFFIYA

MUHAMMAD

ALI

ABU HASHIM

RUQIYA

UMAR

FURTHER READING

Abbott, Nabia, *Aishah: The Beloved of Mohammed*, Chicago, 1942

Ahmad, Fazl, *Omar: The Second Caliph of Islam*, Delhi, 1983

Ahmed, Akbar S., *Discovering Islam: Making Sense of Muslim History and Society*, Routledge, 1988

—— *Islam Today: A Short Introduction to the Muslim World*, I. B. Tauris, 1999

Ali ibn Abu Talib ibn Abdul Muttalib, *Nahjul Balagha: The Sermons, Letters and Sayings of Imam Ali* (2 volumes, trans. Syed Ali Raza), Ansariyan Publications, Qum, Iran, 1971

Ali, Maulana Muhammad, *A Manual of Hadith*, Lahore and Ohio, 1941

Ali, Tariq, *The Clash of Fundamentalisms: Crusades, Jihads and Modernity*, Verso, 2002

Arberry, Arthur, *The Koran Interpreted*, Oxford University Press, 1983

—— *The Seven Odes*, George Allen and Unwin, 1957

Armstrong, Karen, *Muhammad: A Biography of the Prophet*, Victor Gollancz, 1991

—— *Islam: A Short History*, London, 2000

Arnold, T. W., *The Caliphate* (collected lectures), Oxford, 1924

Atiyah, Edward, *The Arabs*, Penguin, 1955

al-Azraqi, Muhammad ibn Abdallah, *History of Mecca*, Leipzig, 1858

Bakhtiar, Laleh, *Sufi: Expressions of the Mystic Quest*, Thames & Hudson, 1976

Ball, Warwick, *Rome in the East: The Transformation of an Empire*, Routledge, 2000

Barlas, Asma, *'Believing Women' in Islam: Unreading Patriarchal Interpretations of the Qur'an*, Austin, 2002

Bodley, R. V. C., *The Messenger: The Life of Mohammed*, Robert Hale, London, 1946

Bonney, Richard, *Jihad from Qur'an to Bin Laden*, Palgrave Macmillan, 2004

Bosworth, C. E., *The Islamic Dynasties*, Edinburgh, 1967

Brockelmann, Carl, *History of the Islamic Peoples*, Munich, 1939

al-Bukhari, *Hadith: The Gathered Collection of the Sayings of the Prophet* (nine-volume edition, trans. Muhammad Muhsin Khan), Kitab Bhaven, 1984

Bulliet, R., *The Camel and the Wheel*, Harvard University Press, 1975

Burton, John, *An Introduction to the Hadith*, Edinburgh, 1994

Cameron, Averil, *The Mediterranean World in Late Antiquity AD 395–600*, Routledge, 1993

Clarke, Peter (ed.), *Islam: The World's Religions*, Routledge, 1988

Cook, Michael, *Muhammad*, Oxford University Press, 1985

—— *The Koran, A Very Short Introduction*, Oxford, 2000

Creswell, K. A. C., *Early Muslim Architecture*, Oxford, 1932

Crone, Patricia, *Meccan Trade and the Rise of Islam*, Princeton, 1987

—— *Slaves on Horses*, Cambridge University Press, 1980

Crone, Patricia and M. Cook, *Hagarism: the Making of the Islamic World*, Cambridge, 1977

Crone, Patricia and M. Hinds, *God's Caliph: Religious Authority in the First Centuries of Islam*, Cambridge, 1986

Delong-Bas, Natana J., *Wahhabi Islam: From Revival and Reform to Global Jihad*, I. B. Tauris, 2004

Donner, F., *The Early Islamic Conquest*, Princeton, 1981

Elahi, Maulana Muhammad Ashiq, *The Wives of the Prophet* (trans. Muhammad Akram), Islamic Book Service, 2002

Epstein, (Rabbi Dr) Isidore, *Judaism*, Pelican, 1959

Esin, Emel, *Mecca the Blessed, Madinah the Radiant*, Paul Elek Books, 1963

Faruqi, Nisar Ahmed, *Early Muslim Historiography: a study of Early Transmitters of Arab History from the Rise of Islam up to the end of the Umayyad Period, 612–750*, Idaarah-i-Delhi, 1979

Fidai, Rafi Ahmed and N. M. Shaikh (consolidated by M. Naqi), *The Companions of the Prophet*, Delhi, 1994

Frye, Richard, *The Golden Age of Persia*, Weidenfeld & Nicolson, 1993

de Gaury, Gerald, *Rulers of Mecca*, George Harrap, 1951

Glubb, John Bagot, *The Great Arab Conquests*, Hodder & Stoughton, 1963

—— *The Empire of the Arabs*, Hodder & Stoughton, 1963

—— *The Life & Times of Muhammad*, Hodder & Stoughton, 1970

Glueck, Norman, *Deities and Dolphins: The Story of the Nabateans*, Farrar, Straus and Giroux, 1965

Grant, Michael, *The Jews in the Roman World*, Weidenfeld & Nicolson, 1973

Groom, Nigel, *Frankincense and Myrrh: A Study of the Arabian Incense Trade*, Longman, 1981

Grunebaun, G. E., *Classical Islam 600–1258* (trans. K. Watson), London, 1970

—— *Muhammadan Festivals*, Curzon, 1976

Guillaume, Alfred, *Islam*, Penguin, 1954

—— *The Traditions of Islam*, Oxford University Press, 1924

—— *The Life of Muhammad* (a translation of Ibn Ishaq's *Sirat Rasul Allah*), Oxford, 1955

Haag, Michael, *Syria & Lebanon*, Cadogan, 1995

Hassan, Masudul, *Hadrat Othamn Ghani*, New Delhi, 1999

—— *Hadrat Ali Murtada*, New Delhi, 1998

Hawting, G. R., *The First Dynasty of Islam, the Umayyad Caliphate, AD 661–750*, London and Sydney, 1986

Henze, Paul, *Layers of Time, a History of Ethiopia*, C. Hurst, 2000

Hitti, P. K., *History of the Arabs* (fifth edition), Macmillan, 1951

—— *History of Syria*, Macmillan, 1951

—— *Lebanon in History*, Macmillan, 1957

—— *Makers of Arab History*, Macmillan, 1968

Horovitz, Josef, *The Earliest Biographies of the Prophet and Their Authors* (ed. Lawrence Conrad), SLAEI, Darwin Press, 2002

Hourani, G. F., *Arab Seafaring*, Princeton University Press, 1995

Hoyland, Robert G., *Arabia and the Arabs: From the Bronze Age to the Coming of Islam*, Routledge, 2001

Insoll, Timothy, *The Archaeology of Islam*, Blackwell, 1999

Irving, Washington, *Life of Mahomet*, Dutton, 1915

Irwin, Robert, *Night & Horses & the Desert: An Anthology of Classical Arabic Literature*, Allen Lane, 1999

—— *Islamic Art*, Laurence King, 1997

Isaac, Benjamin, *The Limits of Empire: The Roman Army in the East*, Oxford University Press, 1990

Ibn Ishak, Muhammad (*c.* 699–761), *The Life of Muhammad* (*Sirat al-Nabi*). The work survives with two different early commentaries: those of Abd al-Malik ibn Hisham and Abd ar-Rahman ibn Abd Allah as-Suhayli. The current preferred English translation is by A.

Guillaume, 1955, but there is also that of the Hungarian-born linguist working in Bombay, Edward Rehatsek (1819–91) from which the Folio Society produced an edited version in 1964.

Jeffery, Arthur, *Materials for the Making of the Text of the Qu'ran*, Leiden, 1937

Kabbani, Rana, *Europe's Myths of Orient*, Macmillan, 1986

Kaegi, Walter, *Byzantium and the Early Islamic Conquests*, Cambridge, 1992

Kattani, Sulayman, *Imam Ali*, Muhammadi Trust, London, 1983

Kennedy, Hugh, *The Armies of the Caliphs: Military and Society in the Early Islamic State*, Routledge, 2001

—— *The Prophet and the Age of the Caliphates*, Longman, 1986

—— *The Court of the Caliphs: The Rise and Fall of Islam's Greatest Dynasty*, Weidenfeld & Nicolson, 2004

Kepel, Gilles, *Jihad: the Trail of Political Islam*, I. B. Tauris, 2002

Khan, Majid Ali, *The Pious Caliphs*, Islamic Book Publishers, 1978

Khan, Maulana Wahiduddin, *Muhammad The Prophet of Revolution* (translated by Farida Khanam), New Delhi, 1986

Khan, Muhammad Zafrulla, *Islam: Its Meaning for Modern Man*, Routledge, 1962

al-Kufi, Abu Muhammad Ahmad ibn A'tham (died 926), *Kitab al-futuh, The Book of Conquests*, recently ed. Muhammad Ali al-Abbasi and Sayyid Abd al-Wahhab Bukhari in eight volumes and published in Hyderabad between 1968 and 1975

Lane-Poole, Stanley, *The Speeches and Table Talk of the Prophet Muhammad*, Macmillan, 1882

Lapidus, Ira, *A History of Islamic Societies*, Cambridge, 1988

Lewis, Bernard, *The Arabs in History*, Hutchinson, 1966

—— *The Assassins: A Radical Sect in Islam*, Weidenfeld & Nicolson, 1967

—— *The Muslim Discovery of Europe*, Weidenfeld & Nicolson, 1982

—— *Music of a Distant Drum: Classical Arab, Persian, Turkish and Hebrew Poems*, Princeton, 2001

Lewis, Bernard and P. M. Holt, 'The Materials Used by Ibn Ishaq' in *Historians of the Middle East*, London, 1962

Lieu, Judith, John North and Tessa Rajak (eds.), *The Jews Among Pagans and Christians in the Roman Empire*, Routledge, 1992

Lings, Martin, *Muhammad, his Life Based on the Earliest Sources*, revised Islamic Texts edition, 1991

—— *What is Sufism?*, Unwin, 1975

—— *The Qur'an* (with Yasin Hamid Safadi), British Library, 1976

Madaj, al, A. M. M, *The Yemen in Early Islam, 9–233 AH, 630–684 AD*, London, 1988

Madelung, Wilfred, *The Succession to Muhammad: A Study of the Caliphate*, Cambridge, 1997

Makiya, Kanan, *The Rock: A Tale of Seventh-Century Jerusalem*, Constable & Robinson, 2002

Margoliouth, D. S., *Mohammed*, Blackie & Son, 1939

Miller, J. Innes, *The Spice Trade of the Roman Empire, 29 BC to 641 AD*, Oxford University Press, 1969

Mokhtar, G. (ed.), *Ancient Civilizations of Africa* (part of the UNESCO General History of Africa), University Presses of California, Columbia & Princeton, 1981

Momen, Moojan, *An Introduction to Shi'i Islam*, Yale, 1985

Muir, (Sir) William, *Life of Mahomet*, first published in four volumes in 1861 but as revised by T. H. Weir, 1923

—— *The Caliphate: Its Rise, Decline and Fall* (third edition), London, 1898

Muzafferedin, Shaikh Shemseddin Halveti al-Jerrahi, *Ninety-Nine Names of Allah*, Sultan & Co.

Nasr, Seyyed Hossein, *Islamic Art and Spirituality*, Golgonooza Press, 1987

Nicholson, Reynold, *A Literary History of the Arabs*, Cambridge University Press, 1930

—— *Translations of Eastern Poetry and Prose*, Cambridge University Press, 1922

Nigosian, Solomon, *Islam*, Crucible, 1987

Norris, Harry Thirlwall, *The Adventures of Antar*, Aris & Phillips, 1980

Norwich, John Julius, *Byzantium: The Early Centuries*, Viking, 1988

Pankhurst, Richard, *The Ethiopians*, Blackwell, 1998

Parrinder, Geoffrey, *Jesus in the Qu'ran*, Faber, 1965

Pawick, Constance, *Muslim Devotions: A Study of Prayer-manuals in Common Use*, SPCK, 1961

Peters, F. E., *Muhammad and the Origins of Islam*, State University of New York Press, 1994

—— *Judaism, Christianity, and Islam*, Princeton, 1982

—— *The Hajj: The Muslim Pilgrimage to Mecca and the Holy Places*, Princeton University Press, 1994

—— *Mecca: A Literary History of the Muslim Holy Lands*, Princeton, 1994

—— *Islam: A Guide for Jews and Christians*, Princeton, 2003

Petersen, E. L., *Ali and Mu'awiya in Early Arabic Tradition*, Copenhagen, 1964

Pitts, Joseph, *A Faithful Account of the Religion and Manners of the Mahometans*, 1731

Qureshi, Sultan Ahmad, *Letters of the Holy Prophet Muhammad*, New Delhi, 2000

Reeces, Minou, *Muhammad in Europe: A Thousand Years of Western Myth-Making*, Garnet, 2000

Robinson, Maxime, A. J. Arberry and Charles Perry, *Medieval Arab Cookery*, Prospect Books, 2001

Rodinson, Maxime, *Mohammed* (trans.), London, 1971

Rogerson, Barnaby, *The Prophet Muhammad: A Biography*, Little, Brown, 2003

—— *A Traveller's History of North Africa*, Windrush, 1998

Ruthven, Malise, *Islam: A Very Short Introduction*, Oxford, 1997

—— *Islam in the World*, Penguin, 2000

ibn Sa'd, Muhammad (764–845), *Kitab al-Tabaqat al-Kabir*, (ed. Eduard Sachau et al.), Brill, between 1904 and 1940

—— *The Women of Madina* (an abridgement of volume 8 of the above, ed. Aisha Bewley), Ta-Ha, 1995

Sardar, Zianddin, *Desperately Seeking Paradise*, Granta, 2004

Schimmel, Annemarie, *Islam: An Introduction*, State University of New York Press, 1992

Sells, Michael, *Desert Tracings*, Wesleyan University Press, 1989

Shah, Ikbal Ali, *Muhammad the Prophet*, London, 1932

Shahid, Irfan, *Byzantium and the Arabs*, Dumbarton Oaks, 1995

Ash-Shanaway, Abdul Aziz, *The Prophet's Children* (trans. Magdy Abdul-Salam and Ibrahim Zaki and revised by Alfwine Acelas Mischler), Umm al-Qura, 2001

Shoufani, E., *Al-Riddah and the Muslim Conquest of Arabia*, Toronto, 1972

Smith, Margaret, *Rabi'a the Mystic*, Cambridge, 1928

Al-Tabari, Abu Jafar Muhammad ibn Jarir (died 923), *Ta'rikh al-Rusul wa-l-Muluk* (*The History of the Prophets and Kings*), ed. M. J. de Goege et al., fifteen volumes, Leiden, 1879–1901. Or a more recent translation, *The History of the Messengers and the Kings*, in the thirty-nine-volume SUNY series in Near Eastern Studies, Albany, State University of New York Press, 1985–99

—— *Jami al-bayan Tafsir ay al-Qu'ran* (thirty volumes, Tabari's Koranic commentary), Cairo, 1903; there is also a more recent translation by E. Yarshater al-Tanataba'I, A. S. M, *Shi'ite Islam* (trans. and ed. Seyyed Hossien Nasr), State University of New York Press, 1975

Thomas, Bertram, *The Arabs*, London, 1937

Thomson, Ahmad, *The Wives of the Prophet Muhammad* (third edition), Ta-Ha, 2004

—— *Fatima Az-Zahra*, Ta-Ha, 1993

Tisdall, W. St. C., *The Original Sources of the Qoran*, SPCK, 1905

Trimingham, John Spencer, *Islam in Ethiopia*, Oxford, 1952

—— *Christianity among the Arabs in Pre-Islamic Times*, Longman, 1979

Uzunoglu, Nurettin, *History of the Prophets*, Istanbul, 1995

Waines, David, *Introduction to Islam*, Cambridge, 1995

Wansbrough, John, *Quranic Studies: Sources and Methods of Scriptural Interpretation*, Oxford University Press, 1977

—— *The Sectarian Milieu: Content and Composition of Islamic Salvation History*, Oxford University Press, 1978

Al-Waqidi, Abu Abd Allah Muhammad ibn Umar, *Kitab al-Maghazi: Waqidi's The Book of Muhammad's Campaigns*, Calcutta, 1856; also the more recent translation by Marsden Jones in three volumes, 1966

Warraq, Ibn (pseud.) (ed.), *The Quest for the Historical Muhammad*, New York, 2000

Watt, W. Montgomery, *Muhammad at Medina*, Oxford University Press, 1956

—— *Muhammad at Mecca*, Oxford University Press, 1956

—— *Islamic Revelation in the Modern World*, Edinburgh, 1969

—— *The Formative Period of Islamic Thought*, Edinburgh, 1973

—— *Early Islam: Collected Articles*, Edinburgh, 1990

Wensinck, A. J., *Muhammad and the Jews of Medina* (trans. W. Behn), Freiburg, 1975

Westermarck, E., *Pagan Survivals in Mohammedan Civilisation*, Macmillan, 1933

Wintle, Justin, *The Rough Guide History of Islam*, Rough Guides, 2003

INDEX

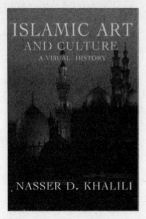
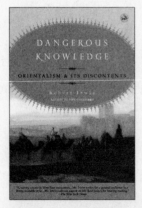